WOMEN'S WORKING LIVES IN EAST ASIA

WOMEN'S WORKING LIVES IN EAST ASIA

Edited by Mary C. Brinton

STANFORD UNIVERSITY PRESS

STANFORD, CALIFORNIA

2001

Stanford University Press
Stanford, California
©2001 by the Board of Trustees of the Leland Stanford
Junior University

Printed in the United States of America on acid-free,
archival-quality paper

Library of Congress Cataloging-in-Publication Data
Women's working lives in East Asia / edited by Mary C.
Brinton.
    p.   cm.—(Studies in social inequality)
  Includes bibliographical references and index.
  ISBN 0-8047-4149-2 (alk. paper)—
  ISBN 0-8047-4354-1 (pbk. : alk. paper)
  1. Women—Employment—East Asia.   I. Brinton,
  Mary C.   II. Series.

  HD6196 .W66   2001
  331.4′095—dc21   2001020377

Typeset by G&S Typesetters in 10/14 Sabon

Original Printing 2001

Last figure below indicates year of this printing:
10   09   08   07   06   05   04   03   02   01

CONTENTS

Tables

Figures

ACKNOWLEDGMENTS

This book has followed me around for a long time. At my dissertation defense (now already over a decade and a half ago), one of my committee members suggested that I do comparative work on gender stratification in East Asia. I reacted with horror. My dissertation had focused solely on Japan—how could this person possibly ask me to make broad comparisons to other countries? In typical graduate student fashion I jumped to the conclusion that I was expected to do this new work right away, adding material to my dissertation before submitting it to the graduate school. No doubt seeing the look of panic spreading across my face, the committee member quickly reassured me that this was meant as a suggestion for *future* research.

The future quickly turns into the present. Over the years I spent at my first job at the University of Chicago, I had the pleasure of working with a number of excellent graduate students from Taiwan and South Korea. They taught me volumes about the contours of gender inequality in their societies. Through them, I became more and more interested in doing what that member of my dissertation committee had encouraged me to do.

A good opportunity came when I was urged in the mid-1990s by a committee at the Social Science Research Council (SSRC) to develop a comparative project on gender in the East Asian region. A Mentorship Award from the Spencer Foundation also provided me funds to use at my discretion for graduate student training in areas related to education; these funds allowed me to partially support the research of Sunhwa Lee and Wei-hsin Yu, both of whom were Ph.D. students of mine. The funding from SSRC and the Spencer Foundation enabled me to convene two workshops, one in Chicago and one in Tokyo, where small numbers of scholars presented drafts of papers and engaged in intensive critique and discussion of one anothers' work.

Those scholars included the authors whose work is presented in this volume, plus two others: Shu-Ling Tsai (Academia Sinica, Taiwan) and Jong-Ha Yoon (then completing his dissertation in economics at the University of Chicago). Subsequent to the workshops, all of the authors revised their papers at least twice before we submitted the manuscript to Stanford University Press. They then undertook further revisions after the press urged me to make the book more comparative. I am grateful to all of the authors for agreeing to "stretch" themselves to be as comparative as possible, for anyone who is a one-country specialist will immediately recognize that trying to make intelligent comparisons to one or more other countries is a challenging enterprise, one that presents different problems from the task of doing intensive work on a single country. At the urging of the press I also solicited two additional comparative papers. I am grateful to Wei-hsin Yu and to Yean-Ju Lee and Shuichi Hirata for rising to the occasion and producing excellent papers in a speedy fashion. The addition of their comparative chapters has significantly strengthened the volume.

Laura Comay, former acquisitions editor at Stanford University Press, and Nathan MacBrien expertly shepherded the manuscript through the editorial process. I also appreciate the assistance of Susan Allan at the University of Chicago and the *American Journal of Sociology*, who provided skillful editorial help at an earlier point on several of the chapters.

This book was completed while I was a fellow at the Center for Advanced Study in the Behavioral Sciences at Stanford during 1999–2000. I am grateful to Cornell University and to the William and Flora Hewlett Foundation for partially supporting my stay there, and to Neil Smelser, Bob Scott, the Center staff, and my fellow fellows for making it such a wonderful home away from home.

Finally, since this book is about women, a word about mothers and daughters. In the middle of the second workshop, held in Tokyo in spring 1996, I received a fax with the first fuzzy-edged photo of my daughter, Emma Baoyan, who was waiting for me in an orphanage in Yueyang, Hunan Province. I trace motherhood to that moment, which I was able to joyfully share with the workshop participants gathered around the table (several of whom also helped me through the accompanying health report in Chinese). This book is respectfully dedicated to Emma, in hopes that her life will be everything she dreams of.

CONTRIBUTORS

Mary C. Brinton
Professor of Sociology, Cornell University

Keiko Hirao
Assistant Professor of Comparative Studies, Sophia University (Japan)

Shūichi Hirata
Senior Researcher, Japan Institute of Labour

Sunhwa Lee
Research Associate, Institute for Women's Policy Research

Yean-Ju Lee
Associate Professor of Sociology, University of Hawaii

Yu-Hsia Lu
Associate Research Fellow, Institute of Sociology, Academia Sinica (Taiwan)

Nidhi Mehrotra
Research Associate, Department of Sociology, Oklahoma State University

Yuko Ogasawara
Assistant Professor, College of Economics, Nihon University (Japan)

William L. Parish
Professor of Sociology, University of Chicago

Wei-hsin Yu
Assistant Research Fellow, Institute of Sociology, Academia Sinica (Taiwan)

WOMEN'S WORKING LIVES IN EAST ASIA

CHAPTER ONE

Married Women's Labor in East Asian Economies

Mary C. Brinton

One of the most dramatic economic changes in the twentieth century was the increase in married women's participation in work roles outside the home. In country after country, regardless of cultural region, late industrialization drew more married women into the labor force.

It is unusual for empirically minded social scientists to have the chance to make such sweeping generalizations, and we generally relish the opportunity. But the empirical regularity of women's increased work opportunities should not blind us to the fact that there nevertheless remain important lines of divergence in highly industrialized countries. One divergence is in gender inequality. There are substantial cross-country differences in the female-to-male wage gap as well as in levels of sex segregation by occupation and employment status (full-time and part-time employment, self-employment, and employment in small family-run enterprises). A second, related line of divergence is in women's employment patterns across the life cycle. In some societies the majority of women leave the labor force at the time of marriage or childbearing; in other countries large numbers of women continue their labor force participation uninterrupted throughout these life-cycle stages. The economic, cultural, and institutional reasons behind the international differences in gender inequality and in women's own work patterns constitute extremely interesting terrain for social scientists.

This volume addresses the nature of women's economic participation in three East Asian "miracles": Japan, Taiwan, and South Korea. In so doing, it asks three questions: First, what is similar or different about women's economic participation in this region of the world compared to others, particu-

1

larly to highly industrialized Western nations? Second, what patterns of convergence and divergence in women's economic participation are evident among East Asian societies themselves? And finally, what accounts for these patterns? The task of this introductory chapter is to offer answers to the first two questions and to advance the general thesis developed throughout the book in answer to the third question: that the different patterns of women's economic participation in Japan, Taiwan, and South Korea stem from key differences in the structure of labor demand and work organizations in each society and their interaction with subtle differences in labor supply.

I have made the conscious decision to center this book on married rather than single women's participation in the economy, although some of the chapters do touch on the work of single women or compare women's work lives before and after marriage (Brinton, Lee, and Parish, Chapter 2; Lee and Hirata, Chapter 4; Ogasawara, Chapter 6; Mehrotra and Parish, Chapter 11). I concentrate principally on married women because it is their work lives that potentially undergo the most dramatic transformation during late industrialization. Exploring why that potential is realized or unrealized in early twenty-first-century East Asia is therefore highly important.

Scholars of women's work in East Asia have produced a strong body of single-country monographs on the lives of factory women in the context of high-speed export-led economic growth (Greenhalgh 1985; Hsiung 1996; Kim 1997; Kung 1983; Roberts 1994; Salaff 1981).[1] These studies examine the complexities and contradictions faced by wage-earning women in patriarchal societies, particularly in negotiating power relationships in the workplace and at home. They also explore how women's work in the labor market impacts their welfare and quality of life. Studies of Taiwan and South Korea in particular are usually framed in the context of a broader debate over whether economic development expands or restricts women's economic opportunities and status. The marginalization literature (also known as the developmentalist, or dependency, literature) argues that export-led economic growth often creates false opportunities for women; capitalism draws more women into the labor market but relegates them to low-paying jobs that recreate the patriarchal gender relations of households (Lantican, Gladwin, and Seale 1996; Pyle 1990; Ward 1984).[2] Central in this literature are the manufacturing jobs in which both single and married women participate, although single women generally work in factories and married women are often involved in home-based piecework.

But the economies of East Asia are rapidly being transformed into post-industrial ones. The Japanese, South Korean, and Taiwanese economies now have large service sectors. As I discuss below, the experience of other countries has amply demonstrated that the expansion of the service sector increases the opportunities for married women, especially highly educated women, to enter the paid workforce in white-collar rather than manufacturing work. The continued development of postindustrial, "information" economies in East Asia means that it is time to pay particular attention to how married women's work is being shaped and transformed, not principally in factories but rather in offices. This argues as well for a focus on women in urban areas, for it is there that the opportunities for white-collar work are greatest.[3] Future changes in women's work and in labor market gender inequality in East Asia will depend principally on how the constellation of opportunities for women expands or constricts in the evolving and complex service sector—ranging from low-paying, dead-end sales jobs to high-skilled, highly remunerated jobs in information technologies.

This volume sets out to be quite different from prior work, then, in its comparative focus within East Asia and in its attempt to theorize and explore how married women's work is being shaped by the nature of work organizations and labor demand in the postindustrial era. While researchers sometimes compare one of these countries (usually Japan) to "the West," little attention has focused on comparisons within East Asia itself. Despite its economic woes in the early twenty-first century, East Asia is and will remain one of the most dynamic economic regions of the world. The region is an inherently important site in which to consider gender inequality. Moreover, I argue in this chapter that Japan, Taiwan, and South Korea afford a marvelous opportunity for comparative work that can untangle some of the key mechanisms structuring women's work. A half-century ago it would have been reasonable to think that gender inequality and the nature of women's work in the three societies would look quite similar at the beginning of the twenty-first century. But as this book shows, there are in fact significant divergences among the three. A central focus of this book, especially in the initial comparative chapters, is how key differences in the nature of labor demand and in the structure and culture of work organizations interact with some subtle labor supply differences to produce different work patterns for women and different levels of gender inequality in these societies. As I show later in this chapter, the cross-society variations in women's work are particularly fascinating given the similar cultural backgrounds and the similar overall contours of female labor supply shared by the three societies.

Before moving to the comparisons among Japan, Taiwan, and South Korea, it is instructive first to locate them within the context of our general knowledge about the changes that occur in women's work lives with industrialization.

INDUSTRIALIZATION AND WOMEN'S WORK

Early comparative studies of women's work by sociologists and labor economists focused mainly on changes in the *level* of female labor force participation with industrialization. This was done by looking at the relationship between level of industrialization and cross-sectional female labor force participation rates (Collver and Langlois 1962; Durand 1975; Pampel and Tanaka 1986; Psacharopoulos and Tzannatos 1989; Semyonov 1980; Ward 1984; Wilensky 1968). These studies often produced conflicting results; some found evidence of rising rates and others found declining rates. As later studies showed, this confusion was produced by the fact that women's labor force participation typically declines during the early stages of industrialization as production moves out of the home and into the factory, and only later increases as a result of the expansion of the service sector (Goldin 1990, 1995). These critical changes in the nature of labor demand are accompanied by typically dramatic changes in labor supply conditions: declines in fertility and increases in life expectancy mean that the average woman in a highly industrialized society has more years available to potentially engage in productive work outside the home than her counterpart in a less-industrialized society.

This combination of changing labor demand and supply factors produces what economists now call a "U-shaped" pattern of female labor force participation over time (Goldin 1995). If one pictures time stretching across the bottom of a graph and the female labor force participation rate on the vertical axis, then the upper left-hand side of the U corresponds to the high labor force participation rates in agricultural society, where the majority of able-bodied men and women alike are engaged in production. The trough of the U (midway across the horizontal axis) corresponds to the transition of the economy to a manufacturing base. During this period, it is typical for some manufacturing industries to be male-dominated and others, particularly textile-related industries, to be dominated by young, single women. The productive work roles of married women are generally limited during this stage of economic development, and thus the overall female labor force participation rate is low. The upward-sloping portion of the U on the right-hand side of the graph corresponds to women's labor force participation during late industrialization. Here the expansion of service sector employment generates more sales, clerical, and other white-collar jobs that are considered "respectable" for married women and that therefore draw them into the labor force (Goldin 1990, 1995; Standing 1976). Typically fertility rates have declined markedly and educational expansion has brought new educational opportunities to women by this stage of economic development as well. Both of these trends also bring more married women into the labor force.

JAPAN, SOUTH KOREA, AND TAIWAN VERSUS
WESTERN INDUSTRIAL NATIONS

The societies considered in this volume all went through the transition from agricultural to service-based economies, as outlined above, with breathtaking speed. Table 1.1 shows the change in industrial structure in each country between 1955 and 1995. Japan is the quintessential postindustrial economy, with a large service (tertiary) sector and tiny agricultural (primary) sector bracketing a declining but still substantial manufacturing (secondary) sector.[4] Taiwan and South Korea, two of East Asia's so-called NICs (newly industrialized countries), industrialized several decades later than Japan and have agricultural sectors that remain somewhat larger than Japan's and manufacturing sectors that are comparable or slightly larger. Among the three societies, South Korea was the latest to industrialize and shows the most rapid and dramatic transformation from an agriculture- to a service-based economy, having moved in the course of three and a half decades from a situation where four-fifths of its labor force was engaged in agriculture to a situation where well under one-fifth is.

Consistencies between East Asia and the West

The panels in figure 1.1 show the change in the overall female labor force participation rate (solid line) as well as the rate in urban areas (dotted line) in Japan, Taiwan, and South Korea since 1960. In each case, women's overall rate of participation in the economy fell slightly at some point and then began a steady increase, mirroring the U-shaped pattern documented in cross-

TABLE 1.1
Industrial Composition of the Labor Force in Japan,
South Korea, and Taiwan, 1955–1995

	Agriculture	Manufacturing	Service	Total[a]
	JAPAN			
1955	43.0	22.8	34.2	100.0
1980	10.4	34.8	54.6	99.8
1995	5.7	32.9	61.0	99.6
	SOUTH KOREA			
1960	79.5	5.8	14.7	100.0
1980	34.0	28.7	37.3	100.0
1995	12.5	32.9	54.7	100.0
	TAIWAN			
1955	60.9	10.0	29.2	100.1
1980	19.5	42.1	38.4	100.0
1995	10.6	38.3	51.1	100.0

SOURCES: Statistics Bureau, Japan, *Labor Force Survey*, various years; National Statistical Office, ROK (Republic of Korea), *Annual Report on the Economically Active Population Survey*, various years; Directorate-General of Budget, Accounting, and Statistics, Executive Yuan, ROC, *Yearbook of Manpower Survey Statistics, Taiwan Area, Republic of China*, various years.

NOTES: All values are percentages. The agricultural sector consists of agriculture, forestry, fishing, and animal husbandry. Manufacturing consists of mining, construction, and manufacturing. The service sector consists of utilities, transportation and communication, sales, finance, insurance and real estate, services, and government.

[a]Due to rounding errors, some rows do not add up to 100.0.

national studies (discussed earlier) that include large numbers of countries. Interestingly, in Taiwan the upturn occurred in the mid-1960s, fully a decade earlier than in its more industrially advanced neighbor, Japan. In South Korea, the female labor force participation rate began its upward trend in the late 1960s.

As one would expect from historical patterns of women's labor force participation in other countries, urban women's rates of participation in East Asia started out lower than those of agricultural women (as evidenced by the gap in the overall rates and the urban rates in figure 1.1), then at some point began to increase more rapidly. This is consistent with the eventual shift from

A. Japan

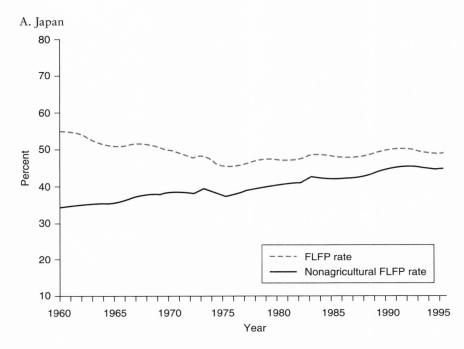

Figure 1.1.   Female Labor Force Participation in Japan, South Korea, and Taiwan, 1960–1995

SOURCE: Statistics Bureau, Japan, *Labor Force Survey*, various years. Figures are based on the population over age 15.

NOTE: FLFP = female labor force participation.

a manufacturing to a service base in urban areas, which opens up increased opportunities for women. Women's labor force participation rates in urban and non-urban areas are a little more similar to each other in Taiwan than in either Japan or South Korea. We come back to this point in later chapters; Taiwan experienced more even geographical urbanization than the other two countries, and the dominant organizational pattern in that society is the small family business, thousands of which are dispersed across the island. This equalizes women's work opportunities geographically more than is the case in Japan and South Korea, both of which have a mixture of very densely populated mega-cities, smaller cities, and villages.

The trends presented so far show nothing particularly unusual about women's labor force participation in East Asia compared to the industrial-

B. South Korea

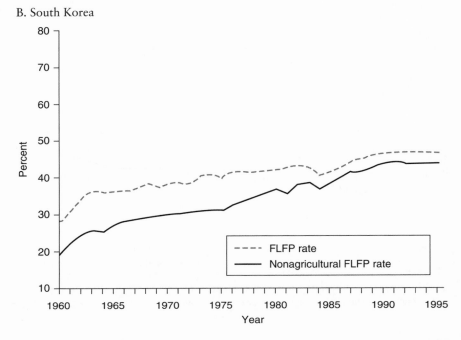

Figure 1.1   (continued)

source: National Statistical Office, ROK (Republic of Korea), *Annual Report on the Economically Active Population Survey*, various years. Figures are based on the population over age 15.

note: FLFP = female labor force participation.

ized West. The overall rate of women's labor force participation in these societies is very similar to that of several European countries (including France, Germany, the Netherlands, and England). Women participate in the economy at substantially higher rates (10 to 30 percentage points more) in the United States, Canada, and the Northern European countries.[5]

Divergences from Western Patterns

It is when we turn to the *type* of women's employment—the proportions of women working as wage/salaried employees, family enterprise workers, or self-employed workers—that East Asia looks quite distinct from either North America or the countries of the European Community. Paid (wage/salaried) employees make up about 90 percent of all working women in nearly every

C. Taiwan

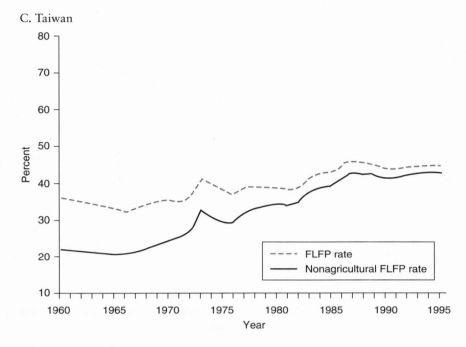

Figure 1.1   (continued)

SOURCE: Directorate-General of Budget, Accounting, and Statistics, Executive Yuan, ROC, *Yearbook of Manpower Survey Statistics, Taiwan Area, Republic of China*, various years. Figures are based on the population over age 15.

NOTE: FLFP = female labor force participation.

Western industrial country, whereas this is not the case in any of the countries dealt with in this book.[6] To be sure, Japan, South Korea, and Taiwan all show a very substantial decline over time in the proportion of working women engaged in family enterprise labor (which is typically, but not always, unremunerated) and a slight decline in rates of female self-employment. There has been a corresponding dramatic increase over time in the proportion of women working as paid employees (figure 1.2). But even so, only a little over 80 percent of Japanese women are paid employees; in Taiwan the figure is under 75 percent, and in South Korea it is under 65 percent.

This means that, compared to their counterparts in North America and the European Community, many more women in each of these East Asian

A. Japan

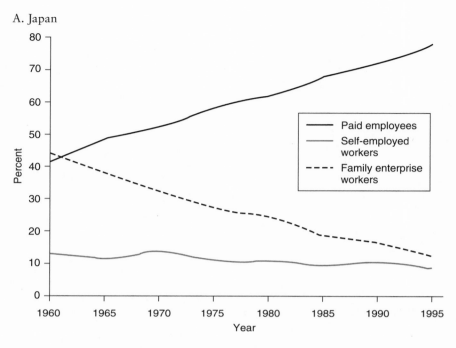

Figure 1.2. Structure of Female Employment in Japan, South Korea, and Taiwan, 1960–1995

SOURCE: Statistics Bureau, Japan, *Labor Force Survey*, various years.

countries work in what is typically called the "informal sector" (self-employment and family enterprises). There is also more divergence on this dimension (women's employment status) *within* East Asia than in the West, with Japan having the smallest informal sector and South Korea the largest. These facts, and the implications of them for women's working lives, are therefore a central focus of several chapters in the present volume.

The second main divergence between East Asia and the West lies in women's work patterns across the life cycle. Figure 1.3 shows that Japan and South Korea exhibit an "M-shaped" curve of female labor force participation with age. Sizable numbers of women withdraw from the labor force in the early years of marriage or childrearing (typically their mid-to-late 20s) and many of them return to work a number of years later, thereby creating the second peak in the M (in their mid-40s). This M-shaped pattern was characteristic of Western industrial countries until recently, but has now been trans-

B. South Korea

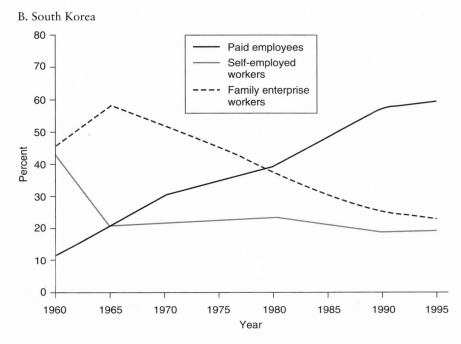

Figure 1.2   (*continued*)

SOURCE: National Statistical Office, ROK (Republic of Korea), *Annual Report on the Economically Active Population Survey*, various years.

formed in North America and nearly all European countries to a smoother, more continuous curve of labor force participation across the life cycle (Brinton 1993; Yu 1999b).[7] For example, the labor force participation rates of mothers with young children (two years old or younger) increased nearly 30 percentage points between 1975 and 1995 in the United States; by the mid-1990s, two-thirds of American mothers of young children were in the labor force (U.S. Bureau of the Census 1997).

The persistence of the M-shaped curve is arguably the most definitive characteristic of women's economic participation in Japan and South Korea compared to Western industrial nations. Moreover, the M-shaped pattern of participation became *more* rather than *less* evident in Japan throughout the entire post–World War II period until at least the mid-1980s (Yamaguchi 1997). Nor has it shown signs of disappearing in South Korea and evolving to the more "Western" pattern. Taiwan, on the other hand, is much closer

C. Taiwan

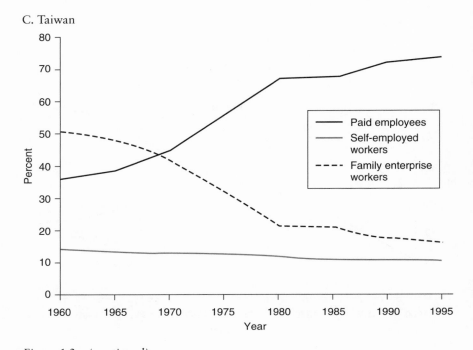

Figure 1.2   (continued)

SOURCE: Directorate-General of Budget, Accounting, and Statistics, Executive Yuan, ROC, *Yearbook of Manpower Survey Statistics, Taiwan Area, Republic of China*, various years.

to the West in exhibiting a "single-peaked" pattern of women's labor force participation across the life cycle (figure 1.3). In this, Taiwan clearly stands apart from its East Asian neighbors of Japan and South Korea, a point taken up by this chapter and others in the volume.

In sum, women's employment in East Asia differs in two significant ways from women's employment in the West: many more women are self-employed or work in family-run businesses, and many more women (especially in Japan and South Korea) withdraw from the labor force at the time of marriage or childbirth and either permanently remain out of the labor force or reenter only after their children are older. These are the two central differences between East Asia and Western industrial countries that this volume takes up; understanding the causes and the implications of these patterns is crucial for understanding women's working lives in the East Asian region.

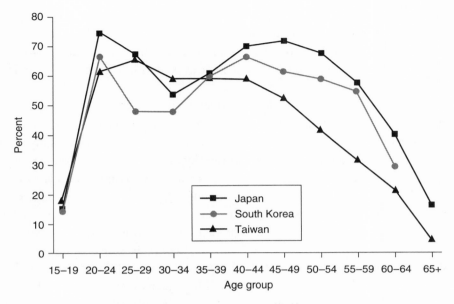

Figure 1.3.   Female Labor Force Participation by Age: Japan, South Korea, and Taiwan, 1995

SOURCES: International Labour Organisation, *Yearbook of Labour Statistics*, 1996; Directorate-General of Budget, Accounting, and Statistics, Executive Yuan, ROC, *Yearbook of Manpower Survey Statistics, Taiwan Area, Republic of China*, 1995.

East Asia as Japan, Taiwan, and South Korea

Before looking in more depth at the differences in women's work patterns *within* East Asia, I should say a word about why I chose to structure this book around a subset of societies in the region and to leave out mainland China, Hong Kong, and Singapore. The reasons are simple. Mainland China is so different from other East Asian societies in its geographical size as well as its political and economic history that bringing it into the picture raises fundamentally different analytical questions, not all of which bear much relevance to the societies in this volume. As shown in table 1.1, agricultural workers make up less than 15 percent of the labor force in South Korea and Taiwan and less than 6 percent in Japan. This compares to a very large agricultural sector in mainland China. The complex and changing mix of state- and privately owned enterprises in mainland China has spawned a lively cottage industry for sociologists in the past decade, but many of the central analytical issues in that literature are not key to understanding Japan, South

Korea, and Taiwan, all of which are dominated by private-sector enterprise. (The larger size of the government sector in Taiwan compared to the other two countries does, however, have some implications for female employment. This is taken up later in this chapter as well as in Chapters 3, 4, and 9 of the volume.)

On the other hand, Hong Kong and Singapore stand at the other end of the spectrum from mainland China in terms of being much smaller, more compact, more urban societies than the three East Asian societies considered here. While relevant comparisons can certainly be made between these two and Taiwan, the comparisons are less relevant to Japan and South Korea.

This being said, readers of this volume who are country specialists, whether of Japan, South Korea, or Taiwan, may still find it jarring to compare the three. Japan specialists in particular may question the utility of comparing Japan with two of its East Asian neighbors, given that Japanese industrialization substantially preceded that of Taiwan and South Korea and stretched over a longer period than the highly condensed trajectories of those two societies. No one in their right mind would have called Japan a "developing country" even a quarter-century ago, while Taiwan and especially South Korea teetered uneasily on the definitional border between "developing" and "industrialized" until quite recently. (South Korea became a member of the Organisation for Economic Co-operation and Development [OECD] only in 1996.) But the East Asian export-led NICs have outgrown their "developing country" status, and this volume is based on the premise (explicitly articulated in Chapter 2) that the broad similarities among these three East Asian cases produce a research opportunity that is akin to a natural experiment. The reasoning behind this premise will become more apparent later in this chapter when I outline the strong similarities in the social, economic, and cultural contexts for married women's labor supply.

CONVERGENCE AND DIVERGENCE IN WOMEN'S EMPLOYMENT IN EAST ASIA: TAIWAN'S EXCEPTIONALISM

When we compare patterns of women's employment across Japan, Taiwan, and South Korea, there are certainly similarities. As outlined above, women participate in nonwage/nonsalaried employment at higher rates in East Asia than in Western industrial nations. Table 1.2 shows the occupational distribution of women workers and likewise demonstrates some likenesses among

TABLE 1.2

Distribution of Female Workers by Occupation, and Percent Female in Each Occupation
in Japan, South Korea, and Taiwan, 1995

Occupation	JAPAN[a]		SOUTH KOREA[b]		TAIWAN[c]	
	Distribution	% Female	Distribution	% Female	Distribution	% Female
Professional/technical	13.1	43.2	13.8	35.2	22.4	42.5
Administrative/managerial	0.8	8.9	2.6	4.4	1.6	15.0
Clerical	29.0	60.5	12.3	50.9	18.8	74.7
Sales and service	26.7	44.8	21.9	58.9	22.2	52.4
Agriculture, forestry, and fishing	6.3	45.5	11.7	46.5	7.7	28.3
Transportation and communication	0.5	5.5	N.A.	N.A.	N.A.	N.A.
Manufacturing, labor, and mining	23.3	30.4	37.7	29.7	27.3	27.4
All*	99.7	40.5	100.0	40.3	100.0	38.6

[a]SOURCE: Statistics Bureau, Japan, *Labor Force Survey*, 1995.

[b]SOURCE: National Statistical Office, ROK (Republic of Korea), *Annual Report on the Economically Active Population Survey*, 1995.

[c]SOURCE: Directorate-General of Budget, Accounting, and Statistics, Executive Yuan, ROC, *Yearbook of Manpower Survey Statistics, Taiwan Area, Republic of China*, 1995.

* Due to rounding errors, some columns do not add up to 100.0.

NOTE: N.A. applies where data are not available—i.e., the category does not exist.

the three economies. More than one-fifth of working women in each society are in sales or service occupations, and about one-quarter (or in South Korea's case, closer to two-fifths) are in manufacturing. But the similarity in women's extent of employment in the informal sector and in certain occupational sectors is outweighed by several other dimensions that clearly seem to group Japan and South Korea together and render Taiwan the divergent case.

First, as discussed above, Taiwan is the only one of the three societies that demonstrates a continuous curve of female labor force participation across the life cycle—many women continue to participate in the labor market throughout their 20s, 30s, and 40s.

Second, as several of the chapters in this book discuss, the link between married women's education and their labor force participation is positive in Taiwan but weak in the other two societies (see Chapters 2, 4, 5, and 7; also see Kao, Polachek, and Wunnava 1994; Kim 1990; Yu 1999b).

Third, wage rates for women relative to men are greater in Taiwan (table 1.3). Taiwan women who work as full-time employees earn on average 69.8 percent of men's monthly earnings. This is substantially above the ratios of 60.4 in Japan and 54.6 in South Korea, and compares quite favorably with the United States (which had a female-to-male weekly earnings ratio of 75 percent in 1992; Bianchi 1995) and a number of European nations (Blau 1993). Table 1.3 further indicates that Taiwan's favorable showing is evident in all major occupational groups. Japan and South Korea also show smaller variation than Taiwan in the relative wage returns for women *across* occupational groups. In contrast, Taiwan women earn considerably closer to what men earn if they are in white-collar jobs (especially professional/technical, clerical, and sales and service) than in manufacturing jobs. This is consistent with other studies that report returns to women's education and work experience in Taiwan that are more consistent with human capital theory than is true for either Japan or South Korea (Brinton, Lee, and Parish, Chapter 2 this volume; Kao, Polachek, and Wunnava 1994; Yu 1999b).

Another way of looking at the female-to-male wage gap is across the life cycle (figure 1.4). The wage rates of young men and women strongly resemble each other in all three East Asian countries and then increasingly diverge with age. But here again, Taiwan is somewhat exceptional because the divergence is less marked than in Japan and South Korea. In those countries,

TABLE 1.3

Female-to-Male Wage Ratio by Occupation among Full-Time Paid
Employees in the Nonagricultural Sector, 1995

Occupation	Japan	South Korea	Taiwan
1. Professional		81.8	86.4
2. Administrative/managerial	64.8[a]	67.8	72.6
3. Technical and assisting professional		58.7	82.2
4. Clerical	68.8	58.0	91.2
5. Sales and service	68.7	66.0	81.3
6. Manufacturing, labor, and mining	50.0	55.0	66.8
Total	60.4	54.6	69.8[b]

NOTES: All values are percentages. Figures are calculated from aggregate data published in the *Yearbook of Labor Statistics*, 1995, prepared by the Ministry of Labor, Japan; *Wage Structure Survey*, 1994, prepared by the Ministry of Labor, ROK (Republic of Korea); and *Yearbook of Manpower Survey Statistics, Taiwan Area, Republic of China*, 1995, prepared by the Directorate-General of Budget, Accounting, and Statistics, Executive Yuan, ROC. Figures for Japan do not include part-time or temporary employees. Figures for South Korea are for 1993; category 6 is "plant and machine operators and assemblers." For Taiwan, category 6 is "production machine operators and related workers."

[a]This figure is for professional, administrative/managerial, and technical and assisting professional occupations.

[b]For Taiwan, the figure for the category "total" includes wages of paid employees in the agricultural sector.

the upward slope of male earnings is steeper past age 25 and women's earnings stagnate or decline during the childrearing years. The female-to-male wage gap remains particularly wide for older workers in South Korea.

Fourth, consistent with the positive link between married women's education and employment in Taiwan and also with the returns generated by their human capital, women are represented more strongly in most categories of white-collar work in Taiwan than they are in Japan or South Korea (table 1.3). This is particularly evident in clerical and administrative/managerial occupations.

What explains the fact that women's work patterns and gender wage inequality in Taiwan stand somewhat apart from what exists in Japan and South Korea and more closely resemble the patterns in the industrialized West?

A. Japan

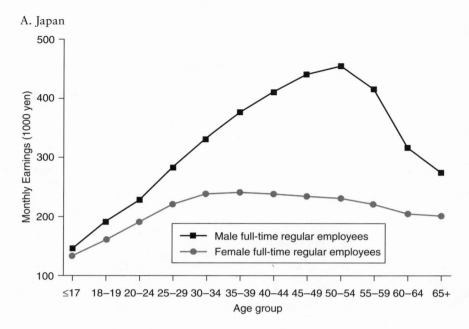

SOURCE: Ministry of Labor, Japan, *Yearbook of Labor Statistics*, 1995.

B. South Korea

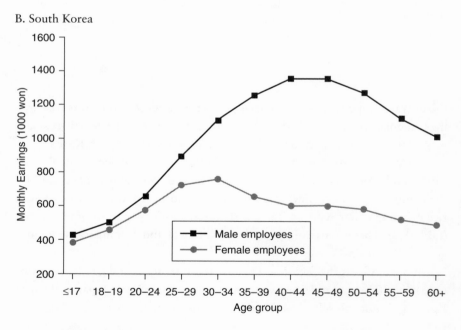

SOURCE: Ministry of Labor, ROK (Republic of Korea), *Establishment-Level Labor Conditions Survey*, 1993. This survey includes establishments with 10 or more workers.

Figure 1.4. Monthly Earnings of Employees by Age: Japan, South Korea, and Taiwan, 1995

C. Taiwan

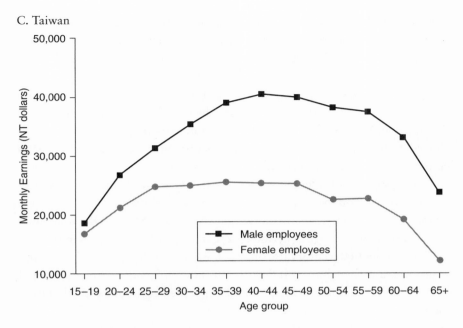

SOURCE: Directorate-General of Budget, Accounting, and Statistics, Executive Yuan, ROC, *Report on the Manpower Utilization Survey, Taiwan Area, Republic of China*, 1995.

Figure 1.4   (*continued*)

THE MACROLEVEL CONTEXT FOR MARRIED WOMEN'S LABOR SUPPLY: COMMONALITIES ACROSS JAPAN, SOUTH KOREA, AND TAIWAN

Women's economic participation is commonly explained by the independent effects of key labor supply and demand factors as well as the intersection of supply and demand (Goldin 1990). Women's educational levels, their marriage and fertility patterns, life expectancies, and household structure are central among the labor supply conditions affecting the decision to enter and remain in the labor force. For example, in highly industrialized societies with large nonmanufacturing sectors and diverse types of white-collar employment in sales and services, women can take advantage of these employment opportunities only if their education levels do not lag far behind men's (Goldin 1995). Large literatures in sociology and labor economics also document the key role that declining fertility rates play in increasing married women's participation in work roles outside the home. The movement of productive work out of the home and into the factory and, subsequently, the office, generally creates incompatibilities for women between childrearing and economic participation. The declines in fertility that almost always accompany industrialization mean that fewer and fewer of a woman's adult years are spent in intensive childrearing activity, and this consequently frees up more of a woman's time for wage labor outside the home. Longer life expectancies do the same. Meanwhile, changes in household structure that occur with advanced industrialization can have contradictory effects on married women's employment, as I discuss below.

The societies considered in this book demonstrate strong similarities in the macrolevel context affecting these important determinants of married women's labor supply. Japan, Taiwan, and South Korea share the following: (1) a Confucian ideological heritage, (2) Japanese administration in the first half of the twentieth century (through colonialism in the cases of Taiwan and South Korea), which heavily influenced the development of their educational systems, and (3) unprecedented rates of export-led economic growth during their respective periods of rapid industrialization.

Confucian Ideology

The common underlying Confucian ideology in the three societies has two types of impact on women's economic roles: it affects the nature of familial relationships and the family expectations placed on women, and it affects societal investment in education.

Confucian patriarchal ideology emphasizes strongly defined, hierarchical relationships between men and women and between generations (Rozman 1991). Women traditionally join their husband's family at the time of marriage and lose membership in their natal family. The division of labor between husband and wife is clearly defined, with wives' primary responsibility being the household and husbands' being the productive work world (Kim 1997; Wolf 1972; Yi 1993). Son preference has traditionally been strong in Japan, Taiwan, and South Korea, and the pressure on women to bear at least one son has at times been extreme. Koreans are frequently referred to as "the most Confucian" in East Asia (Janelli and Janelli 1982). In fact, sex ratios in South Korean elementary schools were reported in the mid-1990s to be as lopsided in favor of males as ratios on the Chinese mainland, where the one-child policy has produced extreme ratios in favor of males. Whereas this was accomplished in mainland China by abandonment and, by some reports, infanticide, of daughters, sex-selective abortion was widespread among upper middle-class South Koreans in the late 1980s and 1990s. While the emphasis on motherhood remains very strong in Japan, Taiwan, and South Korea, son preference has weakened considerably in Japan over the past decade, presumably because affluence has rendered one reason for having a son—support in old age—less compelling. The interaction between patriarchal ideology and economic development and prosperity is not a central theme of this book, but greater changes in the strength of son preference in Japan than in the other two societies are certainly one illustration of this interaction.

The second common effect of Confucianism in the three societies lies in the area of education. Confucian ideology strongly emphasizes the perfectibility of individuals and the possibility of achievement and upward mobility through education. These commonly shared beliefs about the importance of education in the three societies were overlaid by an important bureaucratic commonality as well: Japanese colonial rule in Korea and Taiwan in the first half of the twentieth century.

Japanese Administration

Japanese administration during the first part of the twentieth century resulted in marked structural similarities in the educational systems of the three societies.[8] Furthermore, each society underwent extensive American influence on its educational system in the latter half of the century; they share the basic 6-3-3-4 pattern of educational institutions (six years of elementary education, three years of middle school, three years of high school, and four years of higher education). All three societies experienced rapid educational expansion in the second half of the twentieth century, and this extended to women as well as men. Indeed, if one compares the gender gap in educational enrollments across a broad range of countries, East Asia stands out as having a relatively low gender gap.

Rapid Industrialization and Economic Growth

Finally, all three societies are characterized by high rates of economic growth and rapid industrialization. Industrialization occurred at different time points but was late compared to North America and Western and Northern Europe.

This created, again at different time points in the three countries, rising wages and high demand for labor, both of which impacted female labor supply indirectly and in complex ways (e.g., rising living standards lessened the necessity for middle-class wives to work to help support the family, but at the same time, rising life expectancies lengthened the number of years they were available to work in the labor market).

THE MICROLEVEL DETERMINANTS OF MARRIED WOMEN'S LABOR SUPPLY

The effects of these common macrolevel influences—Confucian ideology, Japanese influence, and late industrialization coupled with rapid economic growth—on the key determinants of married women's labor supply in the three societies can best be understood by looking at a number of indicators: education, marriage and fertility patterns, life expectancy, and household structure. Here we see a picture of striking convergence across the societies, with just a few notable exceptions.

Education

As table 1.4 shows, secondary education is nearly universal for both sexes in South Korea, Taiwan, and especially Japan. In fact, more women than men advance to secondary education in Japan and South Korea. At the higher-education level, Japan and Taiwan show near-parity in advancement rates for the two sexes, and in Japan's case women's advancement rate exceeds men's.

There are, then, significant similarities across East Asia in the arena of education. Women have high levels of education, and there is virtual gender parity at the secondary education level. But there are a few differences that are key for women's potential parity or disparity with men in labor market competition. These lie at the level of higher education.

First, Taiwan is the only society of the three that exhibits gender parity in higher education. In South Korea, men currently proceed on to higher education at nearly twice the rate that women do. Japanese women advance to higher education at similar rates to men, but table 1.4 shows that this masks an important gender difference: as Chapters 5 (Brinton and Lee) and 8 (Lee) discuss, Japanese women advancing to higher education have tended to choose junior college rather than university, whereas year after year only about 2 percent of men have done so (Fujimura-Fanselow 1995). In fact, it

TABLE 1.4
Conditions Affecting Women's Labor Supply in Japan,
South Korea, and Taiwan, 1995

	Japan	South Korea	Taiwan
Educational advancement rates (%)			
Secondary education			
Men	94.8	89.4	83.6
Women	97.1	88.0	87.4
Higher education[a]			
Men	41.9	80.9	18.3
	(2.3)		
Women	24.6	47.6	19.6
	(23.7)		
Marriage and fertility			
Women's mean age at first marriage	26.3	25.4	28.2
Average number of children			
ever born per woman	1.4	1.6[b]	1.8
Women's average life expectancy	82.9	76.0[c]	77.7
Household structure			
Composition of all households (%)			
Nuclear family (two generations)	59.1	66.3	57.7
Extended family (three generations)	15.8	12.2	34.1
Other (one-person households,			
households with nonfamily members)	25.1	21.5	8.2

SOURCES: Ministry of Education, Japan, *Basic School Statistics*, 1996; Ministry of Education, ROK, *Statistical Yearbook of Education*, 1995; Ministry of Education, ROC, *Statistical Yearbook of Education*, 1994; Ministry of Health and Welfare, Japan, *Vital Population Statistics*, 1996; National Statistical Office, ROK, *Population Projection*, 1991a, *Vital Registration Statistics*, 1995b, *Life Table*, 1993; Ministry of the Interior, ROC, *Survey on Women's Living Conditions*, 1998.

[a]For Japan, higher education figures represent advancement to university and, in parentheses, advancement to junior college.

[b]Figure is for 1990.

[c]Figure is for 1991.

was only in 1996 that the number of Japanese women advancing to university inched past the number advancing to junior college (Ministry of Education, Japan, *Basic School Statistics* 1998).

Second, it is important to note that the rate of higher-education advancement for South Korean males currently exceeds that in *any other country,* rendering extreme the surplus of highly educated males in that nation

(OECD 2000a). As we will show in this volume, this has significant ramifications for the likelihood of South Korean women (especially highly educated married women) being able to compete in the labor market for white-collar jobs. Japanese higher-education expansion was tempered to a greater extent by government policy (see Chapter 5, by Brinton and Lee). Similarly, higher-education expansion in Taiwan did not outpace the economy's need for highly educated workers, as occurred so dramatically in South Korea.

The chapters in this volume (especially Chapters 2, 5, and 8) discuss in greater depth the implications of these higher-education patterns for women's translation of education into remunerated work and for gender wage inequality in each society. As I argue later, these higher-education patterns interact in important ways with East Asian employers' preferential demand for educated male (rather than female) workers.

Marriage and Fertility

As in most societies, marriage remains a nearly universal event in the lives of women in Japan, Taiwan, and South Korea, with fewer than 10 percent of women in Japan and fewer than 5 percent in Taiwan and South Korea remaining single throughout their lives (Inoue 1998; Ministry of the Interior, ROC 1998). However, women in all three societies are distinguished by their very high mean age at first marriage (table 1.4), and this age has continued to show marked increases in each society during the past decade. United Nations data show that women's age at first marriage is high in East Asian societies compared to Western industrial nations, and also that the variance in age at marriage is very low (United Nations 1998). This reflects strong cultural norms surrounding the appropriate timing of marriage for women (Brinton 1992).[9]

Women in Japan, Taiwan, and South Korea not only share a pattern of marrying late (and nearly universally), but also show greater educational homogamy than women in any other region of the world, once national economic development level is held constant. (Educational homogamy refers to the similarity in educational levels between marriage partners.) As Smits, Ultee, and Lammers argue in a comparative analysis of 65 countries, "The high level of educational homogamy in Confucian countries is probably due to the combination of a traditional family orientation with a strong emphasis on formal education as a channel of social mobility in these countries" (1998: 282). In other words, marriage in East Asia is typically a decision that matches individuals who are quite similar in terms of social status, especially as reflected by education. In South Korea, employers have attached a very high wage premium to men's education but not to women's (Amsden 1989; Chapters 2 and 8 this volume). Here, educational homogamy and a sex-discriminatory labor market have together exerted a downward pull on highly educated married women's labor force participation; in effect, it is these women's marriage decisions, not their employment, that gives them social status (Kim 1997; Lett 1998; Chapter 8 this volume).

Women in the three societies also show strikingly similar levels and timing of fertility: in each country the average number of children is now below two (table 1.4). The interval between marriage and first childbirth is typically short. In Japan, for example, the interval between the average age at first marriage and at first birth is now only 13 months (Ministry of Health and Welfare, Japan 1998).

Life Expectancy

Just as women's marital and fertility patterns show striking consistency across the three societies, so too do their general levels of health and their life expectancies. As shown in table 1.4, mean life expectancy for women is now very high, exceeding 75 years in all three societies and reaching 83 years in Japan.

Household Structure

Finally, table 1.4 shows the dominant living arrangements in each society, although some caution should be exercised in interpreting these figures because they are based on the entire population rather than just married women. There is one strong similarity and one difference: (1) nuclear family (two-generation) households are the most common living pattern in all three societies, and (2) extended family (three-generation) households are more than twice as common in Taiwan as in Japan and South Korea.

Three-generation households have two potentially contradictory implications for married women. On the one hand, older parents may require care if they are sick or very aged. Because this care is more likely to fall on the shoulders of married women than men, it has a potentially negative impact on married women's ability to simultaneously carry out work responsibilities outside the home. On the other hand, older parents, particularly mothers and mothers-in-law, can provide "built-in childcare" for mothers, freeing up their time for the labor market. The impact of this latter possibility can clearly be seen in Taiwan, as argued in Chapter 3 by Yu, where the availability of grandparents along with higher wage rates for women relative to men (compared to Japan and South Korea) draw more married women into paid employment.

The family patterns I have shown here in statistical form are structural (e.g., age at marriage, household structure, etc.) and are reflective of—as well as significant for—subtle cultural differences in the way patriarchal authority is articulated in these societies. While we delve relatively little into how family norms differ across Japan, Taiwan, and South Korea, we do not mean to imply in this volume that the three societies are completely similar in their specific Confucian "family ideologies" (to use the term employed by Lu in Chapter 10). For example, Chapters 3 by Yu and 7 by Hirao suggest that the central emphasis on the mother-child bond may be stronger in Japan and South Korea than in Taiwan. An intense cultural focus on mothering makes it very difficult for mothers, especially those with young children, to engage in full-time work outside the home. Cultural flexibility in turning the care of children partially over to relatives or to unrelated childcare providers, on the other hand, increases women's range of work options. Of course, these cultural attitudes are of little value unless relatives are close by (as is often the case in Taiwan), children can sometimes be brought to work (also occasionally true in Taiwan), or there are childcare facilities that operate with long hours and are geographically accessible (not the case in any of the societies we examine).[10] The contrasts in childcare norms and availability in Japan and Taiwan in particular are discussed in Yu's comparative chapter (Chapter 3). A number of chapters also discuss the long commuting hours necessitated by full-time work in the major urban centers of Japan and South Korea, which render work and family very nearly incompatible for women given that there is not a strong childcare infrastructure.

THE LABOR SUPPLY SIDE SUMMARIZED

We can summarize the distinctive features of women's labor supply across the three societies as follows. Women in all three have high life expectancies and low fertility, both of which mean that they have many years in their lives to potentially participate in the labor force. Almost all women marry but do so late; the same is true for childbearing. This means that women have several years in their 20s when they are single and can potentially initiate work careers. High levels of educational attainment mean that many women do not complete schooling and enter the workforce until their early 20s, but they do so with a high level of human capital (skills and abilities garnered through their education).

These characteristics of women's labor supply in Japan, Taiwan, and South Korea would be consistent with the life-cycle pattern of female labor force participation common to Western industrial countries, that is, a pattern where the majority of women show continuous participation across the life cycle. Moreover, women's high levels of human capital in East Asia and their high mean age at first marriage would suggest that many women have the opportunity to become committed to jobs in their 20s that further develop their human capital and increase their labor force attachment (or propensity to remain in the labor force).

As I demonstrated earlier in this chapter, though, only in Taiwan do women's working lives approximate these patterns. And notably, it is Taiwan that departs from the other two societies in its gender parity in higher education, tempered rates of higher education expansion, and higher proportion of three-generation households. These supply-side differences are coupled with some marked dissimilarities in the labor demand side between Taiwan on the one hand and Japan and South Korea on the other. Before outlining those dissimilarities, though, we should take a look at one final, political dimension of the labor supply side to see if it too could be producing the emergent pattern of Taiwan's exceptionalism: equal employment legislation. Perhaps it is the case that such legislation in Taiwan makes it easier for married women to work and to receive fair treatment because employers otherwise risk the censure of the government.

Here it is hard not to deliver the punch line first, because it is a striking one: the causality appears to go in precisely the opposite direction from what we would expect. It is Japan and South Korea that both have passed equal employment opportunity legislation, and Taiwan that has not.

The Japanese Diet passed the Equal Employment Opportunity Law (EEOL) in 1985. In 1987 South Korea also enacted an equal employment opportunity law, strikingly similar to the Japanese formulation. As alluded to in Chapter 4, the law has arguably been poorly enforced and has been of little consequence in forestalling gender discrimination by Korean employers. Likewise, it is widely acknowledged that the Japanese EEOL produced little effect in the first decade after its enactment (Hanami 2000).[11] But the "letter" of equal employment opportunity, if not its active enforcement, does exist in both Japan and South Korea. In contrast, Taiwan has no similar legislation. The Labor Standards Law allows women to take 8 weeks of maternity leave, although this was only recently extended (in 1998) to the finance and service industries. (This compares to the 14 weeks of maternity leave that Japanese women are allowed.) Moreover, Taiwanese employers remain free to state their preference for a male or a female worker in job advertisements, whereas this was prohibited in the most recent revisions of Japan's EEOL.

Government equal employment policy, then, cannot account for the differences in married women's economic participation between Taiwan on the one hand and Japan and South Korea on the other.[12] As argued in chapter 2, the tumbling of "marriage bars" in Taiwan occurred due to strong labor demand rather than to government policy. This economic pressure has been much more consequential for married women than have highly centralized legal reforms in Japan and South Korea. (See also Goldin 1990 for a discussion of labor demand vs. legal measures in the United States.)

DIVERGENCE IN EAST ASIA: THE EFFECTS OF LABOR
DEMAND AND WORK STRUCTURES

The central line of divergence in women's work patterns in East Asia, then, is between Taiwan on the one hand and Japan and South Korea on the other. Why does Taiwan rather than the more "advanced" postindustrial Japan exhibit the highest rates of married female labor force activity, the strongest relationship between married women's level of education and their probability of being in salaried employment, the lowest female-to-male wage gap (particularly striking in white-collar jobs), and the greatest representation of women in most categories of white-collar work?

In explaining these cross-country differences, one clearly cannot argue that "stage" of economic development is what matters most (the comparison between Japan and Taiwan defies that logic). Nor can one argue that fundamental differences in the type of economic development, such as import-substitution or export-led, are what matter (Horton 1996), since all three economies have been heavily export-driven. It seems difficult to make the argument that cultural differences in the way Confucian tradition has played out within the families in each society can *alone* account for differences in women's work patterns (see especially Yu, Chapter 3, for an examination of similar gender-role attitudes among women in Japan and Taiwan). In short, the macrolevel conditions affecting female labor supply seem insufficient to explain the divergence.

Likewise, the microlevel conditions of female labor supply are strikingly similar across the three societies, with the exception of the three that emerged from the analysis above—two of them having to do with the over-all level and nongendered character of higher education in Taiwan, and one of them having to do with the greater proportion of extended family house-holds in that society. The chapters in this volume argue that these few labor supply differences interact with strong divergence in labor market structures and organizational forms in the three societies to determine the economic opportunities available to married women. In affecting the economic strate-gies of families and women's own aspirations and attitudes, the demand side of the labor market plays a critical role in shaping women's work roles rela-tive to men's. But we argue not for one-way causation from the demand side of the labor market to women's economic behaviors. Rather, we argue that the few subtle labor supply differences I have outlined among the three soci-eties act in combination with *more extensive differences in the nature of la-bor demand* to produce distinctive employment and gender stratification pat-terns across East Asia.

What are the differences in the labor demand side? Three clearly stand out: (1) firm size and the accompanying internal structure and dynamics of work organizations, (2) the size of the public sector, and (3) the overall level of labor demand, especially for highly educated workers.

Firm Size and the Structure of Work Organizations

Despite a common underlying Confucian ideology and Japan's colonial ad-ministration of Taiwan and South Korea, the size and internal structure of work organizations are highly divergent across the three societies (Hamilton and Biggart 1988; Biggart 1990; Orru, Biggart, and Hamilton 1991). The distribution of employees across firms of different sizes varies significantly. Table 1.5 shows that over half of paid (wage or salaried) employees in Taiwan work in small firms (establishments with fewer than 30 employees). This concentration of employees in small firms is unlike what exists in either Ja-pan or South Korea, where just over one-quarter of employees work in firms of that size. At the other end of the spectrum, the proportion of employees working in very large firms (over 500 employees) in Taiwan is tiny (4 percent)

TABLE 1.5
Distribution of Employees by Firm Size in Japan,
South Korea, and Taiwan, 1995

	Japan	South Korea[a]	Taiwan
Employees by firm size (%)			
1–29	32.9	25.3	55.2
30–99	16.1	26.0	14.3
100–499	16.5	25.4	10.3
>500 and government	34.5	23.3	20.3
>500	24.2		4.3
Government	10.3		16.0

SOURCES: Statistics Bureau, Japan, *Labor Force Survey*, 1995; Ministry of Labor, ROK, *Establishment-Level Labor Conditions Survey*, 1994; Directorate-General of Budget, Accounting, and Statistics, Executive Yuan, ROC, *Yearbook of Manpower Survey Statistics, Taiwan Area, Republic of China*, 1995.

[a]Data for South Korea are for 1994.

compared to Japan (24 percent) and South Korea (23 percent). But this is off-set by the larger size of the public sector in Taiwan than in either of the other two economies, a point to which I return below.

What do these different constellations of firm size signify for the employment of women, especially married women? That the wages paid to employees increase with firm size is well established in the sociological and economics literatures (Brown and Medoff 1989; Brown et al. 1997). This empirical generalization extends to East Asia; wage differentials by firm size are particularly large in Japan and South Korea (Hashimoto and Raisian 1985; Ministry of Labor, ROK 1998; Rebick 1993; Tachibanaki 1993). This means that if women have access to the same jobs as men in large firms, they benefit. But herein lies the rub. While some evidence exists to suggest that large firms are more egalitarian and universalistic than small ones in their personnel practices (Reskin and McBrier 2000), this research is based on the United States, where federal regulation of equal employment opportunity legislation is particularly focused on the large-firm sector. As discussed above, enforcement of equal employment opportunity legislation has been weak in both Japan and South Korea, and the personnel practices of large firms have, from women's point of view, suffered from benign neglect by the government.

In earlier work, I documented that young Japanese men and women enter large firms in relatively equal proportions to each other upon school graduation (Brinton 1989, 1993). In South Korea this is not the case, even for university graduates; Lee documented that among graduates of Seoul universities in the early 1980s, 54 percent of men and only 11 percent of women had entered firms of over 1000 employees in their first job (Lee 1997). But even if entry rates to large firms are the same for the two sexes, as in Japan, tracking by gender produces widely divergent career paths that result in the concentration of women in smaller firms in Japan and South Korea by mid-career (Brinton 1989, 1993; Lee 1997). The managerial logic behind women's near-zero rates of promotion in large Japanese and South Korean firms, while similarly gender-based, has different roots.

Japan: "Permanent" versus Marginal Employment

The existence of firm-internal labor markets or so-called permanent employment for males in large Japanese firms has been extensively documented (Brinton 1993; Brown et al. 1997; Cole 1979; Sakamoto and Powers 1995; Spilerman and Ishida 1996). Japanese management experimented with separating women into a career track (*sōgōshoku*) and a "mommy track" (*ippanshoku*) in the late 1980s after the passage of the Equal Employment Opportunity Law (Lam 1992; Shire and Imai 2000). Nevertheless, the proportion of all working women in administrative/managerial work has increased only marginally in the past 15 years, from 0.9 percent to 1.0 percent (Statistics Bureau, *Labor Force Survey* 1998). Japanese women have first and foremost been viewed by large employers as a reserve army of labor, not a reservoir of managerial potential. The strong inclination to privilege men over women for promotions and indeed for recruitment into the management track in the first place was exacerbated by Japan's most severe post–World War II recession in the late 1990s. Here, the pernicious implications that large firms and their accompanying firm-internal labor markets hold for women became starkly apparent: in an effort to retain as many "core jobs" as possible for men in internal labor markets during a painful period of financial belt-tightening, large Japanese firms decreased their hiring of young female graduates as full-time employees and turned increasingly to employing women instead as part-time, temporary employees.

Most of the increase in Japanese female labor force participation in the final years of the twentieth century came from part-time, not full-time, workers. While it could be argued that this resulted principally from the labor force entrance of greater numbers of married women in age groups where the rate of part-time employment is high (e.g., women in the childrearing years), the data do not bear out such a supply-side explanation. Houseman and Osawa report that nearly two-thirds of the increase in part-time employment between 1982 and 1992 is accounted for by the increased incidence of part-time work *within* age and gender groups. Moreover, the growth in part-time vacancies was faster than the growth in numbers of part-time job-seekers, indicating that employer demand for part-time workers was outpacing the supply (Houseman and Osawa 1997). Thus, while opportunities for part-time work arguably increased for Japanese women at the turn of the century, full-time employment (and the accompanying bonuses and fringe benefits) remained elusive, especially in white-collar work.

Part-time employment is less common in both South Korea and Taiwan, where there is less necessity to maintain a marginalized labor force as a buffer to support permanent male employment in firm-internal labor markets. Fewer than 6 percent of the female labor force in Taiwan worked fewer than 40 hours a week in 1995, compared to the high figure of 39 percent for Japanese women (Directorate-General of Budget, Accounting, and Statistics, *Yearbook of Manpower Survey Statistics* 1995; OECD 2000b). Similarly, only 9 percent of employed South Korean women work part-time (OECD 2000b). Yet women's low rate of part-time employment in South Korea hardly signifies their incorporation into stable "core" employment, as discussed in the next section and in Chapters 2, 4, 5, and 8 of this volume.

South Korean Corporate Culture: "Patrimonial Authoritarianism"

If large firms in Japan restrict married women's full-time employment opportunities due to the prevalence of internal labor markets and the consequent shunting of middle-aged women out of the firm or into unstable part-time work, large firms in South Korea create barriers to women from the start, and for different reasons. Internal labor markets and "permanent employment" are not common in South Korea, and men's labor mobility between firms is higher than in Japan (Amsden 1989; Chung, Lee, and Okumura 1988). Women's difficulties in large South Korean firms can arguably be traced to what has been dubbed "patrimonial authoritarianism" (Biggart 1988; Chung, Lee, and Okumura 1988; Orru, Biggart, and Hamilton 1991). While family ownership is a pattern extending throughout Japan, Taiwan, and South Korea, large firms in South Korea exhibit an extraordinary lack of separation between ownership and management functions, especially as compared to their Japanese counterparts (Chung, Lee, and Okumura 1988). Nepotism is an important feature at the upper levels of management (Janelli and Janelli 1993; Lett 1998). In most *chaebol* (large, diversified business groups), the owner's control is exercised through hiring and promotion based strongly on sex, school affiliation, and, in some cases, region of geographical origin (Biggart 1988).[13]

Moreover, many observers suggest that the hierarchical, nonegalitarian structure of control evident in most large South Korean firms may be related to the fact that all South Korean men go through a period of compulsory military training. In contrast to the more consensus-oriented, egalitarian working environment (at least among men) in large Japanese firms, firms in South Korea are characterized by greater authoritarian control and hierarchy. While Japanese women are excluded from the warm "firm as family" ideology promulgated in large Japanese enterprises, South Korean women are also excluded from the much more "macho," hierarchical organizational culture of large firms in their society (Amsden 1989; Kim 1997; Chapter 4 this volume). Married women in both countries who must work full-time to help support their family, especially if it is in blue-collar jobs, are often openly pitied by their younger single female coworkers (see Ogasawara 1998 and Chapter 6 this volume; Kim 1997).

Taiwanese Small Firms: "Flat" Hierarchy

The different authority structure and the obvious absence of internal labor markets in Taiwan's extensive small-firm sector translate into a different, generally more hospitable organizational culture for married women than in the other two societies. The degree of formalization in job titles is low and promotional trajectories are short in these firms, and employers' need for labor sometimes makes them amenable to allowing working mothers to have slightly more flexible schedules (Yu 1999b and Chapter 3 this volume). Most businesses are family-owned. As Lu discusses in Chapter 10 of this volume in regard to family businesses, depending on their relative abilities, husbands and wives have highly interdependent and sometimes interchangeable roles, and wives often exercise considerable authority given their status as the owner's most trusted worker.

In summary, the greater prevalence of large firms in Japan and South Korea vis-à-vis Taiwan translates into distinctive intraorganizational authority relations and career structures that differentially favor men. Other features of large-firm employment can also create constraints on work opportunities for married women. As the second chapter of this volume argues, Taiwan's pattern of dispersed industrialization and small firms has meant that married women's transportation times to work are generally quite minimal. This contrasts sharply with the long commuting times to corporate headquarters or branches in Tokyo, Seoul, and the other major metropolitan areas of Japan and South Korea. Prevailing childcare arrangements in these two societies rarely accommodate this extension of employed mothers' workdays (see Yu, Chapter 3 this volume). Furthermore, the long overtime hours typically expected of full-time employees in both Japanese and South Korean large firms render long commutes to and from work even more untenable for married women with children (Amsden 1989; Brown et al. 1997; Lett 1998).

Public Sector Employment

In contrast to the rigidities of the work environment in large private firms and the exclusion of women from organizational culture, public-sector employment typically offers more regular work hours and vacations (see Yu, Chapter 3 this volume). The public sector is subject to more careful scrutiny by the government for adherence to legally sanctioned equal employment opportunity rules (Beggs 1995). Entrance to the civil service in Japan, Taiwan, and South Korea is governed by examination, which is a more equal, meritocratic recruitment channel than personal connections.

That women actually do fare better in government employment than in private firms is supported by findings for both Japan and Taiwan showing that female full-time employees earn higher wages in government service (Brinton 1993; Yu 1999b and Chapter 9 this volume; also see Chapter 4 for a comparison of women's jobs in the private and public sector in Japan, South Korea, and Taiwan).[14] The size of the public sector therefore is of significance for women's wage-earning opportunities.

Here again, it is Taiwan that stands apart from Japan and South Korea. As table 1.5 shows, Taiwan has a larger public (government) sector compared to Japan. The South Korean survey that reports the distribution of employees across firms of different sizes does not separate out civil servants; they are subsumed in the 23 percent of employees who work in firms of over 500 employees. Data from other sources, though, specify that just under 8 percent of employees in South Korea worked as civil servants in the mid-1990s (Kim 1995). This figure is even lower than that for Japan.

Level of Labor Demand

Finally, the level of labor demand itself has been quite different in the three societies, arguably working more to the advantage of women in Taiwan than in Japan or South Korea. Chapter 2 of this volume demonstrates that unemployment rates in South Korea, particularly among highly educated men, have been much higher than in Taiwan since 1980. Under conditions of slack labor demand, employers in patriarchal societies can readily exercise their preference for male over female employees (Pyle 1990). This is obviously much more difficult when, as has more often been the case in Taiwan, businesses need to go begging for labor (Yu, Chapter 3, and Lu, Chapter 10, this volume). The interaction with the labor supply side is obvious here, as Taiwan's higher-education expansion did not create the bloated supply of highly educated workers that occurred in South Korea. In Japan, it is not so much the oversupply of highly educated workers that has stalled opportunities for many married women in the white-collar sector, but the slow pace at which labor demand increased in much of that sector (see Chapter 5 this volume). And most recently, the Asian economic crisis of the late 1990s wreaked greater havoc in the labor markets of South Korea and Japan than in Taiwan, lowering labor demand and keeping educated married women in a position far from the front of the labor queue.

CONCLUSION

While Japan industrialized earlier than either Taiwan or South Korea, it is Taiwan that stands out in East Asia as having the employment patterns for married women and the degree of gender equality (although hardly complete) that we associate with the highly industrialized West. This chapter has examined the macrolevel social, economic, and cultural contexts for female labor supply in the three societies and argued that there are strong similarities in these and, likewise, in the microlevel supply-side determinants of women's employment. But there are three subtle ways in which Taiwan differs. Two of these have to do with higher education, and the third has to do with the structure of households and hence childcare availability. Moreover, there are sharp disjunctures on the labor demand side—in the dominant small firm size in Taiwan as compared to Japan and South Korea and hence in the predominant organizational culture; in the size of the public sector; and in the absolute level of labor demand, especially for educated workers.

This chapter provides a framework for the chapters that follow. These chapters testify to the complexities and contingencies of married women's changing employment in East Asia with rapid industrialization. They provide an unusual array of glimpses into how hierarchical gender ideology (permeating households and workplaces), highly competitive educational systems, and the structure of labor markets and work organizations in three East Asian societies influence the work lives of urban married women.

Together with the authors of the research presented in these pages, I have tried as much as possible to knit together the chapters so that readers will be able to trace subthemes and questions throughout the book. To this end the chapters contain many cross-references to one another, and are also presented in two major groupings. The first five chapters (including this one) are comparative. Chapters 2, 3, and 5 each compare the economic roles of women in two of the three societies with each other, and Chapter 4 is comparative across all three societies. This first half of the book is quite quantitative in nature, with the chapters drawing on large-scale survey data. The six chapters of the second half of the book each focus more or less exclusively on either Japan, South Korea, or Taiwan. This part of the book contains at least one chapter for each society that is more ethnographic or descriptive in nature; others combine quantitative and qualitative methods.

Because the chapters throughout the book refer to one another extensively, I expect that readers will gain the most from the volume by reading all of it. For most readers, going through the chapters in order will probably be the best method of reading.

This introductory chapter has explored the central theme of how key labor market differences, along with more subtle labor supply differences, affect married women's working lives in East Asia. A number of subthemes are developed throughout the book as well. These are very much in the form of implicit questions, and although I will close by mentioning here a few of the ones I see as being central, we invite readers to generate others as well from the empirical materials on East Asian contexts that we present in this book. How do we assess the "value" of work available to married women in different countries and cultural contexts? Does wage employment necessarily benefit women more than work in the "informal" sector (work in family-run businesses or in self-employment)? If so, under what conditions? Is full-time work always "better" than part-time work? Is employment itself necessarily a "good" in married women's lives? How can we judge this? These are big questions, and we do not claim to fully answer them. Rather, we hope that readers will not only learn much from the pages that follow but will be stimulated to pursue for themselves some of the myriad questions that our volume raises.

Married Women's Employment in Rapidly Industrializing Societies: South Korea and Taiwan

Mary C. Brinton, Yean-Ju Lee, and William L. Parish

The long-term increase in married women's economic participation in the twentieth century across a range of countries has been a central focus of much recent research in sociology and economics (Goldin 1990; Mincer 1985; Shimada and Higuchi 1985; Smith and Ward 1985). In this chapter we critically evaluate several explanations of the sources of change in married women's economic participation by taking advantage of the semicontrolled "natural experiment" provided by South Korea and Taiwan. Both societies began the push for industrialization roughly two decades ago, and they shared many similar initial conditions. But despite their similarities, these societies subsequently diverged in the patterns of women's incorporation into their economies. By the closing decades of the twentieth century, married women in the two societies showed surprising differences in their age patterns of employment, types of employment, returns to education, and rates of pay compared to men.[1]

The combination of similar initial conditions with differing outcomes in a pair of societies provides a unique opportunity to examine the roles played by the interaction of labor supply, labor demand, patriarchal values, the international division of labor, and export-led economic industrialization in structuring married women's changing labor force participation. We develop an explanation that takes into account the interaction of social and economic forces at both the domestic and international levels. This is especially important for an understanding of the economic role of women in societies in Asia, Latin America, and Eastern Europe that have recently industrialized in the context of an increasingly internationalized world economy. We begin by discussing existing modes of explanation, then evaluate them using macro- and microlevel data on South Korea and Taiwan.

POSSIBLE EXPLANATORY MODELS

The *labor supply* conditions that lead to increased female labor force participation have been well theorized: as age at marriage increases and fertility falls with industrialization, decreasing family obligations free up more of women's time for labor market activities. Increases in human capital (both education and work experience) also generally make women more attractive employees and raise their potential wage rate, pulling more women into the labor market (Goldin 1990). This leads to the hypothesis that differences in the quantity and quality (i.e., wages and working conditions) of women's employment in Taiwan and South Korea hinge primarily on characteristics of women's labor supply: education, prior work experience, and fertility levels.

Labor demand explanations suggest, however, that whether labor supply conditions such as increasing education and decreasing family obligations are translated into labor force participation depends on the nature of local labor markets (e.g., Chant 1991). In developing countries with low labor demand, women with more education may disdain the few lower-paying, less prestigious jobs that are offered, leading to either an inverse or U-shaped relationship between women's education and work (Standing 1981; Smock 1981). Or, if demand for white-collar jobs remains modest, employers may reserve these jobs for men in order that they may earn a family wage. For example, in the United States and Britain before World War II and in Ireland until recently, strong "marriage bars" excluded educated married women from many white-collar jobs (Goldin 1990; Mincer 1962; Oppenheimer 1970; Pyle 1990; Smith and Ward 1985).

A promising way of integrating supply- and demand-based explanations is to analyze the nature of labor queues and women's place within them (Reskin and Roos 1990; Thurow 1969). Researchers who theorize about labor queues argue that workers with different ascriptive characteristics (such as sex) occupy different positions in the queue for jobs; these positions are dictated by employers' preferences. In this view, only when labor demand exceeds the supply of males in the queue will old prejudicial barriers to married women's employment fall. This type of explanation would lead to the hypothesis that differences between South Korea and Taiwan depend primarily on the level of labor demand in each society.

In contrast, explanations of married women's labor force participation that give primacy to *patriarchal values* suggest that regardless of women's qualifications or the nature of labor demand, women are channeled via a myriad of cultural practices into behaviors that either discourage labor force participation or encourage participation in only those jobs with the lowest income and prestige rewards (e.g., Papanek 1990). East Asian cultures such as Taiwan and South Korea are generally considered to be prime candidates for these types of explanations because of their strong extended-family, patrilineal descent traditions (e.g., Greenhalgh 1985; Jones 1984; Salaff 1981). Patriarchal values can affect behavior not only on the supply side but on the demand side as well, with policy makers, employers, and fellow employees making investment, hiring, training, and mentoring decisions that favor males over females (e.g., Pyle 1990). The hypothesis that emerges from this type of explanation is that differences between Taiwan and South Korea may be traced mainly to stronger patriarchal values in one of the two societies.

New international division of labor explanations typically argue that women at the periphery of the world economic system get the worst jobs in that system (see reviews in Beneria and Feldman 1992; Pyle 1990; Tinker 1990; Wolf 1990). One formulation of this idea lays the blame for a large informal sector of makeshift, self-employed, service jobs on multinational corporations that make inappropriately capital-intensive investments in developing countries (e.g., Evans and Timberlake 1980; Frobel, Heinrichs, and Kreye 1980; Kentor 1981; London 1987; Timberlake 1985). Another formulation emphasizes how menial, labor-intensive jobs are increasingly shifted from the core to the periphery of the world system, leading to a "fool's gold" explosion of jobs reserved only for young, single women who are dismissed as soon as they get married and begin childbearing (e.g., Nash and Fernández-Kelly 1983; Sassen 1988). Either framework leads to the hypothesis that societies highly involved in the world economy produce inadequate demand for good jobs and generate employers' preference for young, unmarried women who will work for a few years at low wages and produce competitively priced goods for the world economy.

Finally, *export-led growth* explanations are popular in economic and

World Bank circles. These offer the more optimistic view that suggests that unless local governments distort domestic factor markets (labor, capital, etc.), export production for the world market promotes labor-intensive jobs that eventually soak up so much underemployed labor that employers must raise wages and hire married along with unmarried women (e.g., Fields 1985; Galenson 1992; Krueger 1983; Lim 1990). Only countries that put barriers on imports and exports, who hem in labor with inappropriate legislation, or who mistakenly subsidize capital fail to enjoy these benefits. This type of explanation suggests the hypothesis that economies with higher levels of export involvement and little government distortion of domestic factor markets will generate more and higher-quality opportunities for married female workers.

METHODOLOGICAL APPROACH

We assess the applicability of these competing frameworks with both macro- and microlevel data on Taiwan and South Korea. Our macrolevel analysis attempts to explain society-level differences in urban married women's employment. The microlevel analysis attempts to explain specifically *which* married women get better-quality employment. We therefore combine a discussion of the intersocietal differences in women's employment that need to be explained with a discussion of how the theoretical frameworks outlined above either facilitate or hinder understanding.

We use macrolevel data from commonly available surveys in the two societies and microlevel data from specialized surveys on married women's work. The macrolevel data, mainly from annual government surveys, provide the context for understanding patterns in the microlevel data. The microlevel data are from two nationally representative surveys: the Taiwan Women and Family Survey carried out in 1989 in Taiwan and the Survey of Women's Employment carried out in 1985 in South Korea. The Taiwan sample includes ever-married and never-married women aged 25–59, while the Korean data are for ever-married women aged 15–59. From each sample we select currently married women aged 25–49 who live in urban areas.[2] The emphasis on young and middle-aged married women in urban areas allows us to provide a fine-grained account of the opportunities and difficulties women face in the evolving labor market.

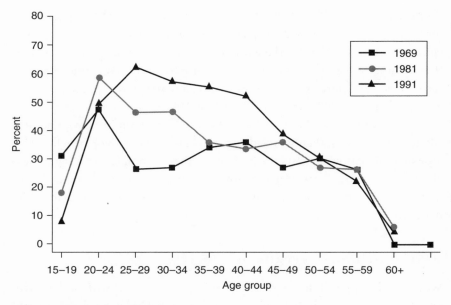

Figure 2.1.   Women at Work, Taipei City

SOURCE: Directorate-General of Budget, Accounting, and Statistics, Executive Yuan, ROC, *Yearbook of Manpower Survey Statistics, Taiwan Area, Republic of China,* various years.

WHAT NEEDS TO BE EXPLAINED

Taiwan and South Korea have shared many conditions in common, including extremely rapid export-led growth that has placed them among the leading "miracle" economies of East Asia. Given many similarities in economic growth patterns and world system position, the existence of three major differences in women's labor force participation is puzzling.

First, the two societies initially had similar female labor force patterns and subsequently diverged. During the early years of export-led industrialization, female labor force participation was very similar in South Korea and Taiwan (figures 2.1 and 2.2, bottom line). In 1970, when one-third to one-half of the labor force remained in agriculture, women in both societies exhibited a pattern of delaying marriage while they worked. This was typically followed by a postmarital exit from the labor force. Despite these initial similarities in women's labor market behavior, the Korean and Taiwan patterns have since diverged (figures 2.1 and 2.2, top lines). Older Korean women

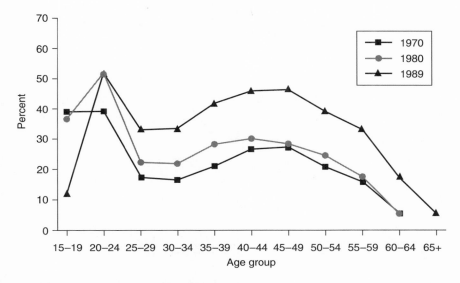

Figure 2.2.   Women at Work, Urban Korea

SOURCE: National Statistical Office, ROK (Republic of Korea), *Annual Report on the Economically Active Population Survey*, various years.

have increasingly entered the labor force once their children start school, a behavior that parallels and even exceeds similar patterns in Taiwan. But in great contrast to Taiwan, many Korean women in the prime childrearing ages of 25–34 remain outside the labor force (see also Cho and Koo 1983).

Second, there are differences not only in the *quantity* of work for young married women but also in the *quality* of work available to all married women. Our microlevel data reinforce the macrolevel data in showing that the age-specific rates of labor force participation for married women are much lower in South Korea than in Taiwan (table 2.1). Korean married women aged 25–29 participate in the labor force at only one-half the rate of their Taiwanese counterparts (27.1 percent compared to 54.9 percent) and women's labor force participation rates remain lower in South Korea than in Taiwan for older age groups as well. Notably, this is mainly a result of the fact that Korean married working women are much less likely to be in formal employment (i.e., working as employees) than women in Taiwan. Why do married women's rates of formal employment at any age in Taiwan so exceed their rates in South Korea? This is a puzzle.

TABLE 2.1

Employment Status Distribution of Urban Married Women by Age: Taiwan and South Korea

Age group	TAIWAN				SOUTH KOREA			
	Employee	Self-employed/ employer	Family enterprise worker	Total FLFP	Employee	Self-employed/ employer[a]	Family enterprise worker	Total FLFP
25–29	36.7	13.0	5.3	54.9	8.1	12.5	6.5	27.1
30–39	29.6	18.3	10.1	58.0	13.8	17.0	8.1	38.9
40–49	30.0	19.8	7.8	57.6	19.8	15.8	11.6	47.2
Total	30.6	18.1	8.8	57.5	13.3	15.4	8.6	37.3

SOURCES: Taiwan Women and Family Survey, 1989; South Korea Survey of Women's Employment, 1985.

NOTE: FLFP = female labor force participation.

[a] Among Korean women who reported themselves as employees, those who worked in their own house (i.e., domestic out-workers) were reclassified as self-employed.

Third, although we save detailed statistics until later, it is striking that *the consequences of education* differ in the two societies. In Taiwan, higher female education leads uniformly to a higher probability of employment. In South Korea, just the opposite occurs. Among Korean married women, more education leads to a lower probability of employment, thereby violating standard models that predict that greater human capital leads to the promise of higher income, which in turn pulls women into the labor force.

These then are the three major differences that emerged for married women in the two societies by the mid-1980s: lower overall labor force participation in South Korea (most strikingly for young married women); lower rates of formal employment (employees working for wages or salaries) in South Korea; and the failure of higher human capital to lead to higher probabilities of employment in South Korea.

MACROLEVEL ANALYSIS

Macrolevel data offer initial clues as to the applicability of the competing explanatory models outlined at the beginning of this chapter.

Labor Supply Conditions

Taiwan and South Korea have shared many similar labor supply conditions (table 2.2). In 1970, mean age at first marriage was slightly lower in Taiwan, but the gap between the two societies narrowed and then disappeared entirely by the end of the 1980s. Likewise, the crude birth rate plummeted in both societies. A parallel rise in marriage age provided more opportunities for women to accumulate work experience before marriage in both countries, and a shortened childbearing period made it possible for women to return to work sooner. Rising educational attainments also provided the conditions for an increase in women's labor force participation in both societies. Levels of female education have been slightly different; a higher proportion of women in Taiwan than in South Korea enrolled in secondary education, but Korean university enrollments overtook those in Taiwan. (Men's education patterns in Taiwan and South Korea diverged, an important point to which we return later.) Examining female life-cycle patterns alone, the common phenomena of increasing age at marriage, declining childcare obligations, and increasing education would lead labor supply explanations to predict not *diverging* but *converging* labor patterns for married women in the

TABLE 2.2
Labor Supply Conditions in Taiwan and South Korea, 1970–1990

	1970	1975	1980	1985	1990
Family obligations					
Age at first marriage, female					
Taiwan	22.2	22.3	23.4	24.4	25.6
South Korea	23.3	23.6	24.1	24.8	25.5
Crude birth rate					
Taiwan	27.2	23.0	23.4	18.0	16.6
South Korea	29.5	24.6	23.4	16.4	15.6
Education					
12–17-year-olds in secondary education (%)					
Taiwan					
Male	N.A.	69.5	71.9	77.9	83.6
Female	N.A.	61.7	70.0	78.6	87.4
South Korea					
Male	51.4	65.9	86.1	91.0	94.3
Female	33.1	48.5	76.1	87.0	90.5
18–21-year-olds in higher education (%)					
Taiwan					
Male	N.A.	11.2	11.9	14.2	18.3
Female	N.A.	8.7	10.2	13.5	19.6
South Korea					
Male	13.9	13.9	25.2	51.0	50.8
Female	4.7	5.6	8.7	23.2	24.4

SOURCES: Directorate-General of Budget, Accounting, and Statistics, Executive Yuan, ROC, *Social Indicators in the Taiwan Area, Republic of China*, 1991; *Statistical Yearbook of the Republic of China*, 1991a; *Report on Fertility and Employment of Married Women, Taiwan Area, Republic of China*, various years; National Statistical Office, ROK (Republic of Korea), *Population and Housing Census Report*, various years; Ministry of Education, ROK (Republic of Korea), *Statistical Yearbook of Education*, various years.

NOTE: N.A. signifies that statistics were not available for this year.

two societies, as discussed in Chapter 1 for all three societies dealt with in this volume. Thus, attention to labor supply conditions is clearly insufficient to explain the societal differences in women's labor force outcomes.

Patriarchal Values

Similarities in patriarchal values in the two societies also render incomplete a value-based explanation. Both societies share a common Confucian cultural tradition that emphasizes patrilineal and patrilocal family patterns. Until recently, it was common for women in Taiwan and South Korea to delay marriage while contributing some of their income to their family of birth, and then to exit the labor market at least temporarily to concentrate on child-rearing and household chores (Greenhalgh 1985; Jones 1984). Though there of course may be some distinctions between Taiwan and South Korea in sex-role values, the two societies have been quite similar (e.g., Arnold and Kuo 1984; Lee 1985). Without the benefit of detailed evidence on systematic, subtle differences between the countries from the initial time point of our analysis (1970) to the late 1980s, it is difficult to see how such differences could have led to the dramatic divergence in married women's work patterns. Based on the cultural commonalities, an explanation giving primacy to patri-archal values would predict similar, not divergent, female labor force pat-terns. Indeed, the initial similarity in work patterns around 1970 suggests that shared cultural values once did lead to similar outcomes. In these ear-lier years, analysts of Taiwan noted that premarital work for one's parental family was followed by a postmarital retreat from the labor force (see Green-halgh 1985; Jones 1984; Salaff 1981). Moreover, employers were eager to hire single women but reluctant to employ women after marriage (Diamond 1979; Kung 1983), illustrating the type of "marriage bar" phenomenon that existed at an earlier point in the United States, Britain, and Ireland (Goldin 1990; Pyle 1990). These patriarchal patterns, however, appear to have had much less impact on later Taiwan work patterns, suggesting that we must move beyond this level of explanation to account for 1980s differences be-tween South Korea and Taiwan.

Labor Demand: The Effects of Government Policy and World Market Involvement

Both societies have been highly involved in the world market. However, as measured by export volume, Taiwan (with exports equal to 60 percent of gross domestic product [GDP] in 1986) has been more highly involved than South Korea (whose exports equal 35 percent of GDP; Ranis 1992: 257; IBRD 1988: 243). Though neither society has had very much direct foreign investment of the sort that might skew capital intensity in production, South Korea has received massive foreign loans through subsidized government channels in ways that could skew production and labor markets.[3] These dif-ferences between the two societies have affected aggregate labor demand, edu-cated labor demand, and job flexibility.

Aggregate Labor Demand   One of the emphases in export-led growth explanations is how government intervention in capital markets can distort the types of industries that are promoted. There are two principal ways that this could have an impact on the labor market for married women: (1) the relative emphasis on heavy versus light industry and (2) the emphasis on more capital-intensive production, leading to lower aggregate labor demand. We examine first the issue of industrial structure and its relationship to women's labor force participation, using 1989 labor force surveys for each country (excluding agriculture). Contrary to expectations, it is *not* the case that Taiwan's industrial distribution is more dominated than South Korea's by light manufacturing or other industries that traditionally employ large numbers of women (appendix table 2.1, column 1). The industrial distributions of the two countries are in fact very similar, with some light industries such as food manufacturing, textiles, insurance, and real estate constituting slightly *more* of the total nonagricultural labor force in South Korea than in Taiwan. It is also striking that the proportion female in each industry is with few exceptions higher in Taiwan; across virtually all industrial categories, there are simply fewer Korean women employed than in Taiwan.

While it appears unlikely that industrial structure per se is related to the lower employment rates of Korean women, it is much more probable that government policies encouraging capital intensity have had a significant effect through lowered labor demand and the concentration of "acceptable" white-collar jobs in large firms (we discuss the latter under "Job Flexibility," below). In the 1970s, South Korean production became more capital intensive while Taiwan production moved in the opposite direction. In South Korea a great influx of foreign capital was funneled through government-subsidized loans to massive urban-centered business conglomerates (*chaebol*) that became more capital-intensive (Amsden 1989; Hong 1979, 1983; Kim 1989; Mason et al. 1980). In contrast, Taiwan experienced little foreign borrowing and few government loans, and initial industrialization involved a myriad of small enterprises scattered throughout small towns and cities (e.g., Amsden 1991; Hamilton and Biggart 1988). By many accounts, the low levels of capitalization and the very labor-intensive methods in these small firms exhausted Taiwan's labor surplus as early as 1968 (Blank and Parish 1990; Galenson 1979; Lundberg 1979; Ranis 1979). Thus, the Korean government's preferential policies toward *chaebol* led to greater capital intensity, while government policies in Taiwan led in the other direction, toward labor intensity.

In short, the observed differences between the two societies are consistent with an export-led growth explanation that emphasizes the capital intensity of firms.

Changes in urban unemployment patterns over time are also consistent with this mode of explanation. In South Korea, urban unemployment continued to be a nagging problem for years (see table 2.3, and Fields 1985; Galenson 1992). The large numbers of migrants who left the industry-impoverished countryside could not all find jobs in capital-intensive industry. In Taiwan, in contrast, urban unemployment remained at extremely low levels, and by the early to mid-1980s employers increasingly complained about labor shortages and the need to hire illegal foreign laborers (e.g., Chang 1987; Speare, Liu, and Tsay 1988). Similar trends in South Korea did emerge but not until the late 1980s, when unemployment began to be replaced by labor shortages, especially in small- and medium-sized firms. This delayed labor shortage coincided with the belated rise in older Korean women's labor force participation in the late 1980s (see figure 2.2). These parallels among the capital intensity of investment, the urban concentration of investment, urban unemployment rates, and married women's employment are consistent with the export-led explanation.

Educated Labor Demand Educated unemployment is common throughout much of the developing world, and explanations of the phenomenon typically emphasize features such as "the diploma disease," where educational credentials become the primary means to enter a modern sector that has dramatically higher incomes than the traditional sector (e.g., Dore 1976). The returns to education in South Korea as contrasted with Taiwan demonstrate the rampant credentialism in South Korea. Heretofore, there has been a greater education premium in South Korea than in Taiwan (table 2.3).[4]

Regardless of its causes—be they the greater capital intensity of large firms or Korean employers' strong preference to hire the best graduates from the best schools—this pattern of educational returns has given parents and children a strong incentive to pressure the government to relax controls over secondary school and college enrollments. Consistent with this pressure, Korean male secondary school and university admissions grew dramatically in the late 1970s and early 1980s (table 2.2; see also Chapter 5 this volume). With the subsequent explosion in the number of secondary school and university graduates entering the labor market, it is not surprising that by the

TABLE 2.3
Labor Market Conditions in Taiwan and South Korea, 1970–1990

	1970	1975	1980	1985	1990
Unemployment rates (%)					
National					
Taiwan	2.1	2.1	1.2	3.2	1.4
South Korea	4.4	4.1	5.2	4.0	2.4
Urban					
Taiwan (Taipei City)	N.A.	N.A.	1.7	3.6	1.8
South Korea (Nonfarm)	7.4	6.6	7.5	4.9	2.9
Unemployment by education					
Taiwan					
Primary school	1.4	1.4	0.5	1.5	1.3
Middle school	2.6	3.6	1.4	3.2	1.7
High school	3.9	5.8	2.7	4.8	2.5
College	3.3	4.3	2.3	4.2	2.2
South Korea					
Primary school	N.A.	N.A.	2.7	1.5	0.7
Middle school	N.A.	N.A.	6.3	4.1	1.8
High school	N.A.	N.A.	9.3	5.9	3.4
College	N.A.	N.A.	6.2	6.6	4.5
Paid-employee female-to-male income ratios					
Taiwan	N.A.	.51	.65	.65	.65
South Korea	N.A.	.42	.43	.47	.53
Paid-employee returns to education					
Secondary/primary ratios					
Taiwan	N.A.	1.47	1.23	1.19	1.12
South Korea	N.A.	1.75	1.45	1.34	1.19
University/primary ratios					
Taiwan	N.A.	2.36	1.94	2.14	1.79
South Korea	N.A.	3.75	3.32	3.03	2.21
Employees in large firms[a] (%)					
Taiwan					
500+ employees	N.A.	N.A.	8.6	7.4	7.7
100+ employees	N.A.	N.A.	26.9	26.5	23.9
South Korea					
200+ through 1975					
300+ starting 1980	52.1	51.9	42.4	36.3	34.6

SOURCES: Directorate-General of Budget, Accounting, and Statistics, Executive Yuan, ROC, *Yearbook of Manpower Statistics, Taiwan Area, Republic of China*, various years, *Monthly Bulletin of Manpower Statistics*, various years, *Social Indicators in the Taiwan Area, Republic of China*, various years, *Statistical Yearbook of the Republic of China*, 1991a; National Statistical Office, ROK (Republic of Korea), *Annual Report on the Economically Active Population Survey*, various years.

NOTE: N.A. signifies that statistics were not available for this year.

[a]Excluding government employment, and including in the denominator only firms with 10 or more employees.

early 1980s unemployment among the educated was much greater in South Korea than in Taiwan, where secondary school and university admissions remained more tightly controlled (table 2.3). As Michell suggests, "the Republic of Korea has a classic case of the diploma disease. . . . The imperfections of the labor market also mean that many well-educated people do not get jobs commensurate with their education" (1988: 104–106). South Korea produced too many college graduates in the 1980s for a society with only modest labor demand in the nonmanual sector (see Amsden 1989; Mason et al. 1980; McGinn et al. 1980). Moreover, when surveyed in 1984, Korean enterprises replied that their labor shortages were not in managerial, clerical, or sales jobs but in skilled manual (40 percent), unskilled manual (17 percent), and engineering jobs (14–18 percent) (Amsden 1989: 225). In short, the queue of job applicants was likely to be the longest for educated applicants, with much of this applicant queue being composed of highly educated males.

From these observations on total labor demand and the long queues of highly educated males in South Korea, the low levels of Korean married women's paid employment begin to make sense. Much as in pre–World War II United States or Britain, an adequate supply of educated males for clerical and other more skilled jobs has provided little incentive for Korean employers to lower traditional marriage bars to women's employment. This is in great contrast to Taiwan, where an inadequate supply of educated males forced employers to alter their patriarchal preferences. As an example, commercial banks in Taiwan abolished the marriage bar in the late 1970s, and by the late 1980s private firms generally no longer asked women to quit upon marriage. In contrast, employer pressure on women to resign from white-collar jobs at the time of marriage has been very strong in South Korea, beginning to diminish only in the late 1980s. With the passage of the Equal Employment Act in 1987, employer pressure on women to resign became more indirect than previously (KAWF 1989).

Job Flexibility

A final aspect of labor demand concerns the types of jobs common in the two societies. In South Korea, one of the consequences of government-subsidized loans to large urban businesses is that nonagricultural jobs are likely to be located in large firms in large cities, which require a lengthy journey to work and long, inflexible work hours (e.g., Amsden 1991; Deyo 1989; Hamilton and

Biggart 1988; Koo 1990). In the 1970s, when many of the work habits of to-day were being established, over half of all Korean private-sector enterprises with ten or more workers had more than 200 workers (table 2.3). Even by 1990, defining a "large" firm as one with 300 or more workers, over one-third of Korean private sector employees have continued to be in large enterprises. In contrast, less than 10 percent of Taiwan employees in private firms with 10 or more workers are in large firms of 500 or more. Even when one uses the very lax standard of 100 or more workers, only one-fourth of Taiwan firms are large. (See Chapter 1 for the comparison with Japan.) Thus, on average, Taiwan employees work in enterprises of a more modest scale, where connections between employer and employee are likely to be more informal and arrangements for working mothers are probably easier to work out.

Commuting times have also remained longer in South Korea. In 1990, the average Korean worker commuted 31 minutes to work, while even in Taiwan's largest city of Taipei, the average worker commuted only 24 minutes to work. In all large cities the Taiwan worker averaged only 18 minutes, and in smaller cities he or she averaged only 13 minutes in commuting to work each day. Thus, for women, the tension between work and family appears to have been greater in South Korea than in Taiwan. These facts fit the export-led growth explanation that emphasizes distortions from government policy and the labor supply explanation that emphasizes the potential role of family responsibilities in keeping women out of the labor force.

In summary, the facts suggest that it is not just supply-side conditions or foreign-loan/government intervention that are important. Rather, it is the intersection of *supply conditions* (similar between the two societies) and the *demand conditions created by government policy and the nature of foreign loan investment* (dissimilar between the two societies). The development of capital-intensive production in South Korea kept aggregate labor demand lower than in Taiwan, while at the same time South Korea's countryside was emptying migrants into the country's largest cities. The excess of educated workers was exacerbated by government policies that allowed the number of places at Korean universities to expand in response to the growing demand for education (see also Chapter 5 this volume). Finally, foreign loans to the Korean government were allocated principally to *chaebol*, thus fueling the growth of large firms. Long commutes and long working hours have been the result. In all of these ways, the nature of labor demand has been shaped in such a way that the opportunities for married women—particularly the highly educated—to work in the formal sector have been hindered in South Korea to a degree that contrasts with the situation in Taiwan.

MICROLEVEL ANALYSIS

If our macrolevel analysis is correct, the effects of women's supply-side characteristics should differ sharply in Taiwan and South Korea because these factors interact with very different demand-side conditions in the two societies. We first show how premarital work experience differently shapes postmarital work for women in Taiwan and South Korea, and then examine the different effects of supply-side factors on married women's current employment.

Work before and after Marriage

Examining young women's work before and after marriage shows how human capital accumulated through prior work experience promotes work in paid (formal) employment in one society but not in the other. The sharp discontinuity between pre- and postmarital work gives further proof of the persistence of a marriage bar in South Korea (table 2.4).[5] The proportion of working women who are employees prior to marriage is very similar in the two societies (93 percent in Taiwan and 89 percent in South Korea). But after marriage, the proportion of working married women who are employees drops to 67 percent in Taiwan; this contrasts with a more precipitous drop in South Korea, down to 30 percent. Conversely, the proportion of Korean working women in family enterprises and especially in self-employment rises sharply after marriage.

Turning to the occupational distribution among the formally employed, about one-third of single female workers in each society are clerical employees, another one-third are manufacturing employees, and the remainder are distributed throughout the major occupational categories. A higher proportion of single female workers in Taiwan than in South Korea are employees in service jobs, but other than that there are few premarital differences. However, the occupational distribution of married women is radically different in the two societies. In Taiwan, the proportion of all married women workers who are employees in clerical jobs is virtually *the same* as for single women workers. But in South Korea, the proportion drops from *37 percent before marriage to 1 percent after marriage*. In short, it is extremely rare for young married female workers in South Korea to be in clerical jobs, whereas

TABLE 2.4

Employment Status and Occupational Distribution before and
after Marriage for Urban Married Women Aged 25–29:
Taiwan and South Korea

| | TAIWAN | | | | SOUTH KOREA | | | |
| | Before | | After | | Before | | After | |
	%	N	%	N	%	N	%	N
Self-employed workers	2.0	(4)	23.6	(27)	4.0	16	45.8	(63)
Family enterprise workers	5.0	(9)	9.7	(11)	7.1	(28)	24.2	(33)
Employees	93.0	(181)	66.7	(76)	88.9	(358)	30.0	(41)
Administrative/ managerial	.0	(0)	.9	(1)	.0	(0)	.0	(0)
Professional/ technical	8.9	(17)	10.3	(12)	11.3	(45)	12.5	(17)
Clerical	32.0	(62)	31.1	(35)	37.3	(151)	1.4	(2)
Sales	3.9	(8)	3.7	(4)	3.4	(14)	.7	(1)
Service	10.2	(20)	8.4	(10)	2.0	(8)	4.6	(6)
Production	38.0	(74)	12.4	(14)	34.4	(138)	10.1	(14)
Farm	.0	(0)	.0	(0)	.5	(2)	.7	(1)
Total in labor force	100.0	(194)	100.0	(113)	100.0	(402)	100.0	(137)
Not in labor force	5.8	(12)	45.1	(93)	20.6	(104)	72.9	(369)
Total women	100.0	(206)	100.0	(206)	100.0	(506)	100.0	(506)

SOURCES: Taiwan Women and Family Survey, 1989; South Korea Survey of Women's Employment, 1985.

NOTE: Educational levels of the two samples are standardized using the Taiwanese distribution as the reference.

about one-third of this population of women in Taiwan are in clerical work. In contrast, the proportion of working women who are professional or technical employees remains about the same in the pre- and postmarital populations of Korean women; this mainly represents women in the teaching profession, one of the few white-collar occupations open to married women.

Do married women eventually return to white-collar work? To investigate this, we examined the premarital and current occupational distribution for women 45–49 years old (not shown). For this cohort also, the proportion of women workers in clerical jobs prior to marriage is similar in the two societies (around 20 percent). But about 14 percent of working women in

Taiwan occupy such positions in their late 40s, compared to only 2 percent of women in South Korea. Thus our conclusions are not restricted only to young married women; older married women in South Korea also show an extremely low propensity to be involved in lower-level white-collar work. The proportions of older women in administrative/managerial work either prior to or after marriage are trivial in both societies, as is the case for the younger cohort as well. These comparisons further strengthen the conclusion that for married women, the differences between the two societies in the quality of employment (specifically, access to white-collar jobs in the formal sector) are as great or greater than the differences in the propensity to be employed.

Current Work

Analysis of whether married women currently work and, if so, in what types of jobs, also demonstrates a very strong interaction between the characteristics a woman supplies to the labor market and the environment she encounters there.

In the quantitative analyses that follow, we emphasize as independent variables the qualities a woman supplies to the labor market. The first group of qualities constitutes her human capital. As already suggested, we infer that because of the greater competition from educated males and a continuing marriage bar in clerical jobs, educational attainment will not be positively related to women's formal employment in South Korea but will be in Taiwan. We also include work experience in the equation and expect a similar result. Educational attainment is measured by four categories: primary school or less, middle school, high school, and college or more.[6] Work experience is measured as whether the woman worked before marriage.

The second group of variables includes husband's income, measured as monthly earnings, and his employment status, which is categorized as employee, self-employed or employer, and not working.[7] We control for employment status because it is expected to have an important effect on the wife's type of labor force participation (e.g., wives of self-employed men are more likely to be family enterprise workers). Our analytical focus is on the effect of the husband's income *net* of this variable, with our expectation being that when labor market opportunities are constrained by a marriage bar the alternative of depending on husband's income will be more common.

The third group of variables represents household structure and family life-cycle characteristics (extended family structure, age of youngest child,

TABLE 2.5
Characteristics of Urban Married Women: Taiwan and South Korea

	Taiwan	*South Korea*
Level of education[a]		
Primary school or less	38.1	31.0
Middle school	16.0	28.5
High school	30.4	33.3
College or more	15.5	7.2
Worked before marriage		
No	11.7	32.7
Yes	88.3	67.3
Average earnings of husband[b]	25,871	403,360
(U.S. dollar values)	743	482
Husband's employment status		
Employee	65.8	64.1
Employer/self-employed	31.1	26.5
Not working	3.1	9.4
Family type		
Nuclear	84.9	88.3
Extended	15.1	11.7
Age of youngest child		
0–2	16.9	24.7
3–5	19.9	24.5
6+	59.8	46.2
No child	3.4	4.6
Age		
25–29	12.3	29.7
30–39	56.0	45.3
40–49	31.7	25.0

SOURCES: Taiwan Women and Family Survey, 1989; South Korea Survey of Women's Employment, 1985.

[a]Values other than averages are percentages.

[b]Units are Taiwanese yuan and Korean won. U.S. dollar values are used for the analysis.

number of children, and women's age). With the exception of age of youngest child, these are included as control variables in the analysis. Household structure is considered extended if respondents lived with their parent(s) or parent(s)-in-law, and nuclear otherwise. Age of youngest child is categorized into three groups: 0–2, 3–5, and 6 or older. Women's age is categorized as 25–29, 30–39, and 40–49. Distributions of the independent variables for the Taiwan and South Korea samples are shown in table 2.5.[8]

For the analysis of the determinants of married women's formal employment, we use a multinomial logit model that contrasts nonwork with formal employment, self-employed work, and family enterprise work. We keep these three categories of work separate because of the major differences in the content and rewards of self-employment, family enterprise work, and formal employment and because much of the implicit emphasis in our analytical models is on societal differences in formal employment. For each society we present two sets of models: a short model that includes women's human capital acquired prior to marriage (education and work experience), husband's employment status, and family life-cycle characteristics; and a long model that adds husband's income.

Results   The multinomial logit results for current types of work demonstrate how women's employment in the two societies is shaped by conditions in the labor market (tables 2.6 and 2.7). As we anticipated, education and premarital work experience affect married women's formal employment differently in the two societies. In the short model for Taiwan, education has a positive linear effect on women's probability of being an employee, with college education having a particularly strong effect. Experience in the labor market before marriage is also positively related to formal employment. The positive linear effect of education does not hold for women's self-employment or employment as a family enterprise worker. Instead, these employment statuses are generally more likely to be occupied by the less educated.

In the short model for South Korea (table 2.7), education is negatively related to formal employment, although this effect is not linear: high school graduates are the least likely to work as employees, and the effect of college education is negative but not statistically significant. Work prior to marriage is not significantly related to formal employment after marriage. The general negative relationship between education and employment persists for self-employment and family enterprise work as well, and work experience bears no relationship to these forms of employment. In both societies, wives whose husbands are employers or self-employed workers are less likely than other women to be employees and are much more likely to work in family enterprises (probably owned by their husbands).[9]

In addition to the direct effects of education, we expected that the link between Korean wives' education and formal employment would be mediated through their husband's income to a greater extent than in Taiwan. As shown

TABLE 2.6

Determinants of Labor Force Participation for Urban Married Women by Their Employment Status: Taiwan

	SHORT MODEL			LONG MODEL		
	Employee	Self-employed	Family enterprise worker	Employee	Self-employed	Family enterprise worker
Education						
Primary school or less	—	—	—	—	—	—
Middle school	-.16	-.21	-.25	-.09	-.17	-.26
	(.21)	(.21)	(.31)	(.22)	(.21)	(.31)
High school	.40*	-.92**	-.67*	.54**	-.83**	-.79*
	(.17)	(.21)	(.29)	(.18)	(.22)	(.31)
College	1.51**	-.64*	-.59	1.73**	-.50	-.83
	(.21)	(.31)	(.45)	(.22)	(.32)	(.47)
Worked before marriage						
No	—	—	—	—	—	—
Yes	.40*	1.04**	.98**	.39*	1.03**	1.01**
	(.20)	(.25)	(.37)	(.20)	(.25)	(.38)
Husband's logged income				-.44**	-.33*	.65**
				(.14)	(.14)	(.24)
Husband's employment status						
Employee	—	—	—	—	—	—
Employer/self-employed	-.36*	.65**	2.71**	-.37*	.66**	2.63**
	(.17)	(.16)	(.27)	(.17)	(.16)	(.27)
Not working	.16	-.14	-.20	-2.71**	-2.25*	4.00*
	(.36)	(.44)	(1.18)	(.95)	(1.02)	(1.96)

	Model 1			Model 2		
Family type						
Nuclear	—	—	—	—	—	—
Extended	.53**	.07	.26	.49**	.04	.37
	(.18)	(.22)	(.30)	(.18)	(.22)	(.30)
Age of youngest child						
0–2	—	—	—	—	—	—
3–5	.39	.04	.36	.37	.04	.39
	(.23)	(.29)	(.41)	(.23)	(.29)	(.43)
6+	.90**	.59*	.20	.90**	.58*	.25
	(.24)	(.29)	(.43)	(.24)	(.28)	(.44)
No child	1.01**	−.24	−.62	.97**	−.29	−.43
	(.37)	(.61)	(.96)	(.38)	(.61)	(.98)
Age						
25–29	—	—	—	—	—	—
30–39	−.39	.13	.72	−.35	.17	.66
	(.22)	(.29)	(.42)	(.22)	(.29)	(.43)
40–49	−.42	−.09	.39	−.35	−.06	.41
	(.27)	(.33)	(.48)	(.27)	(.33)	(.49)
Intercept	−1.38**	−2.08**	−4.44**	1.38	−.00	−8.70**
	(.31)	(.40)	(.62)	(.90)	(.98)	(1.66)
Observed proportion	.31	.18	.09	.31	.18	.09
N	1580			1580		
Log-likelihood	−1859			−1841		

SOURCE: Taiwan Women and Family Survey, 1989.

NOTES: Multinomial regression coefficients, with each of the three types of work being compared to nonwork. Numbers in parentheses are standard errors.

*p < .05, **p < .01

TABLE 2.7

Determinants of Labor Force Participation for Urban Married Women by Their Employment Status: South Korea

	SHORT MODEL			LONG MODEL		
	Employee	Self-employed	Family enterprise worker	Employee	Self-employed	Family enterprise worker
Education						
Primary school or less	—	—	—	—	—	—
Middle school	-.54**	-.38*	-.38	-.33	-.20	-.36
	(.19)	(.18)	(.26)	(.20)	(.18)	(.26)
High school	-1.32**	-1.09**	-1.24**	-.91**	-.72**	-1.19**
	(.22)	(.19)	(.28)	(.23)	(.20)	(.30)
College	-.46	-.83**	-1.46**	.25	-.20	-1.37*
	(.30)	(.32)	(.59)	(.33)	(.34)	(.61)
Worked before marriage						
No	—	—	—	—	—	—
Yes	.22	-.02	-.25	.27	.03	-.28
	(.17)	(.15)	(.22)	(.17)	(.16)	(.22)
Husband's logged income				-.86**	-.80**	-.07
				(.14)	(.13)	(.18)
Husband's employment status						
Employee	—	—	—	—	—	—
Employer/self-employed	-.59**	.03	5.58**	-.61**	.03	5.58**
	(.22)	(.18)	(.72)	(.23)	(.18)	(.72)
Not working	.32	.47*	-6.02	-4.77**	-4.26**	-6.47
	(.23)	(.22)	(39.12)	(.85)	(.82)	(39.2)

Family type						
Nuclear	—	—	—	—	—	—
Extended	.06	.08	.13	.06	.04	.14
	(.24)	(.22)	(.30)	(.25)	(.23)	(.31)
Age of youngest child						
0–2	—	—	—	—	—	—
3–5	.97**	.62**	.59	.95**	.60**	.60
	(.32)	(.22)	(.35)	(.33)	(.22)	(.35)
6+	1.65**	.43	.58	1.71**	.49	.55
	(.34)	(.26)	(.40)	(.34)	(.26)	(.40)
No child	1.52**	-1.31	1.86**	1.42**	-1.42	1.83**
	(.41)	(.74)	(.64)	(.41)	(.74)	(.64)
Age						
25–29	—	—	—	—	—	—
30–39	.16	.05	-.42	.24	.11	-.42
	(.27)	(.21)	(.33)	(.28)	(.21)	(.33)
40–49	.08	-.14	-.34	.14	-.10	-.29
	(.32)	(.28)	(.42)	(.32)	(.28)	(.42)
Intercept	-2.40**	-1.26**	-5.51**	2.44**	3.25**	-5.08**
	(.33)	(.24)	(.79)	(.84)	(.79)	(1.29)
Observed proportion	.13	.15	.09	.13	.15	.09
N		1698			1698	
Log-likelihood		-1486			-1448	

SOURCE: South Korea Survey of Women's Employment, 1985.

NOTES: Multinomial regression coefficients, with each of the three types of work being compared to nonwork. Numbers in parentheses are standard errors.

*p < .05, **p < .01

in the long model for Taiwan (table 2.6), the coefficients for the effects of wife's education on formal employment remain quite stable when husband's income is included in the equation. Husband's income itself is negatively related to the probability of the wife working as an employee. In South Korea (table 2.7), the magnitude of the negative effect of husband's income on wife's formal employment is larger than in Taiwan. Moreover, controlling for husband's income has an impact on the influence of wife's education. Middle school education no longer has a significant dampening effect on wife's formal employment, the magnitude of the high school effect is reduced, and the effect of college education is positive rather than negative (although still statistically insignificant). This offers support for our assumption that married women's education has an indirect effect on their employment via husband's income in South Korea but not in Taiwan. This is because in South Korea an educated woman facing the marriage bar in employment is more likely to use her educational credentials to compete in the marriage market for a husband who will provide an adequate income that frees her from working in one of the lower-status, lower-income jobs open to her (see Lee, Chapter 8 this volume).[10]

Based on aggregate work patterns by age and on information on the lower quality of jobs that are open to married women, we expected that Korean women with preschool children would be less likely to work than their counterparts in Taiwan. (See Chapter 3 for a further discussion of the arrangements sometimes worked out by mothers of young children in Taiwan.) As predicted, though formal employment is positively related to the age of the youngest child in both societies, Korean women with a child under two years old are particularly likely to be nonemployees. The effects of the youngest child's age are stronger for women in South Korea than in Taiwan.

In sum, our analyses strongly support the argument that the differing conditions of labor demand in Taiwan and South Korea shape the work patterns of married women who bring different characteristics to the labor market. Two general questions remain. First, are the country differences in the effects of women's (and their households') characteristics statistically significant—that is, are they truly large differences? Second, to what extent can the intersociety differences in married women's formal employment be attributed to different distributions in the two societies in women's human capital, husband's characteristics, and household characteristics? To answer the first question, we tested for interaction effects between each independent

TABLE 2.8

Estimated Probabilities of Employment for Urban Married Women
by Employment Status: Taiwan and South Korea

	TAIWAN			SOUTH KOREA		
	Employee	Self-employed	Family enterprise worker	Employee	Self-employed	Family enterprise worker
Estimated directly from logit results	.309	.178	.042	.111	.159	.004
Estimated assuming sample composition of the other country	.311	.154	.023	.110	.128	.007

SOURCES: Taiwan Women and Family Survey, 1989; South Korea Survey of Women's Employment, 1985.

variable and a dummy variable (coded "1" or "0") for the society itself. After doing this, the difference in the effects of high school and college education on married women's formal employment is indeed statistically significant for Taiwan and South Korea, and this holds whether the effects are direct or indirect (mediated through husband's income). The effect of husband's income is also significantly stronger in South Korea than Taiwan. Thus our major generalizations receive strong support; the effects of women's labor supply differ significantly in the distinct labor demand situations of Taiwan and South Korea.[11]

To answer the question of whether differences in the characteristics of Taiwanese and Korean women have a strong impact on the intersociety differences in employment probabilities, we calculated the probability of each type of employment based on the logit results in tables 2.6 and 2.7 (substituting the mean for each independent variable) and also calculated the probability of employment in each society using the variable means for the other society. Table 2.8 shows the results. The likelihood of Korean women working as paid employees is roughly one-third that for women in Taiwan, and these probabilities are barely altered when the sample composition of the other society is assumed. Also consistent with the figures presented in table 2.5, the likelihood of self-employment and family enterprise work is quite similar in the two societies. This is not strongly altered by standardizing each society for the sample characteristics of the other. Thus it is not the case that the differences we observe in urban married women's employment in Taiwan and South Korea are produced by differences in women's characteristics; rather, *it is the way these characteristics are translated into employment* that varies by society.

DISCUSSION

Our analyses demonstrate the insufficiency of *labor supply* explanations in explaining married women's employment, consistent with the general theme of this volume as presented in chapter 1. Women's education, premarital work experience, and fertility are very similar in South Korea and Taiwan; labor supply conditions are a constant that cannot explain the different employment outcomes for married women in the two places. Moreover, microlevel analyses show that labor supply conditions (such as education and premarital work experience) lead to opposite outcomes or different magnitudes of outcomes (the case of childcare responsibilities and husband's income) in the two societies. These results can be understood only by paying attention to the intersection between supply and demand factors in each society.

Much the same can be said for *patriarchal value–based* explanations. In earlier periods, such explanations helped account for the very similar female labor market patterns in the two societies. Patriarchal culture supported a rigid marriage bar that kept young married women out of many jobs, particularly the better-paying, more secure jobs as paid employees. But we suggest that one can understand why this marriage bar weakened in one society and remained strong in the other only by paying attention to the intersection between cultural and labor demand factors. When total demand for labor remained relatively flaccid and the supply of educated males was ample, employers found it easy to continue exercising their traditional cultural preference for educated males. But when demand for labor was strong and the supply of educated males became inadequate, old cultural barriers to hiring married women fell, as they had in the United States and Britain after World War II. We do not mean to argue that patriarchal value-based explanations are *wrong*, but that they are insufficient if we do not also pay close attention to the labor demand environment in which values are enacted.

New international division of labor accounts are inadequate for two reasons. First, early versions tend to lead to a uniform set of predictions for societies at the periphery of the world system. A foreign investment-based prediction is not helpful, for direct foreign investment remained minimal in both South Korea and Taiwan. When variation among societies *is* predicted by the new international division of labor, it is inconsistent with many of the observed patterns in the two societies. While the implicit suggestion is that a society with greater world market involvement will have more labor market problems—a formal sector with menial or unskilled dead-end jobs open only to single women and a large informal sector made up of self-employed and family enterprise jobs—this is inconsistent with the two cases we have examined. Taiwan's exports totaled a staggering 60 percent of gross domestic product compared to a figure of 35 percent for South Korea. Yet barriers to married women in the formal sector and the existence of a large informal sector more accurately characterize South Korea than Taiwan.

An *export-led growth* framework proves more productive for explaining the divergence in married women's labor force participation in South Korea and Taiwan. Export-led growth explanations suggest how government distortion of factor markets can weaken otherwise positive effects of export-led growth on women's employment. This is consistent with the labor-intensive, dispersed industrialization pattern of Taiwan versus the more capital-intensive, large urban conglomerate industrialization pattern of South Korea. The Korean government's decision to promote large, capital-intensive enterprises by privileging them with foreign loans does appear to have had important consequences. The prospect of long commuting times and rigid working hours in large enterprises has created difficulties for urban Korean married women to balance work and family responsibilities. Moreover, the government's promotion of large conglomerates in the 1970s raised wages for the more educated, which in turn caused parents to put more pressure on policy makers to relax secondary and higher education enrollments. This led to higher levels of educated unemployment and to longer job queues with males at the front and females at the rear. As a result, the fall of marriage bars to females in white-collar jobs in the formal sector of the Korean economy has been considerably delayed in comparison to Taiwan.

We draw two general conclusions from our analyses. First, we argue for the utility of reviving theoretical attention to the intersection between supply and demand factors in the labor market. Discussions of United States and British labor markets prior to World War II, the Irish labor market in the past few decades, and developing country labor markets show that the analysis of married women's employment can be quite complex during periods of significant economic transition (Goldin 1990; Mincer 1962; Oppenheimer 1970; Pyle 1990; Smith and Ward 1985; Smock 1981; Standing 1981). Our results from Taiwan and South Korea demonstrate clearly that attention to the unique intersection of supply and demand factors is critical in understanding that complexity.

Our second general conclusion is related to the first. In order to properly understand the nature of labor demand, which is a proximate determinant of women's labor force participation, it is important to pay attention to the ways that domestic government policy affects that demand. Accounts stemming from the "new international division of labor" tradition frequently fall short by predicting quite uniform consequences for societies at the periphery of the world market. Though export-led growth explanations are rather skeletal in providing only a checklist of market distortions to search for, they have the virtue of focusing attention on how the interaction between government policies and world market position shapes aggregate, urban, and educated labor demand. This is crucial for understanding the different labor market outcomes for married women in rapidly industrializing societies such as Taiwan and South Korea.

Appendix table 2.1 shows the surprising similarity in the industrial distribution of the labor force in Taiwan and South Korea. Moreover, there do not appear to be systematic industrial differences in the proportion of employed females in the two countries; in nearly all cases, there is a higher proportion female in Taiwan.[12] When we standardize each country's industrial distribution to the other's, surprising results are produced (see Durand 1975 and Pyle 1990 for similar analyses for other countries). South Korea's overall 34.6 percent female share *declines* to 32.2 percent after standardizing to Taiwan's industrial distribution, and Taiwan's 39.0 percent share *increases* to 40.7 percent when the industrial distribution is standardized to South Korea's. This is the opposite of what would be expected if it were South Korea's greater emphasis on heavy industry (or conversely, Taiwan's emphasis on light industry) that was producing country divergence in female employment. Only minor shifts occur when one standardizes on occupational rather than industrial categories, and the direction of change is once again in the opposite direction than one would predict. In short, across virtually all categories (other than a few limited categories such as restaurant and retail trade), be they heavy or light manufacturing, social services, or public administration, there are simply fewer Korean working women than in the comparable sector in Taiwan.

APPENDIX TABLE 2.1

Nonagricultural Industrial Distribution and Women's Employment
Share in Taiwan and South Korea, 1989

	INDUSTRIAL DISTRIBUTION (%)			FEMALE SHARE (%)		
	Taiwan	*South Korea*	*(T − K)*	*Taiwan*	*South Korea*	*(T − K)*
Primary products						
Coal mining	0.1	0.3	−0.2	11.1	5.4	5.7
Petroleum	0.1	0.0	0.1	20.0	0.0	20.0
Metal ore mining	0.0	0.1	−0.1	0.0	0.0	0.0
Other mining	0.1	0.2	−0.0	10.0	10.0	0.0
Light manufacturing						
Food	2.1	2.8	−0.7	35.8	41.2	−5.4
Textiles	7.3	9.2	−1.9	65.5	51.3	14.1
Wood	2.0	1.3	0.7	27.9	19.0	8.8
Paper	1.9	1.8	0.1	31.1	25.6	5.6
Chemicals, petrol. prod.	5.6	2.6	3.1	41.1	26.6	14.5
Nonmetallic	1.3	1.3	0.0	34.7	20.5	14.3
Heavy manufacturing						
Basic metal	0.9	0.9	0.0	15.9	6.2	9.7
Fabric. metal, machinery	15.4	11.3	4.0	36.2	22.5	13.8
Other manufacturing	2.5	2.2	0.3	53.1	45.8	7.3
Public utilities						
Electricity, gas	0.4	0.3	0.0	10.7	6.7	4.0
Water	0.1	0.1	0.0	28.6	12.5	16.1
Construction						
Construct.—general	5.9	7.3	−1.4	13.0	7.2	5.8
Construct.—special	2.8	1.7	1.1	6.0	7.8	−1.8
Commerce						
Wholesale	5.0	3.2	1.8	61.6	29.1	32.5
Retail	13.2	18.0	−4.8	43.6	46.3	−2.7
Restaurants	4.2	7.2	−3.0	49.0	61.7	−12.7
Transport, bus. services						
Transport and storage	5.4	5.7	−0.3	13.4	5.9	7.4
Communication	0.8	0.6	0.2	24.6	21.8	2.8
Financial institutions	1.7	1.8	−0.1	47.9	39.3	8.6
Insurance	0.7	1.0	−0.3	61.2	64.7	−3.4
Real estate, bus. serv.	1.9	2.7	−0.8	42.9	21.3	21.6

APPENDIX TABLE 2.1
(continued)

	INDUSTRIAL DISTRIBUTION (%)			FEMALE SHARE (%)		
	Taiwan	South Korea	(T − K)	Taiwan	South Korea	(T − K)
Services						
Public administration	4.3	3.4	0.9	32.5	15.3	17.2
Sanitary services	0.1	0.2	−0.1	40.0	19.2	20.8
Social services	7.7	6.8	0.9	54.3	43.6	10.7
Recreational services	0.8	1.2	−0.4	45.5	34.6	10.8
Personal services	5.7	4.8	0.9	48.9	54.7	−5.8
International bodies	0.0	0.1	−0.1	0.0	11.8	−11.8
Average/total	100.0%	100.0%	0.0	39.0	34.6	4.4

SOURCES: Directorate-General of Budgeting, Accounting, and Statistics, Executive Yuan, ROC, *Yearbook of Manpower Survey Statistics, Taiwan Area, Republic of China*, 1989; Ministry of Labor, ROK (Republic of Korea), *Wage Structure Survey*, 1989.

NOTES: (T − K) = Taiwan percent minus Korean percent, with a plus result meaning more in Taiwan and a minus result meaning more in South Korea. Female share = female as a percent of all employees in each industry.

CHAPTER THREE

Family Demands, Gender Attitudes, and Married Women's Labor Force Participation

Comparing Japan and Taiwan

Wei-hsin Yu

Attitudinal support for nontraditional gender roles and gender equality has increased in industrial societies along with the upswing in married women's labor force participation. Research has shown that women's gender role attitudes are closely connected to their work experiences and lifestyle choices (Gerson 1985; Glass 1992). Employed women tend to express more support than full-time homemakers for nontraditional gender roles, and full-time employed wives are more likely than part-time ones to disagree with traditional gender roles (Cassidy and Warren 1996; Gerson 1985, 1987; Glass 1992).

Although a strong connection between gender-role ideology and married women's employment decisions is found in many societies, *across* societies the link between gender attitudes and work experiences is sometimes confounded by the national context and the overall degree of gender inequality in the society (Baxter and Kane 1995; Panayotova and Brayfield 1997). The comparison between Japan and Taiwan demonstrates this type of inconsistent relationship between gender attitudes and wives' employment; married women in Taiwan are generally more active in the labor force, but at the same time, they are as conservative in their attitudes towards husbands' and wives' household roles as their Japanese counterparts. Given the positive association between gender-role ideology and married women's employment in many societies, the comparison between Japan and Taiwan presents a puzzle.

This chapter sets out to explain why it is that labor force participation among married women, especially married women with young children, is much higher in Taiwan than in Japan when gender attitudes do not differ markedly between the two societies. It has been argued elsewhere that wives' employment does not necessarily reflect unconventional attitudes toward breadwinning (Potuchek 1992). Rather, because gender boundaries are constantly created and recreated in daily experience depending on situational factors, the meaning of wives' employment and its connection with traditional gender roles—that is, husbands being breadwinners and wives being caretakers—needs to be explained with reference to the cultural and socio-economic context (Potuchek 1992; West and Zimmerman 1987). This chapter takes the importance of context seriously and examines the situational factors that determine the meanings of labor force participation for married women in Japan and Taiwan. In this way I try to provide an answer to the puzzle of why gender role attitudes and women's employment have a different relationship to each other in these two societies.

DATA FOR THE STUDY

Data regarding gender attitudes in Japan are from the Social Stratification and Social Mobility (SSM) Survey, conducted in 1995.[1] For Taiwan I use the second part of the Social Change (SC) Survey, conducted one year later. In order to make the data sets comparable, I use data from the SSM Survey on women aged 25–60, the age range for the SC Survey. As a result, the SSM survey data contains 1080 cases, while the SC survey data contains 1379 cases.

    In addition to the survey data, I employ data from interviews I conducted in the Tokyo and Taipei metropolitan areas from 1994 to 1998. I interviewed 73 women in total in these two areas; all were married and working at the time. The age range was 35 to 50 years old. Interviewees were found through snowball sampling. Questions I asked included information about their work histories, reasons for job shifting, their own evaluations of these job changes, expectations for future career advancement, and attitudes toward family vis-à-vis career.

THE DISCREPANCY: GENDER-ROLE ATTITUDES
AND WOMEN'S EMPLOYMENT

It has been discussed in both Chapters 1 and 2 that despite their economic, cultural, and social similarities, female workers in Japan, South Korea, and Taiwan differ in their labor force participation over the life course. It is common for Japanese and South Korean women to withdraw from the labor force in their mid-to-late 20s, when they are likely to marry or give birth. Despite

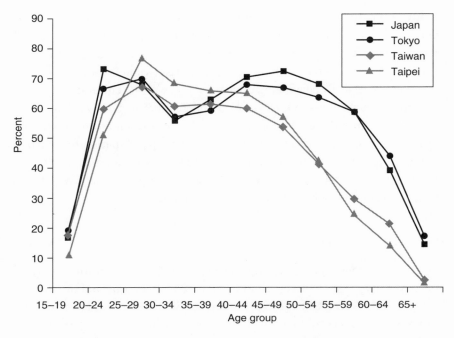

Figure 3.1. Female Labor Force Participation by Age, 1997

s o u r c e s : Ministry of Labor, Japan, *Yearbook of Labor Statistics*, 1997; Statistics Bureau, Japan, *Employment Status Survey*, 1997; Directorate-General of Budget, Accounting, and Statistics, Executive Yuan, ROC, *Yearbook of Manpower Survey Statistics, Taiwan Area, Republic of China*, 1997.

the increase in numbers of women in the workplace, there is little change in the trend of leaving the labor force upon marriage or childbearing among Japanese women (Brinton 1993; Yamaguchi 1997; Yu 1999a). In contrast, the proportion of Taiwanese women who continue working after marriage or childbearing has increased for every successive cohort (Yu 1999a).

Chapter 2 focused on explaining the difference in married women's labor force participation between South Korea and Taiwan. The current chapter concentrates on the puzzling relations between women's gender-role attitudes and employment behavior in Japan and Taiwan. Figure 3.1 illustrates the female labor force participation rate by age group in the two societies as well as in Tokyo and Taipei, the largest cities. While the difference between women's labor force participation patterns in the two societies is visible in the national figures, it is yet more striking when we eliminate the variation caused by different degrees of urbanization in Japan and Taiwan by looking

TABLE 3.1
Responses to Whether Men Should Work Outside of Home
and Women Should Stay In

	Agree	Somewhat agree	Somewhat disagree	Disagree
Japan				
All women	12.9	24.2	24.4	38.5
Women with junior college education	8.2	25.9	29.6	36.3
Women with university education/more	3.4	19.3	21.6	55.7
Taiwan				
All women	9.5	40.0	45.2	5.3
Women with junior college education	4.5	35.3	54.1	6.0
Women with university education/more	6.3	28.4	56.8	8.4

SOURCES: Japan: 1995 SSM Survey, part A; Taiwan: 1996 SC Survey, part II.

NOTES: All figures are percentages. Some rows do not add up to 100.0 because of rounding errors.

only at urban employment patterns. Taiwanese women (especially in urban areas) are far more likely than Japanese women to continue working through marriage and the early stages of childrearing (i.e., ages 25–40), while Japanese women are more active in the labor force when they no longer need to care for preschool children (after age 40).[2]

The difference in married women's labor force participation patterns in the two countries is puzzling when we look at gender-role attitudes. Traditional gender roles assume men as the primary breadwinners and women as the primary caregivers. This is no different in East Asian societies. In both Japan and Taiwan there exists a saying that wives should manage domestic affairs while husbands are in charge of business outside. Both the SSM and SC surveys specifically asked for opinions regarding this traditional saying, although the former asked only female respondents to answer the question. The distribution of answers is shown in table 3.1.

Japanese women's answers indicate that they are *not* more traditional than their counterparts in Taiwan. Fewer than 40 percent of Japanese women agree with the traditional division of labor between men and women, that is, men out working and women staying home, whereas nearly 50 percent of Taiwanese women agree. Due to the difference in the level of economic development in Japan and Taiwan, the average level of education for Japanese women is higher than that of Taiwanese women in the survey samples. Because education usually mutes the belief in traditional gender roles, it is possible that the higher level of education of Japanese women is responsible for the more liberal attitudes overall in Japan. I therefore separate out in table 3.1 the responses of highly educated women. As expected, the percentage of women who agree with traditional gender roles is lower in both Japan and Taiwan for women with higher education than for all women in the sample. However, the cross-cultural result is the same: the percentage of highly educated Taiwanese women who completely or somewhat agree with traditional gender roles is higher than that for their Japanese counterparts.[3]

In addition to the survey data, my interview notes also indicate that Taiwanese women are as likely to be expected to be the primary caregiver (compared to their husbands) in the household as their Japanese counterparts. For example, a middle-level manager in an investment bank in Taipei told me this story regarding her role in the family:

> My mother-in-law takes care of my son while I am at work, since we live together. . . . One day my son injured his leg while playing with other kids. My mother-in-law called me at the office and asked me to take off, so I could take him to a doctor. I did. See, it's me whom she called. She didn't call her son (i.e., the husband) and tell him to go home and take care of the child. She didn't even bother to call him to inform him of the accident. She would tell him what happens to our son only after he gets home after work.

As I discuss at greater length later in the chapter, grandparents often play key roles in childcare in Taiwan. But this does not mean that they bear the ultimate responsibility for children; this rests, as in Japan, with the mother.

Given that Japanese women's employment patterns better fit the image dictated by traditional gender-role ideology than Taiwanese women's, it is surprising that they are not as supportive of that ideology. How can we explain this? Why is the proportion of married women who work continuously much higher in Taiwan despite gender attitudes that are as conservative or more conservative than in Japan?

THEORIZING MARRIED WOMEN'S EMPLOYMENT DECISIONS

The puzzle shown in the previous section suggests that the meanings of married women's labor force participation may differ in Japan and Taiwan, and that there is no necessary link between female labor force participation and gender-role ideology. It is necessary to consider the situational factors that may affect the meaning of women's labor force participation. I argue for a closer examination of the structural factors that generate household demands on wives, as these demands—in addition to gender-role attitudes—play a crucial role in married women's employment decisions.

Household members consume certain commodities in the process of moving through the life cycle. In addition, supporters of the "new home economics" argue that a family is also a unit that produces "commodities," such as children, prestige and esteem, health, altruism, envy, and pleasures of the senses for the family's own consumption (Becker 1981; Berk and Berk 1983). Consequently, a family places demands on individuals who form the household—household members are not simply consumers, but have to contribute as well. Becker argues that traditional gender roles that encourage husbands to specialize in market activities and provide financial resources and wives to specialize in homemaking and provide housework and nurture are the result of this being the most efficient arrangement of household production (1981, 1985).

Becker's gender-neutral approach of explaining gender roles has been criticized for its neglect of real household dynamics and the unequal status of husbands and wives within households (Berk and Berk 1983; Brines 1994; England and Farkas 1986; Folbre 1988). However, it is useful to understand a married woman's lifestyle choices (continuous employment versus full-time homemaking) within the context of her family's demands. Even though married men generally are under pressure to provide resources to ensure the functioning of the household, the pressure on wives to accommodate family demands is arguably even greater because their bargaining power in the labor market as well as in the remarriage market is likely to be less than their husbands'. This relatively low bargaining power leads to the greater dependence of married women on their spouses than vice versa. As a result, married women have to take the family's needs into account in making employment decisions.

In short, a married woman's decision about labor force participation is not only a reflection of her own gender attitudes but also a reflection of the family's demands on her. When a family demands more care (i.e., childcare, care for the aged or disabled) and housework labor than financial support, the wife is likely to withdraw from the labor force. In contrast, if a family has a sufficient amount of labor for providing care and accomplishing house-work, the wife is likely to spend more time on market activities and provide financial resources for the family. This is why we find that middle-aged married women, even in very ideologically conservative societies, sometimes participate in the labor force when their children are old enough to provide some care and household labor to the family.

Structural conditions make certain resources quite accessible for households and others not so easy to get. The accessibility of the various resources needed by a family determines the family's demands on its members. Therefore, structural differences between societies that contribute to the accessibility of various types of resources should help explain married women's employment decisions and the relative strength of the connection between gender-role ideology and female labor force participation across societies.

The discussion so far has questioned the equation of women's labor force participation with changes in traditional gender roles, especially when we compare societies, because structural contexts in different societies may determine the meanings of wives' employment. The increase in married women's labor force participation may be a result of changing gender boundaries (i.e., redefining employment to be acceptable feminine behavior) due to situational factors, rather than a reflection of fundamental changes in gender role attitudes concerning breadwinning or homemaking.

Finally, it is worth noting that the importance of resource accessibility and family demands in determining married women's employment decisions should be greater in societies that exhibit strong patriarchal values and low marriage dissolution rates, since both of these encourage married women to place their family's needs over their own. Both Japan and Taiwan have relatively strong patriarchal cultures and low divorce rates. Therefore, the approach I propose that considers the interlinked relations among gender-role ideology, family demands, and female labor force participation should be quite applicable in these two societies.

EXPLAINING THE PUZZLE

Although households demand more than financial resources and domestic work (including childcare and homemaking), I discuss only these two dimensions because they are the most likely determinants of women's deci-

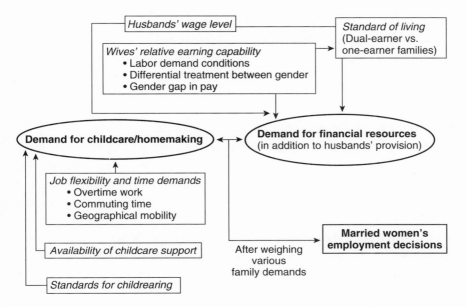

Figure 3.2.   Determinants of Household Demands on Wives

sions about whether to continue employment upon marriage or childbearing, a key issue in the Japan-Taiwan comparison. Figure 3.2 illustrates factors at the macrolevel that affect family demands on wives in a society.

For factors that influence a family's demand for financial resources, I focus on a husband's income level relative to the average living standard as well as a wife's relative earning capability. Whether a husband is able to provide for the family inevitably determines the family's financial demands on the wife. Moreover, at the societal level, overall labor demand in the economy, the gender gap in pay, and the differential treatment of men and women in the workplace all determine wives' earning capability relative to their husbands'.

With respect to factors that affect the household demand for childcare and homemaking, I will discuss job flexibility and time demands, the accessibility of childcare facilities, and average childrearing standards. Although job flexibility and time demands are an outcome of labor demand conditions, I consider them factors that shape the household demand for childcare and homemaking because they directly determine the amount of time employed wives have for these activities. Further, high childrearing standards in a society increase the demand for care within the household. Whether childcare support is easily accessible also determines the extent to which families demand mothers to engage in intensive childcare (see Hirao's Chapter 7 in this volume). The following sections discuss these conditions in Japan and Taiwan.

Demand for Financial Resources

Prior research has shown that whether wives participate in the labor force or not does not change the fact that they bear the main responsibility for housework and childcare (Berk 1985; Hochschild 1989). Nevertheless, the increase in married women's employment in late industrial societies has made dual-earner families more common. Whether a husband's wage is sufficient or not determines the extent to which the family needs extra income. Also, if married women are able to provide a relatively large amount of income to the family through working outside the home, this increases the incentive for families to encourage wives to work.

Husband's Wages   Husbands are still likely to be considered normatively as the primary income providers for families, so the financial demand on wives tends to be determined by husbands' wages relative to the prevailing living standard. The more insufficient a husband's earnings are to maintain a family's living, the greater the household pressure for the wife to bring in earnings as well. Labor compensation in Taiwan is relatively low because of the scale of most enterprises as well as the labor-intensive methods of production. In 1995, the average annual consumption expenditure per household in Taiwan was NT$591,035 (New Taiwanese dollars), while the average monthly earnings of paid employees were NT$35,450, according to *Reports on Social Indicators*, prepared by the Executive Yuan in Taiwan. Therefore, with twelve months of wages, one employee in Taiwan can on average pay for only 70 percent of the annual consumption expenditure of a household.

By contrast, male employees in Japan on average received ¥361,000 per month in 1995, and the average monthly consumption expenditure per household in the same year was ¥329,092. In addition to their monthly wages, Japanese employees receive an annual bonus equaling three to six months of wages. Hence, a male employee's wage in Japan is likely to be enough to cover the household consumption expenditures. In short, it is easier for Japanese than Taiwanese families to survive on the wages of one earner.

Given the ratio of the wage level and household expenditures in Japan and Taiwan, dual-earner families are more able to afford an average standard of living in Taiwan, while one-earner families in Japan can usually meet the average standard of living. Insufficient income from husbands' wages increases the demands for wives' financial contribution in many Taiwanese households. Thus, married Taiwanese women are under more financial pressure to work even though they seem to be more traditional in their gender attitudes than their Japanese counterparts. A Taiwanese woman in her late 40s who had worked in textile factories since the age of 13 put it this way:

> Why did I choose to continue working after marriage and childbearing? Hey, I didn't choose it. I didn't have a choice. You young kids have no idea how difficult it was in the old times (laugh). We were so poor. If I didn't work, where did the money come from? We couldn't live solely on my husband's wage.

The shift of family financial demands to the shoulders of wives in Taiwan can be illustrated further with the following two examples. First, according to a report in the *United Evening News* on September 26, 1998, recent research on urban middle-class men reported that more than 90 percent of middle-class men prefer their wives to work because "housing is really expensive in Taiwan, and it is helpful to have another earner in the household to pay the mortgage." Second, a comment from a young professional woman in Taiwan expressed current social expectations toward women:

> All my married female friends' mothers-in-law tell them not to quit their jobs after marriage or childbearing. The mothers-in-law say things like: "Don't worry, all you need to do is give birth and I will take care of everything else from then on. I will raise your children. And you can just focus on work. We need you to make money so my son doesn't need to be so hard-working and tired for the purpose of paying the mortgage. . . ." Of course all these female friends of mine are professionals and are really good at making money (laugh).

Wives' Relative Earning Capability   To understand the difference between Japan and Taiwan in married women's relative opportunities in the labor force, it is necessary to take into account labor demand conditions and the gender gap in pay. Chapter 2 discussed the high labor demand over the past several decades in Taiwan. Married women's labor became critical in the economy due to the labor shortage, which became more severe after educational expansion. As an example of Taiwan's labor shortage, the government used the slogan "making the living room a factory" in the late 1970s to encourage more housewives to be involved in home-based piecework (Cheng and Hsiung 1994). For the same reason that the government initiated such a campaign, many firms became willing to accommodate married women as workers (Salaff 1994).

While the demand for labor in Taiwan was greater than in South Korea, the contrast to Japan is even sharper because Japan moved away from labor-intensive production much earlier than either of the other two countries. Despite a low unemployment rate, labor surplus conditions characterized the first two decades of the postwar Japanese economy (Cole 1971). Labor demand did not increase very much after the early 1970s; labor force growth slightly slowed and unemployment increased slightly from the previous decades (Yu 1999b). In contrast, the labor force has grown at a much faster pace in Taiwan over the past four decades, and the unemployment rate has been lower than Japan's since the 1970s (Yu 1999b). As in most advanced economies, specialization in capital- or skill-intensive commodities in Japan discouraged growth in overall labor demand but created a keen demand for skilled labor (Wood 1994). The fact that Japanese management encountered a labor surplus (for semiskilled or unskilled labor) and a labor shortage (for skill-intensive labor) at the same time reinforced long-term employment, high pay, and extensive benefits for "core workers" (Crawcour 1978; Koike 1987), but led to little effort to accommodate the rest of workers.

Furthermore, the seniority-based wage system adopted by most Japanese companies encourages management to keep the noncore labor force young. Be it management's patriarchal preferences, the socially assumed work-family conflict for women, or the improbability of women being household breadwinners, Japanese women are rarely considered core employees in Japanese firms (Brinton 1989; Kalleberg and Lincoln 1988). That is to say, women are likely to be in the track where high turnover is expected. Moreover, to save on labor costs, Japanese management often pressures female workers to leave the firm upon marriage or childbearing (Ogasawara 1998 and Chapter 6 this volume; Roberts 1994).

Partly due to the unequal treatment of men and women in Japanese firms, the Japanese gender gap in earnings is greater than that in Taiwan (Chapter 1 this volume). Among all full-time employees, female employees in Japan earned about 60 percent of the wages of their male counterparts in 1995 compared to a ratio of 68 percent in Taiwan (Yu 1999b). The difference in the wage gap by occupation is even more striking. In Taiwan, female employees in professional, technical, semiprofessional, clerical, and sales and service occupations earned more than 80 percent of their male counterparts' wages in 1995, whereas Japanese women in all these occupations made under 70 percent of the wages of their male counterparts (Yu 1999b; Chapter 1 this volume). This shows that the earnings capability of women in white-collar jobs relative to their male counterparts is generally greater in Taiwan than in Japan. The earnings gap between men and women is even greater in Japan if we include all types of employment, because a large proportion of married Japanese women are in part-time employment (discussed in Chapter 1 this volume). This category shows the largest gender gap in earnings (Yu 1999b).

To summarize, Japan in comparison to Taiwan provides fewer opportunities for married women to shoulder the responsibility of being income providers. Relatively low labor demand, discriminatory treatment of women in the workplace, and a large gap between men's and women's earnings all decrease the earning capability of Japanese married women relative to their husbands. By contrast, the labor shortage and the relatively high female-to-male wage ratio in Taiwan increases married women's earnings ability relative to men's. Therefore, Taiwanese women need to shoulder more financial responsibility in the family than their Japanese counterparts because their husbands' earnings are likely to be insufficient and their own chances of providing a substantial contribution are great.

Demand for Childcare and Homemaking

Traditionally, childcare and homemaking have both been "women's work." The demand for childcare tends to conflict more with married women's labor force participation than does the demand for housework. While married women continue to spend considerable time on housework, the invention of modern appliances and the increase in purchasable services has helped. Moreover, childcare cannot be taken care of simply by lowering standards (as is conceivable with housework).[4]

Because the difference between Japan and Taiwan in women's labor force participation exists mainly among women with young children, it is critical to examine the structural factors affecting the demand for childcare.

Job Flexibility, Time Demands, and Job Rotation   The flexibility and time demands of a job determine whether a married woman can take the job without completely sacrificing the household demand for care (usually child-care). At the macrolevel, we are likely to see relatively high female labor force participation rates in a society that allows great job flexibility. For example, Brinton, Lee, and Parish argue in Chapter 2 that job flexibility is one of the factors leading to higher female labor participation rates in Taiwan than South Korea. Flexibility and the time demands of jobs are generally different between Japanese and Taiwanese workplaces as well. As Japanese management applies a familistic ideology to the workplace (Cole 1971), the "family members," that is, regular, full-time employees, in return devote extremely long hours at work to the corporate family, regardless of the number of hours they are required to work according to the Labor Standards Law. A full package of fringe benefits provided to standard, full-time employees also legitimates management's demand for long hours of work. Overtime work thus becomes, as much as fringe benefits, part of the standard employment contract in Japan.

Extremely long hours of work make regular employment particularly difficult for the mothers of young children. A 35-year-old married Japanese woman who works part-time in a family-owned dental clinic told me why full-time employment is not suitable for married women:

> When I first went back to work (after giving birth), I tried to find a full-time job. I had obtained my license for denture making then, so I tried to find a job in one of the medium-sized firms that make dental materials. I told every employer during my job interviews that I could only work until seven o'clock in the evening because I needed to be home by then to cook dinner and take care of my kids. I told them that I didn't mind getting less pay but I couldn't do overtime work. So I started to work at a firm that said yes to me. But right after I went to work, I found it impossible to avoid overtime work. I wanted to leave by seven, but they always kept me late. There was so much work to do. I went to tell my employer that I couldn't stay that late, and he was really upset and said it was my responsibility. He expected me to finish the work, no matter how long it took me. I was angry and told him that he had lied to me about the working conditions. I only worked there for a month before quitting. Then I thought, that's it. Full-time jobs don't work. I would have to do overtime work anyway—they always lie about it. So I didn't try again to look for a full-time job after that.

At the time of the interview, this woman had an additional part-time job from midnight to six o'clock in the morning, making *bentō* (box lunches) for convenience stores nearby. The two part-time jobs added up to 11 hours of her everyday life. She explained that she had to take two part-time jobs because part-time jobs did not pay well enough to support her family, since her husband was self-employed and had suffered greatly during Japan's severe economic recession (of the mid-1990s). It was obvious that she would have preferred to take one full-time job rather than two part-time jobs, if only she could find a full-time job that demanded less overtime work at night.

Another woman with whom I spoke told a similar story, but from a different angle: when excessively long work hours are not part of the standard employment contract, women are as willing to continue employment as men. This woman worked in a local ward office and told me that unlike anywhere else in Japan, it is common for women to continue their full-time employment in the public sector (see also Chapter 1 this volume). She explained:

> Women in the ward office seem to all work through marriage and childbearing. I asked them, particularly those who have kids, why they are able to continue their work for so many years. They said it is because they are always able to get as many days of annual leave as they should. You know, in many large companies, you don't get annual leave regularly, even though you are entitled to. You are too busy to take any time off. That doesn't happen in the public sector.

Statistically speaking, Taiwanese workers do not spend much less time at work than their Japanese counterparts. Until very recently, workers in Taiwan were required to spend 8 hours a day from Monday to Friday and at least 4 hours on Saturday in the workplace, adding up to at least 44 hours of work per week. Manufacturing jobs sometimes require 48 hours of work per week. Nonetheless, overtime work at night is less common than in Japan. Smaller businesses in Taiwan usually do not provide overtime pay, nor offer enough in fringe benefits to demand workers' devotion after regular work hours.

Furthermore, the arrangements between management and employees are relatively informal and personal in small- to medium-sized enterprises in Taiwan, which constitute the majority of businesses. Mothers in Taiwan with young children are often able to negotiate with small-firm employers to ease work-family conflict.[5] A woman who did bookkeeping in a small international trade company provided such an example:

> I usually do not need to work overtime, but sometimes we get busy and I have difficulty finishing work by six o'clock. My boss lets me bring the work back home and finish it outside the office. I've worked for him for more than 20 years and he trusts me. He knows that I have to take care of my family. Sometimes

we older workers, the ones with children, are late for work because of sending children to school, and he doesn't say anything. Last year, during the summer vacation of my daughter's elementary school, for a while I couldn't find any-body to look after her, and at the time we had an empty desk in the office, so I took my daughter to the office and asked her to sit there all day while I worked. . . . In a small firm, if the boss doesn't like you, he can show you a long face every day and very soon you will want to quit. But if he trusts you, it's usually pretty much okay to negotiate.

Another Taiwanese woman told me that she would sneak out of the of-fice to pick up her daughter from a nearby elementary school, bring her back to the office, and ask her daughter to wait there until she could leave the office. These stories are generally unimaginable in Japanese workplaces. Ironically, while Japanese management explicitly makes an analogy between the work-place and the family, the distinction between the public and private spheres is much more rigid than in Taiwan. One Japanese woman told me that her company arranged an overseas trip without inviting employees' family mem-bers because it was a "company tour," as if acknowledging the existence of one's actual family will interfere with one's loyalty to the corporate family. It is impossible for female employees to bring young children to the work-place in Japan as a way to handle unusually great demand for childcare. The contrast in job flexibility between Japan and Taiwan means that Taiwanese women are more able to assume extra financial responsibility in their house-holds without jeopardizing their traditional roles as caretakers.

Job rotation, a common practice in large Japanese firms to provide on-the-job training (Koike 1987), also creates conflict between family and work for Japanese women because it often requires geographical mobility. In con-trast, geographical mobility is rarely an issue in Taiwan because the average firm size is small and job rotation is not common. A Japanese woman in the *sōgōshoku* (managerial track) in a large firm told me that she had seen a greater proportion of married women in this career track quit than their counterparts in the clerical track (*jimushoku*) because the former track re-quires transfers to different parts of the country.

While job rotation is rarely offered to women (Brinton 1989), a hus-band's relocation often forces the wife to quit her job and follow him (Bielby and Bielby 1992). Several labor union officials of large Japanese enterprises that I visited stated that male employees in their firms are transferred to another city and another type of job about every two to three years. Such frequent job rotation further increases wives' difficulty in managing work and family at the same time. Moreover, the existence of the job rotation system per se sometimes is enough to encourage a wife to give up her job. The following example, coming from a Japanese woman in her 40s, illustrates this:

> I met my husband in the company when he was assigned to my branch as a result of job rotation (*tenkin*). Our firm is a huge insurance company. I quit when we got married because we worked in the same firm, and I knew that job rotation was common and frequent for male employees. If I had stayed in the same job—there is no opportunity for job rotation in that kind of job—he would have been transferred to other regions and I would have stayed in Kyushu. We would not have been able to have a family life. We would have needed to live separately. My husband has told me stories about couples in the firm who have to live separately because one or both of them was relocated.

City Size and Commuting Time   The commuting time to work adds to the time demands of jobs. The population density and size of cities determine commuting time to work and therefore exacerbate the time conflict between work and family for married women. Although the overall population density in Taiwan is much greater than in Japan, major cities in Japan are on average larger than Taiwan cities. While the population density in major cities in both countries is extremely high, Japan is more able to expand its cities because the total land area of the country is greater. As high population density in metropolitan areas increased the price of land, city residents in Japan moved to suburban areas for less expensive housing. The ever-present threat of earthquakes also prevented urban residential housing from developing vertically. Residential buildings in Taipei, for example, are generally taller than residential buildings in Tokyo. Moreover, earlier and better development of mass transportation systems in metropolitan areas allowed cities in Japan to expand outward; this is less the case in Taiwan.

The comparisons between Tokyo and Taipei, the biggest cities in Japan and Taiwan, respectively, illustrate the differences in city size between these two countries. The population density in Tokyo is 5384 people per square kilometer, whereas it is 9560 people per square kilometer in Taipei, according to recent census data in both countries (Statistics Bureau 1997c; Directorate-General of Budget, Accounting, and Statistics, *Social Indicators, The Republic of China* 1997). The absolute population size in the Tokyo municipal area, however, is four and a half times that of the Taipei municipal area. With four and a half times more residents and half the population density, the Tokyo municipal area is more than eight times larger than the municipal area of Taipei. In addition, more than 3 million people who do not live within the Tokyo municipal area commute to work in the city every day, according to census reports in 1995. All these figures indicate that the distance to work in Tokyo is usually much greater than in Taipei.[6]

According to a survey done in 1995 by the research institute of NHK (the abbreviation for the Japan Broadcasting Association) on the everyday time use of Japanese people (*Kokumin Seikatsu Jikan Chōsa*), the average commuting time for all Japanese workers sampled, regardless of area, was one hour and fifteen minutes a day. The average commuting time for residents in the 13 largest Japanese cities was about 10 minutes longer than the national average. In contrast, commuting time in Taiwan, according to the Time Utilization Survey done by the Directorate-General of Budget, Accounting, and Statistics in 1994, is 50 minutes per working day on average for all workers.

During my interviews, the issue of long commuting time was brought up frequently. For example, one woman with whom I spoke quit her job at a hospital in Tokyo because of the long commuting time. After marriage, she and her husband moved to Saitama, a prefecture adjacent to Tokyo where young couples can afford to buy a house. She then had to spend three hours a day on the train, getting to and from work:

> I felt so tired when I was working. I needed to spend three hours in total a day on commuting. There was never a seat on the train. And after a full-time job, I need to do housework. My husband doesn't do any. He comes home too late. I did that for a while and I became really tired. So I quit my job. When I worked, we both were so tired and we could hardly talk. . . . Oh, I am looking for a new job. I don't know. I want to find a job closer to home but it is really difficult. I think I may need to get a part-time job.

Long commuting time also causes time conflict for working mothers with young children, in particular when daycare centers operate on schedules that are unrealistic for full-time employees in Japanese firms (see the discussion of daycare facilities following). A young Japanese mother who worked in a private daycare center said that she was considering quitting her job sometime soon for her daughter, who was a little over one year old at the time. She explained:

I live in Kamakura and work in Yokohama. It's a long distance for commuting. Right now I put my daughter in a daycare center near home, and my parents-in-law, who live next door to us, pick her up in the afternoon before I get home. They have to send her to the daycare in the morning for me, too, because I leave home early. If I leave my office at 6 P.M., it is almost 8 P.M. when I get back home. My daughter is usually already asleep by the time I get home. With help from my in-laws, it works out okay. But I feel that I don't spend enough time with my daughter. When she is older I want to be able to spend more time with her. If I have to spend so much time on transportation, I hardly have time to talk to her. That's why I am thinking about quitting this job and finding something closer—I don't know whether I can, though. Maybe a part-time job. Well. I've commuted this far for several years, ever since I was single, but it didn't bother me before. Now I have a child. It's different.

As this woman admitted, the long commuting time was not an issue when she was single, because then she did not need to handle the dual roles of wage earner and caregiver. This supports my argument that married women's labor force participation, unlike men's or single women's, results from weighing the family's conflicting needs for care and financial resources. I asked this woman whether she had considered bringing her daughter to the daycare center where she worked, so that she could keep her job and spend time with her in the meantime. She replied: "I don't think so. Can you imagine bringing a young child onto a crowded train for two hours, without a place to sit? It is too difficult for children." As she points out, it is almost impossible to bring a preschool child on a rush-hour train in Tokyo. For urban residents in Japan, trains or buses, which are extremely crowded during rush hour, are the only means of transportation. Driving a child or taking a taxi to a daycare center is rarely an option because the cost is extremely high. Working mothers with young children have to send their children to daycare centers near their home, not their workplace. As a result, the schedules of daycare centers need to accommodate working mothers' commuting time, but this is usually not the case.

Availability of Childcare Facilities   The accessibility of childcare facilities has a great impact on women's labor supply during the early stage of childrearing. In Japan, providing childcare facilities is the responsibility of local governments. Local governments set up kindergartens (*yochien*) and daycare centers (*hoikuen*) as well as manage applications and admissions to public childcare facilities every year. Kindergartens accept older children, whose mothers are likely to be full-time homemakers, because children stay there for only a short amount of time (e.g., from 10 A.M. to 1 or 2 P.M.). Day-care centers, designed for full-time employed mothers, provide care for children aged 0 to 6, and stay open until 5 or 6 P.M. in most cases. Local governments also subsidize privately owned childcare facilities and require them to operate exactly the same way as public ones. Public daycare centers, including government-subsidized ones, charge based on parents' income level and therefore are relatively inexpensive. While private childcare facilities do exist, their high cost means that public ones are what most working mothers rely on.[7] There are also nannies and baby-sitters, but the number is small because examinations for licenses are required if they work through agencies.

According to my interviews with mothers and care providers at daycare centers in Japan, there has been and is still a great lack of childcare centers provided by local government in almost all urban areas. A 45-year-old woman told me her story:

> I had my mother-in-law take care of my first child. At the time we lived with my parents-in-law. I was able to work because of their help. Then my mother-in-law got sick, so we moved out of their house and they could not help us anymore. I didn't want to quit. But it was extremely difficult to find a daycare center nearby. I tried all the possibilities. But I was told that I had to be on the waiting list for several months to a year before I could put my child into a day-care center. So I had no choice. I had to quit.

While a decrease in the birth rate in Japan has reduced the shortage of public childcare support, it is still difficult for Japanese women to continue working after childbearing because the shortage of childcare for children under age three remains a problem. A worker in a public daycare center spoke to me about how difficult it has been for young working mothers to find childcare support:

> We do not have enough facilities to take all children under three years old. There is always a long waiting list for babies between birth and three years old to enter our center. After age three it gets easier, because older children require fewer caretakers around and hence we can accommodate more of them. I know many young mothers on the waiting list are really worried. They are allowed to take unpaid childcare leave (*ikuji kyūgyō*) for one year after giving birth, as the law says. But some of them still cannot get in after waiting for nearly one year. They tell me how worried they are. They are not able to go back to work if they don't find a place for their babies before the leave ends. People like us,

who work in a daycare center, know how difficult it is to get in. So we apply to the ward office—it is the ward office, not us, that decides which children we accept—as early as possible. But many women don't know that. They have a whole year of leave but they don't apply until the seventh month or so. By then it is too late. Not enough waiting time. Moreover, the ward office releases admissions every April, so the timing of childbearing also determines how soon the child can be admitted.

The other problem with daycare facilities in Japan is that they do not operate according to the schedule of many employed mothers. Most of them are open from eight o'clock in the morning to five or six o'clock in the afternoon. As discussed above, full-time work in Japan often requires long working hours and long commuting time. As part of their gender roles, mothers are likely to be the ones to take children to and pick them up from daycare centers (see Hirao, Chapter 7 this volume). Long commuting time and frequent overtime work make it extremely difficult for working mothers to arrive at daycare centers by six o'clock in the evening. When I asked a *kachō* (section manager) in a ward office, who was responsible for women's welfare within the ward, whether the local government had considered extending the operating hours of public daycare centers to accommodate working mothers' schedules, she replied: "We don't have any plan like that. I don't think it's right for Japanese corporations to make employees work this late. Shouldn't corporations shorten employees' working hours, rather than daycare centers extending their hours?"

Her reply to some extent reflects the government's effort to promote leisure and shorten working hours. However, the upper limit for working hours set by the Labor Standards Law is *tatemae* (the "principle," which does not necessarily reflect the underlying reality) for both management and employees. To comply with the law, many overtime hours are simply unreported. When both corporations and childcare providers show no intention of changing the current system, it is working mothers who have to leave the labor force in order to fill the childcare needs in their family.

By contrast, childcare is arranged in a much more informal way in Taiwan. Grandparents and nannies are the main resources of childcare support for working mothers with young children. As shown in figure 3.1, a much higher proportion of women over age 45 are in the labor force in Japan than in Taiwan. This reflects the fact that more grandmothers are available to do childcare (i.e., are not in the labor force) in Taiwan. Furthermore, about one-third of households in Taiwan were constituted by extended families in 1995 compared to only about 16 percent of Japanese households (Yu 1999b; Chapter 1 this volume). Nor did these statistics include, of course, those families living next door to or in the same building with grandparents. Several women to whom I spoke in Taiwan were able to seek support from their own parents or parents-in-law by choosing to live nearby. This is less possible in Japan, especially in metropolitan areas, because of the larger size of cities and because young couples have few choices for residence areas due to the extremely high housing costs.

In fact, according to the report of the Ministry of Internal Affairs, about two-thirds of women in Taiwan prefer to have parents or grandparents as the primary caregivers for preschool children (1993). This is less the case in Japan; I found in my interviews that many women believed that professional daycare workers do a better job. Given that most childcare givers are not professionally trained in Taiwan, it is not hard to understand why most Taiwanese women whom I interviewed stated that they consider grandparents to be the most reliable and trustworthy. By contrast, during my interviews, I found that it is common for Japanese women to feel that it is inappropriate to cause trouble to their parents or parents-in-laws by asking them to take care of grandchildren.

These varying attitudes can be partly attributed to the older generation's different degree of financial dependence on the young in Japan and Taiwan. Many older people in Taiwan rely on financial support from children in addition to their own savings, as retirement pension programs have been unavailable to the majority of them (Parish and Willis 1993; Lee, Parish, and Willis 1994). Using survey data from the late 1980s, Lee, Parish, and Willis show that the average amount of financial support Taiwanese parents receive from their children after retirement is quite substantial (1994). In contrast, the retirement programs of large firms and the public pension program make financial dependence of the older generation on the young weaker in Japan. For example, when the *Yomiuri Shimbun* (*Yomiuri Daily* newspaper) asked respondents in a national poll in 1990 to list multiple sources of old-age financial support, only 9 percent of respondents cited children as one of their sources. The financial dependence of older people in Taiwan strengthens the ties between generations and thereby legitimates grandparents' roles as caregivers for their preschool-aged grandchildren. In fact, I sometimes overheard

Taiwanese women complain in public about their parents-in-law being unwilling to take care of their children; grandparents' help was taken for granted.

With grandparents conveniently serving as caregivers, for many married women in Taiwan the household demand for them to generate financial resources surpasses the demand for them to provide intensive childcare. The economic dependence of old people and the low average wage level both contribute to this increasingly popular household division of labor *between generations* in Taiwan.[8] In three-generation households, grandparents play the role of the primary caregiver, while the middle generation, including the husband and wife, focus on their roles as income contributors; this is despite the common belief in the traditional gendered division of labor. The example given above about mothers-in-law who encourage their daughters-in-law to give birth but stay in the labor force illustrates this household division of labor.

Taiwanese women without parents or parents-in-law close by may hire nannies or baby-sitters. In the absence of state regulation, hardly any qualifications are required for baby-sitters in Taiwan. Working mothers usually find nannies who live nearby, through neighbors. As a Taiwanese woman put it, "If one is not picky, that is, if one does not care too much about the quality of a nanny, it's pretty easy to find one. Any woman who does not have a job can do it."

Having grandparents or housewives in the neighborhood provide childcare allows more flexibility than daycare centers. Since in the former cases children are usually taken care of in the caregiver's home, the arrangements tend to be more personal than institutional and the time to leave and pick up a child can usually be arranged based on the mother's work schedule. Staying overnight at the nanny's or grandparents' place is also possible when the workload is extremely high.

Standards for Childrearing Prevailing standards of childrearing are another reason why differences exist between Japan and Taiwan in the household demand for mothers' childcare vis-à-vis their income from working. To illustrate the standards for childrearing in Taiwan, "weekend parents" have become increasingly popular and acceptable for dual-earner families in metropolitan areas. That is to say, some Taiwanese parents rely on nannies or grandparents during the workweek and take their preschool children home only on weekends. This is unheard of in Japan for two reasons. First, 24-

hour childcare is unavailable in Japan. Second, and more importantly, the standards of childrearing make weekend parents unacceptable in Japanese society.

It may not be surprising that, between Japan and Taiwan, it is the more developed society where people generally pay more attention to child welfare. Hirao discusses prevailing childrearing standards in Japan and the *kyōiku mama* (education mother) phenomenon in greater length in Chapter 7 of this volume. Being a *kyōiku mama* requires that a mother devote a great deal of time facilitating children's study in and after school. In contrast, the image of mothers as educators barely comes to mind in Taiwanese society. The following interview note represents a common sentiment among Japanese mothers about raising children:

> I think women ought to work. A job is important for a woman. But family is important, too. Sometimes I look at those women who spend all day in the office and put their children in daycare centers from eight o'clock in the morning to six or seven o'clock at night, and I wonder what their children will grow up to be. These women don't get time to be with their children. Their children have to grow up without having their mothers around much.

As high standards for childrearing increase the family's demands on mothers for childcare, married women in Japan encounter tremendous pressure not to continue working outside the home. A young mother who had just given birth and gone back to her *sōgōshoku* job in a large company recounted to me her experience of this kind of pressure:

> I have been told by many people that staying at work may hurt my relationship with my daughter. They also say it can hurt my daughter psychologically if she doesn't have her mother with her 24 hours a day. People kept telling me that I should quit my job when I was pregnant. Everybody says things like "what a poor baby! (*kawaisō*)" when they know I put my daughter in a daycare center until 8 P.M. every day. . . . I know women who quit because other people keep saying things like that.

The higher standards for childrearing in Japan contribute to greater tension between work and family for Japanese women than for their Taiwanese counterparts. The childrearing standards in Japan make the relative demand for childcare in an average Japanese household greater than in an average Taiwanese household. As a result, married women in Taiwan are more able to address the financial needs of the family and participate in the labor force.

CONCLUSION

In this chapter I have shown that Taiwanese women, though agreeing with traditional gender roles that characterize women's responsibility as being in the home, are more likely to cope with employment and rear preschool children at the same time than their Japanese counterparts. While many studies have shown that within a society there is usually a strong connection between gender attitudes and women's labor force participation (e.g., Cassidy and Warren 1996; Gerson 1985; Glass 1992), this cross-national study shows that structural conditions that affect the balance between the family's demands for childcare and its need for financial resources play an important role in determining whether women leave the labor force at marriage or childbearing. This is true *despite* the gender-role ideology that prevails in the society.

In Taiwan, childcare is easily accessible and relatively costless. Due to a low average wage level, a single earner is usually insufficient to meet a family's demand for financial resources. High labor demand in the economy also means that it is relatively easy for women to find jobs. In addition, job flexibility is quite high because employers have to adapt to the labor shortage by hiring women. These factors together encourage families to emphasize wives' earnings more than their time on childcare or housework. Women's roles are in a sense transformed to incorporate the family's financial needs, and the responsibility of childcare is transferred to grandparents or nannies, whose help is relatively easy to get.

By contrast, Japanese families often have higher demands for care than for the income generated by wives and mothers. Male employees' wages are relatively high compared to the standard of living, and the relative earning capability of married women is low (due to the labor surplus and the large gender gap in pay). The childcare system is rigid and spaces in it are scarce. General standards for childrearing are high. As a result of all of these conditions, women's role in providing childcare becomes much more important than the role of offering supplementary income as far as Japanese households are concerned. This is particularly the case when there are young children in the family. Therefore, the predominant types of household demands, conditioned by structural factors, determine Japanese women's labor force withdrawal as well as Taiwanese women's continuation of employment after marriage and childbearing.

It is worth noting that this chapter demonstrates that meeting a family's financial needs does not necessitate a complete change of gender-role ideology. The fact that many married women in Taiwan play a role in supporting the household economy does not seem to actually shake their belief that a wife should be the primary caregiver in the household; contributing money to the family is also one way of taking care of the family. While mothers who cannot arrange childcare will withdraw from the labor force, women in high-paying white-collar jobs in particular often find staying at work and increasing household income to be the best way to take care of the family.

Although the primary responsibility of providing for the family and being the person representing the household to the "outside" world still belongs to husbands, married women's roles in Taiwan have extended to include the role of supplementary provider (see also Chapter 10, this volume, on wives' key roles as "inside persons" in family businesses). This explains why we see a relatively active female labor force and at the same time a relatively high approval rate for the traditional gendered division of labor in Taiwan. As the role of supplementary provider becomes added to women's image, the pressure in society shifts to be against women who choose to ignore the family's demand for extra income. As a result, the office atmosphere for female white-collar workers in Taiwan regarding marriage, pregnancy, and work is remarkably different from Japan. During my field research in Taiwan, I noticed several pregnant women in service occupations wearing company-made uniforms. This indicates that continuing work during pregnancy is common enough for firms to make uniforms for pregnant women. During my 1½-year stay in Tokyo, I did not see any pregnant woman working in department stores or as tellers in banks. A comment by a Taiwanese woman who had a one-year-old daughter and worked in a large commercial bank evidences the very different office atmosphere in Taiwan for young mothers with white-collar jobs:[9]

> I actually don't mind quitting my job and being a full-time mother. I think it's important to spend time with my daughter before she turns three. But the fact is, these days there is hardly anyone who quits upon childbearing. If women leave it is usually for a better job, not for giving birth. I've seen one woman who used giving birth as the reason to quit—but three months later I found her in another bank. If you quit, your coworkers may wonder: Why? What's wrong? Why are you quitting a job if nothing is really wrong? It's as if quitting a job because of giving birth is not acceptable.

The comparison between Japan and Taiwan supports the idea that the actual content of gender roles is dynamic (Potuchek 1992; West and Zimmerman 1987). Structural conditions that shape family demands can encourage changes in the meanings attached to married women's employment. This also means, of course, that increases in married women's employment may occur in the absence of fundamental changes in either gender-role ideology or gender inequality in society. The transformation of married women's roles in households in Taiwan needs to be understood in a context that necessitates women's provision of additional income and dampens the need for mothers' provision of childcare as a means to this end. Rather than a reflection of increasingly egalitarian gender-role ideology, married women's labor force roles reflect the family demands placed on women's shoulders. It remains to be seen whether women's roles outside the home will feed back *into* gender ideology in Taiwan in the long run.

CHAPTER FOUR

Women, Work, and Marriage in Three East Asian Labor Markets

The Cases of Taiwan, Japan, and South Korea

Yean-Ju Lee and Shuichi Hirata

In Japan and South Korea, almost two-thirds of women in the labor market quit their jobs at the time of marriage, and many later reenter the labor market in middle age. As previous chapters have demonstrated, this M-shaped pattern of labor force participation by age has persisted for the past few decades, ever since the size of the female labor force in the formal sector came to exceed that in the informal sector in these countries. In contrast, fewer women (about half) in Taiwan quit at marriage. Taiwanese women's rate of labor force participation peaks during their late 20s and then declines gradually, with the most rapid declines in the early 30s and then again from the mid-40s on (Chapters 1, 2, and 3 this volume; Hirata 1998a).

The comparative chapters of this volume suggest that women's prelabor market human capital, that is, education, cannot explain these differences in married women's employment across Taiwan, Japan, and South Korea. In Taiwan, for example, where educational levels are the lowest among the three societies, the rate of married women's labor force participation is the highest. This suggests that women's opportunities for employment as well as for on-the-job training and promotion are crucial for cross-country differences in married women's employment. Differential family circumstances may also contribute to these country differences.

This chapter explores the factors associated with women's separation from their jobs at the time of first marriage in Taiwan, Japan, and South Korea. This job separation may be either voluntary or involuntary; we are interested in examining what is associated with either type.[1] By focusing on job separation, we can examine differences and similarities among the three societies in how the labor market and the family affect married women's labor force participation. Specifically, we ask whether job separation at the time of first marriage seems to be mainly the outcome of women's cost-benefit considerations of their time use, or the result of more structural constraints posed by labor markets. Neoclassical economic models mainly emphasize the former, that is, women's relative productivity at work and home. Labor-market structure theories, on the other hand, explain women's labor force participation with reference to labor market structures and women's positions in them.

In looking at how the predictions of neoclassical economic and labor market models play out in Taiwan, Japan, and South Korea, we pay special attention to the relationship between the *timing* of marriage and women's job separation. We do so because women in different labor market circumstances may choose when to marry partly based on the structural constraints posed by work. The relationships between marriage timing and job separation may therefore provide insight into women's work motivations.

TWO THEORETICAL FRAMEWORKS FOR MARRIED WOMEN'S LABOR FORCE PARTICIPATION

In the following, we present two broadly defined perspectives on married women's labor force participation and discuss how they might be relevant in Taiwan, Japan, and South Korea. One emphasizes women's cost/benefit calculations, and the other highlights structural circumstances that women face in the labor market.

The New Home Economics

The new home economics model explains various family processes, including marriage, divorce, childbearing, and wives' employment based on neoclassical economic concepts. The model explains married women's labor force participation based on their relative productivity in the labor market and in the home. It posits that married women will work outside the home if their market wages are higher than the wages associated with their home production (Heckman 1974; Mincer 1962; Schultz 1980). Reservation wage refers to the (shadow) value of women's time in nonmarket activities, and it is determined mainly by spouse's income. Women's high market wages in effect lower the household's demand for their nonmarket time, whereas husbands' high market wages have the opposite effect of *increasing* this demand (Heckman 1974;

Schultz 1980). According to the model, a large gender wage gap will discourage married women's labor force participation. This prediction is consistent with macrolevel data from Taiwan, Japan, and South Korea. In Taiwan, where the gender wage gap is the smallest, the rate of married women's labor force participation is the highest (Chapter 1 this volume). The nature of women's roles as wives and mothers also affects the value of their time in household activities (Mincer 1962; Schultz 1980). For example, in Japan and South Korea, the mother's role is heavily emphasized because of the tense competition children face in the educational system (Hirao, Chapter 7 this volume; Lee 1994). This increases the value to the family of women's home time.

The new home economics model also suggests that in Japan and South Korea, where the gender wage gap is large and the mother's role is strongly emphasized, a husband's earnings will have a strong positive effect on whether his wife will leave her job at marriage. Likewise, in Taiwan, where the gender wage gap is smaller and the mother's role in day-to-day childcare is somewhat less emphasized (see Yu, Chapter 3 this volume), a husband's earnings will have a weaker positive effect on his wife's job separation. In making decisions about women's job separation at the time of marriage, couples will take into consideration their earnings potential after marriage rather than their earnings at the time they marry. Thus, we predict a strong positive effect of a husband's education (a measure of his earnings potential) on his wife's job separation at the time of marriage in Japan and South Korea, and the same effect but weaker in Taiwan.

Sociological studies suggest that women's education not only measures their potential market wages but also affects the value of their time for home production. It is argued that more educated mothers are more effective in maintaining family members' health and well-being (e.g., Desai and Alva 1998). Even so, we expect the relationship between women's education and their earnings potential to be stronger than the relationship between women's education and the value of their time for home production; women with greater education will be less likely to leave their jobs. But because of the stronger emphasis on the mother's role in Japan and South Korea than in Taiwan, this negative effect may be weaker in the former countries.

Labor Market Theories

The new home economics model does not explicitly take into account the difficulty married women may have in moving in and out of the labor market.

Labor market theorists, on the other hand, suggest that structural constraints may be crucial. In segmented labor markets, married women face institutional or structural constraints unique to them. For example, job competition theory (or job queuing theory) postulates that job skills are acquired mainly through on-the-job training. In this model, employers do not hire workers based on prior job skills, but rather, they hire workers with certain background characteristics who appear to cost a minimum for their job training (Thurow 1975). Employers sort on gender and marital status because women show high rates of turnover and decreased productivity during childbearing and childrearing; these are key factors that would increase the cost of job training and retraining for female workers (KMA 1995; Reskin and Roos 1990).

Related to this, in some labor markets, notably in Japan, entry-level jobs are open to new school graduates wishing to enter large work organizations, and other jobs in these organizations are filled mainly by employees who went through the necessary on-the-job training (Doeringer and Piore 1971; Koike 1983; Sakamoto and Powers 1995). In these closed labor markets, workers' first jobs have strong effects on their lifetime employment outcomes such as social status and income. Those who enter career-track jobs, that is, entry-level jobs in internal labor markets, are promoted and move up job ladders. Women in Japan rarely enter the internal labor markets of large private firms. Women who enter the noncareer-track jobs of private firms reach the ceiling early on, and are often forced to leave their jobs (Brinton 1989, 1993; Ogasawara, Chapter 6 this volume; Takahashi 1997). The South Korean labor market shows similar features (e.g., Kim 1995). Women who work in the informal sector or in the public sector face fewer such institutional barriers (e.g., Lu 1991; Yu, Chapter 9 this volume).

In the next section, we explore the labor market contexts of the three countries and assess the likelihood of job separation for women in different labor market positions.

LABOR MARKET CONTEXTS AND WOMEN'S JOB SEPARATION AT MARRIAGE

Newly married women's job separation has been documented cross-culturally and at different time periods (Pyle 1990). Until the 1950s in the United States, the majority of female clerical workers quit their jobs at the time of marriage. A significant change in this trend then occurred. Currently in Japan, which is obviously well past the industrialization stage of the 1950s United States, female clerical workers still commonly exit the labor market at marriage. Brinton (1998a) points out two reasons for such a persistent pattern. One is the organizational culture of Japan, which defines jobs more broadly than in the United States. Japanese firms prefer hiring generalists over specialists. Japanese workers in large firms do not stay in the same jobs over their career, but move through a wide range of jobs within the organization. Within this organizational culture of job rotation, Japanese female clerical workers do not monopolize particular functions. In contrast, female white-collar workers in the United States who do not occupy managerial positions still perform some key functions such as word processing, filing, and bookkeeping. This monopoly guarantees their indispensability. They move up job ladders, albeit short ones, based on their acquired job skills and seniority. In Japan, female clerical workers do not have any job ladders to move up (Brinton 1998a).

The second crucial force that leads to Japanese married female clerical workers separating from their jobs is common conceptions about age and gender relations in Japan. Since age and the status of being a married person command respect, it is awkward for both parties if young male workers have older married women as their subordinates. This status inconsistency becomes a fatal force for female clerical workers, who do not have long job ladders to move up; as women enter their 30s, interpersonal relationships in the workplace often become quite strained (Brinton 1998a; Ogasawara, Chapter 6 this volume).

The Japanese employment system is known for features such as long-term employment, a tenure-based seniority wage system, and enterprise unionism (Cole 1979; Koike 1983; Sakamoto and Powers 1995). The system of long-term employment refers to the practice of recruiting new graduates who are expected to work continuously in the same company until a fixed retirement age (see Rosenbaum and Kariya 1989). The seniority wage system means that the length of employment in the company, not in a particular job, is important in determining wages and promotion.[2]

Until 1986, when Japan's Equal Employment Opportunity Law went into effect, most female workers were assigned to different career tracks from those for male workers.[3] Only male regular workers were promoted along career ladders. The secondary workforce—female workers, part-time workers, and dispatched workers—was excluded from career tracks (Sano 1988: 86). Generally it was assumed that female workers would resign at marriage or childbirth. Japanese companies emphasize firm-specific skills and knowledge and hence on-the-job training. Such employment practices drive women into a disadvantageous position in a twofold way. First, women and men are assigned to different career tracks with different training opportunities. Second, once women quit their jobs, it is difficult to find another job commensurate with their career and education.

South Korea's organizational culture shares some features with Japan. Since the promulgation of an equal employment law in 1987, overt gender differentiation in work assignments has gradually declined. But in the new, supposedly more flexible hiring systems, gender differentiation continues, albeit in a more subtle way. White-collar workers with college or high school education who enter large firms choose between two types of tracks, "general" and "clerical" tracks, analogous to internal labor markets and noncareer tracks in Japan. Job descriptions for the former include planning and managerial as well as clerical tasks, whereas the latter is limited to clerical work and assistant tasks. The key difference between the two types of tracks that affects women's career choices, however, is the place of work. The generalist track requires that workers be rotated to any branch of the firm regardless of their preference or convenience (Kim 1995). Leaving parental households before marriage or living separately from their husbands and children is not a respectable arrangement for the majority of South Korean women, for many reasons—from Confucian values to such economic circumstances as expensive housing and low wages.[4] As a result, most South Korean women end up choosing the clerical track.

Deprived of promotional opportunities and suffering from low wages, many frustrated South Korean female workers quit their jobs voluntarily (or leave involuntarily) when they undertake new family roles upon marriage or childbearing (KAWF 1989; Kim 1995). Although increasing proportions of female workers continue their work until first childbearing, a dominant pattern is still to quit at marriage. Asked in a survey why they are reluctant to hire female workers, South Korean employers report three main reasons—women's lack of commitment, their lack of responsibility, and conservative labor laws that legislate a broad range of protective measures for female workers, for example, a ban on overtime work (KMA 1992). Thus, though the causality is not totally transparent, women's family roles interact with the structural barriers in labor markets in pushing married women to quit their jobs. The recent movement to supposedly more flexible hiring systems in South Korea has increased the proportion of part-time and subcontracted jobs where female workers are concentrated, resulting in yet deeper gender stratification (Chung and Yoon 1994).

There is less literature directly discussing the organizational barriers to Taiwanese female workers compared to the barriers in Japan and South Korea. Although studies suggest such barriers for women workers in large firms in Taiwan (e.g., Kung 1983), the female disadvantage seems substantially smaller than in Japan and South Korea because of the predominance of small-sized firms and a large government sector (e.g., Chapter 1 this volume; Galenson 1992; Lu 1991; Yu 1999a and Chapters 3 and 9 this volume). The vast majority of private enterprises are small, family-based businesses that hire their relatives based on informal agreements (Lu, Chapter 10 this volume). Many private-sector employees, hence, are like informal-sector workers. In 1980, 54 percent of both male and female employees in Taiwan worked in firms with nine or fewer workers. At the same time, the government sector comprised almost one-quarter of the female labor force, most of whom are white-collar workers. Legally bound, the government practices equal employment policies and guarantees job security in general.

In each country, female production (manufacturing) workers are in situations similar to those of clerical workers. In Japan and South Korea, a large proportion of the blue-collar labor force works in the same large companies (often in the manufacturing industry) as clerical workers, and they face similar organizational barriers in their job training and promotional opportunities (Kim 1996; Roberts 1994). In Taiwan, production workers rarely work in the government sector (although many clerical workers do); the majority work in small firms where contracts are often informal and personal (Lu 1991, Chapter 10 this volume; Yu, Chapter 3 this volume). In all three societies, the majority of unmarried women work in these two occupations, clerical or production. Thus, the different organizational cultures of the three countries can be expected to be a major force responsible for differences in job separation among newly married women who work before marriage.

Female professional workers in Japan and South Korea do not face the same problems of organizational culture as clerical and production workers, because their jobs are based on specialized skills and also because most of them do not work in large private firms. Being mostly teachers or medical workers such as nurses and pharmacists, on-the-job training or promotional opportunities in the organization are less of a problem. Less gender disparity in these opportunities is particularly the case since professional jobs are highly gendered (Lee, Chapter 8 this volume). In Taiwan, the majority of teachers are government employees, and their job security is unquestioned.

Sales and service workers are in quite different positions in the three societies. In South Korea, even after excluding the agricultural labor force, the informal-sector labor force remains large (Chang 1995; Yee 1990). About 60 percent of female sales and service workers are self-employed or family workers. The percentage among Taiwanese sales and service workers is smaller, but it is still much higher than in Japan (appendix tables 4.1, 4.2, and 4.3). Self-employed workers, being outside the domain of organizational culture, have a greater chance for job continuation than paid employees. Furthermore, the flexible work schedules of self-employment are more compatible with family roles (see Yu, Chapter 9 this volume). We would thus expect that female sales and service workers in South Korea are less likely to quit their jobs than clerical workers. In Taiwan, as they are less likely to be in the government sector, sales and service workers will likely show a *higher* rate of job separation than clerical workers. In Japan, because they tend not to be self-employed or to be in the government sector, sales and service workers are expected to be no different from clerical or production workers in their rate of job separation. In all three countries, most agricultural workers are not paid employees, and so we expect them to be the least likely of all to quit work at marriage.

To summarize, we expect country differences in women's rate of job separation at marriage to be greatest among clerical and production workers because they are the ones who face the most serious organizational barriers. Their rates of job separation will be lower in Taiwan than in Japan and South Korea due to differences in organizational culture. Country differentials in job separation are expected to be smaller among professional workers, as professional skills will help women overcome structural constraints in the labor market. Country differences in job separation among sales and service workers are expected to differ from the overall country patterns because of the uniqueness of their positions in the labor market of each country.

MARRIAGE TIMING AND JOB SEPARATION

In the labor market circumstances of these three societies, what do women do to maximize their well-being? Does marriage timing influence their careers? The literature on the timing of marriage and women's work has not explored the case of women in these labor markets. Some researchers argue that women are likely to marry later (if at all) if they do not need a male's income for support (e.g., Sorensen 1995). Oppenheimer (1988, 1997) argues that as more women have come to participate in the labor force, an increasing number of them delay marriage until they clarify their career paths, just as men do. Both of these models implicitly assume noninterrupted career patterns and, although the reasons are different, both postulate that women who are working or who pursue careers will marry later than women who are not working and do not pursue careers. Basically, they suggest that women who marry later have a stronger work attachment than those who marry earlier.

However, these models were formulated in the social context of the United States where marital status is not as major a determinant of women's employment as in East Asia (Chapter 1 this volume). Where marriage poses a substantial barrier to women's work, the prospect of discontinued work due to marriage may play a crucial role in determining the timing of marriage. First, if women can expect little chance of continuing work after marriage but nevertheless do wish to keep working, then delaying marriage may be their choice. In the same way, if women can continue work after marriage, they may not delay their marriage in East Asian societies, where marriage is nearly universal and women's age at first marriage is concentrated in the mid-20s (Choe 1998; Retherford, Ogawa, and Matsukura 1999; Thornton et al. 1994). According to these scenarios, there will be a positive relationship between working women's timing of marriage and the probability of quitting their jobs, that is, the later women marry the more likely it will be that they then leave their job. This reasoning is supported by country-level data, that is, higher ages at marriage in Japan, where women face a greater disadvantage, than in Taiwan, where a greater percentage of married women participate in the labor force (Choe 1998; Retherford, Ogawa, and Matsukura 1999; Thornton et al. 1994). Whether individual-level data also support this hypothesis, which we could call the hypothesis of "work extension," will be examined later.

It is noteworthy that later age at marriage among working women also means longer duration of work until marriage. Longer work duration before marriage, that is, longer labor market experience, increases women's market wages and should have a deterrent effect on job separation at marriage.[5] If longer work duration leads to promotion or change of jobs from noncareer to career tracks, this deterrent effect will be even stronger (see Felmlee 1984; Petersen and Spilerman 1990). However, if women are outside the internal labor markets of organizations, long work duration would not bring about such transitions. A different reason for a negative relationship between work duration before marriage and job separation may be selectivity in the nature of jobs or in women's work attachment. That is, jobs in which unmarried women workers can remain for a longer time may be the ones that allow them to continue after marriage. Jobs at small-sized firms are an example. In any case, this discussion shows that the effects of work duration on women's job separation may very well be contingent on the occupational sector where they work.

We speculate that women's decision on job continuation/separation at marriage may be based more on their choice of age at marriage than on their choice of duration of work, due to the strong norms regarding age at marriage in East Asian societies. In our analysis below we explore both variables and examine their effects on job separation.

RESEARCH QUESTIONS

We can summarize our key questions as follows: (1) Does the new home economics model explain newly married women's job separation in East Asia?[6] Specifically, how important is husbands' education for wives' job separation at marriage? How important is women's own education? (2) How does women's labor market position affect their job separation at marriage? What are the effects of women's occupation before marriage? Is duration of work before marriage an important factor affecting job separation at marriage? (3) Lastly, what is the role of the timing of marriage in women's job separation at marriage? Is there any systematic pattern in the relationships between age at marriage and job separation, before or after taking into account the duration of work?

DATA AND METHODS

Data are from nationally representative sample surveys from the three countries. These surveys were not originally conducted for comparative purposes and do not use the same questionnaires. Still, they provide quite similar information and we can construct the same variables for our analysis. The Taiwan data are from the Survey of Women's Employment and Fertility that focuses on women's employment and fertility history. The Taiwanese census bureau (DGBAS) conducts the survey annually; we use data from the 1993 survey. For Japan, we use data from the 1991 National Survey of Occupational Mobility and Careers of Women. Although the number of cases in Japan is smaller than the numbers for the other two countries, the survey contains rich information on women's career transitions. For the South Korean sample, we combined data from two household surveys conducted five years apart, in 1992 and 1997. The South Korea Women's Development Institute carried out both surveys with similar questionnaires, focusing on women's employment history. To increase the South Korean sample size, we merged the two data sets.

For the analysis of the South Korean data, we include in the sample only urban residents, 89 percent of the original national sample. Consistent with the other chapters in this volume, a major purpose of this study is to compare women in the different labor market and organizational contexts of the three societies. Including rural residents (who mainly work in agriculture) would obscure the effects of labor market circumstances in South Korea. (We could also exclude rural residents in Taiwan and Japan, but their percentages are so small as to not affect the overall results.)[7]

Table 4.1 shows the percentages of women respondents aged 25–49 who worked before marriage. Consistent with macrolevel data on the age profile of women's labor force participation (see Chapter 1 this volume), the percentages are similar across the three societies. Among women aged 25–34, the percentages who worked before marriage are 86.2, 92.2, and 89.2 in Taiwan, Japan, and South Korea, respectively. Between the two broad age cohorts in the table, labor force participation before marriage increased in all three societies, by the largest percentage in South Korea and the smallest in Taiwan (20.1 and 7.4 percent, respectively). In Taiwan, the increase is generally larger at the lower end of the educational distribution, middle-school

TABLE 4.1
Married Women Aged 25–49 Who Worked before Marriage:
Taiwan, Japan, and South Korea

| | TAIWAN | | JAPAN | | SOUTH KOREA | | | |
| | | | | | Urban | | National | |
	25–34	35–49	25–34	35–49	25–34	35–49	25–34	35–49
Education								
Primary school	79.0	72.5	0.0	0.0	76.3	62.2	79.8	69.0
Middle school	84.4	82.4	96.7[a]	72.9	84.2	67.7	85.7	67.8
High school	88.9	89.2	93.8	86.4	92.2	73.0	92.0	73.2
Junior college	91.9	91.7	90.7	82.0	88.9	70.5	87.9	71.1
4-year university	91.9	89.5	85.7	75.0	86.2	73.3	86.2	73.3
Total	86.2	78.8	92.2	82.2	89.2	69.1	89.1	70.4
Number of women who worked	4355	5856	389	819	1390	1227	1492	1441
Total number of women	5050	7428	422	997	1559	1777	1674	2047

NOTE: All figures are percentages except in last two rows.

[a]For this cell, the number of cases is only 30.

and primary-school educated women. In Japan, women at the two ends of the educational distribution show a slightly greater increase in labor force participation than women at the middle two levels. In South Korea, the increase is substantial for all educational groups.

For the analysis, we restrict the samples to ever-married women aged 25–49 at the time of the survey, and to those who worked before marriage.[8] This means that we have 10,211, 1107, and 2617 cases in Taiwan, Japan, and South Korea, respectively.

Variables and Analysis

The dependent variable is dichotomous, coded 1 if women quit their jobs at the time of marriage and 0 if they continue their work.[9] Women's education and that of their husbands are the measures of earnings potential. Wives' education also measures the value of their time for home production. For Taiwan and South Korea, women's and their husbands' education are categorized as primary school or less, middle school, high school, junior college, and four-year university or more education. For Japan, primary- and middle-school education are combined into one category due to the small number of cases in those categories.

Following the classification schemes used in the Taiwanese and South Korean surveys, we group women's occupations before marriage into six categories: professional, semiprofessional, clerical, sales and service, agriculture, and production occupations. Very few women had managerial occupations in any of the three countries, and they are included in the professional category. The Japanese data did not separate out semiprofessional occupations from the professional category.

For the total duration of work before marriage, the Taiwan survey asked the question directly. The Japan survey had the length of each spell of employment before marriage, while the South Korean survey recorded the number of months worked yearly by age. For both, we sum the total months worked before marriage. Age at marriage is categorized in two- or three-year intervals: age 19 or less, 20–22, 23–24, 25–27, 28–30, and 31 or older. We construct age at marriage as a categorical variable rather than a continuous variable to examine any nonlinear effects on the dependent variable, job separation. Current age represents the birth cohort of women and is a control variable. Ages are grouped into five-year intervals: 25–29, 30–34, 35–39, 40–44, and 45–49.

For the multivariate analysis of women's job separation at marriage, we use a logistic regression model. We present two regression models, one with all the independent variables, and the second with interaction terms between occupation and work duration.[10]

Descriptive Statistics

The characteristics of the women who worked before marriage are shown in table 4.2. The distribution of women's education is quite distinctive among the three samples. Taiwan shows the lowest levels of education, with high percentages of women in the lowest two levels (primary- and middle-school education, totaling 57.3 percent). In Japan a majority of women received high school education, and junior college is the next modal category. The two extremes, middle school and college, are small. Among South Korean urban women, as in Japan, a majority received a high school education. The percentage of primary and middle school together and the frequency of four-year university-educated women are both 10 to 15 percent higher in South

TABLE 4.2

Sample Characteristics of Married Women Aged 25–49 Who Worked
before Marriage: Taiwan, Japan, and South Korea

	Taiwan	Japan	South Korea (urban only)
Education			
Primary	37.0	0.0	10.8
Middle	20.3	15.4	20.4
High	30.6	57.3	50.1
Junior college	7.1	21.1	4.2
4-year university	5.0	6.2	14.6
Husband's education			
Primary	23.5	0.0	5.5
Middle	19.1	14.9	12.3
High	27.4	45.1	44.3
Junior college	11.3	5.3	4.8
4-year university	9.6	26.2	29.0
Missing	9.0	8.5	3.9
Occupation			
Professional	5.5	13.9	7.8
Semiprofessional	11.2	N.A.	9.6
Clerical	16.8	48.3	31.8
Sales/service	13.1	18.8	14.1
Agriculture	10.3	1.0	8.3
Production	43.1	17.9	28.3
Duration of working years	4.9	5.2	4.6
Duration by occupation			
Professional	4.3	5.0	3.8
Semiprofessional	4.9	N.A.	4.2
Clerical	4.8	5.0	4.5
Sales/service	4.8	5.5	4.5
Agriculture	4.4	6.9	5.9
Production	5.0	5.3	4.7
Age at marriage			
To 19	8.6	1.0	3.3
20–22	25.8	16.0	18.9
23–24	23.9	16.4	28.7
25–27	28.2	36.8	38.0
28–30	10.3	12.9	9.0
31+	3.2	4.6	2.1
Age			
25–29	17.7	10.7	23.3
30–34	25.0	17.7	29.8
35–39	25.0	24.4	23.2
40–44	20.6	28.1	14.5
45–49	11.7	19.1	9.2
Quit job at marriage	34.4	68.9	70.1
Number of cases	10,211	1107	2617

NOTES: For South Korea, we use only the urban sample in the analysis (refer to the methods section). All figures (except those for work duration) are percentages; work duration figures are years.

Korea than in Japan (also see Chapters 1 and 5 this volume). The frequency of junior college education is smaller in South Korea than in Japan by 17 percentage points. Husbands' education is generally higher than women's education, and shows somewhat similar but smaller country differentials as for women's education.

Women's occupations before marriage show greater variation across countries. As we expected, a majority of women aged 25–49 who worked before marriage had clerical or production occupations. In each country, about 60 percent of women worked in these two occupations before marriage, with Japan having the largest percentage of clerical workers and Taiwan the largest percentage of production workers. In South Korea, the percentage of clerical workers is a few points higher than the percentage of production workers. The percentages of professional and semiprofessional workers combined, as well as those of sales and service workers combined, are similar across the three societies. The percentage of urban South Korean women who were in agricultural occupations before marriage is almost as large as the comparable percentage for Taiwanese women in the whole nation (8 and 10 percent, respectively). The analogous percentage among Japanese women is only 1 percent.

The average duration of work before marriage is quite long, around five years, in all three societies. It is longest in Japan, 5.2 years, and shortest in South Korea, 4.6 years. Age at marriage is more dispersed toward younger ages in Taiwan; about one-third of women marry by age 22.

Finally, the cohort distribution is skewed toward younger ages in South Korea because of the rapid increase in women's rates of labor force participation in recent years.

Employment Status by Occupation

Table 4.3 gives more insight into the characteristics of women's occupations before marriage, showing the distribution of employment status by occupation. As mentioned earlier (and in Chapter 1 of this volume), women's work in the informal sector is more prevalent in urban South Korea (19.3 percent) than in Taiwan and Japan (13.1 and 4.2 percent, respectively). It is striking that in every occupation, urban South Korean women are more likely to be in informal employment than Japanese or Taiwanese women. The country differences are particularly conspicuous in sales and service occupations,

TABLE 4.3

Distribution of Employment Status by Women's Occupation before Marriage:
Taiwan, Japan, and South Korea

| | TAIWAN | | | JAPAN | | SOUTH KOREA | |
| | Self- | Paid employees | | Self- | Paid | Self- | Paid |
Occupation	employed[a]	PUBLIC	PRIVATE	employed[a]	employees	employed[a]	employees
Professional	1.8	54.7	43.5	2.6	97.4	8.8	91.2
Semiprofessional	2.2	10.9	86.9	N.A.	N.A.	11.5	88.5
Clerical	1.1	20.1	78.8	1.1	98.9	3.7	96.3
Sales/service	16.9	2.8	80.3	10.6	89.4	42.7	57.3
Agriculture	91.3	0.3	8.4	100.0	0.0	96.8	3.2
Production	2.3	1.6	96.1	2.0	98.0	8.1	91.9
Total	13.1	8.7	78.2	4.2	95.8	19.3	80.7

NOTE: Figures are percentages.

[a]The self-employed category also includes unpaid family workers.

where the percentages of women in informal employment are 42.7 percent in South Korea compared to only 16.9 and 10.6 percent in Taiwan and Japan, respectively.

FINDINGS

Based on the results from the multivariate analyses, we discuss which of the two alternative theoretical models presented earlier is more relevant. The findings suggest that women face sharply different labor market circumstances in the three countries.

The New Home Economics Model

The results from the multivariate analyses of job separation are presented in table 4.4. In both Taiwan and Japan, the new home economics model seems to fit the data, albeit in different ways. In Taiwan, where the gender wage gap is relatively small, husbands' education has no effect on newly married women's job separation. Rather, women's *own* education has a significant negative effect on job separation: the more educated a woman is, the less likely she is to quit her job at the time of marriage. That is, women's market wages dominate the decision on job separation rather than their reservation wages.

TABLE 4.4

Logit Coefficients of Women Quitting Job at Time of Marriage: Taiwan, Japan, and South Korea

Model	TAIWAN		JAPAN		SOUTH KOREA[a]	
	A	B	A	B	A	B
Education [high]						
Primary	0.32***		—		0.02	
Middle	0.33***		1.06***		0.05	
Junior college	−0.58***		−0.75***		−0.08	
4-year university	−1.05***		−1.10***		−0.80***	
Husband's education [high]						
Primary	0.01		—		0.03	
Middle	0.09		−0.03		−0.07	
Junior college	0.01		−0.32		0.33	
4-year university	−0.12		0.49*		−0.30*	
Missing	0.03				−0.38	
Occupation [clerical]						
Professional	−0.71***	−1.05***	−1.16***	−1.76***	−1.33***	−1.09**
Semiprofessional	−0.14	0.09	—	—	−0.47**	−0.56
Sales/service	0.21*	0.12	0.14	−0.14	−0.78***	−1.22***
Agriculture	−0.61***	−0.99***	−1.26#	−2.41	−0.18	−1.35**
Production	−0.03	−0.15	−0.30	−0.47	0.06	−0.33
Duration of work (DW)	−0.08***	−0.11***	−0.22***	−0.27***	−0.21**	−0.26***
Duration by occupation[b]						
Professional*DW		−0.04		−0.15*		−0.34***
Semiprofessional*DW		−0.12***		—		−0.25***
Sales/service*DW		−0.09***		−0.21***		−0.15*
Agriculture*DW		−0.02*		−0.10*		−0.05**
Production*DW		−0.08***		−0.24***		−0.18**

Age at marriage [23–24]						
To 19	−0.24**		−1.74*		−1.26***	
20–22	−0.05		−0.41		−0.73***	
25–27	−0.01		0.33		0.06	
28–30	0.28**		0.94***		0.15	
31+	0.41**		1.61***		1.21**	
Age [25–29]						
30–34	−0.07		−0.05		0.42***	
35–39	−0.08		−0.08		0.37**	
40–44	−0.02		0.07		0.38*	
45–49	0.16#		−0.04		0.31	
Intercept	−0.26	−0.17	1.95	2.17	2.09	2.40
−2 Log-likelihood	12,704	12,697	1169	1166	2906	2893
N	10,211	10,211	1107	1107	2617	2617
Mean of dependent variable	0.344	0.344	0.689	0.689	0.701	0.701

NOTES: We do not present the coefficients of other independent variables in model B because they are almost identical to those in model A. Words and numbers in brackets represent the omitted category, for categorical variables.

# p < .10, * p < .05, ** p < .01, *** p < .001

[a]The South Korea equation also includes a dummy variable representing the year of the sample.

[b]The coefficients represent the slope of work duration for each occupation.

In Japan, where the gender wage gap is relatively large, husbands' education has a significant positive effect; husbands' college education increases the probability of wives' job separation. A high reservation wage, or the high price of time for home production, reduces the probability of married women's work outside the home. After controlling for husbands' education, women's greater human capital resources increase their chances of work in Japan. In fact, the negative effect of Japanese women's education on their job separation is even stronger than in Taiwan. This does not support our speculation that women's education may increase their reservation wages more in Japan and South Korea than in Taiwan.

The new home economics model seems less applicable to South Korea. Neither market wages (i.e., women's education) nor reservation wages (i.e., husbands' education) have as strong effects as in Japan or Taiwan (table 4.4). Contrary to our predictions, husbands' higher education, that is, college education, *decreases* the probability of Korean women's job separation, which means that high reservation wages do not discourage women from working outside the home (see Chapter 8 this volume for a more in-depth discussion of marriage and work among highly educated Korean couples). In South Korea, it may be that husbands' education more strongly represents egalitarian attitudes than earnings potential, thus indicating moral support for wives' work outside the home. That is, higher education may demarcate some South Korean husbands from adhering so strongly to the prescribed cultural norms against married women's employment, which appear to be even stronger than in Japan (Liao 1998).[11] Women's own education is also less important in determining job separation in South Korea than in Taiwan and Japan. Only college education significantly reduces South Korean women's probability of job separation, and there is no significant difference among other educational groups (again, see Chapter 8 for detailed discussion of university-educated Korean wives' working patterns). In sum, the economic consideration of costs and benefits appears less relevant to the employment decisions of South Korean than Japanese and Taiwanese married women.

Labor Market Structures

The patterns of job separation by occupation are consistent with our predictions. In all three countries, clerical and manufacturing workers are among the most likely to separate from their jobs, whereas professional workers are among the least likely to do so (tables 4.4 and 4.5). Some minor exceptions

TABLE 4.5
Predicted Probability of Women Quitting Job at Marriage,
by Occupation: Taiwan, Japan, and South Korea

	Taiwan	*Japan*	*South Korea*
Professional	0.22	0.55	0.44
Semiprofessional	0.33	N.A.	0.65
Clerical	0.36	0.79	0.75
Sales/service	0.41	0.81	0.58
Agriculture	0.24	0.41	0.72
Production	0.36	0.74	0.76
All occupations	0.34	0.76	0.70

NOTE: These probabilities are calculated from the logit results in table 4.4, assuming the mean values for all the independent variables other than occupation.

to this pattern include the fact that agricultural workers in Japan are slightly less likely to quit their jobs than professional workers, and sales and service workers in Taiwan are even more likely to quit their jobs than clerical and manufacturing workers. Gender-segregated job tracks in the large firms of Japan and South Korea do not allow promotional opportunities for female workers in clerical and manufacturing sectors, and many frustrated female workers quit their jobs upon assuming new family roles. As discussed earlier, when younger male workers are promoted earlier than their female counterparts and then have older, married female subordinates, this creates cognitive dissonance in a cultural context where elders are treated with respect. Both employers and female workers themselves assume that these workers will quit at marriage (Ogasawara, Chapter 6 this volume). Female professional workers in Japan and South Korea, such as teachers, nurses, and pharmacists, are not as constrained as clerical workers by organizational barriers in their promotional and on-the-job training opportunities.

On the other hand, in Taiwan, equal employment policies of the large government sector and informal contracts in small businesses allow female clerical and manufacturing workers more opportunities to continue work after marriage compared to their Japanese and South Korean counterparts. Generally, the predominance of small-sized firms and the overall labor shortage in Taiwan give female clerical and manufacturing workers an advantage. In contrast, the relative instability of sales and service sector businesses in Taiwan results in higher rates of job separation than among clerical and manufacturing workers (table 4.4). Still, their predicted probability of job separation is lower than sales and service workers in Japan and South Korea (table 4.5).

In Japan, sales and service workers are as likely as clerical and manufacturing workers to quit their jobs; in South Korea, they are significantly less likely to do so. As we showed earlier (table 4.3), a large percentage of female sales and service workers in South Korea are either self-employed or family workers, and we argue, consistent with other chapters in this volume, that work-family compatibility is generally higher among self-employed workers than among paid employees in large private firms.

Women in semiprofessional jobs such as accounting, legal and other administrative clerks, technicians, instructors, and assistant nurses are in a situation that represents a mixture of professional and clerical work (tables 4.4 and 4.5). Their rates of job separation reflect this, but are closer to those of clerical workers in Taiwan and professional workers in South Korea. This is understandable given the high rate of job separation among South Korean clerical workers. In Taiwan, semiprofessional workers are much less likely to be employed in the government sector than professional workers (table 4.3). This explains the large disparity in the rates of job separation between professional and semiprofessional workers in that society. But still, the professional nature of their jobs leads semiprofessional workers to have a lower rate of job separation than clerical workers. Agricultural workers, as expected, are among those least likely to quit their jobs, except in South Korea where the sample includes only urban women.[12]

The effects of work duration are rather unexpected but quite interesting. Duration of work shows a strong negative relationship with job separation in all three countries (table 4.4). A one-year increase in experience reduces the predicted probability of job separation by .018, .041, and .046 in Taiwan, Japan, and South Korea, respectively (calculated from the logit results in table 4.4, model A, assuming the mean values for each independent variable). The magnitudes of probability change are similar and substantially larger in Japan and South Korea than in Taiwan. In labor market circumstances where women face strong organizational barriers to their promotional opportunities (Japan and South Korea), longer work duration significantly reduces the probability of job separation. But when gender inequality is relatively small (as in Taiwan), longer duration makes less difference in women's job separation. Surprisingly, the interaction effects between occupation and work duration show that these negative effects are *strongest* among clerical workers in all three countries, although the occupational differentials in the effects of work duration are not large (table 4.4, model B). Given the literature documenting female clerical jobs as being outside the internal labor markets of organizations, this is unexpected.

As discussed earlier, however, the negative effect of work duration on job separation may also be due to differences in women's work attachment or in the nature of jobs within each occupation. Women who work for a long period before marriage may be the ones who have strong attachment to work, making them more likely to pursue employment after marriage too. Or, it could be that some jobs where unmarried women can work for a long period (such as jobs in small firms) are also receptive to married women. This selectivity explanation is also consistent with country differences. For example, in Taiwan, because a large percentage of women continue their work anyway, we would expect such selectivity to be weaker than in Japan and South Korea. And indeed, work duration has a smaller effect in Taiwan than in the other two countries.

The interaction models also show that for all occupations besides agriculture, work duration has a negative relationship to job separation (table 4.4, model B). The magnitude of the effect is consistently larger in Japan and South Korea than in Taiwan. The deterrent effect of work duration on job separation is stronger in those sectors of the market where institutional barriers are higher.[13]

Timing of Marriage

Age at marriage shows no systematic relationship to job separation in any of the three countries when duration of work is not controlled (results not shown). When duration of work *is* controlled, age at marriage has a significant positive relationship with job separation in all three countries (table 4.4). That is, the later women marry, the more likely they are to quit their jobs. Time pressure for childbearing may be the prime reason for this result in these Confucian societies, where childbearing is as universal as marriage. Whether those who marry early and continue their work eventually quit their jobs at the time of childbearing and show the same rates of quitting over the process of family formation is not clear, and needs further study. In any case, it is not surprising that this positive effect of age at marriage on job separation is somewhat weaker in Taiwan than in Japan and South Korea. The effect is strongest in Japan. These results confirm the idea of greater work-family compatibility for married women in Taiwan than in either Japan or South Korea. They are also consistent with the strong negative effect of husband's education on wife's job separation in Japan, suggesting a generally stronger role of family circumstances in married women's employment decisions in Japan than in South Korea or Taiwan, once labor market circumstances are held constant.

This positive relationship between age at marriage and job separation could be seen as supporting the work extension hypothesis that women delay marriage to extend their employment in labor market circumstances where women cannot continue their work after marriage. However, this interpretation seems implausible. First, as discussed earlier, women's longer duration of work before marriage does not increase but instead *decreases* the probability of job separation. Second, if work extension were the driving force for delayed marriages, age at marriage should also have a positive effect on job separation in the equation that does not control for duration of work. But in fact, with work duration not controlled, no such relationship is found. Last, there is a possibility that the higher rate of job separation among women who marry later is because late-marrying women participate in the labor force simply due to longer exposure to employment. That is, some women who marry later may not be delaying their marriages for work. Rather, *because* of their late marriage, they may have participated in the labor force. Such women would have low work commitment and are likely to quit at marriage.

Overall, in all three societies women's timing of marriage does not seem to be based on their employment prospects after marriage. When not controlling for duration of work, age at marriage shows no systematic relationship to job separation. Also, unlike the effect of work duration, relationship between age at marriage and job separation does not vary by occupation (results not shown).

Given these findings, it is unlikely that women in these countries choose the timing of marriage by considering both their age and work duration and at the same time taking into account their prospects of employment. Rather, it appears that the timing of marriage is chosen irrespective of the prospects for employment, and job separation is determined by the two conflicting forces of time pressure for childbearing and the labor market advantage accruing to work experience. This summary is strikingly consistent across all three societies. In other words, women's work attachment does not explain country differences in job separation. This finding is consistent with the fact that women's gender-role attitudes are no more traditional in Japan than in Taiwan (Yu, Chapter 3 this volume).

Age measures the birth cohort of women. Controlling for various relevant factors, it is not surprising to find no net effect of birth cohorts in Taiwan and Japan. The secular trends of increasing rates of women's employment are explained largely by other variables in our models. Also, while work attachment may be stronger among younger cohorts, at the same time, the fact that more jobs have become full-time, paid employment outside the home (rather than in the informal sector) has heightened the incompatibility between women's work and family roles (Yamaguchi 1998). These forces may therefore offset each other. In South Korea, members of the youngest cohort are significantly less likely to separate from their jobs than those in earlier cohorts, but this may simply be because these women are still young (rather than being a genuine cohort trend).

CONCLUSION

This chapter examined the factors associated with working women's job separation at the time of first marriage in Taiwan, Japan, and South Korea. Married women's labor force participation rate is higher in Taiwan than in the other two countries, and this is not easily explainable with macrolevel data such as industrial and occupational structures and per capita GDP, or with overall supply-side factors such as education and fertility levels (Chapter 1 this volume). We have tried to clarify the operation of labor market, familial, and individual forces that affect women's decisions about job separation during the transition to marriage. Our empirical results are consistent with the predictions we made based on the greater degree of gender inequality in the Japanese and South Korean labor markets than in the Taiwanese. The results support the idea that there are fundamental differences in the labor market structures of the three countries, especially between Japan and South Korea on the one hand and Taiwan on the other. Consistent with the argument in Chapter 1, these structural characteristics of labor markets include the average firm size, the size of the public sector, and the gender wage gap in the economy.

Looking first at the test of the new home economics model, husband's education, a measure of women's reservation wages, has different effects on women's job separation at marriage in the three societies: zero, positive, and negative in Taiwan, Japan, and South Korea, respectively. Considering the levels of gender inequality in the labor market, the Taiwanese and Japanese results are consistent with the predictions of the new home economics model. That is, in these two societies the consideration of economic costs and benefits appears to be a significant aspect of women's employment decision process. In Japan, the gender wage gap is large and higher reservation wages increase the probability of job separation. Women's own education, a measure of women's market wages, has a significant negative effect on job separation in all three countries, but again, the effect is stronger in Taiwan and Japan than in South Korea.

In South Korea, the cost-benefit consideration of women's time at home and at work appears less relevant in their decisions about job separation. The fact that husband's high education decreases the probability of job separation seems to reflect the effects of more egalitarian attitudes of highly educated husbands. The results suggest stronger normative resistance in society overall to married women's employment outside the home in South Korea; we think that the effect of education shows up as significant because highly educated husbands are somewhat outside this normative structure.

Our second main question concerned how labor market structures and women's positions in them affect job separation at marriage. Here, there are many similarities and a few important differences among the three countries. These findings are again consistent with the argument of greater overall gender equality in Taiwanese labor markets (due to such structural features as smaller firm sizes, a smaller gender wage gap, and a large government sector) than in the other two countries. Clerical and manufacturing workers are the most likely to quit at marriage *except* in Taiwan, and professional and agricultural workers are the least likely. Clerical and manufacturing workers in Japan and South Korea tend to work in large private firms and face severe organizational barriers in their choices of job tracks and in the opportunities for on-the-job training and promotion. In contrast, in Taiwan, sales and service workers show a higher rate of job separation than clerical and manufacturing workers. Sales and service occupations are the ones most distinct from the public sector in Taiwan, whereas clerical workers are often employed in the public sector. In South Korea, self-employment among sales and service workers means that they tend to remain in their jobs after marriage, resulting in a significantly lower rate of job separation for them than for clerical workers. Overall, the predicted probabilities of job separation are considerably lower across occupations in Taiwan than in Japan and South Korea.

Also common among the three countries is that the longer women work before marriage, the less likely they are to quit their jobs at the time of marriage. A surprising commonality among the three countries is that the negative effect of duration is strongest among clerical workers. Women in large companies have limited opportunities for job training and promotion in Japan and South Korea because they are almost always in positions outside internal labor markets. Yet longer duration of work is still associated with a higher likelihood of continuing work. From these findings, it is not clear how much of this is due to some improvement in a woman's labor market position with work duration and how much is due to selectivity either in terms of women's work attachment or in terms of the nature of the job. Two important factors related to the job may be the size of the firm where a woman works and whether she works full-time or part-time. Further research definitely needs to explore whether these are producing the result we find.

Within these similar patterns, there are some differences among the countries in the magnitude of the work duration effects. The effects are considerably smaller in Taiwan than in Japan and South Korea. When a majority of women continue work after marriage (as in Taiwan), the premium for a longer duration of labor market experience is smaller than such a premium in societies where only a minority of women continue work after marriage. These cross-country patterns hold for women in all occupations.

The third and last research question concerns the role played by marriage timing in women's job separation. The relationship between age at marriage and job separation again shows a striking similarity among the three countries. Supporting neither the hypotheses developed in the West nor the hypothesis of "work extension," the data suggest that in all three societies the timing of marriage is determined *irrespective of women's employment prospects*. Controlling for duration of work, age at marriage is positively related to job separation in all three countries. This is consistent with the time pressure for childbearing in these societies, all of which have short intervals between age at first marriage and first birth. The magnitude of the positive

relationship goes down starting with Japan, then South Korea, and then Taiwan, confirming the particular importance of family circumstances for Japanese women (also see Yu, Chapter 3, and Hirao, Chapter 7, this volume).

Overall, there is not a major difference across the three societies in the
effects of the factors we examined in influencing women's job separation at
marriage. The patterns of effects are quite similar; most of the country differences are a matter of degree. The large gaps in the intercepts (table 4.4)
suggest that factors other than the ones we looked at are responsible for the
country differences in job separation. We believe that the predominance of
small, family-type businesses may be the prime reason for the high rates of
labor force participation among Taiwanese married women. A relatively
large government sector in Taiwan also contributes to women's job stability
regardless of marital status. Large private firms appear to be the worst place
for married women's employment. This is probably true in all three societies,
but Japan simply has more of them (see table 4.5 and Chapter 1 this volume).

Work-family incompatibility among married women makes husbands'
high earnings a dominant factor in discouraging wives' employment in Japan. Together with the results on the effects of age at marriage, we conclude
that familial circumstances are especially important for Japanese married
women. South Korea shows more overall similarity to Japan than to Taiwan,
but not in the effect of familial circumstances.

We predict that these country patterns of married women's labor force
participation will remain stable in the coming years as long as strong organizational barriers to married women continue to exist in large private firms.
Our findings clearly support the conclusion that such barriers are stronger
in Japan and South Korea than in Taiwan. In South Korea, changes in values and attitudes regarding the gender division of labor may bring about
some increases in married women's labor force participation. But if the informal sector labor force in South Korea declines (and with it, the extent of
work-family compatibility), this may offset such trends.

Women's Employment Status by Occupation, Taiwan

	Self-employed	Unpaid family workers	Paid employees	
			PUBLIC	PRIVATE
Professional	16.3	0.6	28.8	54.3
Semiprofessional	3.2	3.5	12.2	81.1
Clerical	0.8	5.9	20.8	72.5
Sales/service	24.0	29.4	1.7	45.0
Agriculture	24.2	66.9	0.6	8.4
Production	3.8	8.5	3.2	84.6
Total	9.7	15.4	8.9	66.0

SOURCE: Directorate-General of Budget, Accounting, and Statistics, Executive Yuan, ROC, *Report on Fertility and Employment of Married Women, Taiwan Area, Republic of China*, 1993.

NOTE: Women aged 15–49.

Women's Employment Status by Occupation, Japan

	Self-employed	Family workers	Executives	Regular workers	Part-time workers	Dis-patched workers	Others
Professional	9.2	1.7	1.0	68.7	15.8	0.3	3.2
Managerial	3.8	0.0	86.0	9.3	0.4	0.0	0.4
Clerical	0.7	7.3	4.9	57.6	26.3	2.0	1.2
Sales	15.1	12.5	3.1	36.2	32.2	0.1	0.8
Service	12.0	12.7	1.3	28.8	43.3	0.2	1.7
Protective service	0.0	0.0	0.0	71.4	26.2	0.0	2.4
Agriculture	14.0	77.5	0.2	2.2	5.2	0.0	0.9
Transportation	0.7	3.7	0.7	53.3	37.0	2.2	2.2
Production	11.5	8.0	1.1	30.6	47.3	0.2	1.2
Don't know/ not applicable	1.4	1.0	2.9	36.8	54.1	0.0	3.8
Total	8.4	12.0	3.2	42.8	31.4	0.7	1.5

SOURCE: Statistics Bureau, Japan, *Employment Status Survey*, 1997.

Women's Employment Status by Occupation, Urban South Korea

	Self-employed	Unpaid family workers	Paid employees
Professional	12.1	1.6	86.3
Semiprofessional	11.4	3.0	85.7
Clerical	1.0	6.7	92.4
Sales/service	33.1	26.0	40.9
Agriculture	17.9	80.3	1.8
Production	6.5	10.3	83.2
Total	15.6	16.3	68.1

SOURCE: National Statistical Office, ROK (Republic of Korea), *Korean Census*, 1995.

NOTE: Two percent sample of women aged 15–49.

CHAPTER FIVE

Women's Education and the Labor Market in Japan and South Korea

Mary C. Brinton and Sunhwa Lee

Women's participation in higher education and in the labor force both increased dramatically in industrial societies during the second half of the twentieth century. As Chapter 1 of this book outlined, the rapidly industrializing societies of East Asia were no exception to these aggregate trends.[1] But in addition to the macrolevel changes in women's education and labor force participation, the link *between* them at the level of the individual has also become stronger over time in most Western industrial societies. In the United States, highly educated women have been more likely than the less educated to participate in the labor force in every decade since the 1940s. This tendency became even stronger after the 1970s (Goldin 1990; McLaughlin et al. 1988). But at this level of individual behavior, the similarity between much of the industrial West on the one hand and East Asia on the other is much weaker than at the societal level. Chapter 2 and others in this volume demonstrate that while there is a close link between women's education and their labor force participation in Taiwan, this is not the case in Japan and South Korea. In each of those two countries, women's rates of higher education attainment are considerably higher than in Taiwan but their rates of labor force participation are considerably lower.

This chapter takes up the issue of why there is an apparent mismatch between women's human capital and their employment in Japan and South Korea. We do this by examining the economic, political, and cultural reasons why women's higher education attainments have risen so dramatically in both societies over the past several decades. We question in particular the applicability of a dominant approach to explaining why educational attainments increase as an economy industrializes, an approach based on a human capital rationale that individuals invest in education principally for the purpose of labor market returns. We first lay out this approach and examine the support it has received in empirical studies of women's increasing educational enrollments in the United States in the twentieth century. We then turn to women's increasing educational levels in Japan and South Korea and consider the degree to which they have been driven by increasing opportunities for women in the labor market, on the one hand, or by reasons related to the political economy of educational expansion and to the cultural and social meanings of education in the two societies. Our endeavor leads us to address some of the cultural complexities that may be involved in the link between women's education and work, especially in societies such as Japan and South Korea with patriarchal traditions that ascribe strongly gendered roles to men and women.

LONG-TERM EDUCATIONAL EXPANSION FOR WOMEN

While much research has addressed the issues of how, why, and when higher education attainments increase as an economy industrializes (Osterman 1979; Trow 1961; Walters 1986), few studies have considered educational expansion separately by gender (Durbin and Kent 1989; Walters 1986).[2] Walters examined the hypothesis, based on ideas generated by human capital theory, that young people invest in education to prepare for roles they anticipate playing in the labor market. In this scenario, educational attainments rise as the demand for educated workers increases in an economy.

Walters tested this argument by empirically examining the link between macrolevel occupational change and the higher education enrollments of American men and women in the period 1952–1980. Her study produced considerable support for the perspective that individuals' educational choices are responsive to changing labor demands. Moreover, *women's* educational enrollments were much more affected than *men's* by changes in the mix of occupations in the economy during the several decades following World War II. Increases in the proportion of the labor force in white-collar occupations and, more specifically, in professional/technical and clerical occupations led to increases in women's but not men's higher education enrollments.[3] Walters noted that while the rise in women's labor force participation during this period might mean that the effect of occupational transformation is spurious, this is empirically not the case—the statistically significant effect of occupational transformation remains even when women's labor force participation is taken into account. Michael also found that the increase in American women's labor force participation preceded increases in women's higher education attainments in this period (1985). This suggests that young women were motivated to attain a higher education credential by the prospect of joining the ever-greater numbers of women entering the workforce.

Empirical findings such as those of Walters and Michael support the ideas that (1) more and more young women will go on for higher education as women's overall participation in the economy increases, and (2) growth in clerical, professional/technical, and other white-collar occupations will also lead to growth in women's higher education attainments. The appeal of white-collar work for women has also been extensively argued by Goldin, who shows for a broad range of countries in different cultural areas of the world that there is a strong association between women's education and the proportion of the labor force in clerical work (Goldin 1995).

But shifting the focus to East Asia raises the question of whether the connections among change in the occupational mix of economies (toward white-collar, service-sector work), women's labor force participation, and educational expansion might not vary both *historically* and *cross-culturally*. We suggest that it is entirely possible that there is no ironclad set of relationships. Instead, relationships at the macrolevel among these may be contingent upon the societal context, because this context affects the structure of choices and constraints under which individual women operate.

We suggest three sources of contingency that need to be taken into account in analyzing how rapid economic and occupational change may be related to the expansion of women's education, especially at the higher education level: (1) the extent of sex discrimination in the labor market, (2) how the state responds to the popular demand for higher education, and (3) what we shall call the "cultural demand" for education as opposed to the economic, utilitarian demand based on labor market opportunities. In the cases of Japan and South Korea, we expect these contingencies to render the connection between economic change and women's education looser than it was found to be in the United States during the several decades following World War II. Furthermore, for reasons we explain below, we expect the connection to be weaker in South Korea than in Japan, and weakest in both countries at the level of women's university education (rather than junior college).

JAPANESE AND SOUTH KOREAN EDUCATION
IN AN ERA OF RAPID SOCIAL CHANGE

The structure of the educational system and the expansion of higher education in each country provide a backdrop for our theoretical expectations.

Japan

In the post–World War II period, education has been compulsory in Japan through the junior high school level. Prior to junior high school graduation, students wishing to enter public high school must choose a particular one in their district to apply to. A typical district has a vocational school and several academically oriented high schools of varying quality. Thus, the "tracking" of students begins at the high school stage (Brinton 1993, 1998b; Rohlen 1983). After high school, students have a variety of educational options: *senmon gakkō* (specialized two-year training schools oriented toward the acquisition of vocational skills), junior college, or university. Demand for university education, especially for men, has consistently been high because a degree from a "good" university is viewed as a ticket into a large company and a secure job (Brinton 1993; Ono 2000).

Figure 5.1 shows the trends in Japanese men's and women's advancement rates to high school, junior college, and university since 1955.[4] As shown in panel A of the figure, the rate of high school advancement has risen dramatically for both sexes and is now nearly universal. At the level of higher education (panel B), 1955–1975 constituted the major period of expansion. Two principal sex differences exist: women's advancement rate increased faster than men's, and junior college became a "female" track (Fujimura-Fanselow 1985). Few men or women (less than 5 percent) advanced to junior college in 1955, and the situation for men was no different in 1996. But women's junior college advancement rates increased tenfold, from 2.4 percent in 1955 to over 20 percent in 1996. Meanwhile, the increase in men's higher education was concentrated completely at the university level. Women's university advancement rates also increased substantially in an early time period (1965–1975), remained stable, and then increased. But until very recently these were superseded by the increase in women's advancement rates to junior college.

These figures show that higher education expansion occurred in very different ways for Japanese men and women, with university being the most

Panel A. High School Advancement Rates

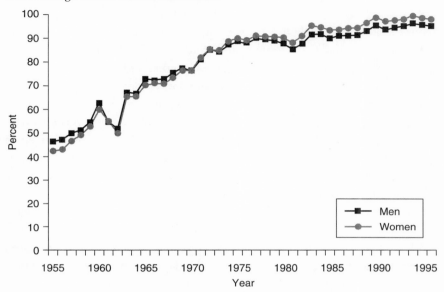

Panel B. Junior College and University Advancement Rates

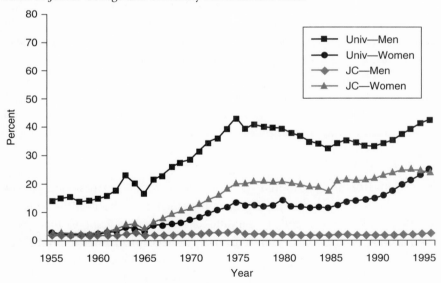

Figure 5.1. Educational Advancement Rates for Japanese Men and Women, 1955–1996

SOURCE: Ministry of Education, Japan, *Basic School Statistics*, various years.

common type for men and junior college being the most typical for women until just a few years ago. Given the sex-discriminatory nature of Japanese labor markets, especially toward very highly educated women, these differentiated educational paths for men and women would seem to be in line with the human capital perspective, that is, the view that higher education choices are influenced by the structure of labor market opportunities. Japanese women with or without a university credential have been heavily discriminated against in managerial labor markets (discussed later in this chapter). And as Ogasawara discusses in Chapter 6 of this volume, when they enter clerical work instead, university-educated women occupy a highly ambiguous role; their years of education are greater than high school- and junior college-educated women but their years of full-time work experience are generally lower. This restricts the sectors where a woman's university education will potentially pay off to professional/technical occupations and work in the government sector. (But as shown in Chapter 1 of this book, the size of the government sector is quite small in Japan. Among new female university graduates in 1996, only 6 percent entered government service upon graduation; Ministry of Education, Japan 1996).

To summarize, we expect that a model linking occupational change and female labor force participation to increasing educational enrollments will work fairly well in Japan at the high school and junior college levels and less well at the university level. At the latter level, employer discrimination against women has been strong, but the indicators of economic change that have conventionally been used in models of educational expansion (female labor force participation and change in the occupational structure of the economy) do not incorporate this social process, sex discrimination.

South Korea

The South Korean educational system is similar to the Japanese one, except that compulsory education was through elementary school until the early 1980s and then was extended to middle school. Figure 5.2 shows changes in high school, junior college, and university advancement rates in South Korea for the period 1965–1998. As in Japan, high school advancement has become nearly universal for both sexes (panel A). The period of steepest growth in South Korea was in the decade 1973–1983, when rates for both men and women more than doubled. The greatest increases at the level of higher education began four or five years later, in the late 1970s (panel B).

Panel A. High School Advancement Rates

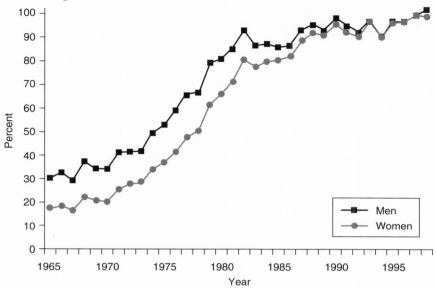

Panel B. Junior College and University Advancement Rates

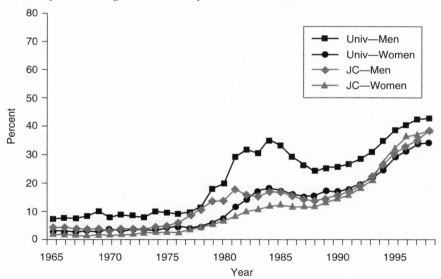

Figure 5.2.   Educational Advancement Rates for South Korean Men and Women, 1965–1998

SOURCE: Ministry of Education, ROK (Republic of Korea), *Statistical Yearbook of Education*, various years.

Sharp growth occurred in both junior college and university advancement rates in the short time span between the late 1970s and the mid-1980s. This was true for men and women alike.

Comparing these trends with those in Japan, the major similarity is at the high school level, where growth rates were fairly smooth in both countries. Increases in Japan preceded those in South Korea, which is what we would expect given Japan's earlier "economic takeoff." By the mid-1980s, high school was almost universally attended by men and women in both countries.

Trends in women's higher education expansion in Japan and South Korea, though, are distinctly different from each other. South Korean women follow paths in higher education that are much more parallel to men's than is the case for Japanese women. Panel B in figure 5.2 shows that there is only a slight difference in the slopes of South Korean men's and women's advancement rates to junior college, although men's rate of increase during the period of rapid expansion in the late 1970s to early 1980s was slightly greater. The same holds true for university advancement. This contrasts sharply with trends in Japan, where women's junior college rates increased sharply and men's remained very low.

The similar patterns of change in men's and women's higher education attainment in South Korea have occurred despite the fact that discrimination against women in white-collar labor markets—implying discrimination against highly educated women—is strong (Brinton, Lee, and Parish, Chapter 2 this volume; KAWF 1989; Lee, Chapter 8 this volume; Park 1992; Sohn and Cho 1993). South Korean urban labor markets had a surplus of male university graduates in the late 1970s and early 1980s, and the unemployment rate for that group was relatively high. To the extent that employers had an inherent preference for hiring male over female workers into white-collar jobs, they were well able to exercise that preference given the oversupply of highly qualified males (see Brinton, Lee, and Parish, Chapter 2 this volume). Highly educated South Korean women have had strikingly low rates of employment following graduation and across the life cycle, whether compared to Japanese women or to less educated South Korean women (Brinton 1989; Brinton and Choi forthcoming; Choi 1994; Kim 1990). All in all, then, it is hardly likely that increases in South Korean women's advancement rates to university have been based on a rising, unmet demand for white-collar workers.

In sum, the human capital approach leads one to expect close linkages between increases in women's educational attainment and in their labor market opportunities. Looking at the patterns of educational expansion for women in Japan and South Korea over the past 30 years, it appears at first glance that this approach may better fit the case of Japan than South Korea. Japanese women have traditionally "specialized" in going to junior college in the post–World War II period, nearly monopolizing this level of education. Until recently, fewer women have gone to university. Correspondingly, junior college-educated women in Japan have had considerable opportunity in the labor market, and university-educated women have had some, albeit more limited, opportunity as well.

These interpretations are further supported by data from both countries on the employment rates of new female junior college and university graduates over the past 10 years. The top lines in figure 5.3 show that from the mid-1980s to the mid-1990s, new female junior college graduates in Japan had consistently higher employment rates than university graduates.[5] The female-to-male earnings ratio also demonstrates that the immediate marginal payoff to university education over junior college is hardly significant for Japanese women; starting wages for junior college-educated women were 96.1 percent of men's, and for their university-educated counterparts the rate was 96.3 percent. A slightly larger difference existed between high school– and junior college–educated women (Ministry of Labor, Japan 1995).

We showed above that South Korean women have experienced a much more rapid trajectory than Japanese women over the past three decades in increasing their rates of university attendance, and throughout the 1980s and early 1990s university was a more likely destination than junior college for South Korean female high school graduates. However, the lower lines in figure 5.3 show that in South Korea, university-educated women have entered the labor market at markedly *lower* rates than junior college graduates. While female South Korean university graduates enter graduate school at slightly higher rates than Japanese women, this cannot explain the low employment rate for university graduates because the calculation of the rate takes this into account (see note to the figure). Moreover, the female-to-male ratio for the starting wages of South Korean female university graduates in 1998 was actually slightly *lower* than for high school graduates (74.8 vs. 75.8 percent) and below that of junior college graduates (81.1 percent; Min-

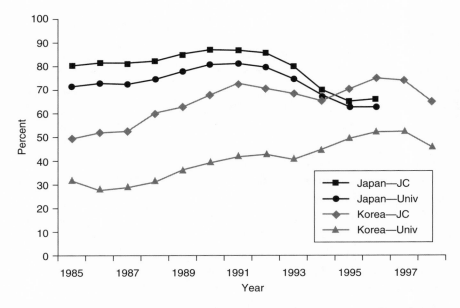

Figure 5.3.   Employment Rates for New Female Graduates: Japan and South Korea

SOURCES: Ministry of Education, Japan, *Basic School Statistics*, various years; National Statistical Office, ROK (Republic of Korea), *Statistical Yearbook of Education*, various years.

NOTES: The employment rate is calculated as (Employed/(Graduates − Advanced)). "Junior colleges" in South Korea excludes teachers' colleges.

istry of Labor, ROK 1998). What accounts for this seeming mismatch between South Korean women's high rates of university advancement on the one hand and their strikingly low rates of employment and marginal wage benefits vis-à-vis men on the other hand?

REASONS FOR PREDICTING LOOSE COUPLING BETWEEN WOMEN'S HIGHER EDUCATION AND LONG-TERM OCCUPATIONAL CHANGE

It appears to us that the connection between economic change and women's increasing rates of higher education advancement is moderated in Japan and South Korea by several contingencies inherent in the social, political, and cultural contexts of the two countries. More specifically, we attach significance to the high degree of labor market sex discrimination, national strategies of higher education expansion, and a strong popular desire for higher education for its own sake.

Sex Discrimination in the Labor Market

We argue that the discrimination against university-educated women in both Japan and South Korea suggests that there will be at best a loose coupling between economic change and university advancement rates, especially in the latter country. Despite the demand for well-educated workers in the two economies in the past few decades, the labor market returns to university education for women have been questionable (Brinton 1989, 1993; Lee, Chapter 8 this volume; Osawa 1988; Tanaka 1987). In Japan, discrimination has been due mainly to the prevalence of internal labor markets and employer investment in workers' human capital in large firms, which has biased employers toward hiring men—viewed as more stable employees—over university-educated women (Brinton 1993; Lam 1992; Saso 1990; Upham 1987). This has meant that the prospects for white-collar employment have been limited for female university graduates. As Ogasawara discusses in Chapter 6 of this volume, employers can hire high school– and junior college– educated women into low-level, noncareer-track clerical jobs at lower wages than university-educated women, who frequently want such jobs because they are generally excluded from managerial-track ones (*sōgōshoku*) or are frustrated by the rigidity of company demands on managerial workers (e.g., for overtime work, domestic and international transfers, etc.). This pattern showed signs of breaking down in the late 1980s as a result of the passage of the Equal Employment Opportunity Law in 1985 and, probably more critical, the development of a severe labor shortage. As figure 5.1 (panel B) shows, Japanese women's university advancement rates did rise sharply after 1986. This suggests that university enrollment rates began responding to the possibility of greater opportunities in the labor market. However, the expansion of economic opportunity was considerably slowed by the recession of the early 1990s, and by the late 1990s Japan was experiencing its highest rates of unemployment in the entire post–World War II period. This closed some of the doors that the labor shortage of the late 1980s had opened for highly educated women.

   In South Korea, it is not so much the prevalence of internal labor markets as it is the oversupply of university-educated males that has allowed employers to continue to practice sex discrimination against university females for white-collar jobs (see Chapter 2 this volume). Many South Korean women are "discouraged workers"; the jobs available to them fall considerably short of their aspirations (Kong and Choe 1989). Standing captured this phenomenon well in a perceptive (albeit relatively uncited) article on conditions affecting the link between women's education and labor market activity in industrializing countries (1976). His points merit quoting at length:

> The work available to educated women is often of a lower status and less well paid than that to which they feel entitled and for which their education qualifies them. In many cases they have to accept jobs inferior to those of men with levels of education comparable or even inferior to their own. Whatever the causes, this may lead to a pronounced "status frustration" effect, whereby many women who feel entitled to a certain level of income (sometimes known as the "reservation" or "aspiration" level) withdraw from the labour force rather than accept some lower-paying, low-status job. In these circumstances the tendency to withdraw is probably strongest for educated women whose husbands have high-income, high-status jobs. (286–287)

In sum, in both Japan and South Korea, sex discrimination in white-collar labor markets and against the most highly educated women in particular would suggest that the relationship between economic change and educational attainment will be weaker at the university level than at the junior college level. This may have begun to change in the mid-to-late 1980s in Japan as the demand for highly educated workers exceeded the supply of new male graduates; likewise, prior to the onset of the Asian economic crisis in the late 1990s, there were signs of change in this direction in South Korea as well. But these trends have now reversed with the economic downturn in both countries. Moreover, our subsequent statistical analysis covers the past three decades of change. So overall, we expect to see a weak relationship in Japan and no relationship in South Korea between economic change and women's university advancement rates.

In addition to these predictions, there are compelling reasons to expect that the coupling of education and economic change will generally be weaker at all higher education levels in South Korea than in Japan. These reasons include the strong influence of South Korean government policy on the number of spaces in higher education institutions and what we term the "cultural demand" for education, commonly known in South Korea as the "zeal for education."

Government Educational Policy

A government's posture toward secondary and higher education affects the degree to which educational demand can be institutionally accommodated. In South Korea, major policy shifts over time made education more and more available to the populace. We expect this to result in a looser fit between economic expansion and the popular demand for education than in Japan or in the United States.

Educational reform measures have been undertaken by the South Korean government since the 1960s, concentrated principally on the admissions process at each level of schooling. In 1968 the Ministry of Education eliminated the entrance examination in junior high schools (middle schools). This was replaced with a computer lottery system in which students were assigned to a school in their own school district. As a consequence, enrollments at middle schools increased dramatically in the 1970s. A similar reform was passed for the high school entrance system in 1973, ushering in a period of rapid growth in high school advancement rates between 1973 and the early 1980s.

At the level of higher education, demand intensified in the late 1970s as more South Korean students graduated from high school. Up until the 1980s a restrictive enrollment policy was in effect, and the admissions process was based on a two-stage entrance examination process: a preliminary, nationwide exam that determined a student's eligibility to apply to university, and a university-specific entrance exam. The government instituted reforms in 1980 that removed some autonomy from individual universities by putting in place a standard scholastic achievement test and abolishing the entrance examinations administered by each university. The government mandated that universities, both public and private, admit students based mainly on their scores on the nationwide standardized exam and on their high school grades. The effect of these policy changes was to loosen the strict, university-specific admissions system and open up more spaces in universities to meet the popular demand for education. This allowed university enrollments to expand rapidly in the early 1980s (see again panel B, figure 5.2). As one observer noted in the late 1980s, "the Republic of Korea has a classic case of the diploma disease" (Michell 1988: 104).

Since 1985 there have been recurring changes in the nature and format of the standardized university entrance examination in South Korea. The college-specific test has been restored, along with some autonomy being given to each institution in defining its own admissions procedures. As Joo notes, "Over the years, the Korean government has tended to take steps that increased its influence on student selection for higher education. However, since the late 1980s, higher education institutions have been recovering autonomy with respect to student selection" (Joo 2000: 98).

The fluidity of state policies toward universities in South Korea should not obscure the fact that university enrollments were allowed to virtually explode over the past two decades, in response to the huge demand on the part of the "new" urban middle class in particular, whom the political regime had every reason to attempt to satisfy (Cheng 1993). Public expenditure on education has been low relative to a number of other countries. Instead, South Korean parents have amply demonstrated their willingness to come up with expenditures for their children's education, at a level approximating 15 percent of gross national product (Sorensen 1994).

Japan provides a strong contrast. There, governmental policies have tended to *restrict* rather than encourage rapid expansion in higher education enrollments. The Ministry of Education has periodically tightened the rules for chartering private universities in an attempt to control the quality of higher education (Nakata and Mosk 1987). Even so, the private sector has been allowed to expand much more rapidly than the prestigious public universities, where the number of places has risen slowly. Japanese citizens remain acutely aware that a degree from one of the handful of national universities or the highest-prestige private universities is important in securing a job in a prestigious company (Ono 2000).

The Japanese government's controls on higher education, especially in the prestigious public sphere, mean that educational demand has not outpaced the demand for white-collar workers, as happened so strongly in South Korea. An indication of the contrast between the two societies is the persistently higher unemployment rate for university-educated men in South Korea than in Japan, even prior to the devastating impact of the Asian financial crisis on South Korea in the late 1990s. In the early 1990s, the unemployment rate for male South Korean university graduates hovered around 24 percent, whereas Japan's was closer to 5 percent (National Statistical Office, ROK 1998; Ministry of Education, Japan, 1998).

TABLE 5.1
Mothers' University Aspirations for Sons and Daughters

	Sons	*Daughters*
South Korea	88.3	81.2
Japan	73.0	27.7
United States	68.9	65.8
Sweden	31.3	30.8
West Germany	19.6	14.3
Great Britain	48.1	44.1

SOURCE: Korea Survey (Gallup) Polls Limited, 1987.

NOTES: Figures indicate the percentage of mothers who aspire to university education or above for their sons and daughters. This survey was sponsored by the Prime Minister's Office of Japan in 1982 and conducted in Japan, the United States, Sweden, West Germany, and Great Britain. Respondents were a random sample of approximately 1200 married women in each country. The Gallup organization in South Korea replicated the survey for a sample of Korean married women in 1987.

Cultural Demand for Education

Finally, we argue that what one can call the "cultural demand" for education has been much higher in South Korea than in Japan. By this we mean the value of education for reasons other than as a means to obtain "good" employment. These reasons include education for its own sake, for the marriage market, and for the prestige of the family (Sorensen 1994). South Korean parents demonstrate a remarkably strong preference for higher education for their children. This preference extends to daughters as well as sons—something that would not seem to make a great deal of economic sense given South Korea's highly sex-discriminatory labor market. It is difficult to find recent cross-national surveys including Japan, South Korea, and other nations, so we must rely here on results from the 1980s. Table 5.1 shows the results of a cross-cultural survey carried out by the Prime Minister's Office in Japan and repeated in South Korea by the Gallup organization. Two points are striking: A higher percentage of South Korean mothers than any others aspire to university education for their children, and South Korean mothers are much more egalitarian than Japanese mothers. These aspirations mirror the trends in actual university attendance in the two countries: as we demonstrated, the shape of the growth curve in university advancement for men and women is much more similar in South Korea than in Japan (figures 5.1 and 5.2).

The very high levels of educational aspirations in South Korea and the sex-egalitarianism of aspirations do not fit well with a narrow conceptualization of education-for-the-labor market. Instead, we suggest that especially in the case of women, other concerns are relevant. One of these is the marriage market returns to education. South Korea has a very high rate of educational homogamy in marriage (Kim 1990; Lee, Chapter 8 this volume; Smits, Ultee, and Lammers 1998). This is an important reason why parents aspire to have their daughters attend university. As Lee documents in Chapter 8 of this volume, the "returns" to a prestigious university education for a woman in South Korea are significant in terms of the economic and social standing of her potential husband. In the same vein, university attendance on the part of women has been deemed more and more necessary by parents and by young women themselves as a way of competing in the marriage market because rates of graduate school attendance by South Korean men have become so high. Graduate school remains a rarity in Japan, and men's rates of attendance at graduate schools in the United States and other foreign countries also remain far below the comparable rates for South Korean men. The significant overeducation of young men in South Korea is thus an important social pressure affecting young South Korean women and their parents, making a university education an important credential for women's competition in the marriage market. The status rewards to the woman's own family and to her future husband are important signifiers of middle-class status, particularly in South Korea's large urban centers (Lett 1998).

We argue that in contrast, educational motivations in Japan have tended to be quite economically instrumental, in the sense of being attuned more to labor market rewards than to social status concerns (Brinton 1993; James and Benjamin 1988; Nakata and Mosk 1987). Nakata and Mosk argue that in particular, "the Japanese tend to choose as measures of the benefit of educational investment indicators such as the probability of entering a large firm" (1987: 402). This distinguishes Japan from South Korea, where an abundance of cases suggest that social status concerns often override the economic benefits that a university education bestows. Sorensen cites the example, unimaginable in Japan, of a director of a successful South Korean construction company who attends night school to obtain a Ph.D. in economics. As Sorensen puts it, "Even economically successful persons find it difficult to attain high social status without education." He continues, "when I mentioned this director's situation to another Korean of my acquaintance, he smiled and remarked, 'Oh ho, of course! Otherwise people will talk behind his back. They will say he makes all this money, but he is really only an uneducated *sajang-nom*,' a derogatory term for uneducated, coarse businessmen" (1994: 24).

There also seems to be stronger concern in Japan than in South Korea that women may become "overeducated" for the marriage market. The fact that education is helpful to men in both the labor and marriage markets but may be detrimental to women in the marriage market is reflected in the asymmetry of Japanese parents' educational aspirations for sons and daughters (Brinton 1990).

In sum, two educational factors—government policy that allowed South Korean secondary and higher education enrollments to expand at a speed disproportionate to that of economic and occupational change, and a very high demand for education on the part of the populace to fulfill social status concerns—suggest that South Korean women's higher education advancement rates have been more decoupled from economic change than Japanese women's. Finally, Japan and especially South Korea have undergone industrialization in a very compressed period of time, and it is possible that this too may cause deviations from the more tightly coupled pattern of economic and educational changes observed in post–World War II United States.

ANALYSIS OF CHANGE OVER TIME IN WOMEN'S HIGHER EDUCATION ATTAINMENTS AND THE ECONOMY

To examine the link between changes in women's education and the economy in Japan and South Korea, we carry out a time-series analysis for each country. For the Japanese analysis we begin in 1955; we were able to obtain data for South Korea beginning in 1965. We predict women's entrance to high school, junior college, and four-year universities based on the occupational structure and on existing patterns of female labor force participation. We are only secondarily interested in high school compared to higher education because high school is not compulsory in either country, and as we have shown, rates of attendance rose dramatically for both sexes during the period we are considering.

Our basic model assumes the following form:

Educational advancement = (age-eligible population) + (number of graduates at the prior schooling level) + (lagged changes in occupational structure) + (lagged changes in extent and type of female labor force participation)

Measurement of Educational Advancement

We measure education at each level as the number of people who advanced to that level in a particular year. We use advancement rather than enrollment because it is a more precise measure of changes by year. Moreover, the drop-out rate at each level of education is very low in both countries, so advancement is a good indicator of eventual graduation (and certainly better than it would be in the United States).[6] For high school advancement, we use the age-eligible population (15-year-olds) as an independent variable, to investigate how it affects the numbers advancing. Both the dependent variable and this control variable are logged. We also control for a "floor effect," measured as the logged number of people who graduated from junior high school that year (and were thus eligible for high school). Similarly, advancement to junior college is calculated as the logged number of people admitted to junior college. We control for the age-eligible population (logged number of 18-year-olds) and the number of high school graduates (logged) in that year.

Measuring yearly entrance rates to four-year universities in Japan and South Korea is more problematic. This is because there are many late entrants—students who fail the university-specific admissions tests in one year and retake them in a later year.[7] The number admitted in a particular year therefore includes students who graduated from high school that year in addition to some students who graduated from high school in previous years. Unless the late entrants are subtracted from the total number admitted, the university advancement rate for a given age-eligible cohort is inflated. We correct for this by estimating the number of direct entrants to university for each high school graduating class and the number who entered university in the subsequent year. These two are then added together to make up the number of high school graduates in a given year who advanced directly or indirectly to university.[8] The number of 18-year-olds is used as an independent variable (as in other equations, where we used the age-eligible population).

The floor effect is the logged sum of the number of high school graduates in the current year and in the previous year. This takes into account the fact that any late entrants will normally be drawn from the previous year's high school graduates.

Measurement of Occupational Structure and Labor Force Participation

We use three measures of occupational structure to measure the effect of economic change on educational advancement: the percentage of the total labor force (male and female) engaged in nonclerical white-collar work, the percentage engaged in clerical work, and the percentage engaged in service work.[9] Nonclerical white-collar work refers to professional/technical and managerial/administrative work. These categories are combined because separate figures are not available for South Korea between 1969 and 1982, and this would limit the analysis to too few years. The rate of female labor force participation in nonagricultural industries is used to measure women's level of economic participation.[10] We prefer this over the total rate of female labor force participation because the former is more representative of women's entrance into urban wage employment.

The models take changes in women's educational advancement to high school, junior college, and four-year university as a function of changes in the occupational structure and changes in women's extent of participation in the economy. We lag occupational and labor force participation variables by one and three years, testing for the best-fitting model. In each equation we employ the same lag structure for the occupational variables as we do for the labor force participation variables. Our rationale for using short lag structures is that the speed of economic development has been very rapid in both countries. We therefore expect changes in the occupational structure and in the participation of women in the economy to have short-term effects, if any.

Generalized least squares is used to estimate all models. Time-series regression models were estimated using the Cochrane-Orcott iterative procedure. We have 41 observations for Japan (1955–1995). One-year lagged variables reduce the number of observations in the models to 40, and three-year lagged variables reduce the number of observations to 38. For South Korea, we begin with 31 observations (1965–1995), which are subsequently reduced in the same way as the Japanese case.

TABLE 5.2
Models of Educational Attainment for Japanese Women, 1955–1995

	Junior college advancement			University advancement		
	(1)	(2)	(3)	(4)	(5)	(6)
Constant	1.512 (1.518)	2.976 (1.965)	-.852 (1.648)	-29.595** (6.384)	-29.172** (6.476)	-18.381** (4.189)
Age-eligible population	-1.433** (.134)	-.463** (.150)	-.789** (.193)	1.373** (.363)	1.297** (.374)	1.089** (.393)
Floor effect	2.138** (.130)	1.034** (.171)	1.568** (.184)	1.492** (.488)	1.466** (.497)	.777* (.414)
Percent of labor force in non-clerical white-collar work	.010 (.016)	—	—	.106* (.055)	—	—
Percent of labor force in clerical work	—	.069 (.043)	—	—	.103 (.081)	—
Percent of labor force in service work	—	—	.157** (.048)	—	—	.323** (.106)
Percent of labor force in blue-collar work	—	—	—	—	—	—
Nonagricultural female labor force participation rate	.026* (.014)	.007 (.014)	.027** (.009)	-.002 (.041)	.011 (.045)	.032 (.020)
Rho	.145 (.158)	.940** (.028)	.405** (.138)	.715** (.115)	.679** (.117)	.246 (.151)
Durbin-Watson statistic	1.92	1.99	1.84	2.22	2.16	1.97

NOTE: Numbers in parentheses are standard errors.

* $p < .10$, ** $p < .05$ (two-tailed)

EMPIRICAL RESULTS

Because our main focus in this chapter is on the expansion of women's higher education, we summarize the results of the analysis of high school advancement in a note and turn instead to the principal analysis on junior college and university advancement.[11]

Tables 5.2 and 5.3 show these results for Japan and South Korea, respectively. For each level of schooling, three equations are presented. Each includes the age-eligible population, the floor effect, and the nonagricultural female labor force participation rate; the three occupational variables are entered in turn. In both the Japanese and South Korean cases, the zero-order correlations between the independent variables (labor force participation and indicators of occupational structure) were not large enough to prevent their use in the same model. At all three levels of education in both countries, one-year and three-year lagged models either produced very similar results or the one-year lagged model produced statistically significant coefficients that were not evident in the three-year model. For this reason, we show only the results for the one-year lagged model.

Starting with the models for Japan (table 5.2), the floor effect and the female labor force participation rate are both positively related to young women's advancement to junior college over the 40-year period for which we have data. This shows that increases in the numbers of high school graduates led to increases in junior college advancement, and that greater participation of women in the labor force seems to have spurred young women's interest in junior college. The latter is consistent with the data we showed on the relatively high economic participation rate of female junior college graduates in the labor force. The age-eligible population is *negatively* related to junior college advancement. This might be because the rate of junior college advancement leveled off in the second half of the period (while cohort size increased). Among the occupational variables, only the proportion of the labor force in service-sector jobs has a positive and statistically significant relationship to women's junior college advancement rates.

Given that the major increase in the popularity of junior colleges occurred before 1975 and that the advancement rates were quite stable in the subsequent 20-year period, we also separated the data into two time periods (1955–1975 and 1976–1995) and ran a time-series analysis for each period. The results from these analyses (reported here but not shown) demonstrate

TABLE 5.3
Models of Educational Attainment for South Korean Women, 1965–1994

	Junior college advancement			University advancement		
	(1)	(2)	(3)	(4)	(5)	(6)
Constant	-2.165 (3.536)	.600 (3.936)	9.979** (3.016)	5.380 (3.443)	6.540* (3.239)	5.309* (3.114)
Age-eligible population	-.008 (.295)	-.021 (.278)	-1.171** (.322)	-.985* (.355)	-1.050** (.349)	-.898* (.337)
Floor effect	.971** (.193)	.714** (.248)	1.117** (.146)	1.420** (.156)	1.375** (.190)	1.302** (.167)
Percent of labor force in non-clerical white-collar work	.123** (.035)	—	—	.041 (.039)	—	—
Percent of labor force in clerical work	—	.119** (.034)	—	—	.027 (.041)	—
Percent of labor force in service work	—	—	.020 (.034)	—	—	.062 (.038)
Percent of labor force in blue-collar work	—	—	—	—	—	—
Nonagricultural female labor force participation rate	.001 (.014)	.005 (.013)	.044** (.013)	-.015 (.020)	-.009 (.019)	-.011 (.016)
Rho	.748** (.131)	.821** (.125)	.026 (.164)	.273 (.187)	.252 (.189)	.207 (.199)
Durbin-Watson statistic	1.26	1.06	1.84	1.73	1.75	1.80

NOTE: Numbers in parentheses are standard errors.

*p < .10, **p < .05 (two-tailed)

more clearly the underlying dynamics of the relationship between women's junior college attendance and occupational changes in the economy. In the initial period, when women's junior college advancement rates were rapidly increasing, all three measures of change in white-collar labor markets (nonclerical white-collar work, clerical work, and service sector work) were positively and significantly related to junior college advancement and so were the female labor force participation rate and the age-eligible population. The "action" in the junior college-economy interaction therefore occurred during this early period. In the later period, only the female labor force participation rate was statistically significant (and none of the occupational variables). Thus when we periodize the history of change in junior college advancement rates, the relationship between Japanese women's educational participation and labor market incentives becomes clear for the period of rapid educational expansion (1955–1975).

At the level of university advancement, both the size of the age cohort and the floor effect have positive and statistically significant effects. The female labor force participation rate has no bearing on whether women proceed in higher numbers to university; this is what we would have expected given the weak connection between university education and employment for women in Japan over the past several decades. That is, one would not a priori expect that the demonstration of more women participating in the non-agricultural labor force would generate greater motivations on the part of Japanese women to attend university. Holding this variable constant, though, growth in the white-collar and service sectors is related to women's higher advancement rates to university. It is not clear why this is not also the case for clerical work (nor was it the case in the junior college analyses), except that that sector did not grow as quickly as nonclerical white-collar jobs, especially professional/technical ones.[12] When we ran the model for university advancement separately for the two time periods (1955–1975 and 1976–1995), the effect of the occupational variables remained largely unchanged from the analysis of the longer time span. In effect, Japanese women's advancement to university has indeed been affected by the growth of white-collar and service-sector jobs. It was also somewhat affected in the later period by overall growth in female labor force participation, which may possibly reflect the influence of the Equal Employment Opportunity Law from the mid-1980s on and its greater encouragement of women to enter the labor market after they leave higher education.

Turning to the models for South Korea, the floor effect is positive and statistically significant in the case of junior college advancement. Women's labor force participation rate is not, but the growth of the labor force in both nonclerical white-collar and clerical occupations has a positive effect on drawing more women to junior college. The white-collar category in all of our models includes the teaching profession. Given that this has been a popular vocational choice for South Korean women and that a junior college education offers preparation for the lower levels of teaching, these empirical results make sense. It also is logical to us that service growth is unrelated to growth in junior college advancement. The service sector in South Korea includes many self-employed women (see Chapter 1), and advancement to junior college is not a strong prerequisite for this type of employment.

In the model for university advancement, none of the economic variables (women's labor force participation and variables reflecting the white-collar composition of the labor force) are statistically significant; only the floor effect is. Consistent with the historical trajectory of university enrollments in South Korea that we outlined earlier in the chapter, this shows that the more high school graduates there were, the higher were the numbers of people going on to university. The lack of any statistically significant relationship between economic/occupational change and change in university advancement rates in South Korea is ironically similar to the case of high school advancement in Japan (see note 11). That is, whereas the high school level in Japan expanded and became "normal" irrespective of change in the economy, this occurred at the *top* of the educational hierarchy (university) in South Korea.

In summary, the white-collarization of the occupational structure in Japan appears to have had positive and statistically significant effects on increases in women's advancement to junior college in the period when junior colleges were undergoing their most rapid expansion. The general increase in female labor force participation has also been related to increases in junior college attendance, again especially in the early period of expansion. Women's labor force participation has not had a statistically significant effect at the university level except in a few of the equations in the later period. But there have been effects of occupational change on women's university advancement.

In South Korea, the model linking economic change to women's educational advancement performs quite well at the junior college level and very poorly at the university level. These results are very consistent with our data and discussion of the South Korean case earlier in the chapter and in other parts of the book, especially Chapters 2 and 8. University education is highly valued for South Korean women as well as men, but the utilitarian value of it seems to be strongly directed toward social status. For men, a university credential has become essential for entrance to a white-collar job, but for women, the sex segregation in the labor market and the oversupply of highly educated men has meant that unless a woman graduates from a very prestigious university, the credential does not open many doors in the labor market. It does greatly increase the possibility that she will be able to marry a highly educated man, however.

CONCLUSION

If one expects to find close linkages between increases in women's educational attainment and changes in the economy, our findings for Japan offer some support but our findings for South Korea offer less. In the United States, changes in the demand for white-collar workers (especially in the clerical sector) and changes in women's labor force participation spurred growth in women's educational attainments. In Japan, increases in women's junior college and university advancement rates have followed growth in the white-collar and service sectors of the economy and to some extent, growth in women's overall labor force participation. In South Korea there is some support at the junior college level for a model linking economic change and women's education, but the applicability of the model breaks down at the university level.

The experience of Japan and South Korea in the past few decades compresses economic change that spanned many more decades in the twentieth-century United States. The history of many of the early employment barriers to American women is repeated in the contemporary experiences of these countries.[13] In the United States, these barriers fell partly because the demand for educated labor necessitated changes in employers' discriminatory attitudes (Goldin 1990). If the supply of highly educated males is sufficient to meet economic demand, employers' preferences that men fill many of the white-collar jobs in the economy can be maintained.[14] If the supply is not sufficient, employers must increasingly turn to women, which should encourage more women to attain higher education. There is some evidence that this process began to occur in Japan in the mid-to-late 1980s. The cumulative effects of small birth cohorts entering the labor market produced a labor shortage that was predicted to become more severe in the coming decades. Japanese economic growth stalled in the 1990s, but if this is temporary (which is not clear at the time of this writing), in the long run university-educated women's employment prospects should once again improve by virtue of continuing low birth rates and a resurfacing labor shortage.

But even if one included educated male labor supply in a more fully elaborated model of women's educational advancement based on the labor market returns to education, we remain doubtful that the model would fully explain educational expansion for women in Japan and South Korea. We expect that it would remain more accurate for the Japanese than the South Korean case, where we have argued that government educational policy and the cultural demand for education have significantly diminished the direct effect of economic change on women's education, especially at the university level.

We argue that it would be useful for future research to focus on the development of a more comprehensive conceptual model of the link between women's education and labor market change that attempts to incorporate the factors we have discussed in this chapter: educational policy changes, the extent of labor market discrimination against women, and the culturally embedded nature of educational demand. Moreover, several of the chapters in this book demonstrate that research using individual-level data on the link between education, work, and marriage patterns in East Asia can fruitfully test assumptions drawn from theoretical and empirical research in the United States. Our findings suggest to us that in industrializing countries where employers use marriage bars, the link between economic change and educational attainment will most likely percolate upward through the educational system over time. That is, because marriage bars historically are found more typically in white-collar jobs than in the manufacturing or service sector, women's enrollment in high school and possibly junior college may be tied to opportunities in the labor market long before such a logic operates at the university level. The availability of enough highly educated males to fill white-collar jobs will delay the development of the economy-education link for women at the highest schooling levels. But if labor demand at this level outpaces the supply of males (as it did in Taiwan; see Chapter 2), then the link will become stronger and will come to resemble what initially occurred at the lower levels of schooling.

CHAPTER SIX

Women's Solidarity

Company Policies and Japanese Office Ladies

Yuko Ogasawara

Trends in Japanese female employment by occupation show that over the last thirty years, the proportion of women in blue-collar jobs has decreased. Accompanying this change has been the rapid increase in the proportion of women in clerical jobs. Clerical workers have come to account for more than one-third of the total women employed, and in fact, more Japanese women hold clerical positions than any other occupation.

The increase in the number of women in clerical jobs is not unique to Japan. The expansion and feminization of clerical work have occurred in many industrialized and rapidly industrializing countries.[1] The major difference seems to lie in the opportunities clerical work provides or does not provide for women to continue and develop their careers. In the United States, women in clerical jobs are more likely than women in many other occupations to work continuously across the life cycle or to resume working after a short spell out of the labor force (Goldin 1990). In contrast, the majority of young female clerical workers in Japan retire from the labor market upon marriage or childbirth, and many do not return to the labor force.

In her study comparing female clerical workers in the United States, Japan, and South Korea, Brinton points out that among all Japanese women with clerical work experience, 65 percent worked only before marriage (Brinton 1998c). In South Korea, the tendency for young unmarried women to monopolize clerical positions is even stronger, with women above the age of 30 accounting for only 15 percent of the total number of female clerical workers.

Similarly, Brinton, Lee, and Parish (Chapter 2) show that the proportion of working women in South Korea who are clerical employees drops sharply from 37 percent before marriage to 1 percent after marriage. They analyze the lower rate at which married women overall work as employees in South Korea compared to Taiwan by considering the different patterns of industrialization followed by these two societies. Because of the South Korean government's decision to promote more capital-intensive, large urban conglomerates, many South Korean women face the prospect of long commuting times and rigid working hours. This makes it more difficult for married women to balance work and family responsibilities.

Japanese women face similar barriers to South Korean women in white-collar work. In his study of Japanese women's occupational careers, Hirata (1998b) shows that the proportion of women in clerical jobs falls from over 40 percent to under 20 percent when comparing their initial and current occupational status. Moreover, he documents that women who begin their career as clerical workers are more likely to exit the labor market than those in other occupational categories. Tanaka (1999) estimates that approximately 20 percent of Japanese women remain employed full-time throughout their childrearing years. In Japan as in South Korea (as discussed by Lee in Chapter 8 of this volume), the association between women's higher-education attainment and labor market participation after marriage, which can be observed in the United States and most other industrialized societies, is weak (Akachi 1998; Hirao 1999; Imada 1996; Tanaka 1997, 1998).

One of the major differences between women workers in Japan and those in South Korea lies in the opportunity for them to work as clerical employees in middle age. Although such opportunities are rare in South Korea, this is not the case in Japan. The tendency for women to retire from clerical jobs remains higher in Japan than in the United States, but even so, an increasing number of middle-aged Japanese women are in white-collar work (Brinton 1998a). Today, women aged 35 or older account for approximately half the total number of female clerical workers (Inoue and Ehara 1999). However, this does not imply that young unmarried women and older married women enjoy the same status in the workforce. The majority of middle-aged Japanese women who reenter the labor market do so as part-time employees and/or work in small companies (Akachi 1998; Ogasawara 1998; Seiyama 1999).

When the Equal Employment Opportunity Law (hereafter EEOL) went into effect in Japan in 1986, quite a few firms—especially large ones—introduced a two-track system composed of managerial (*sōgōshoku*) and clerical

(*ippanshoku*) tracks. The introduction of the system and the subsequent recruitment of a small number of women into the managerial track allowed
these corporations to insist that they were equal opportunity employers.
However, improvements in women's employment conditions in the first
10 years after the EEOL were minimal, partly due to the weak enforcement
provisions (Hirata 1995; Imada 1996; Lam 1992; Tanaka 1996, 1997; Okuyama 1996). In order to respond to the claim that the law was ineffective,
various amendments, including vesting the law with greater enforcement
power, were introduced in 1999.

In this chapter, I look at young Japanese women's experience of working as clerical employees in large enterprises. This group constitutes a distinct category of working women in Japan. These "office ladies" (often
shortened to "OLs"), a vernacular expression commonly used to describe
young female clerical workers, are recruited immediately upon graduation
from universities and two-year colleges. In the past, many were also hired
straight from high school. But the number of OLs with a high school education has decreased, especially in large corporations in urban areas, as more
and more women have attained higher education.

Tasks assigned to OLs usually involve word processing, elementary accounting, and doing photocopying or facsimile tasks. They are also often responsible for various chores such as serving tea to their male colleagues or
to company visitors, wiping desks, cleaning ashtrays, or answering telephone calls. Sometimes they are asked to run errands, ranging from delivering documents to buying train tickets. Opportunities for these women to be
promoted into management are very limited.[2]

OLs rarely protest openly against the company authority structure that
discriminates against them.[3] It is difficult to understand, though, how well-
educated women can be satisfied with such dead-end jobs. Why is it that OLs
so seldom form a united front in demanding improved working conditions?

In his study of how individuals may indicate dissatisfaction with an organization, Hirschman (1970) identified two options: withdrawal from the
unhappy situation ("exit"), or protest against authority ("voice"). He argued
that the availability of the exit alternative limits the use of voice: whereas exit
is simply an either-or decision, voice is an art, and therefore must be learned
and developed. I will show in this essay that many Japanese companies successfully engage in what Hirschman calls "conspiracy in restraint of voice"

(1970: 61) by prompting women's early exit from the workplace. I will argue, moreover, that the asymmetry in the expectations that companies hold about the primary activity of men and women potentially has an important effect on each sex's ability to resort to the voice option. I contend, therefore, that we must examine not only the effects of the length of women's service on their readiness to organize for the collective good, but also examine the nature of their service. Women's work lives differ from men's not only in quantity but in quality. I begin by reviewing existing explanations of OL quiescence.

THE STUDY OF OFFICE LADIES

Popular conceptions about essential differences between men and women are one ready explanation for the lack of organized OL movements. There is a general belief among the Japanese public that women's capacity for comradeliness is somehow inferior to men's. The phrase *otoko no yūjō* (male comradeship) is frequently referred to, while a similar expression for women does not exist. *Otoko no yūjō* is highly prized, while friendship among women is often considered to be either shallow or false. Sadly, many women are themselves skeptical of the sincerity of their capacity for friendship. For example, one OL I talked to suggested that jealousy, which she considered to be an intrinsically female quality, inhibits women's solidarity.

Contrary to such popular conceptions, a number of scholars have elucidated the mechanisms in the structure of the workplace that produce so-called female emotions and reactions. In their classic sociological works, Hochschild (1983) and Kanter (1977) both argued that what often become labeled as female emotions are in fact natural human responses to situations that afford limited alternatives for reaction. According to this view, it is not that OLs are intrinsically more jealous than male workers. Rather, it is the structure of the workplace and the work process itself that differentially affect men and women, leading one sex (women) into circumstances that tend to prompt jealousy.

Indeed, researchers on OLs have attempted to account for OL quiescence by paying more attention to structural factors and relying less on purely psychological explanations. Some scholars present OLs as passive victims of an all-embracing system of gender discrimination in the workplace. For example, in his influential research on OLs in a general trading company, McLendon (1983) argues that the position of OLs is either a "way station" on the road to marriage or a "blind alley" for those who have failed to find a husband. Similarly, Lo (1990) portrays OLs working in an electric equipment manufacturer as childish and submissive employees who have no alternatives and thus must accept whatever the company requires of them. In their description of the conflict-ridden conditions faced by female clerical employees, Carter and Dilatush (1976) likewise emphasize how OLs suffer from exploitation.

The view of OLs as being largely receptive to their position in the workplace despite stark structural inequality is shared by Saso (1990), who writes that, except for a few professionals, Japanese women seem to be passive and accepting of discrimination. According to her analysis, "Women connive in their own exploitation," because for many "the ideal picture of a wife is one of gentle disposition, who by her devotion to her family sacrifices her own interests" (1990: 134).

In a strange way, the thought that Japanese women are passive and accepting of discrimination is comforting, for it is usually assumed at the same time that their views of women's roles are still restricted by tradition. Defenders of this opinion hypothesize that once women are liberated from the "premodern" ideal, they will stand up and protest. It is argued, in short, that overt sex discrimination and women's acquiescence are simply manifestations of Japan's cultural lag behind the United States and other Western nations. This assumption implies that it is only a matter of time before these attitudes disappear.

Some other researchers, on the other hand, maintain that OLs are more creative and expressive than conventional accounts allow. According to their view, OLs need not use confrontational tactics to fight discrimination because they enjoy various types of constructive play made possible by the freedom ironically associated with their second-rate employee status. Condon (1985) points out that OLs are relieved from serious work and family responsibilities, and that their shorter working hours and considerable financial resources permit them to enjoy extensive shopping, various hobbies, gourmet dinners, and overseas travel.[4] Similarly, Kelsky (1994) describes how OLs use their large expendable income to support a vibrant subculture of their own through which they find opportunities to defy as well as to escape traditional gender hierarchies. This is not an isolated view of observers of OLs. Iwao (1993), in her overview of contemporary Japanese women, explains the "nonconfrontational strategy" favored by many Japanese women:

> [Women] have not occupied positions of significance in policy-making and business and their existence and voices have been pretty much ignored by men in formal arenas, but there has been some advantage in this state of "inequality." It has exempted women from having to fit into the frameworks set down by the public or private organizations (corporations) of society and has allowed them the margin of freedom to explore their individuality in ways not permitted to men. One manifestation of this is that outside the corporation one is more likely to find an adventurous or creative spirit in women than in men. (7)

Iwao concludes that today it is husbands who are being controlled and who ought to be pitied, because their lives are confined and regimented by their jobs to a degree not experienced by most women.

Although the above three modes of explanation present diverse interpretations of the OL life, they have one thing in common: they all argue that the reasons for OLs' failure to organize open rebellion reside in the women themselves. According to the first genre of literature, women are incapable of acting in solidarity because their psychological dispositions, notably the tendency toward jealousy, get in the way. The second view stresses OLs' victimization in a sex-discriminatory workplace and therefore attributes weak solidarity less explicitly to women's inherent nature. Writings in this group provide much in the way of understanding the dilemmas for women of working in a male-biased career structure, but they nonetheless ascribe passivity and submissiveness to OLs.

In contrast, the last group of scholars insists that OLs actively seek an independent lifestyle that allows them to criticize and even defy traditional male values. However, even this literature is not successful in totally doing away with the idea that passivity is highly typical of OLs. For according to this analysis, women do not directly challenge unequal working conditions. As Kelsky notes, they are at best temporarily enjoying a unique space within Japanese culture and at worst making the best of a bad situation. Without a good explanation of why OLs choose (or are forced to choose) the circuitous method, the claim that OLs are not merely trying to escape from the reality of male domination is less convincing. Indeed, Iwao remarks that "[Japanese women] have not completely shed their characteristic passivity and, to a certain degree, resignation to their fate" (1993: 10).

In the end, all three modes of explanation attribute women's quiescence to their intrinsic nature, whether that is described as jealousy, submissiveness, or passivity. This is, in my view, blaming the victim for her inability to organize or join a united front. What the above observers fail to recognize is that OLs find themselves in an environment that is extremely hostile to the cultivation of the "cultures of solidarity" (Fantasia 1988) that make it possible to stage formal protest actions. In this essay, I argue that company employment policies differentially affect male and female workers' capability to cooperate for the collective good; company policies are generally detrimental to women's solidarity and beneficial to men's. Specifically, I show that management's reluctance to promote female university graduates results in women with different educational backgrounds having to perform similar types of jobs, which creates undue tensions among them. In addition, I describe how an overt emphasis on women's family responsibilities and early retirement promotes conflicts of interests. Feeling lonely and atomized, most OLs seek solitary solutions to their problems of working in Japanese firms by adopting the exit strategy instead of attempting to voice protest.

After a brief description of the research methodology I used, I discuss tension created among OLs who must cope with status differentiation processes that are less explicit than those faced by men. Four potential criteria for determining seniority (tenure, education, job transfer, and youth/attractiveness) are contradictory, due to inconsistent company policies. Next, I look at the decisions a woman must make in order to overcome various obstacles she faces in continuing her work. Women find themselves increasingly alienated from each other depending on the ways they have chosen to proceed. I conclude that employment policies that make work and family decisions inseparable for women but not for men have important effects on an individual woman's ability to cooperate for the collective good.

DATA

The first set of data for this research consists of my own participant observation in a large financial institution in Tokyo, which I will refer to as the "Tōzai Bank."[5] The bank was founded about three-quarters of a century ago. It has an extensive network of branches covering the entire nation and extending overseas. At the time of my research, the bank employed about 4000 men and 3000 women. I worked at the headquarters of Tōzai Bank, which is located in the central business district of Tokyo. My position was as a temporary employee, giving miscellaneous assistance to 49 businessmen and 13 OLs across three departments.[6] While in the office, I worked closely with OLs but avoided asking questions that did not fit naturally with the flow of daily conversation. Sharing the drudgery of OL work day in and day out, I became very intimate with some of the OLs. I was able to keep in touch with them after I quit my job at Tōzai. What I learned through phone calls, letters, and mutual visits about the most recent developments in the office proved extremely useful for the research.

Although my experiences at the Tōzai Bank were eye-opening, it was important for me to assess the universality of what I observed in a particular workplace. For this purpose, additional interviews were indispensable. After completing the participant observation, I spoke to 30 *sararīman* and 30 OLs employed in various large Japanese firms.[7] Although I had to rely on a non-random method of identifying my informants, I attempted to compensate for the limitations of the data as much as possible by contacting informants who differed, among other things, in their age, tenure, position, education, lines of business, and types of industry. Above all, I made sure that no two interviewees worked for the same firm. I should point out, however, that the claims I make for large companies in Tokyo do not necessarily hold true for smaller firms or for organizations in more rural areas of Japan.

CONTRADICTORY CRITERIA OF SENIORITY

Someone new to the office would have received the impression that the OLs at the Tōzai Bank were on extremely good terms with each other. They always seemed to do things as a group: they ate lunch together, took their tea break together, and visited various places together during nonwork hours. More than a few times I heard men use the expression "Girls flock together." I, too, believed that the OLs got along very well with each other until one day one of them admitted to me that she sometimes got tired of trying to chime in with other women's conversation. She then secretly told me how she carefully read TV columns in the newspaper everyday in order to become familiar with the story of popular dramas. This way she was able to follow other women's conversation without actually watching the program. TV programs, travel, and men were decidedly the most popular things women talked about during lunch. Until then I had assumed that OLs *liked* to talk about these matters. This woman's remark therefore took me by surprise. I realized then that the OLs might not be enjoying talking about these matters or be enjoying each other's company as much as it had seemed at first.

Closer observation revealed a surprising degree of friction, frequently experienced between OLs paired for work. One OL, for example, described how she often had a dream at night of being scolded by her older colleague, who used to summon her into the tea room and give various warnings, such as to pick up the phone more quickly. Another OL told me that she had to "dump," mentally, her university diploma in order to get along with other OLs. One OL summarized, "You don't care what men think about you, but you must watch out what other girls might think."

Division among OLs was not confined to the bank; it seemed to be a fairly typical phenomenon in many of the large Japanese corporations where my interviewees worked. Women often disclosed during the interviews that they could never be completely at ease in their female colleagues' company and that they paid considerable attention to what they said to one another. Indeed, when talking about their current problems and future dreams with me, many OLs commented that they generally did not talk about these matters with their colleagues at work except within a closed circle of a few intimate friends. It seemed ironic that they should share personal feelings with me, whom they had met for the first time, and not with their female colleagues, with whom they spent such long hours day after day.

Relationships among OLs were structured hierarchically and were indicated by their frequent use of the terms *senpai* (one's senior) and *kōhai* (one's junior), much valued phrases not only in the bank but in Japanese society in general. Being *senpai* and *kōhai* is considered something different from being a friend. This was illustrated by women's conversation about a stranger who mistook two women in a *senpai-kōhai* relationship to be friends. Apparently the OLs thought this was both awkward and funny. A similar distinction between being friends and being *senpai-kōhai* was made by an ex-OL of a general trading company: "If you become very intimate with your *senpai*, you become friends. But if you don't, then she remains your *senpai*." Although friendship is possible with one's *senpai*, it is not inevitable. The primary determinant of seniority among OLs was the length of service in the company.

Tenure

Generally speaking, the longer the tenure, the higher the status in the OL group. Because all of the OLs at Tōzai were recruited immediately from school, two women with the same length of tenure would have started working in the same year. Thus which year a person had joined the bank was considered important and was reflected in employees' incessant concern over the composition of their *dōki* (coworkers who entered the firm in the same year). This word was used frequently by both male and female workers to describe their relationships to one another. Persons outside one's *dōki* were either *senpai* or *kōhai*.

The rule of hierarchy was solemnly observed among women, who paid respect to *senpai* OLs. A woman showed deference to her senior OL by addressing the person by her last name and the suffix "-san," and by speaking to her in polite language, using *desu* and *masu* and sometimes even honorific terms such as *nasaru* and *sareru*. In turn, a senior woman addressed her junior OL either by speaking in casual terms and by using her nickname without any honorific suffix or by nickname, last, or first name with the suffix *-chan*. The OLs themselves judged the relationship between two persons by how they spoke to one another. This was apparent in a conversation between two OLs talking about another woman they did not know well. "You know this woman with long hair? I think she's Kei-chan's *dōki*," said one woman. The other responded, "I see, you heard them speak on equal terms with each other."[8]

Language, however, could not be isolated from the other ways in which people indicated respect. I noticed this when the other temporary employee, who began working at the bank after I did, firmly insisted on letting me walk in front of her whenever we proceeded through the narrow aisles between the desks. Kondo finds in her study of a small, family-owned factory in Tokyo that "awareness of complex social positioning is an *inescapable* element of any utterance in Japanese, for it is *utterly impossible* to form a sentence without *also* commenting on the relationship between oneself and one's interlocutor" (1990: 31; emphasis in original). Similarly, it was impossible for the OLs not only to talk, but to walk through doors and aisles, get on elevators, and take seats at a meeting without first sorting out the hierarchical relationships among them. Junior OLs also typically relied upon their more experienced colleagues to guide them through their daily routines of work. Men were aware of this, and therefore it was customary for more complicated tasks to be assigned to senior OLs.

If length of service had been the sole criterion determining one's position in the bank, relationships among OLs would have been more straightforward than they actually were. In fact, the OLs' world was complicated and strained by the existence of other criteria (i.e., education, length of service in a certain section or department, and physical attractiveness) that did not neatly correspond to the confines of one's *dōki*.

Education

An OL's official rank at the bank was determined not only by her length of tenure but also by her educational background. The third-year university graduate was regarded as being equivalent to the fifth-year junior college graduate and the seventh-year high school graduate in terms of compensation and promotion. This is a typical practice in many other large Japanese firms, quite a few of which started hiring female university graduates on a regular basis only after the implementation of the EEOL in 1986. In the mid-to-late 1980s, the Tōzai Bank as well as other large companies began offering employment opportunities regularly to female university graduates (partly as an antidiscrimination measure), but they were not prepared to give these women the jobs and duties for which they were qualified.

Because the management at Tōzai did not treat this new group of highly educated women exactly the same as junior college graduates in terms of compensation, it was an improvement over the old practice. Before the implementation of the EEOL, only women who had a special connection with the bank were hired from university, and these were offered the same amount of compensation as that paid to junior college graduates. Even after the implementation of the EEOL, however, the company continued to ignore the human capital investment that these women had made in obtaining higher education: while her university counterpart paid tuition, a junior college graduate made money and was nonetheless able to receive the same amount of compensation at the same age, presuming that they had both left school at the customary ages of 20 and 22 years old, respectively.[9]

The treatment of female university graduates was thus extremely ambiguous and contradictory. Because they deserved better jobs and more challenging duties, many of them of course felt mistreated. They often resented being given the same tasks as junior college and high school graduates. How-

ever, from the point of view of the latter, it was unfair that university graduate *dōki* should receive better pay when they were doing the same job.

At the bank, it was typical for high school and junior college graduates
to regard university graduates as arrogant, while university graduates tended
to feel unfairly bullied by *senpai* with high school or junior college education. For example, there was a famous incident the OLs called the "open
bank book case" that occurred a few years ago in a different section of the
firm. According to the tale told to me, a junior college graduate said repeat-
edly to her university graduate *kōhai* how nice it must be to receive a large
salary until the university showed the *senpai* her bank book in order to con-
vince her that the difference in their compensation was not as large as her
senpai thought it to be.

Similarly, a university graduate woman remembered an offensive remark
made by a senior OL who had graduated from junior college. A man received a letter written in English and asked the senior woman to translate it
into Japanese because he had difficulty understanding the language. The
woman looked at the junior OL who happened to be standing nearby and
recommended that he ask her instead, since she was a university graduate.
Despite it being common knowledge, the man had to remind her that he was
also a university graduate. The man's having a university diploma was not
the target for the senior OL's sarcasm, but the junior OL's educational background was.

Does similar tension exist between male high school and university graduates? (There are very few male junior college graduates in Japan.) Although
uneasy feelings often do exist between these two groups of men, antagonism
usually does not become as apparent as among women. One of the reasons
for the peacefulness seems to be that, in the case of men, university graduates
are generally understood to have considerable advantage over high school
graduates in terms of promotion. The former personnel manager of a bank
explained the situation to me:

> Although everybody has a chance for advancement, university graduates tend
> to be promoted faster than high school graduates because they have deeper
> knowledge and more extensive experience. But there are some exceptionally
> capable high school graduates who are in no way inferior to university gradu-
> ates. These people are promoted—perhaps not at the same speed as university
> graduates—but they are nevertheless advanced, and some even make it to the
> position of branch manager.

But even in the long run the most talented and hardworking high school graduate cannot hope to be promoted as far as a university graduate. Similarly, another man working for a shipping company told me the following:

> When university graduates join a firm, high school graduates of the same age have already been working for four years. Naturally, they [high school graduates] know more about the job and are respected accordingly. But both university graduates and high school graduates know that in several years their positions will be reversed, with the university graduates in higher offices. It would be unwise for high school graduates to put on airs with university graduates because retaliation would be easy later on. So they don't do such a thing.

Both men's statements make clear that a high school graduate rarely has the chance to compete on an equal footing with a university graduate even if their tenure with the firm is the same. Men with different educational backgrounds, therefore, usually do not engage in an apparent struggle over their positions.

Enmity was similarly absent among women employed in a few firms where education, rather than sex, determined one's job and duties within the organization. In these rare cases, female university graduates received equal treatment with male university graduates, while female junior college graduates worked as their assistants. Junior college graduates working under this system also expressed dissatisfaction, but they did not bear malice against the university women as happened in other firms. Instead, they indicated frustration against the company authority, which refused to give them the opportunity to do more than routine clerical work. The following comment made by a junior college graduate OL working under the more gender-neutral arrangement in an electronic giant was illustrative:

> I don't have any grudge against university graduates, really, but I do have complaints against the company system. There are really no hard feelings between junior college and university graduates in our department, or in other sections of the company that I know of. It's probably because we don't do the same job [that we don't have any bad feelings].

In short, men's and women's experiences in a more gender-neutral arrangement suggest that it is management's indecisive and inconsistent policy concerning the recruitment of highly educated women that makes it difficult for women with different educational backgrounds to get along with one another. University graduates are given the same or similar tasks but are paid more than junior college graduates. This contradictory policy pits the two groups of women against each other.

Job Transfer

The second factor that sometimes contradicted the hierarchy produced by tenure was the length of service in a particular section. Two women with the same educational background and the same length of tenure with Tōzai were working in pairs for a department. They talked in casual terms to each other, but one woman was often given an order by the other OL to do things in a certain way. One day when the woman was given such instructions, she explained to me that because the OL was her senior concerning work, she had to follow her ways. This woman was new to the section. She was transferred to the office three months ago and had to learn how things were done there. The two women were *dōki*, but when it came to work, she had to respect the other OL as her *senpai*.

It was apparent that the woman did not particularly enjoy complying with her *dōki*'s requests. She said she sometimes wished she had been able to stay in one section. If she had, she would have been someone everybody else would count on and respect. Being taught how to do things was all right for her when she was younger, but she found it hard at her current age.

Seniority based on length of service in a particular section was also a typical OL phenomenon. At the bank, as in many other Japanese firms, job rotation was considered important for men as an opportunity to accumulate extensive knowledge and the experience necessary to become competent managers. Men therefore were transferred routinely from department to department. Women, however, were transferred less frequently. Their transfer became necessary only when the number of OLs between departments had to be redistributed.[10] Consequently, transfers did not confer the benefits to OLs that they did to men. What was considered important for OLs was not extensive knowledge and experience, but to remember such details as where certain documents were stored and how they were filed.

Indeed, one of the men I interviewed working in another bank described to me how they came to speak of *onna no ko oboe* (girls' way of remembering):

> What women do everyday is pieces of a job that must be processed quickly without any mistake. They don't know how a certain job fits into the entire

picture, or why they must do the job. We men would hate it if we didn't know the meaning of the jobs we were doing. So, among us, we call it "*onna no ko oboe*" [girls' way of remembering]. They just memorize mechanically what to do if a certain item is marked X and if another is marked Y. I guess their [different ways of learning] do not really reflect differences between men and women, but are more related to what the company expects from us. But people tend to think that women cannot make sound and comprehensive judgments.

When mechanical memory is much of what is expected of OLs, some of the knowledge that a woman gains in a certain department becomes of little use when she is transferred to a different department. The OL has to start from the beginning, making her position weak in the new environment.

Youthful Attractiveness

Youth carries positive value for women in the Japanese workplace. Many workers, both men and women, used the expression *chiyahoya sareru* (to be puffed up by others' attention; to be danced attendance on) to describe how much young women were waited upon by men in their office. A woman who worked in a general trading company explained to me the meaning of *chiyahoya sareru* in the following way: "It means to be invited incessantly to play tennis, to go skiing, go to parties, etc. by men [in the company]. Even if you don't try hard, you're invited to some sort of a gathering on Friday evenings."

However, such invitations stop coming after a few years when men characteristically turn their attention to the fresh supply of young women who enter the organization every year. An OL of a food processing company described how older women were no longer able to attract men's attention: "When you go to a drinking party, it's only the new women whom the men pay attention to. Other women are treated as though it didn't matter whether they came or not. Men don't even look at you." A banker expressed his sympathy for older women who were abruptly abandoned by men in the office and explained why younger women might be more popular: "Younger women are more popular because they are novel to the workplace. People get tired of being together all the time. When a new woman joins, men are curious to find out what sort of a person she is." The man added falteringly that younger women also tended to be prettier.

How the situation becomes progressively intolerable for older OLs was brought home to me one day when I was talking with my fellow temporary worker, who worked as an OL at a prominent general trading company for eight years before her marriage. I asked her why she had decided to retire from the firm and become a temporary worker. Clearly she was making much less money than before. In addition, a temporary worker was genuinely at the bottom of the office hierarchy, doing bits and pieces of work, often at the bidding of female regular employees. I wondered how she felt being bossed around by OLs, when she herself used to enjoy OL status. To my surprise, she looked at me in bewilderment that I should ask a question whose answer was self-evident: "Do you really find it strange [that I am working as a temporary worker instead of continuing to work as an OL]? It just means that it's difficult working as an OL when you grow older. The way people look at you and treat you—you begin to think it's better if you quit." According to her, people at the workplace continued to treat older OLs in the same way on the surface. However, when she went for a drink after work, she heard many people say horrible things about older women.

In spite of the seniority rule that women observed dutifully among themselves, a *reverse-seniority system* was at work in their relation to men: younger OLs, judged to be more attractive, were more popular than older OLs.[11] Therefore, although women paid deference to older colleagues as their seniors, both were at the same time keenly aware that a premium was placed on youth. This reversal of the rule of seniority added further complications to the already complex and difficult relationships among them.

In sum, solidarity among OLs is undermined because there are potentially many lines of cleavage. Men find that their standing in the hierarchical order and the path their goals should follow are clearly delineated at each stage of promotion. However, for female employees, there is little status differentiation. Although women with longer tenure receive respect, the essential quality of their jobs and responsibilities often do not differ from those of the less experienced. Even in the case where experienced women are given more difficult assignments, they do not necessarily make more money, because university graduates are offered higher pay than junior college graduates regardless of job content. Because their work centers around remembering mechanically what to do, women also carry the risk of losing their status due to a transfer. Furthermore, women find it hard to prevent the depreciation of their value as they age, as there are few other features to distinguish them, in men's eyes, besides youth and attractiveness. It is extremely difficult for women to work harmoniously, let alone cultivate cultures of solidarity, when they must cope with such contradictions.

INSEPARABLE DECISIONS: WORK AND FAMILY

It has often been pointed out by the Japanese public and in literature on OLs that OLs are one of the richest groups of people in society (see, e.g., Kelsky 1994 and Condon 1985). It is said that because most OLs live with their parents, who pay for their living expenses, they can spend the majority of their earnings on luxuries. Indeed, many of the unmarried OLs I came to know at Tōzai lived with their parents, and they seemed to enjoy comfortable lives.[12]

For example, many OLs found pleasure in traveling abroad. Within the year that I worked at Tōzai, OLs in the office visited Hawaii, Paris, Australia, Canada, Tibet, and Hong Kong. Even those women who decided to travel domestically took vacations in remote places like Okinawa (the southernmost island of Japan) and Hokkaido (the northernmost island). In addition, many enjoyed long weekends by the seaside in the summer and in ski resorts and hot springs in the winter.

The OLs, however, did not seem to regard their generous spending on travel to be a permanent phenomenon. They would often justify their current luxuries with, "It's only for now." Many considered their carefree lifestyle to be permissible only for the several years before their eventual retirement from the firm. In fact, although they seemed to be fully enjoying their lives outside of work, they appeared restless, as though each one was somehow not yet her true self.

Marriage

An important recent demographic change, especially in urban Japan, is the rise in the average age of first marriage. In 1960, it was 24.4 years of age for women and 27.2 years for men, but it reached a historic high in 1998: 26.7 years of age for women and 28.6 for men. In 1995, 48 percent of women and 67 percent of men in their late 20s had never married. Never-married women in their late 20s increased 8 percent in just five years. Accompanying the rise in the average age of first marriage is the increase in women's years of service in a firm. On average, in 1998 women had been working continuously for 8.2 years (up from 4.0 in 1960).

This evidence may seem to imply that OL status is no longer a "temporary bench" on the road to marriage, or, on the other hand, for those who have failed to find a husband, a "blind alley" as McLendon suggested (1983). We must not forget, however, the fact that the overwhelming majority of OLs intend to get married and retire from the workplace. According to research conducted by a life insurance company, almost three-quarters of 575 OLs who were currently working in the headquarters of large companies located in the central business district of Tokyo (Chiyoda-ku, Chūō-ku, and Minato-ku) intended to retire from work upon marriage or childbirth (Fukuhara 1992).[13] The finding is consistent with women's life-course analyses conducted by Imada (1996) and Manabe (1998) in which both researchers compare cohorts born between the 1920s and 1960s. They report that although there is a tendency for younger women to continue working at the time of marriage, an increasing number of them retire with the arrival of their first child so that the total number of women who continue working throughout marriage and childrearing has not increased in the last forty or so years.

The marriage of female coworkers was always of paramount concern for the OLs at Tōzai. Young OLs tended simply to take interest in the future husband of their colleague, but older OLs appeared to have ambivalent feelings. Although they unanimously congratulated the bride-to-be, many at the same time seemed unable to avoid the feeling of being somewhat left behind. After it was made known that one of the women in the workplace was soon to marry and resign, an OL who had been working for 10 years murmured sadly, "The time you feel lonely and desolate being an OL is when one of your fellow workers marries and leaves." Similarly, an OL who used to work at a general trading company remarked: "There's always a feeling of fear that you'll be left behind. Especially when your *dōki* start to leave one by one, you begin to feel the pressure. You certainly don't want to be the last one to go! You also compare the social standing of your fiancé—which company he works for, for example. If his company is not well known, you feel a bit embarrassed. Marriage to a man of good social standing becomes the most important goal of your life." Because women were, in a sense, competitors in the race for marriage, she thought solidarity among OLs was difficult.

Perhaps because there were no young men in the workplace, rivalry among the Tōzai OLs did not seem to be as strong as among the women in the general trading company described above. Upon joining the bank, male graduates were first usually assigned to a position in a branch, and by the time they were transferred to the headquarters, most were older and married.[14] It is important to note, therefore, that how strongly OLs regarded one another as contenders varied partly according to the particularities of the workplace.

The fact remains, however, that few OLs embraced their jobs; the jobs provided them little prospect for promotion and a lifetime career. The older the OL, the more she felt that her time was running out. For example, a 34-year-old, single OL working in a real estate company did not have any immediate complaint about her current comfortable life because she lived with her parents and made a handsome salary. However, she felt uneasy about her future. The following is her response to my question about her coming plans:

> Future? That is the biggest problem. When I joined the company, I expected to work for only four years or so. I thought about quitting [the company], for instance, working as a temporary staff. But that's only keeping up appearances and deceiving yourself. You quit because you want to get away from the inquisitive eyes at your workplace which silently say things like, "She can't get married," or "How long does she intend to stay on?" I feel lonely and helpless going on working like this. I didn't intend things to turn out this way. It's especially painful when your *dōki* quit.

This woman's story graphically illustrates that a woman may find life as an OL comfortable for a short period of time until her eventual retirement, but may feel miserable when she fails to follow the expected path. Consequently, some women quit their jobs in large firms for reasons other than marriage, as I discuss below.

Job Change

As age at marriage rises in Japan, the tight coupling between marriage and early retirement that once existed is disappearing. More women abandon OL status and venture into new jobs. An increasing number of them seek employment in foreign affiliated companies (*gaishikei*) where opportunities are believed to be more equitable than in Japanese firms (Kelsky 1994). One of the five ex-OLs I interviewed resigned from an automobile manufacturer and started working for a *gaishikei* management consulting firm. While working as an OL in her former office, she became responsible for arranging a tour of Japan for American auto dealers. In spite of the fact that she presided over a luncheon meeting, many dealers treated her as though they had met her for the first time when they saw her without the company uniform at night. The incident led her to recognize that a uniform makes women invisible: "I realized that no matter how hard I worked, I would only be one among many clerical workers so long as I wore a uniform." The meeting with the American dealers left a very strong impression on her, which ultimately contributed to her decision to change to a workplace where she did not have to wear a uniform.

Some women did not yet have language skills sufficient for work in a foreign company. For them, one alternative was to study overseas. Indeed, it has become popular among OLs to leave employment and go abroad for study. Most of these high-spirited women are said to be in their mid-to-late 20s and to have worked for a large company for about five years. Although some obtain degrees, many hope to acquire language skills by studying in English-speaking countries for about a year (Taga 1991).

Other women sought opportunities in professional occupations. One of the married OLs I came to know at Tōzai went to accounting school two nights a week and on Saturday afternoon to prepared for her eventual retirement from the bank. She had already passed the second-grade qualifying examination for commercial bookkeeping, and she hoped to pass the first-grade exam the next fall. She wanted to become a tax accountant in the future. Because she considered it difficult to continue working full-time and at the same time to study to obtain necessary qualifications, she planned to look for a part-time job in a small accounting office once she moved up a grade in bookkeeping. She explained in the following way why she had decided to become a tax accountant:

> If you want an ordinary clerical job, I know it's better to stay with this bank. If you change jobs, your pay decreases. If you haven't learned some trade, you feel miserable like Tanaka-san [one of the temporary employees at Tōzai who always complained of her current position, comparing it to her former OL status in another large financial institution]. . . . They [the company] would transfer me to some other department if I become pregnant, so I have to think about what to do when I quit. My husband's pay is not enough for the two of us.

The OL firmly believed that her current job at Tōzai was not compatible with childrearing. However, she also knew that without any specific skills, her employment prospects as a woman in her 30s were slim in the Japanese labor market. She therefore decided to obtain qualifications that would help her combine work and family by doing tax accounts part-time. She added that she usually avoided talking about her plans with her female colleagues because few of them seemed to share her thoughts.

Although she may not represent the majority of OLs, this woman is certainly not alone in attempting to change her vocation to one requiring a certain level of specialization. One of the five informants who once worked as OLs in a general trading company passed the examination to teach high school social studies. Although she initially suffered a reduction of 1 million yen (approximately 10,000 U.S. dollars) in her annual income when she started her teaching career, she was glad she had entered a profession that enabled her to better integrate family into her working days. She became a mother of two children and was satisfied that she had been able to take a one-year childcare leave at the birth of each of her daughters. In contrast, women who continued to work for Tōzai seemed less fortunate in their struggle to juggle the roles of OL, wife, and mother.

Family

At Tōzai, it was customary for a woman to retire upon marrying a fellow banker. When I asked the OLs whether it was the company rule, they did not know if it was formally stated, but they were sure that that was what was expected. OLs talked of a woman who had married her colleague and had protested against leaving the firm. However, she gave up in the end when it was hinted that her staying with the company would "hurt" her husband's career.

It was possible, on the other hand, for a woman to continue working after marriage so long as her husband was not also a member of the bank. However, she had to be prepared to face many difficulties. One of the first obstacles a married woman faced in continuing her work at Tōzai was her *sararīman* husband's possible transfer to offices outside of Tokyo. With their emphasis on job rotation as an important form of training, Japanese firms including Tōzai regularly changed the location of where their male employees worked without giving any consideration to their family situation. It was also generally understood that a man must be prepared to receive a heavy penalty if he refused a company request to move. An OL who got married shortly before I started working at Tōzai eventually retired when her husband's company transferred him to an office in Osaka.

Increasingly, Japanese families have coped with husbands' transfers to distant places by their *tanshin funin* (literally, "to leave for the new post alone"), leaving behind other family members. Although the arrangement is more popular among parents with school-aged children—who choose living apart as a necessary evil for their children to stay in the same schools and obtain a quality education—it is also an option for dual-career families. However, the family sacrifice is greater the longer and the further away the husband must go for *tanshin funin*. Many women must give up their jobs when their husbands are assigned a transfer overseas. Thus even if one company agreed to adopt a policy that made it easier for women to combine work and family, women would still have to retire from the workplace given the circumstances of men's employment in Japan.

Another major obstacle to women's working at the Tōzai Bank for an extended time was the difficulty in combining career and motherhood. The bank was equipped with fine systems that would, if utilized, greatly help working mothers, such as a 14-week maternity leave and a year-long child-care leave. However, in reality, those systems were difficult to use. For example, because no special arrangement was made for a section in which a woman took maternity leave, the burden of making up for the temporary labor shortage in the workplace was imposed on her female colleagues. During the period of my research, a woman in a nearby section took maternity leave, which meant that her three fellow OLs were forced to put up with extreme inconvenience. Upon witnessing their trouble, several OLs in my section announced that they themselves had no intention of taking maternity leave and continuing work. The following sentiments voiced by an OL were typical: "You can't help feeling ill at ease for annoying other OLs, and I don't know if this job is worth all that trouble." The OLs concurred that although a woman had the right to take maternity leave, she nonetheless would be under great pressure to avoid causing so much annoyance to other women.[15]

Sometimes a company attempted to discourage a mother from continuing at work by transferring her to another section or by assigning her a difficult job after she returned from her maternity leave. The former personnel manager of a bank expressed this strategy in a typically convoluted Japanese way:

> At a convenient moment, such as after the return from maternity leave, the company might transfer the woman to a section where it's not easy for her to manage work. Then it's more likely for her to quit. After all, we cannot fire

employees, and so if we could have the person quit in a natural way through such personnel relocations, it's better for the company. Yes, I must admit it isn't true if we say that management doesn't have such intentions at all.

At Tōzai, a married woman expressed her determination to take a maternity leave and continue working and then requested a transfer to a suitable section to carry out her plans. Her request for relocation was indeed granted. However, there was a problem. The new workplace was known to be much busier than the previous one, making it even more difficult for her to take a maternity leave. Although there was no way to find out for sure, the OLs in our office came to the conclusion that it was in effect *katatataki* (tap on the shoulder suggesting retirement).

Even fewer women took the year-long childcare leave at Tōzai. A woman who managed to take the leave remembers the pressure put on her. She was summoned by her boss several times and was asked to return to work after taking only a maternity leave. She refused: "Now that I think of it, I don't know how I was able to stick to my plans!" The woman firmly believed that, although a childcare leave was available, the managers did not actually want OLs to take it. She thought they preferred OLs to quit so that they could hire younger women.

This woman's story illustrates how difficult it was for an OL to take a childcare leave that, in theory, every woman was entitled to take. It is small wonder that only a few women exercised this option at Tōzai. Having the system and actually using it are two completely different matters.

Finally, women who continued to work after marriage and childbirth sometimes had to face prejudice from their coworkers, both male and female. A married woman, especially with children, was generally believed to have more important commitments at home than in the labor market. If she nevertheless continued her work, this implied either that she found the work greatly fulfilling or that she should be counted among the lower classes who must work even after marriage.

With the influence of Western feminist thinking, the Japanese public has increasingly come to acknowledge that some women prefer to work for a sense of accomplishment and for personal happiness. However, the kind of work performed by OLs was generally considered to provide little satisfaction. So it was assumed that if someone continued in a job that was unsatisfactory, then it must be for economic reasons.

This explains the ambivalent attitudes the OLs in our workplace held toward Yamada-san. Yamada-san was a woman in her 40s with unusually long tenure with the bank. She was much respected for her experience and knowledge; some younger women even said they were apprehensive about speaking to her. But, at the same time, the women whispered behind her back that she was separated and had to work to raise two children. They also believed that she went out drinking after work with different men because she was lonely. It was evident from the way the OLs talked about Yamada-san that they did not particularly envy her life.

My fellow temporary worker shared the view that a decent housewife should not continue to work as an OL. She thought she was lucky because she could rely on her husband and did not have to work full-time to make a living like Yamada-san. She explained: "It's a privilege to work temporarily, and not something that you should be ashamed of. It might be a little unpleasant being asked to do odd jobs here and there by other women, but it's only a side job. The fact that I'm married is much more important." This temporary worker was able to justify her subsidiary position in the office because she was a woman successfully married to a dependable husband. According to this view, a woman's marital status is more important than the type of job she holds.

COMPANY POLICIES AND THEIR IMPLICATIONS

At first glance, OLs in the office, some of them wearing identical uniforms and performing similar tasks, may seem as if they have much in common. But detailed examination reveals a surprising degree of variation among them: some women are considering marriage, some are attempting to change jobs, and others are starting a family. As discussed in the following section, company employment policies are not necessarily helpful for women as they struggle with their individual agendas.

Employment Policies

Before the implementation of the EEOL, many firms openly urged OLs to retire after several years of service. According to the custom called *katatataki*, male managers approached the OL from behind and tapped her on the shoulder, suggesting that it was time for her to quit. Although most Japanese firms have abolished the notorious custom of *katatataki* since the implementation of the EEOL, some, as we have seen, continue to put pressure on older married women to leave the company.

Firms by and large prefer OLs to leave after several years of service, for both direct and indirect economic reasons. From a purely economic point of view, it is costly to keep employing older women, since even women's wages rise gradually with tenure. In addition, a retirement allowance is normally determined by multiplying the length of service by a certain fixed amount, so the company must pay more to a woman with a longer length of service. Because most firms expect no more than low-level clerical work from OLs, it is more economical to employ younger women at lower rates than experienced and skilled but more expensive workers (Machiko Osawa 1993; Mari Osawa 1993).

It is also generally believed that younger women work more enthusiastically because, being newer and junior members of the organization, they feel less distaste for menial jobs. However, as women accumulate tenure, they become increasingly frustrated doing the same kind of jobs day after day, year after year, as their male *dōki* begin to rise in importance.

At the Tōzai Bank, male employees were older than women (except for one exception—an OL with 25.5 years of tenure); only men with a certain length of tenure were assigned to the positions in the three departments where I did participant observation of OLs. Older women talked of the day when, finally, the youngest men on the floor would be their *dōki*. They apparently did not find the idea of having a male *dōki* on the floor agreeable and hoped to retire before the day came. At first I did not understand why they did not want to work with their male *dōki*, but I gradually began to see that serving tea or making copies was easier when carried out for someone's *senpai*, rather than for *dōki*.

Not only did companies prefer young women because they constituted cheaper and more docile labor, but because all workers were better able to justify younger women's engagement in menial jobs. According to this view, it is not primarily sex but age that relegates women to low-paying clerical jobs. Indeed, in many Japanese firms, young men similarly start their careers as clerical workers, often running errands for their bosses (Shirahase and Ishida 1994). The potential for feelings of unfairness was greatly alleviated by employing only older men as bosses. Although companies in most cases did not intend to promote women even if they stayed on, they were spared the embarrassment of actually not promoting them. As discussed, those few women who did not quit were simply labeled either as social failures who could not marry or who were divorced, or as social inferiors married to husbands who could not support their families.

Preferring young women as cheaper, more docile, and more suitable labor for dead-end jobs, some companies encouraged OLs' "harmonious separation" (*enman taisha*) from the workplace. For example, I was told that a woman at Tōzai was given a maternity allowance upon retiring at childbirth. Similarly, according to an OL working in a general trading company, a premium was added to the retirement allowance for women who left at the end of April or May after a smooth transfer of work to the new recruits. In fact, there were quite a few Japanese companies that customarily offered a monetary incentive to women who decided to retire early upon marriage or childbirth (*Nihon Keizai Shinbun* 1993; Saso 1990).

Implications for Female Solidarity

What seems particularly important when we think about OLs' quiescence is that a woman's work life is made inseparable from her private life. Whatever decision she makes in one sphere has profound impact on her activities in the other area. Does a woman intend to marry soon? If not, does she wish to continue working in the present company, or does she plan on looking for opportunities elsewhere? If she is to marry, what is her partner like? Is he a member of the same firm, necessitating her to retire from the workplace? Is he a *sararīman* who is likely to be transferred to distant places? Is it possible to live on his earnings alone? Do she and her husband plan on having a child soon? Does she intend to take a maternity leave and come back to the workplace? What about childcare leave? Which path a woman chooses to take at each of the decision-making points will make her work life differ entirely from her fellow colleagues who select a separate way. Accordingly, women have different agendas to consider, different goals to seek, and different problems to solve even as they hold similar jobs in the same workplace. A Japanese woman's work life is to a large extent contingent on her family life.

Because their expectations for work differ according to their private lives, one woman's desired improvements at the workplace will often be at variance with another's. In her study of a large garment manufacturer in Japan, Roberts (1994) describes how difficult it was when women with diverse backgrounds—young and old, unmarried and married, childless and with children—were expected to work harmoniously. Moreover, she observes that organizing for an issue that did not affect all women equally was problematic for female workers, because those who asked for improved working conditions were frequently accused of being indulgent. Because women's work lives differed considerably in relation to their age, marital status, and family circumstances, it was difficult to organize and push for desired reforms.

In contrast, a man's work life varies less according to his family life. Men, too, differ in many aspects of their private lives. Some marry early, and others marry late or never marry. Some marry a woman who is working; others marry a woman who will stay at home. Some will have many children; others will have a few or none. Individual decisions men make in their family lives, however, have less influence on their work lives. Whomever they marry, most *sararīman* will continue to work for the large firm they joined upon graduation. Whatever their family circumstances, the majority of men will agree to relocate to remote areas if asked to do so. However many children they may have, few will consider applying for childcare leave. A man's work life, in short, is less contingent on his family life.

Furthermore, company policies tend to promote the permeability of work and family decisions for women, but they discourage it for men. Most Japanese firms' employment policies make it difficult for women to combine work and family. Whatever decisions a woman makes in the private sphere are going to have an immediate effect on whether or not she will be able to continue working and in what form. Many companies also emphasize the connection between work and family lives for women by their constant reminder that women's ultimate place is at home.

However, for men, companies generally insist that their private lives not interfere with their work lives. The common assumption is that families are taken care of by wives, so men do not have to let private matters influence their work lives.[16] Many researchers have observed that the separation of work and family lives is especially marked for Japanese *sararīman*, who are expected to give priority to their company and their work over their relationships at home (Allison 1994; Lebra 1981; Mari Osawa 1993; Rohlen 1974; Vogel 1963). It is said that as *kaisha ningen* (company persons), men devote so much to working hard that they spend little free time at home. Without such an intense commitment to work, their prospects for promotion are likely to suffer. Wives, on the other hand, are supposed to provide various domestic services to these hardworking husbands and keep distractions from them.

Because a successful businessman is expected to give himself whole-heartedly to his work, the men at Tōzai seemed keen to stage themselves as "company persons," playing down their roles as husbands and fathers as well as other aspects of their private lives. They often spoke boastfully of how late they had worked the previous night, and were generally reluctant to talk about home and family. Allison (1994) similarly observes how a Japanese white-collar worker turned his absence from home into evidence of hard work and made it the subject of competition among his colleagues.

In sum, a man's work in a large Japanese company is predicated on the assumption that his day-to-day needs and those of his family are taken care of by his wife at home. As Akaoka argues, "Firms find it relatively easy to order men to work and entertain clients late into the night and on weekends, and to go on business trips and transfer to remote places. Men can readily comply with these company requests because there are wives who take care of all aspects of their home and social life" (1996: 9). For such a man, work and family can be separate spheres. However, *somebody's* life must become flexible in order for a man to give such extraordinary precedence to work. In most cases it is women who adjust their roles and expectations to make it possible for men to pursue rigid work lives. How a woman works, if at all, is to a large extent subject to her family's needs. We must take into account this asymmetry in the degree of separability of work and family lives for men and women when considering the strength or weakness of women's solidarity. It is difficult for women to reach agreement on improving the workplace when they find themselves coping with problems that are distinct from those of others because of differences in where they are in their own life cycle.

CONCLUSION

OLs in contemporary Japanese firms have difficulty organizing formal protest movements. I have argued that their weak solidarity is related to company policies that divide and atomize them. Many OLs suffer from the stress of trying to get along with one another, a goal made difficult by employment policies that reward women with different educational backgrounds unequally in spite of their performance of the same or similar jobs. Due to the inseparability of Japanese women's work and family lives, OLs are also typically alone in their agendas, goals, and problems even though they share work in the same office. In my opinion, failure to examine carefully the structures of work that differentially affect men's and women's ability to cultivate cultures of solidarity has led many observers to the erroneous conclusion that Japanese women are largely content with the current discriminatory treatment or are passively resigned to their fate. When there is no direct exercise of power to quell protest movements, it is easy to misinterpret a subordinate group's silence as arising from its consent.

CHAPTER SEVEN

Mothers as the Best Teachers
Japanese Motherhood and Early Childhood Education

Keiko Hirao

Previous chapters have pointed out that the so-called M-shaped curve of female labor force participation remains prevalent in Japan, with a large number of women temporarily leaving the labor force during the parenting stage. While just over 70 percent of women aged 20–24 are in the labor force, the participation rate plunges to 54 percent in the 30–34 age group. Most working women in the latter age group are in part-time jobs (Statistics Bureau 1997a). The major reason given by women of this age for leaving jobs is the need for childcare (Statistics Bureau, Japan, *Basic Survey on Employment Structure,* 1992).

This labor force participation pattern is widely supported by the Japanese public. Even among single women, the most popular stated choice of life-course pattern is leaving the labor force either upon marriage or upon childbirth (National Institute of Population and Social Security Research 1997). Despite the glamorous image of working mothers in the mass media, women are expected to take care of domestic work. The vast majority of Japanese women (85 percent) continue to agree with the idea that "It is all right for a woman to hold a job, but she must properly do the housework and childcare" (National Institute of Population and Social Security Research 1997). Although the level of female labor force participation has increased over time, the preference for the M-shaped participation pattern across the life course appears to remain very strong.

This M-shaped curve implies the incompatibility of work and family life in Japan. The difficulty of balancing the two spheres and the high cost of raising children are often cited as the main reasons for delayed marriage and, as a consequence, the sharp decline in the total fertility rate to a level as low as 1.38 (Ministry of Health and Welfare 1998). In response to the low birth rate, the Japanese government has started to take many initiatives to create a more "gender-equal" society. A few examples of government initiatives are the establishment of the Council for Gender Equality, revision of the Equal Employment Opportunity Law, and a proposal for a "Fundamental Law Designed to Promote a Gender-Equal Society." In March 1999, the Ministry of Health and Welfare carried out a campaign to encourage husbands to participate in childcare. As part of the campaign they ran a huge advertisement in major newspapers that read "We don't call a man a father if he doesn't participate." Moreover, six ministries, including the Ministry of Education and the Ministry of Finance, jointly launched the New Angel Plan starting in 2000. The plan aims to establish a more "family-friendly" society by doing things such as increasing the number of daycare facilities and making afterschool daycare programs more accessible.

In spite of these governmental initiatives, the normative and ideological constraints for young Japanese mothers have not relaxed; instead, they continue to exert a strong pull on women to leave the labor force when they start a family. One reason is that young Japanese mothers are faced with an ever-intensifying agenda to carry out at home: providing an excellent education for their children.

The intensity and the depth of involvement of many Japanese mothers in their children's education has received considerable attention (Boocock 1991; Ellington 1992; Uno 1993; White 1987a). The phenomenon of the *kyōiku mama* (education mother), in which a woman devotes a major part of her life to her child's academic career, is both praised as the source of Japanese students' impressive academic success and criticized for depriving children of their free time. The description of the *kyōiku mama* phenomenon, however, has been limited by a lack of attention to how Japanese education has been privatized in the past 20 years and how the role of *kyōiku mama* has been shaped and influenced by the reality of the educational system in Japan.

According to a survey by the Ministry of Education, over 35 percent of schoolchildren attend *juku* (private educational institutions) that provide supplemental academic training (Ministry of Education 1994). The rate of attendance is highest among older children: in 1993, an amazing 67 percent of Japanese ninth graders were enrolled. Between 1985 and 1993, *juku* attendance increased from 17 to 24 percent for elementary school children and from 47 to 60 percent for middle school children. These *juku* statistics, however, tell only a small part of the story, which includes correspondence courses, tutoring services, and various private lessons available to children. When these services are included, 82 percent of all Japanese schoolchildren are enrolled in one or a combination of private educational programs (Ministry of Education 1994).

South Korea and Taiwan share a similar educational environment with Japan, with private educational services at a high demand. In South Korea, 75 percent of students at elementary and secondary schools attend cram schools or tutoring services (Choi and Kim 1995). The percentage is lower in Taiwan, but even so, 55 percent of elementary and secondary school students in Taipei are enrolled in outside-school cram services. The number of cram services in Taipei rose from 985 in 1997 to 1180 in 1999 (Taipei Ministry of Education 1999). It is beyond the scope of this chapter to discuss in depth the similarities and differences in maternal roles in these three East Asian countries. But the statistics above are compatible with other chapters in this volume (Brinton, Lee, and Parish, Chapter 2; Yu, Chapter 3; Lee and Hirata, Chapter 4), suggesting that the expectations on mothers in South Korea and Japan are similarly high; the centrality of mothers' role in Taiwan may be slightly less. South Korean mothers have been criticized for "overprotecting their children or having unrealistic expectations for them" (Choi 1994: 197), a comment that is strikingly similar to those heard in Japan.

A recent notable development in educational competition and the *kyōiku mama* phenomenon in Japan is that ever-younger children are becoming involved in educational activities outside of school. Approximately 42 percent of Japanese preschool children are enrolled in some kind of educational program outside of kindergarten and day nurseries (Ministry of Health and Welfare 1991). As Norma Field notes, childhood in contemporary Japan has become streamlined as a series of preparatory steps to productive adulthood (Field 1995), and parents—especially mothers—play a vital role as the agents of human capital investment.

This chapter illustrates how the market in private educational services and changes in women's roles interact to make young children in Japan the objects of education. I focus mainly on the recent development of privatized education at the preschool level, as this illustrates the interaction between profit-seeking market intentions and the educational agenda expected to be carried out by mothers, particularly in white-collar, urban communities.

How is the ideology of motherhood constructed in contemporary Japan? How are young women socialized into the role of mother? What are the cultural contradictions in Japanese women's roles? These are the main questions addressed here.

DATA

This chapter is based on interviews conducted on the parenting behaviors of mothers in the Tokyo area during 1991–1992 and in Nagoya (Aichi Prefecture) in 1994–1995. The samples for the Tokyo interviews were recruited through three parenting classes sponsored by local governments and play-group networks. The parenting classes involved approximately 80 participants in total. As I served as the coordinator/instructor, I was able to request the names of participants who were willing to cooperate in the interviews. I then added to the samples through snowball sampling methods. Twenty women from the classes were contacted for the in-depth interviews. I also utilized the discussions in the classes as a means of participant observation. Because the parenting classes were offered in the daytime, the participants were limited to full-time housewives and part-time workers. The format of the interview was mostly open-ended, with some structured questions about personal background.

The Nagoya interviews were conducted as part of the pretest for a survey on Japanese women's work and family histories (Hirao 1997). Twenty women were recruited through personal networks and snowball sampling methods. The initial objective of contacting these women in Nagoya was to test questions in the survey, which included information on detailed family and work histories, a measure for parents' investment in children's education, and participation in community networks. The interview was formatted in such a way that as the participant filled out the questionnaire, I discussed with her the items, wordings, and format of the instrument. This turned out to be a valuable opportunity to learn about participants' family relations, parenting styles, and attitudes toward children's education.

The interviews in both cities lasted for one to two hours and took place in the participants' homes or in nearby coffee shops. Most of the interviews were tape-recorded with the permission of the interviewees, and the parts that were pertinent to mothers' involvement in children's education were transcribed and analyzed for this chapter. The discussions in the parenting classes could not be tape-recorded, but detailed notes were taken with the help of assistants. The average age of the participants was 28 years in the Tokyo sample and 35 in Nagoya. All were married and had at least one child, and most came from middle-class families and had completed either junior college or four-year university education, except for two mothers who had only high school diplomas.

Educational competition is keener in large cities, as are *juku* attendance rates and household expenditures on extra-school education (Ministry of Education 1994). *Kyōiku mama* are more likely to be urban than rural residents. Moreover, as a deep involvement in children's education requires a tremendous amount of time and human capital, *kyōiku mama* tend to be highly educated women who are not employed full-time. The mothers I interviewed are not representative of the entire Japanese population, but I would argue that given my purposes, it was appropriate to have my samples drawn from Tokyo and Nagoya. Interviewing a relatively small number of women also made it possible for me to have extensive contact with them and to better understand the ecology of *kyōiku mama* and the ways that school, family, and private educational enterprises are related to each other.

DEVELOPMENT OF EARLY EDUCATION PROGRAMS: AN OBSESSION WITH PRODIGIES

The educational role played by Japanese mothers starts when children are very young. Kindergartens and nursery schools expect mothers to incorporate an educational agenda into the routine of daily life (Allison 1996). The intensity of this responsibility is illustrated by the recent development of *sōki-kyōiku*, early educational programs that are given either at home or at private, extra-school institutions. These are geared explicitly toward the development of cognitive skills in preschool children.

These programs are "extra-school" in the sense that they are independent from formal kindergartens and accredited day nurseries. Kindergartens and day nurseries operate under the auspices of the Ministry of Education and the Ministry of Health and Welfare, respectively.[1] Because more than 93 percent of preschool children are enrolled in one or the other of these institutions, kindergartens and day nursery programs have now become comparable to formal schools (Statistics Bureau 1997b). Private enterprises that provide educational services for preschoolers can be compared to the preschool version of *juku* for school-aged children. *Juku* is distinguished from extracurricular activities as it is administered outside the school system. In the same manner, early education programs function externally to the formal system of kindergarten and nursery schools.

Sōkikyōiku can be literally translated as "early education." Very few providers of these services, however, use this term; instead they claim, "It is never too early to start." Translating *sōkikyōiku* as a "head-start program" might help draw an analogy for U.S. readers, but the political and social context for *sōkikyōiku* is very different from that for U.S. head-start programs. *Sōkikyōiku* can be seen as a kind of intervention program in the sense that it is not necessary for the development of normal competence, according to psychologists' point of view. Its objectives are to enhance positive aspects of children rather than to combat learning problems that can hinder children from low-income backgrounds. With these caveats in mind, I will use "extra-preschool curricula" when including nonacademic programs and use "early education" and "early intervention programs" interchangeably when the program is geared specifically toward developing the cognitive skills of preschoolers.

The course content offered in the extra-preschool curriculums varies widely, ranging from music lessons to reading and writing, simple mathematics to foreign languages. Some courses are purely academically oriented, some specialize in preparatory training for entrance examinations for prestigious elementary schools, and others emphasize artistic skills and music lessons. Many boast a combination of some or all of these benefits.

Kumon, a prominent *juku*, for example, invites preschoolers to work on mathematics, English, and Japanese. Founded by Toru Kumon in 1958 in Osaka as a small neighborhood *juku* for schoolchildren, Kumon is now one of the largest *juku* establishments in Japan, with more than 18,000 branch classroom locations all over the country and a total enrollment of 1.5 million (Kumon Kyōiku Kenkyūkai 1998). (It should be noted that Kumon reports only the total number of enrollments, not the actual number of children. If a child is registered for Japanese, mathematics, and English, this is counted as three enrollments. This system of counting gives the impression that more children are enrolled in Kumon's program than truly are.)

During the late 1980s, Kumon expanded its programs to include the enrollment of preschoolers. In 1990, they started a correspondence course through which they delivered monthly educational kits such as videos, flash cards, and workbooks to children between the ages of two and five. In the mid-1980s, Kumon began to commend their high achievers. Among them were preschool children who could work out differential and integral calculus. These youngsters had already finished the high school level mathematics curriculum, and some of their mothers were reported to have started the program while they were pregnant.

The Association of Early Childhood Development, founded by Masaru Ibuka, the founder of Sony, states its mission as assisting in the sound development of the mother-child relationship. Its operation includes developing teaching materials, such as electronically prerecorded flash cards called "talking cards." Courses are offered to children aged 12 to 24 months old. Courses are also available to pregnant women on how to enhance the potential abilities of their unborn children.

The Child Academy, founded by Makoto Shichida, offers comprehensive programs such as storytelling, flash-card learning, haiku, arts and crafts, and music. The Ishii School of Kanji Education focuses on the teaching of reading and writing Chinese characters for preschoolers, offering correspondence courses as well as instruction in classrooms.

There are very few statistics on private educational programs for preschoolers, because neither the Ministry of Education nor the Ministry of Health and Welfare is in control of such services. Therefore, very little is known about nationwide enrollment or geographical distribution of the programs. As *juku* attendance is higher in urban areas, it is likely that early education programs are more prominent in large cities. Available data suggest that the increase in early education programs began in the late 1980s and continued through the early 1990s (Ishihara 1993; Shiomi 1996). Shiomi reports that there are more than 1000 schools that provide nonacademic programs and 150 schools that provide academic training for preschool children in the Tokyo metropolitan area. As the number of academic schools reflects only the headquarters, there may be hundreds or even thousands of branch schools in the Tokyo area (Shiomi 1996). A survey by the Japan Association of Child Health reports that 30 percent of four-year-old children are enrolled in some kind of educational program, among which 23 percent are known to have an academic component in their curriculum (Takahashi, Amino, and Kashiwame 1996). A longitudinal survey of 5400 households in Tokyo and Osaka revealed that the percentage of five-year-olds whose parents paid for them to receive cognitive training either through extra-preschool institutions (*yōji kyōshitsu*), correspondence courses, or private tutors increased from just over 9 percent in 1989 to 27 percent in 1997 (Tōkai Ginkō 1997).

The spur for early education began in 1976 when Ibuka published a sensational book titled *Yōchien de wa Ososugiru* ("Kindergarten Is Too Late"). This book became a best-seller and was followed by a flood of publications that advocated early intervention in order to develop the cognitive and verbal skills of infants. Such publications include Shichida's *Miraculous Education for the Zero-Year-Old* (1983) and *Tips on Raising an Intelligent Baby* (1985), Mitsuishi's *Creating Prodigies* (1988), and Ōshima's *Prenatal Education* (1988). The acceleration of early education can be seen through the titles of Ibuka's successive books: *Kindergarten Is Too Late* (1976), followed by *Zero-Year-Old* (1991) and *From Embryo* (1992). We can see the shift in the messages. Kindergarten was too late in the 1970s. But in the 1990s mothers were instructed to be concerned about their children's academic achievements *from conception*.

The accelerated education in Japan parallels, to some extent, the proliferation of educational programs for preschool children in the United States. Programs with heavy educational components for prekindergarten children are also on the increase in the United States. The well-publicized "superkid" practice by Glenn Doman, *How to Teach Your Baby to Read* (1964) and *How to Multiply Your Baby's Intelligence* (1984), for example, resonates with many of the publications by Ibuka, Shichida, and Ishii. They share the common premises that children's IQ is not fixed at birth but is determined by environment and intellectual stimulation, that children's potential for learning has long been underestimated, and that intellectual growth is very rapid during early childhood. In other words, the cognitive potential of children, according to both Doman and Ishii, can be significantly boosted by early intervention programs.

Criticism has been leveled against accelerated education in both countries. Psychologist David Elkind (1987), for example, calls it "miseducation" and warns of possible long-term damage to a child's self-esteem, which may result in a loss of positive attitudes toward learning. Japanese specialists in education such as Toshiyuki Shiomi (1993, 1996) have also begun to raise questions about the effects of excessive early intervention programs. But developmental psychologists and educators in Japan have done little research on the long-term effects of intervention programs; the findings are still limited to clinical cases (Takara 1996), those reported by journalists (e.g., Hosaka 1994), and those focused on small samples of individuals and using limited observation periods (Nakano 1990, 1993).

In spite of the similarities in the expansion of early childhood education in the United States and Japan, it is located in very different social and political contexts in the two countries. Elkind asserts that the idea of the malleability of a child's IQ was first applied in the 1960s in the United States to disadvantaged children, who presumably lacked proper intellectual stimulation. It was initially intended to remedy social inequality by giving a "head start" to low-income children. In Japan, however, social inequality was never an issue in the debate over early intervention. Instead, its implementation took place as younger and younger children were being introduced into educational competition. In other words, accelerated education for preschoolers in Japan was not initiated to narrow the learning gap between children from wealthy and less wealthy families. Nor does it function as extra enrichment for gifted prodigies; "gifted children" has not been a concept in Japanese educational philosophy. Japanese parents are more likely than their American counterparts to place importance on the role of "effort," "perseverance," and "diligence" in modifying the course of human development, and to deemphasize individual, innate differences in potential (Stevenson and Stigler, 1992). In other words, children are thought to have equal potential for success at birth. What counts is effort, by children and by their parents. This is believed to result in substantial differences in children's outcomes. The proliferation of early intervention programs in Japan can be seen as a popularization of the ideal of a "high-quality" child, or, more accurately, the popularization of parents' dreams for having such a child.

PRESCHOOLERS AS A NEW MARKET

One of the factors that spurred the early education boom in Japan was the rapid shift in demographic structure. The total fertility rate has steadily declined in Japan from 4.72 children on average in 1930, to 2.14 in 1973 and 1.38 in 1998. Compared with the size of the cohort born 20 years ago, the cohort born today is only half as large. In the beginning of the 1980s, the size of the age cohort entering elementary school fell to its lowest level since the World War II baby boom. An upsurge in births occurred as the second baby boom generation passed college age,[2] but currently there is no prospect of a demographic increase. The implication of this demographic change is

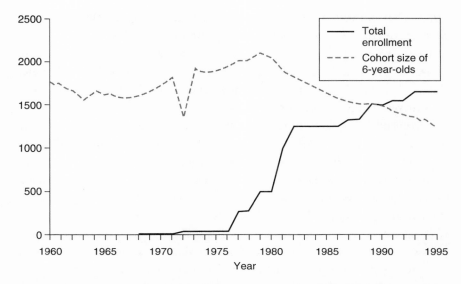

Figure 7.1. Total Enrollment in *Kumon* Program and Cohort Size of 6-Year-Olds (in 1000)

sources: Kumon Kyōiku Kenkyūkai 1998; Ministry of Health and Welfare, *Vital Population Statistics*, various years.

clear: the number of school-aged children in the educational marketplace is rapidly declining and the shrinking size of the school-aged cohort has had a direct impact on educational industries. They have been forced, quite simply, to seek a new market.

Preschoolers were identified as a new market frontier for educational industries in the market crisis shared by both formal and informal educational institutions. Figure 7.1 plots the total enrollment in the Kumon Program and the sizes of six-year-old cohorts. It shows that the total enrollment of Kumon increased sharply in the late 1970s and then plateaued in the early 1980s. This time period coincides with the beginning of the decline in the size of the school-aged cohort. It is also the period when Kumon made major revisions in their teaching materials to facilitate the inclusion of preschoolers in their program.

Once education for preschoolers proved to be a profitable business for *juku* industries, other sectors began to enter the market. For example, a company that sells underwear and other home-related products through direct-mail catalogs decided to go into the extra-preschool education business in

1992. They converted their customer list into a mailing list through which they delivered educational materials each month for children under the age of six. It is not unusual, especially in urban areas, for mothers of newborn babies to receive a direct-mail advertisement of courses offered to "enhance the academic ability" of their offspring. The early education "boom" was thus driven by the supply of these services.

Ironically, this development took place outside the public school system just as the Ministry of Education was trying to relax school schedules to remedy the excessive competition for entrance examinations. The public schools have taken to heart the criticism that excessive academic competition causes poor health among children, school violence, and bullying. Contrary to the common belief that Japanese schools are driving their students with relentless pressure for academic success, they are now shifting their emphasis to "creativity," "sociability," and "whole development" and away from rote learning. Approximately one-fourth of the time spent at Japanese schools is now devoted to nonacademic activities, such as recess and club activities (Stevenson 1992). Moreover, the Ministry of Education decided to reduce the time spent in school by 70 hours per year for elementary school students and 35 hours for junior high school students. The ministry also stipulates in the new curriculum guidelines that the content be cut by 30 percent, beginning in 2002.

In spite of the ministry's attempt to give children more free time and develop their creativity, the reforms have not extended to broad changes in the entrance examination system for colleges. As a result, many parents feel that school classrooms have become a place to confirm what children already know instead of a center for learning and mastering new subjects. This concern has prompted them to plan ahead out of the fear of having their children fall behind.

For example, Natsuko, who is age 36 and has three school-aged children, comments that

> I was too naive when I was raising my first child. You can't believe how smart today's children are. Most first graders already know several *kanji* [Chinese characters], not to mention being able to read and write *hiragana* [the Japanese phonetic syllabary]. My daughter was the only one in the class who could not write her name. Although we are told that teachers don't expect children to have mastered these things by the time they enter school, the fact that all the other children already know them makes the slow starters fall behind.

Another problem with the educational reforms is that all schools must meet minimum standards, but private schools are not bound by the curriculum guidelines stipulated by the Ministry of Education. That is, private schools can use more advanced materials than those used in public schools. They can also allocate more hours to important subjects, such as English, which carries more weight in the college entrance exams. Given that a sizable portion of students admitted to the University of Tokyo, the most prestigious university in the Japanese educational hierarchy, come from private high schools with admission tracks tied to their own attached junior high schools, parents are reminded that educational competition starts at a very young age. Many of these schools push their curricula forward so that students can devote their entire senior year in high school to preparing for college entrance examinations. Private elementary schools are also attractive to parents who worry that their children will not fare well in the intense competition for junior high schools: many of these private institutions provide an admission track all the way up to high school. Consequently, the age for competition has been lowered, and the competition for a better school career has involved young preschool children.

Chisato is married to a computer engineer and has a three-year-old son. She is planning to send him to a private elementary school. He is attending a weekly preparatory program for the screening test. He also has to do workbook exercises at home with his mother. Chisato comments on their decision as follows:

> I know it is a pity that a small boy like him has to work so hard, but it is for his own good. It is much easier to push him now than it will be later. If he can avoid the pressure of the entrance examination for junior high and high school, he can devote more time to developing his talents during the 12 years [he is in school full-time].

Kumiko, who is married to a physician, had a son just three weeks before I interviewed her. When I asked her how she felt about having a baby, she said,

> I am glad Satoshi was born in April. Of course it's the best time for having a baby! The weather is nice, and I can take him outside and let him breathe fresh air. You know, oxygen is very important for brain development. Also, he will be one of the oldest in his class [the school year starts in April in Japan], and that will make him ahead of most children. Kids born in spring have better school records. I think that's why children born in April and May are overrepresented among students in the University of Tokyo.

I wish I had asked her where she got this idea about the birth month and the chance of being accepted to the University of Tokyo. When I met her a year later, she had put Satoshi in an enrichment class for infants run by one of the large *juku* establishments. She escorted Satoshi every week and joined an hour-long class with him. She commented bashfully,

> Well, I don't mean to raise him as a "super kid." It's just a play group sort of program where children play with toys and listen to songs and so on. I just think it is important to let him play with other babies, because he has to know how to cooperate and socialize with his peers by the time he goes to kindergarten.

Although Kumiko's example may be an extreme case, there are three points that represent the ideas shared by many *kyōiku mama* today. First, a child has to go through keen academic competition in order to obtain a decent educational background. Second, a child's educational success depends on how much the parent puts into it. Third, the younger the child, the better the time for preparation. It is almost always the mother who is responsible for seeing to the provision of these opportunities and who is expected to be closely involved in the process.

CONSTRUCTION OF MOTHERHOOD IDEOLOGY

What factors shape Japanese mothers' keen interest and deep involvement in their children's education? To answer this question, it is necessary to discuss how parenting norms have been constructed in relation to the motherhood ideology that developed in postwar Japan.

The Ascendance of Motherhood in Postwar Japan

The "good wife, wise mother" concept (*ryōsai kenbo*) emerged as the ideal of womanhood when Japan was restructured as a modern nation-state during the Meiji Restoration in the late nineteenth century. A good wife efficiently manages domestic affairs and serves to meet the needs of adult family members; a wise mother devotes herself to bringing up her children so that they can become productive members of society. Women under the rule of Imperial Japan were expected to serve the nation in these ways (Buckley 1993; Fukaya 1977; Koyama 1991; Uno 1993). The modern version of *ryōsai kenbo* places more emphasis on the role of "wise mother" than on the role of "good wife." This new ideal emerged in the postwar period and was intensified during the high economic growth period of the late 1960s (Fujii 1975).

The new primacy of motherhood was not at all unique to postwar Japan. In fact, the issue of mothering formed one of the crucial themes in the Western feminist literature of the time. There are varied arguments about the definition and role of motherhood in the framework of male-female relations. For example, Dinnerstein (1976), Firestone (1970), and Rich (1976) have all hypothesized that mothering is a cause of male dominance, Chodorow (1978) has asserted that it is a mechanism reproducing female oppression, and O'Brien (1981) sees it as a source of female liberation and power. Regardless of these differences, the fact that the institution of motherhood has instigated profound feminist discourse signifies its definitive power in the social construction of gender. The works of social historians clearly demonstrate that motherhood is a learned social construct, and neither an innate instinct nor a universal feature of women (Badinter 1981). The emphasis on maternal affection and nurturing care for children, along with permissiveness in childrearing, came into existence as the family came to be seen as a private sphere (Aries 1962). In this sense, the prominence of motherhood emerged as one aspect of a long-term change in family patterns.

The Mother-Child Relationship and Parental Norms

Although the importance of motherhood can be found in modern societies in general, the construction of motherhood and the ideal of "the good mother" provide important clues as to how parenting (mothering) norms are constructed in Japan.

The theme of psychological proximity between a mother and a child appears repeatedly in the literature that describes the Japanese mother-child relationship in comparison with that of Western societies. There is a strong emphasis on the special "bond" that makes mothers and children inseparable. The mother-child bond is seen as unique among all relationships in Japan, more so than in a society that values independence and autonomy, such as the United States. It is seen in Japan as the prototype of a relationship in which the wish to be "dependent" is fulfilled. Dependence, or *amae*, is a psychological concept defined by Doi as a "desire to be passively loved" and to be taken care of unconditionally. Doi, a clinical psychiatrist, argued that many psychological problems in later life can be traced back to the unfulfilled dependency on mothers in early childhood (Doi 1973).

The concept of *amae* elucidates a different way in which the "self" is constructed in Japan than in the United States. The Japanese mother is believed to see her infant as an extension of herself, and she interacts with the infant to strengthen and promote the mutual dependence between them. The American mother, on the other hand, is presumed to see the relation with her infant as a developmental stage in which the infant learns to seek separation (Bornstein 1989; Caudill and Weinstein 1969; White 1987a).

The Japanese notion of the mother-child bond has significant implications in the formation of parenting norms. Because mother and child are seen as an inseparable pair, the childhood outcomes—be they related to social, cognitive, or physical development—are seen as a function of how much of herself the mother has invested in bringing up her child. The child's actions and personality, both positive and negative, are seen as reflecting the mother's personality, intelligence, behavior, and resources.

Mothers as the Best Caretakers

When maternal deprivation theory and attachment theory on mother-infant interaction (Bowlby 1969; Klaus and Kennell 1976; Klaus, Leger, and Trause 1975) were introduced to Japan in the late 1970s, they quickly lent "scientific" support to existing beliefs on mother-child bonding. They were also often cited to support the idea that maternal employment is harmful to a child's development. The how-to books on parenting in the late 1970s and early 1980s, most of which were written by male pediatricians or psychologists, conveyed a similar message: problems in a child's behavior and mental health can be traced back to the ways in which the mother raised the child.

One prominent example of such books is *Bogenbyō* ("Mother-Caused Diseases"), written by Shigemori Kyūtoku, a pediatrician specializing in asthma treatment for children (Kyūtoku 1979). *Bogenbyō*, coined by Kyūtoku, consists of three characters: *Bo* (mother), *gen* (origin), and *byō* (diseases). With its shocking title, it was no wonder that the book was a best-seller and that several sequels were produced in the 1980s by the same author. Kyūtoku observed certain similarities in the parenting styles among mothers coming to his clinic with children who had respiratory problems such as asthma and bronchitis. These mothers, according to Kyūtoku, were either too protective or too manipulative of their children, both of which he saw as problematic.

Kyūtoku asserted that many of the problems in a child's physical and psychological well-being are related to a mother's overprotection: "Almost 100 percent of the health problems in children . . . are attributable to parenting disorders, where parents failed to provide proper training to build up physical and mental strength in children." Kyūtoku sees mothers as "the central figures responsible in parenting" and names asthma, asthmatic bronchitis, and other respiratory disorders as *bogenbyō*, because he believes that "they are caused by mothers" (Kyūtoku 1979: 2–3). Although he sees a mother's overprotection as problematic, Kyūtoku does not suggest the independence of mothers from the mother-child bond as a remedy. Nor does he investigate the possible reversed causal link, in which mothers of children with respiratory problems tend to be more protective *because* of their children's health problems. Instead, Kyūtoku labels mothering disorders as a sign of "disturbed maternal instinct."

Bogenbyō is not exceptional in the how-to parenting literature published in Japan in the 1970s and 1980s. On the contrary, we can readily find similar messages in contemporary parenting books by physicians, psychologists, clinical counselors, hygiene practitioners, and specialists in education (e.g., Hirai 1984; Kawai, Kobayashi, and Nakane 1984; Sasaki and Ishizuki 1988) that emphasize the links between parenting (mothering) style and child outcomes. The importance of the mother-child bond and of maternal care is emphasized so strongly that any physical or psychological problem in a child is seen as a reflection of "disordered" maternal care, such as using disposable diapers (e.g., Taniguchi 1988), bottle-feeding (e.g., Oketani 1987), and a lack of mutual dependence (e.g., Kawai 1989). Although parenting advice books with more relaxed messages began to appear in the late 1980s (e.g., Yamada 1989), the messages conveyed in the majority of parenting books can still be summarized in two phrases: "What a child learns by the age of three will remain until he reaches the age of one hundred" (*mitsugo no tamashī hyaku made*) and "Mothers should stay at home at least until the child reaches three years of age" (*sansai made wa haha no te de*).

JAPANESE WOMEN IN THE COMMUNITY

While the publication trends in popular books set the tenor of public discourse on "good parenting," they also mirror what the public wants to read. The increased demands for parenting advice reflect the social context in which adult socialization takes place for young Japanese mothers.

Adult Socialization and the Role of the Mass Media

Assuming the parental role is a totally fresh endeavor for most Japanese women, who generally become mothers without any firsthand experience of taking care of small children (given that Japanese families typically now have few children). Unlike in the United States, baby-sitting is not a socially accepted way for teenagers to earn money. So it is not unusual for a mother to start parenting with no experience in changing diapers or bathing babies. Parenting, or mothering specifically, is a performance without rehearsal.

Japanese women learn parenting from several socializing agents: parents and in-laws, friends, neighbors, older siblings, books, magazines, television programs, parenting courses sponsored by local governments, and kindergartens and daycare centers. Among these sources, the mass media is of increasing importance as a socializing agent. When asked where they obtained information on infant care, 35 percent of mothers surveyed in Tokyo named the mass media (books, magazines, and television) as the primary source of information, 34 percent named friends, and 17 percent answered kindergartens and daycare centers (Shirasa 1990). Parents and kin networks still play a major role in providing emotional support, but apparently they are somewhat secondary in the transmission of parenting knowledge.

Given the rapid pace at which childrearing practices have changed over the past decades, it is understandable that what grandmothers did 30 years ago is not often applicable to today's childrearing. For example, women in their 60s raised children when bottle-feeding was predominant; it was regarded as superior and as the "modern" way of feeding. Now the trend has reversed. Today more mothers opt for breast-feeding if it is possible (Katsuura-Cook 1991).

The arrival of parenting magazines is a rational consequence of this "information gap." They began to be published in the early 1980s and now provide detailed, up-to-date information on childrearing practices based on children's ages. Opposite to the decline in the birth rate, the circulation of parenting magazines has steadily increased. The total circulation of the major 12 parenting magazines is estimated to be as high as 2,710,000 (Shiomi 1996). Almost all of these parenting magazines contain advertisements and paid publications by companies that provide extra-preschool curricula and educational materials. No single issue appears without their advertisements and their sponsored articles on early intervention programs.

The effect of the mass media on the early education boom can be seen in a survey that showed a positive relationship between mothers' reliance on published materials for parenting know-how and their attitudes toward extra-preschool curricula. The more they are exposed to parenting information through the mass media, the more they are likely to be influenced to provide enrichment "stimulus" through extra-preschool curricula (Shirasa 1990). These mothers are also more likely to feel uneasy about their child's development if other children of the same age are more advanced in writing Chinese characters and in computations. Thus reliance on the mass media for parenting information seems to go hand in hand with the popularization of early education.

Isolation and Anxiety: Childrearing behind Closed Doors

Another prominent aspect in the lives of Japanese mothers who stay at home full-time is their isolation with their children. Because the social spheres of Japanese men and women tend to be so distinctly separated, there are very few opportunities for full-time housewives of salaried workers to socialize. The husband is busy with long working hours and rarely has spare time to help around the home with chores and childcare. Baby-sitters are not readily available in the neighborhood, and commercialized services are often too expensive. A mother is not qualified to have her baby enrolled in an accredited daycare center if she is not working or does not have another "legitimate" reason, such as illness. Commenting on her days with her baby, Toshiko, a full-time housewife married to a "salaryman," says: "A day, a week, and a month could easily pass without talking to any adult except for people in the market or with a salesperson who comes to our door to sell educational toys and *futon*."

In spite of the great emphasis placed on close mother-child relationships in Japanese families, literature in psychology and sociology has long ignored the situation of young mothers. The focus of attention has always been on *children* and on how the mother-child relationship affects the development of a child's personality, well-being, and so on. Little has been written or known about how the mother-child relationship affects mothers.

The isolation of mothers from other adult interaction is another precondition for the development of the early education boom. Ironically, extra-preschool courses provide lonely mothers with a place to meet people. Toshiko said that she decided to put her son in an enrichment program because she wanted to meet people and make friends. The "friends" she was talking about were not for her son, but for herself. Kumiko, mentioned earlier in this chapter, also said that chatting with other mothers in the waiting room while their children took classes provided a nice change of pace.

Many mothers are aware of the suffocation of lonely childrearing and many of them do try to get out of the isolation. Ochiai (1989) argues that a new type of network among mothers is emerging in urban areas in response to the lack of support from husbands and kin. They are of a spontaneous nature, usually composed of mothers who meet each other in neighborhood parks or parenting classes sponsored by the local government. These neighborhood networks provide mutual support in parenting and supplement kin networks. However, my observation is that much of what Ochiai calls "networks" tend to be exclusive, rarely involve fathers, and limit concerns to matters revolving around children.

Yoshiko used to work as a secretary at a trading company until she became pregnant. She decided to leave her job and take care of her son at home. The change in her lifestyle and the routines of a full-time housewife were "a kind of culture shock" to her. She described her days as follows:

> I usually take my son to a neighborhood park in the morning so that he can play with other children. Mothers chat while children play in the sandbox. If the kids move to the swings, we move with them and chat around the swing, or slides, or whatever. Then we usually go to one of the mothers' houses, order pizza or noodles for lunch, and then chat in the afternoon while the children play in the house. When daddies are on business trips, we sometimes eat supper together. The members are the same and the topic of our conversation is the same. At first I enjoyed being with these people, but I am getting tired of it. It's so suffocating!

After several months, she decided to have her son enroll in Suzuki violin and Kumon so that she could avoid this situation.

> I was getting tired of this, but did not want to be ostracized and to be left alone with my kid. Having a private lesson for him gave me a good excuse for keeping some distance from other mothers. They won't feel bad about me if I just say, "I can't join you today because I have to take my kid to a violin lesson."

Again, extra-preschool courses are meeting the demands of their patrons. They provide a place to meet other mothers—and to avoid them.

"A GOOD MOTHER" AS A STATUS: THE CULTURAL CONTRADICTIONS IN WOMEN'S ROLES

Mothers receive mixed and conflicting messages from the M-shaped model of labor force participation: you have to be a good mother, but childrearing will not occupy you for your entire life. On the one hand, mothers are pressed to stay home at least until their children reach the age of three. On the other hand, mothers are aware that they have to be prepared to pursue their "own lives," for their children will grow up and leave the nest. Men and women, especially those who have pursued higher education, have been exposed to contemporary cultural values that emphasize the significance of achievement.

The contradiction can be seen clearly in the relationships between Japanese women's educational level and the employment pattern of Japanese women. As discussed in earlier chapters of this volume, previous research on Japanese female labor supply has reported an ambiguous picture of the relationship between women's educational levels and their likelihood of being employed outside the home. The majority of studies have shown either negative or insignificant effects of a woman's educational level on her propensity to be in the labor force (Brinton 1993; Hirao 1997, 1999; Machiko Osawa 1993; National Institute of Employment and Vocational Training 1987; Okamoto and Naoi 1990; Tanaka 1998; Yano 1982). The labor-force participation rate of four-year university graduates has notably increased among younger cohorts (aged 25–29 and 30–34); however, among the cohort aged 35–39, the participation rate of four-year university graduates is lower than that of women with less education (Seiyama 1998).

Over 80 percent of Japanese women join the labor force upon graduating from school, but more than 80 percent of these women have withdrawn from the labor force for one year or longer by the time they reach the age of 34. The probability of leaving one's job is not necessarily lower for women with higher education (Brinton 1993; Hirao 1997). That is, highly educated women are as likely to be out of the labor force as their less-educated counterparts during the prime parenting years. Moreover, the probability of coming back to the labor force after initial "retirement" is not necessarily higher for four-year university graduates (Hirao 1998). In other words, Japanese women's human capital is very much underutilized in the labor force.

The most striking thing that I noticed throughout my interviews was the frustration shared by many young mothers. "What depresses me is the social trend that gives praise to career women," said Yuko, a graduate from a prestigious four-year university. She used to work at a large department store as a sales assistant and resigned from her job when she had her second daughter.

> They say it's good to be "at the top," pursue your career, and earn money. Super moms who can handle both work and family appear as attractive figures in TV dramas. I used to have self-confidence. I was always at the top both in school and work. My grades were higher than those of my male classmates. I thought I was in a career track until I left it to take care of my kids. Now, I ask myself, "What am I doing here?" I feel trapped and left behind by the rest of the world.

Emiko, who also has two children, expresses her frustration more clearly.

> I used to have everything except kids: study, work, travel, and love. I was imbued with the pleasure of achieving what I deserved. But now, I am doing nothing but raising children, feeding them, bathing them, chasing them around, and yelling at them. My speculation is that, in spite of the primacy given to mothering by childcare experts, the perceived value of childrearing is declining.

These women, particularly those with higher education, have experienced an egalitarian school environment and have internalized, to some extent, the idea that it is crucial even for women to have status in society. Upon becoming mothers, however, the role of mother becomes their primary social identity.

Ōhinata (1982) reports changes in mothers' attitudes toward the value of childcare. She compared the attitude of two cohorts of highly educated mothers, one in their 60s and the other in their 30s. Both cohorts shared the idea that childrearing is physically and emotionally demanding. A significant difference was observed, however, in how they viewed the value of childrearing. A majority (74 percent) of the older cohort agreed that childrearing is a worthwhile and wonderful job, while only 40 percent of the younger cohort shared this view. The majority (61 percent) of the younger cohort asserted that their reasons to live exist outside childrearing, while only 20 percent of the older cohort expressed this view.

The ambivalence toward parenting among young mothers is a natural consequence of changing lifestyles. Being a mother no longer necessarily provides a sense of achievement. Becoming a "good mother," however, is a different story. The ideology of the good mother has exerted a strong normative force on Japanese women during the last two decades. This is because mother and child have been seen as an inseparable pair, the mother and child relationship has been conceptualized as an extension of a mother's "self," a substantial proportion of a child's achievement is believed to result from his or her "effort" rather than from innate individual capabilities, and a child's outcomes have become more easily measurable at an early stage of childhood (e.g., school records and results in entrance examinations to prestigious elementary schools).

Mothers can learn where their child stands relative to other children at quite an early stage through various assessments. The results are thought to reflect how hard the child—and the mother—worked. When we take into account the presumably close psychological proximity between mother and child in Japan and the beliefs related to the causal link between maternal care and child outcomes, it is logical to see being a good mother as a status, one that is achievable depending on how much effort one makes.

Natsumi works part-time as a shop clerk in a confectionery store. She feels that her parenting is constantly being assessed. In her view, "'a good child' is necessary for becoming 'a good mother.'"

> When I talk with other mothers, I often feel that they are evaluating each other's "worth" by the "quality" of the child. A good child is what makes you proud. It isn't your career, your achievement, or what you do as an individual. These things don't count in the world of mothers!

Tomoe, a physician's wife and the full-time mother of one daughter, described early intervention programs as "addictive."

> I wasn't serious when I started sending my daughter to a *yōji kyōshitsu*. I was just curious about the program when I saw their flyer in the newspaper. After I enrolled her, however, I soon learned that such a program has an addictive power. She liked going there, and it was exciting to see how quickly and how much a child can learn. This excitement makes you feel as if it was you who took the test and scored so well. Once you feel this excitement, it is very hard to stop; you don't want to feel that you have failed in something.

The *kyōiku mama* syndrome is not an irreversible process: Tomoe began to notice that she was seeking a vicarious sense of achievement.

> One day, I was telling my daughter to do her homework. She must have thought I was nagging her too much. She stared at me and said, "Mom, it's

my homework, not yours. Don't talk to me like that." I realized that I was pushing her too hard and that being an extreme *kyōiku mama* can be its own form of child abuse.

CONCLUSION

As I have discussed, few official statistics chart the nationwide enrollment or geographical distribution of early intervention educational programs in Japan. It may be that the market-seeking activities of the educational industry and the information proliferation in the mass media, along with women's surplus human capital during the early parenting stages (when they are typically not in the labor force) have combined to create the "boom" in extra-preschool education. It is not clear whether extra-preschool programs will continue to mushroom, for some of the medium-sized and small extra-preschool institutions are reportedly being weeded out through competition. In fact, even Kumon stopped video-delivery services in 1998. Moreover, the prolonged recession in Japan in the past several years means that many families find it difficult to put additional expenses toward their children's education.

The privatization of education, however, is expected to persist, as *juku* has become an even more integral part of the Japanese education system. While the majority of parents criticize the excessive academic competition and decry the extreme emphasis placed on achievement in school, they admit that *juku* is necessary in helping their children to achieve good school records (Ministry of Education 1994). As I described earlier, it has become common for parents to feel that their children are expected to be able to read by the time they enter first grade. In this respect, parents' involvement in creating and carrying out an educational agenda for their children will continue to be crucial. An implication of this trend is that children's educational careers may become more and more dependent on their parents' financial resources.

On the other hand, many of the heavily involved mothers I interviewed did not want to be identified as *kyōiku mama* because of the negative connotations implied. Their hesitation can be interpreted as ambivalence toward women's assigned roles. Based on this, it appears that the role of stay-at-home *kyōiku mama* is likely to be debated and challenged more than ever before.

This chapter has illuminated some important areas for further investigation regarding the ecology and etiology of *kyōiku mama*. Is the heavy involvement of many Japanese mothers in their children's education a reflection of their own suppressed desire for achievement? Is the *kyōiku mama* phenomenon a transition or bridge between *ryōsai kenbo* and future women's roles in Japan? If Japanese women decide to pursue their happiness independent from their roles as mothers, will *kyōiku mama* become an endangered species?

It is also important to investigate the long-term effect of early intervention programs on children. Very little is known about the effectiveness—or the side effects—of early exposure to cognitive training. Most of the discourse on the pros and cons of early intervention programs has been conducted without sound scientific evidence. Psychologists and sociologists will need to investigate how children's long-term social and psychological adjustment is affected by the ways in which human capital is transmitted through school, family, and private institutions.

Finally, an important topic for future research is the comparison of maternal roles in three East Asian countries. The M-shaped curve of female labor force participation remains in South Korea but not in Taiwan (Brinton, Lee, and Parish, Chapter 2 this volume). The difference in married women's employment patterns between these two countries is examined in detail in Chapter 2 from the viewpoint of labor demand and its structure. But how are the roles of mothers shaped by the intersection of work, family, and education patterns? Japan, South Korea, and Taiwan share very similar educational environments, with families keenly competing to have their children enter the best schools. Private educational services are also in high demand in all three countries.

Given such a context, what is expected of mothers, especially as educational agents at home? Little has been done to investigate the similarities and differences in the ideologies of maternal roles in these countries and how they relate to female employment patterns. It is my hope that this chapter will provide an impetus for research in that area.

CHAPTER EIGHT

Women's Education, Work, and Marriage in South Korea

Sunhwa Lee

Educational opportunities have expanded tremendously in South Korea over the past four decades, along with the rapid pace of economic and social change in the society. When the Republic of South Korea was established in 1948, nearly four out of five South Koreans were illiterate. In the ensuing decades, the combination of traditional Confucian respect for learning, the government's emphasis on human resource development, and the perceived social and economic benefits of education to individuals all became engines for rapid educational growth. Higher education attendance rates increased dramatically beginning in the 1970s, outpacing those in other East Asian societies such as Taiwan at a similar stage of economic development (see Chapter 2 for the comparison of educational growth between South Korea and Taiwan). As shown in figure 8.1, prior to 1980 fewer than 20 percent of South Korean men and 10 percent of women aged 18–21 were enrolled in some type of higher education. By 1998 the enrollment rate had reached almost 80 percent for men and 50 percent for women, exceeding the rates for other East Asian countries and most Western countries as well.

A considerable gender gap in higher education enrollments still exists in South Korea, in spite of the remarkable growth of women's educational attendance during the past 20 years. But it is important to underscore that women have very much followed men in the *type* of higher education they have pursued. The experiences of other countries such as the United States and Japan show that women's opportunities for higher education often expand initially through their attendance at two-year junior colleges rather than four-year institutions (Bianchi and Spain 1986; Brinton 1993; Fujimura-Fanselow 1995). In Japan, over two-thirds of women's higher education en-

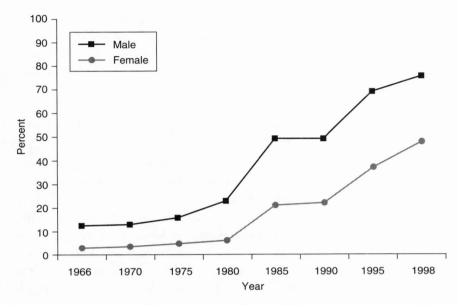

Figure 8.1.   South Korean Enrollment Rates in Higher Education by Sex, 1966–1998

SOURCES: Ministry of Education, ROK (Republic of Korea), *Statistical Yearbook of Education*, various years; National Statistical Office, ROK (Republic of Korea), *Population and Housing Census Report*, various years.

NOTES: The enrollment rate is calculated as the number of students enrolled in higher education divided by the total population aged 18–21. Higher education includes junior college, teachers' college, university, and other miscellaneous undergraduate institutions.

rollments were concentrated in two-year junior colleges until the early 1990s, whereas almost all men pursuing higher education were at four-year universities (see Brinton and Lee, Chapter 5 this volume). Not until 1996 did Japanese women's enrollments at universities overtake their enrollment at junior colleges. In sharp contrast, over two-thirds of South Korean women's enrollments, as well as men's, have been concentrated in four-year institutions.[1]

This diverging pattern of women's higher education growth in South Korea and Japan leads us to ponder the social and economic value of university education in South Korean women's lives, especially given that these two societies have many similarities in terms of the structure of their higher education systems, cultural values regarding gender roles, women's work patterns, and the degree of sex discrimination in the labor market (see Chapter 1 and other chapters in this volume). The higher education systems of South Korea and Japan are both characterized by competitive entrance examinations, generating an almost identical phenomenon of "examination hell" among youngsters and equally prevalent practices of exam preparation studies after regular school hours—known as *kwawe* in South Korea and *juku* in Japan (see Hirao, Chapter 7 this volume). This intense competition for college entrance has been further fueled by the hierarchical structure of higher education in both countries. The clear hierarchical ranking of prestige among universities emerged due to an admissions process emphasizing students' academic performance on the entrance examination and also due to differing career patterns of graduates. In each country, the belief is widely held that a degree from a highly prestigious university is essential for a successful career, particularly for men. In this competitive higher education environment, South Korean women have pursued a similar path to men by aspiring to attend prestigious four-year universities. Many Japanese women, on the other hand, have traditionally chosen a distinctly different path—junior colleges—from their male counterparts.

But South Korean women's university education has not necessarily corresponded to their involvement in the labor market or reflected major changes in the economy, whereas Japanese women's preference for a two-year junior college education has mirrored the differential employment opportunities for junior college and university graduates in that country (see Brinton and Lee, Chapter 5 this volume). The employment rate among unmarried South Korean women with a university education has risen considerably in recent years (to 85 percent in 1995), exceeding the rates for less-educated women. Yet the employment rate among *married* women with a university education is still no greater than the rates for their less-educated counterparts. Moreover, it is less than half the rate for single women (Korean Women's Development Institute 1999). As discussed by Brinton in the introductory chapter, despite substantial increases in women's overall participation in the labor force, the M-shaped pattern of life-cycle participation persists in both South Korea and Japan; a large number of women still withdraw from the labor force as they get married and have children. Female university graduates' labor force behavior is consistent with this pattern, although they are much less likely than less-educated women to later reenter the labor force (Kim 1996; Tanaka 1995).

The relatively low level of postmarital employment among highly educated women in both countries suggests that the traditional emphasis on women's roles as wife and mother has not abated despite recent increases in women's higher education attainment. Cultural traditions and social norms in both societies have highlighted the virtues of women as "wise mothers and good wives" whose main role is to support the husband's career and to be the primary investor in children's education (Brinton 1993; Hirao, Chapter 7 this volume). At the same time, sex-discriminatory practices in the labor market and the resulting lack of appropriate employment opportunities for female university graduates have been severe impediments to their pursuit of a lifelong career. Female university graduates in South Korea and Japan have only limited access to career-track jobs—the same jobs that are taken for granted among their male counterparts.

Under these social norms and labor market circumstances, Japanese women's preference to enroll in junior colleges has represented a rational response to their perceived opportunities in the labor market (Brinton 1993; Fujimura-Fanselow 1985). Women's junior college education has at least provided good access to short-term white-collar jobs (euphemistically known as "office ladies"), whereas university education has not necessarily guaranteed better career opportunities (see Brinton and Lee, Chapter 5, and Ogasawara, Chapter 6, this volume). In contrast, South Korean women's increased attendance at four-year universities seems to have been motivated more by its value in the marriage market than in the labor market. Women's university education is commonly viewed in South Korean society as a prime route for meeting high-status men and as a cultural credential necessary for marrying a man with high socioeconomic potential. Empirical studies show that there is a high degree of educational homogamy among South Koreans in general and among the highly educated in particular. There is also a strong positive association between women's levels of education and their husband's incomes (Kim 1990; Park 1991).

Given that South Korean women's university education is closely associated with their marriage prospects on the one hand and more loosely related to their postmarital employment on the other, this chapter examines whether female university graduates make up a homogeneous group or whether there are distinct subgroups of women who have different career and possibly marriage patterns. Tanaka (1995) has suggested that rather than Japanese female university graduates being a homogenous group, they tend to be polarized into two groups: women who have long-term career commitment, and women who become full-time housewives after a brief employment period before marriage. Do South Korean women show the same polarized employment patterns or not?

Many dimensions such as innate ability, family background, and field of study can affect university graduates' opportunities. Among these, this study focuses on the prestige ranking of the university a woman attended. Numerous studies have shown that not just a university education but the *prestige* of the university attended is crucial in determining the occupational outcomes and career opportunities for South Korean men (Amsden 1989; Choi 1989; Lee 1994; Lee and Brinton 1996).[2] But no existing studies on South Korea or Japan have examined how university prestige affects women's labor market participation patterns, the occupations they enter, or their marriages.[3]

The research presented in this chapter begins to fill this void by analyzing a unique data set from an original survey (the Survey of Employment Experiences of University Graduates) conducted in Seoul, South Korea, in 1992. The survey contains extensive information on the employment and marital histories of approximately 1000 women and men who graduated from universities of different prestige rankings in the early 1980s.[4]

SURVEY DATA

Most of the studies in South Korea that argue for male graduates' differing employment opportunities by university prestige have either used employment data on graduates from a few universities or have relied on recruitment data from select business corporations. In contrast, the survey used here was specifically designed to assess the importance of university prestige in the lives of female as well as male university graduates, based on a systematic sampling of universities and their graduates.

Sampling consisted of the random selection of approximately 1000 men and women from the alumni directories of 14 universities (including three women's universities) distributed among the three distinct rankings of university prestige. The respondents graduated in the early 1980s, and the survey collected extensive information on family background, education, marriage, and work histories up to the survey date. The survey was conducted through personal interviews in May–August 1992. Since female university graduates made up only about one-third of the total number of university

graduates in the early 1980s, female and male graduates were sampled separately in order to secure sufficient numbers of women and men from each
university prestige ranking. This resulted in a total sample of 435 women
and 468 men. The universities from which we sampled are all located in
Seoul, which has a high proportion of all South Korean universities.[5] The
four coed universities and the one women's university that are regarded as
the most prestigious in South Korea are located in Seoul. We included this
women's university and three of these coed ones in our sample. All the universities included in the sample except Seoul National University (regarded
as the most prestigious in South Korea) are private.

Since the respondents were selected from graduates of the early 1980s,
they represented a cohort of university graduates in their mid-30s who potentially had about 10 years of employment experience by the survey date.
The average age of respondents was 33 years for women and 35 years for
men. More than 90 percent of both female and male respondents were married by the survey date, and their mean age at first marriage was 26 for women
and 28 for men. Most of the married respondents had at least one child, with
the average number of children being 1.6 for both women and men.

Because the admissions process for each university is based strictly on
individuals' academic performance on the entrance examination, there is a
prevailing ideology of meritocracy. The majority of students as well as parents from different social classes firmly believe that they or their children can
enter a prestigious university as long as students study hard and parents are
willing to support their efforts (Hong and Koo 1993). The social background
characteristics of the respondents in the survey, however, suggest that female
university graduates of the early 1980s came from quite privileged social
backgrounds (see table 8.1). Moreover, social background varied by university prestige. The proportion of women whose fathers were university-
educated increased from 33 percent for third-ranked university graduates
to 45 percent for second-ranked and 54 percent for top-ranked university
graduates. A similar pattern held for men, although the percentages were
lower than for women. Considering that fewer than 10 percent of the male
population in the parental generation even had a university education, it is
striking how many university graduates in this cohort came from high social
backgrounds.

The academic abilities of university graduates also differed substantially

TABLE 8.1
General Characteristics of the Survey Sample

	WOMEN				MEN			
	University prestige ranking				University prestige ranking			
	FIRST (N = 159)	SECOND (N = 150)	THIRD (N = 126)	TOTAL (N = 435)	FIRST (N = 167)	SECOND (N = 160)	THIRD (N = 141)	TOTAL (N = 468)
Father's education (%)								
University or more	54.1	44.7	32.5	44.6	35.9	23.1	22.0	27.4
Less than university	45.9	55.3	67.5	55.4	64.1	76.9	78.0	72.6
Examination score								
Average minimum	262.89	242.04	224.88	244.69	284.83	251.09	236.90	258.86
(SD)	(16.03)	(12.70)	(13.39)	(20.94)	(13.98)	(15.41)	(10.20)	(24.27)
Graduate degree (%)								
Master's	24.5	21.3	7.9	18.6	22.1	13.1	19.2	18.2
Doctorate	8.8	1.3	0.8	3.9	9.6	3.8	2.1	5.3
Total	33.3	22.6	8.7	22.5	31.7	16.9	21.3	23.5

by university prestige ranking. The precise entrance examination score for each individual was not available, but the estimated score for each department in each university is published every year.[6] These scores indicate the level of difficulty and the degree of competition in entering each department in each university. As shown in table 8.1, scores differ significantly by university prestige, indicating that university prestige ranking closely approximates individuals' academic abilities (general human capital). The apparent difference in human capital by university prestige can also be illustrated by the proportion of women and men who pursued graduate education. Almost one-third of women and men from top-ranked universities obtained a graduate degree by the survey date, while the proportion was lower among those from lower-ranked universities.[7]

Men's scores are higher than women's, primarily due to the fact that the fields men tend to enter, such as engineering, business, and law, require higher examination scores than female-dominated fields. Despite the tremendous growth in South Korean women's university attendance, there remains a tendency for men and women to specialize in different fields. Over three-quarters of all male university students in 1995 were in social and natural science fields, including business, law, and engineering. Only 1 out of 10 men majored in humanities and very few (only about 3 percent) majored in education. In contrast, a substantial proportion of all female students in 1995 majored in traditional female fields such as humanities (23 percent), education (11 percent), and arts (13 percent), although the proportion of women majoring in social sciences (21 percent) and natural sciences (23 percent) has steadily increased since 1980.

GENDER AND EDUCATION IN THE SOUTH KOREAN LABOR MARKET

Educational attainment plays a prominent role in the South Korean labor market. A central reason for the rapid growth of higher education in South Korea lies in the fact that higher educational attainment has become a key means to upward mobility in income, class, and social status. As South Korea entered the era of rapid economic development in the 1960s, work opportunities expanded in the white-collar sector and educational attainment became the most critical determinant of occupational status and earnings (Cha 1992; Koo and Hong 1990; Park and Park 1984). The earnings of male four-year university graduates in the period 1975–1985 were 2.2 times greater than those of high school graduates and 1.7 times greater than those of two-year junior college graduates; since then, the earnings differential has narrowed somewhat due to increased earnings among high school graduates (National Statistical Office, ROK 1998).

The high premium attached to a four-year university education, especially for men, is closely related to an industrialization process in South Korea in which large manufacturing companies competed during the 1970s to recruit a highly capable group of managerial personnel, in the midst of a relatively short supply of university graduates (Amsden 1989; Kim 1992; Park 1982). Because university enrollments have grown dramatically since the early 1980s, however, the lucrative employment opportunities previously enjoyed by university graduates have decreased considerably. The employment situation for university graduates has shifted, lessening the advantage of a mere four-year university education while elevating the importance of the *prestige* of one's educational credential. As an illustration, the proportion of university graduates who had not secured a job by the time of graduation nearly doubled in the 1980s, from 27 percent in 1980 to 50 percent in 1989 (Choi 1989). But this proportion varied substantially by the prestige of the university: in 1988, 30 percent of all four-year university graduates in Seoul did not have a job at the time of graduation, whereas this was true for only 10–17 percent of graduates from the top three universities.

Some of the advantages associated with university education apply to women as well as men. But this does not necessarily mean that women enjoy equal benefits to men from their university education. The average monthly earnings of female university graduates in 1990 were only about two-thirds of the earnings of their male counterparts (Korean Women's Development Institute 1999). In fact, the earnings differential by sex in South Korea is one of the largest in the world (along with Japan), according to the 1989–1990 ILO *Yearbook of Labor Statistics* (cited in Bai and Cho 1996: 186). The gender gap in earnings among university graduates is in large part associated with occupational sex segregation. Most male and female university graduates are engaged in nonclerical white-collar occupations (including professional/technical or administrative/managerial positions), but the majority of female graduates are concentrated in traditionally female professions or semi-professions such as teaching and nursing, while male graduates are found in a variety of other white-collar jobs.

The persisting gender differentiation in major fields of study no doubt plays a part in the later occupational sex segregation among university graduates. But female university graduates also face discrimination in the labor market, including entry barriers to high-wage occupations, biased job assignment in firms, and differential wages, all of which steer them into diverging career paths from their male counterparts. In the South Korean labor market, sex and educational attainment are considered the two most important determinants of earnings (Lee 1984; Park 1982). Hyo-Soo Lee (1984) has argued that the South Korean labor market is structured by four strata based on sex and educational attainment, which provide distinctly different chances for pay raises and promotions. While male university graduates make up the highest stratum with the highest earnings potential and the greatest possibilities for promotion, female university graduates constitute the second highest stratum—along with male junior college and high school graduates—which offers some increases in pay but limited promotional chances. Lee further contends that there is little mobility between the strata: female university graduates rarely move into the upper stratum occupied mainly by male university graduates.

Under these labor market circumstances, it is not clear whether university prestige has an important influence on the employment patterns and occupations of women graduates, as is commonly assumed for men. Do women from highly prestigious universities face better employment opportunities than those from less prestigious ones, producing a heterogeneous pattern of career commitment and economic rewards for women based on university prestige ranking? Or do women, regardless of their university prestige, encounter very similar employment opportunities in the discriminatory environment of the South Korean labor market? Does sex discrimination vary across occupational fields? Is women's university prestige important to employers as a measure of human capital? These questions are examined below through empirical analyses of the survey data.

Patterns of Work Experience among Female University Graduates

The vast majority (85 percent) of women in the survey ($n = 435$) had employment experience between the time of university graduation and the time of the survey. The proportion of women with work experience was positively associated with their university prestige, increasing from 78 percent for third-ranked university graduates to 86 percent for second-ranked and 91 percent

TABLE 8.2

Married Women's Work Patterns by University Prestige
and Major Field of Study

By university prestige	First	Second	Third	Total
Worked only before marriage	18.7	23.4	25.2	22.1
Worked only after marriage	8.0	5.5	7.0	6.9
Worked both before and after marriage	63.3	54.7	44.4	55.0
Did not work	10.0	16.4	23.5	16.0
Total	100.0	100.0	100.0	100.0
N	150	128	115	393

By major field of study	Humanities/ arts/home economics	Social/ natural sciences	Education	Nursing/ pharmacy
Worked only before marriage	22.9	27.3	19.4	9.3
Worked only after marriage	8.9	2.7	8.1	2.3
Worked both before and after marriage	43.9	64.9	62.9	86.1
Did not work	24.3	5.4	9.7	2.3
Total	100.0	100.0	100.0	100.0
N	214	74	62	43

for top-ranked university graduates. This positive association was also evident in the experience of postmarital employment. Among married women ($N = 393$; table 8.2), a greater proportion of top-ranked university graduates (63 percent) had some work experience both before and after marriage, compared to second-ranked (55 percent) and third-ranked (44 percent) university graduates. Conversely, the percentage of married women who had worked only before marriage was higher for those from lower-ranked universities.

In addition to these differences by university prestige, there were also differences by women's major fields of study. Women who had majored in the humanities, arts, or home economics were the least likely to have been employed, while women who had majored in education, nursing, or pharmacy were the most likely to be employed both before and after marriage. But even when we accounted for different major fields, women from the top-ranked universities were the most likely to be employed after marriage. In other words, although university-educated South Korean women in general exhibit a relatively low level of postmarital labor force participation, there seems to be significant variation in both premarital and postmarital labor force participation according to university prestige. Given that university prestige in South Korean society closely approximates students' academic ability or human capital, the varying employment patterns by university prestige suggest that women's human capital is important for their labor market participation. Employers may also use the credential of a prestigious university degree as a screening criterion in the hiring process.

The data show that South Korean female university graduates, similar to their Japanese counterparts, tend to be polarized into two groups of women: those who are long-term labor market participants (with continuous employment), and those who are temporary participants only up to the time of marriage. If female university graduates are homogeneous in their career commitment or if they all have a similar tendency to move in and out of the labor force, women's work histories should not vary much depending on whether or not they were working at the survey time. On the other hand, if women have significantly different degrees of career commitment, their work histories should diverge depending on their current employment status at the survey time.

At the time of the survey, a little over half of the women who had initially entered the labor force were still working. Of the women who were *not* working at this time, over half had left the labor force before marriage and another one-third left soon after marriage, all without reentering the labor force. These women were employed only about 30 percent of the time between university graduation and the survey date. In sharp contrast, four out of five married women who were working at the survey date had worked continuously since the time they initially entered the labor force. This indicates that there is indeed considerable heterogeneity in university-educated women's work patterns across their early life course.

Continuity of Work Experience among Female University Graduates

The issue of whether women have continuous or intermittent work experience after marriage has been an important theoretical concern in sociology as well as in economics. Mincer and Polachek (1974) argue that married women tend to have intermittent patterns of employment because of their childbearing and childrearing responsibilities. Polachek (1975, 1981) further contends that predominantly female occupations tend to penalize women's intermittent employment less in terms of lifetime earnings than do male occupations, making it rational for women who anticipate intermittent employment to choose female occupations. Conversely, he expects women who anticipate continuous employment to be in predominantly male rather than female occupations.[8] But in the case of South Korean female university graduates, we find a different pattern than the one predicted by this theory.

Female university graduates' first jobs were concentrated in "traditional" female occupations such as teaching, nursing, and pharmacy (see table 8.3). Nearly half of all women had their first job in an education-related field, including teaching in regular schools, exam preparation schools, or doing private tutoring. Fewer than one-third had their first job in a professional occupation other than teaching, nursing, or pharmacy. (Hereafter I will use the term "other white-collar occupations" to refer to white-collar jobs other than teaching, nursing, pharmacy, and secretarial jobs.)[9] One out of ten female university graduates held a secretarial job. There was no significant difference at all by university prestige in the distribution of these major occupations.

The occupational distribution by major field further illustrates that even the majority of women who had majored in humanities/arts/home economics or social/natural sciences held their first job in education-related occupations, although these women were also more likely to have entered other white-collar occupations (excluding secretarial jobs) than women who had majored in either education or nursing/pharmacy. Except for the women with nursing/pharmacy majors, whose specialized training led into the corresponding occupations, some form of teaching was the main occupation held by female university graduates regardless of their university prestige and major. The extent of women's concentration in these occupations becomes very clear when the occupational distribution of their male counterparts is examined. The vast majority of men—about three-quarters—held their first job in what I have called "other white-collar occupations," mainly entry-level jobs in private or public firms, the jobs that are commonly considered the first career step for male university graduates. Just as for women, there was no significant difference in men's occupational distribution by university prestige.

South Korean women's concentration in traditional female occupations, especially in teaching, seems to arise from both push and pull factors. The

TABLE 8.3
Women's and Men's First Jobs by University
Prestige and Major Field of Study

By university prestige	WOMEN				MEN			
	First	Second	Third	Total	First	Second	Third	Total
Education-related	46.5	47.3	48.0	47.2	17.4	12.5	17.7	15.8
Nursing/pharmacy[a]	12.5	11.6	8.2	11.1	1.2	5.0	0.0	2.1
Other white-collar	25.7	32.6	30.6	29.4	78.4	78.1	78.0	78.2
Secretarial	14.6	7.8	10.2	11.1	0.0	0.0	0.0	0.0
Sales/service	0.7	0.8	3.1	1.4	3.0	4.4	4.3	3.9
	100.0	100.0	100.0	100.0	100.0	100.0	100.0	100.0
N	144	129	98	371	167	160	141	468

By major field of study	WOMEN				MEN			
	Human.	Sciences	Educ.	Nursing/pharm.	Human.	Sciences	Educ.	Pharm.
Education-related	48.6	51.2	67.2	6.7	21.0	10.7	67.7	9.1
Nursing/pharmacy[a]	0.0	0.0	0.0	91.1	0.0	0.0	0.0	90.9
Other white-collar	37.7	36.6	16.4	0.0	74.2	85.2	32.3	0.0
Secretarial	12.0	12.2	13.1	2.2	0.0	0.0	0.0	0.0
Sales/service	1.6	0.0	3.3	0.0	4.8	4.1	0.0	0.0
	100.0	100.0	100.0	100.0	100.0	100.0	100.0	100.0
N	183	82	61	45	62	364	31	11

[a]There were no men in nursing jobs.

teaching profession in South Korea has traditionally been a popular choice for educated women, not only because of the high social respect and social status accorded to teachers but also because the work environment is relatively conducive to women's dual responsibilities at home and at work. The work environment of other white-collar workers—commonly called "salary-men" in South Korea, as in Japan—is typified by long working hours and the demanding nature of the job (see Brinton, Lee, and Parish, Chapter 2 this volume). Typical South Korean salarymen in their 30s spend more time at work than at home, with work beginning at eight o'clock in the morning and ending around seven o'clock in the evening—without including commuting time or the frequent social gatherings required for many entry-level office workers (*Weekly Economist* 1995). Compared to this, the teaching profession offers relatively flexible schedules as well as vacation. This makes teaching attractive for women who want to pursue long-term careers while carrying out family responsibilities.

In addition, the degree of sex discrimination tends to differ between traditional female and other white-collar occupations. Since other white-collar occupations are in great demand by male university graduates, female graduates encounter various types of discrimination in this particular job market. The Equal Employment Opportunity Law (EEOL) of 1987 prohibited employers from explicitly specifying gender as a job criterion, but informally it is often still used (Jeong 1994). The hiring process also tends to differ for men and women in most white-collar occupations. Male university graduates tend to be hired through an open application process (called *gongchae*) which combines written tests and interviews, while female university graduates are less likely to be hired through *gongchae* than through a combination of school recommendations and interviews (Bai and Cho 1996; Lee 1984; Park 1992). Despite government efforts since the passage of the EEOL to promote the hiring of female university graduates into career-track jobs in large corporations, female graduates in 1996 constituted only 12 percent of the new employees hired by the top 50 largest corporations in South Korea (an increase from 5 percent in 1990).[10]

Even when the selection of female and male university graduates is based on the same criteria, women tend to be assigned to positions of lesser importance such as public relations, product design, or secretarial positions, whereas men are assigned to more important positions such as marketing or management. This differential job assignment leads naturally to differential promotional opportunities and earnings. Moreover, women engaged in many white-collar jobs face serious obstacles in continuing their employment once they marry, as many firms in South Korea still pressure women to quit upon marriage. Although the explicit practice of "marriage bars" is no longer prevalent since the enactment of EEOL, subtle and informal pressures on married women still persist in many white-collar occupations, as is true in Japan as well (see chapters in this volume by Brinton, Lee, and Parish; Lee and Hirata; and Ogasawara; also see Sohn and Cho 1993).[11] For college-educated women working in white-collar occupations, discrimination at the workplace, particularly the lack of promotional potential, is the second most cited reason for wanting to leave the job, closely following childcare concerns (Sohn and Cho 1993). The strenuous nature of the work environment and the various discriminatory practices against women in white-collar occupations therefore undermine women's potential long-term commitment to work.

The difference in women's potential long-term opportunities in traditional female versus other white-collar occupations is illustrated in the survey data by the different distribution of occupations for women who were still working at the survey time and those who had left their jobs. Over two-thirds of married women who were working at the time of the survey were employed in teaching, nursing, or pharmacy jobs. In contrast, fewer than half of married women who left the labor force had been in these traditional female jobs; about half of those who had left had instead been employed in secretarial or other white-collar jobs. (Also see Lee and Hirata, Chapter 4 this volume.)

Multivariate analyses verify that occupational type is indeed an important determinant of the continuity of South Korean women's work experience throughout the early life course. Appendix table 8.1 presents the results of event-history models that estimate the hazard rate of women's leaving the labor force given that they had entered the labor force after university graduation.[12] The specific type of occupation held by a woman has a strong, statistically significant effect on the rate of leaving the labor force, controlling for other characteristics such as university prestige, marital status, and family attributes. Women engaged in traditional female occupations were significantly less likely to leave the labor force, and those working in secretarial jobs were significantly *more* likely to do so, both compared to women working in other white-collar occupations. Contrary to the predictions of Mincer and Polachek for women in the United States, university-educated South Korean women who entered traditional female occupations were the most likely to be continuously employed. Women in full-time jobs and those who had accumulated substantial years of work experience were also less likely to leave the labor force. But women who had changed jobs frequently were more likely to exit the labor force.

Women's marital and family characteristics also have a significant impact on their likelihood of continuous participation in the labor market. Marital timing in particular has a strong effect on women's leaving the labor force. Two measures of women's marital status indicate that compared to being single, women's marriage increases the odds of leaving the labor force by 15.5 times, whereas once women are married there is no significant difference in their odds of leaving the labor force compared to single women's. This is consistent with the fact that most South Korean female university graduates who left the labor force did so around the time of marriage. Women's pregnancy and childbirth during the job period significantly increases the rate of leaving the labor force, relative to having no children. Yet women with preschool children are no more likely to leave the labor force than childless women, and women with school-aged children are significantly *less* likely to leave than childless women. These results contradict the common social science expectation that having preschool children hinders married women's continuous labor force participation, especially highly educated women's, since they are most likely to be concerned with investing in children's human capital (Hill and Stafford 1974; Leibowitz 1975). In the South Korean context, women who lack a strong career commitment tend to exit the labor force at the time of marriage rather than during the period of childbearing and childrearing. Since married women who remain employed throughout this period are those with a strong career commitment, having preschool or school-aged children does not seem to be much of a deterrent for their continuous participation in the labor market. Consistent with other studies, husband's socioeconomic status has a negative influence on married women's continuous labor force participation. Married women whose husbands are in high-prestige professional/administrative occupations[13] are more likely to leave the labor force compared to single women or to married women whose husbands are in other occupations.

Finally, with all of the occupational and family variables controlled, multivariate analyses show that top-ranked university women are significantly less likely to leave the labor force than third-ranked university women (whereas there is no significant difference between second- and third-ranked university women). This effect of university prestige is weak once the effect of graduate education is added (model 2), suggesting that the greater tendency for continuous employment among top-ranked university women is due in part to the fact that many of them obtain advanced degrees that lead them into the labor force. (One-third of top-ranked university women went on to graduate school.) The importance of top-ranked university education along with the strong significant effect of graduate education illustrates that elite women who attended the most prestigious universities were significantly more likely to be continuously employed than women who attended less prestigious ones. In other words, women's human capital—reflected in both university prestige and graduate education—is crucial in producing differences in long-term career commitment.

In sum, these analyses demonstrate that female university graduates in South Korea are *not* a homogeneous group of women with respect to employment patterns and career commitment. Similar to the case of Japanese women, South Korean women university graduates are polarized into two groups: those who seek long-term careers, and those who seek temporary work mostly before marriage. Marriage timing in particular is important in demarcating who has long-term versus short-term labor force participation (though this may be even more important for less-educated women; see Lee and Hirata, Chapter 4 this volume). Women's university prestige contributes to these heterogeneous career patterns, as shown by the greater propensity for continuous employment as well as postmarital labor market participation among women from the most prestigious institutions. In addition to university prestige, occupational type is very critical for women's career patterns. Traditional female occupations tend to facilitate women's long-term continuous employment, largely because of their more women-friendly work environment and the lesser degree of discrimination compared to other white-collar occupations.

Can we expect to find a similar heterogeneity in the labor market rewards to university degrees of varying prestige? This issue is explored next, by examining characteristics of the jobs held by women and men such as the female composition, the promotional potential, and earnings. This gender comparison is included in order to assess how the economic benefits of education differ not only by university prestige or type of occupation among women, but also by gender.

Gender, University Prestige, and Occupational Outcomes

Although women from the most elite universities are more likely than other women to work after marriage and to work continuously over time, their occupational characteristics are not much different from those of other women. But female graduates overall tend to be in distinctly different occupations compared to male graduates from the very beginning of their careers. As described earlier, regardless of university prestige, the majority of women are engaged in traditional female occupations whereas the vast majority of men are concentrated in other white-collar occupations. Women's jobs overall differ significantly from men's jobs even when they are in the same type of occupation, particularly with respect to the female composition of the job, promotional opportunities, and earnings potential. Moreover, women's attendance at the most elite institutions does not generate any career advantage, whereas men's elite university attendance clearly produces advantages in career prospects and economic rewards.

The female composition rate of the first job (table 8.4) illustrates that women and men are segregated not just in terms of broad occupational categories but in terms of the specific jobs they perform. Women report that almost half of their colleagues in the workplace who are performing jobs similar to their own are female. By contrast, men report that only 16 percent of their colleagues are female. This female composition rate does not vary much by university prestige or by occupational category for either sex.

The female composition rate in other white-collar occupations further suggests that women's entrance to such white-collar occupations does not mean that they work in predominantly male jobs. In fact, there is no significant difference in the female composition rate of women's first jobs between education-related and other white-collar occupations. This supports the general observation that jobs in South Korean organizations that are assigned to entry-level office workers are highly gender-segregated. Even among women and men in teaching positions in higher education, the female composition rate is higher for women than for men. Why? Most men hold the position of professor while most women are instructors, even if women entered teaching with the same graduate degree as men.

Women also anticipate significantly fewer promotional opportunities than men in their first jobs (table 8.4). Since the organizational structure of each occupation involves different hierarchies, promotional expectations may vary by the type of occupation. But even within the same occupation, there are gender differences in anticipated promotional chances. According to multivariate analyses (appendix table 8.2), women's university prestige has no significant effect on their promotional expectations (controlling for occupation). In contrast, the promotional opportunities men anticipate are significantly greater among top-ranked and second-ranked university graduates

TABLE 8.4

Characteristics of First Jobs among Female and Male Employees

| | FEMALE COMPOSITION RATE[a] | | | | | |
| | Women | | | Men | | |
	MEAN	(SD)	(N)	MEAN	(SD)	(N)
Total	44.9**	(30.6)	(359)	16.1	(17.0)	(461)
By university prestige						
First	44.6**	(31.1)	(140)	14.8	(16.4)	(167)
Second	45.9**	(30.6)	(127)	17.2	(17.7)	(156)
Third	43.8**	(30.2)	(92)	16.6	(16.8)	(138)
By occupation						
Teaching at higher education level	34.1**	(27.3)	(28)	15.8	(13.1)	(18)
Teaching at other education level	47.7**	(26.3)	(141)	22.0	(19.3)	(56)
Nursing/pharmacy	57.3*	(36.6)	(39)	28.6	(29.4)	(7)
Other white-collar	40.1**	(32.0)	(106)	15.3	(16.4)	(366)
Secretarial	41.3	(31.4)	(41)	—	—	—
Sales/service	58.8**	(37.7)	(4)	8.6	(9.9)	(14)

| | EXPECTED PROMOTIONAL OPPORTUNITIES[b] | | | | | |
| | Women | | | Men | | |
	MEAN	(SD)	(N)	MEAN	(SD)	(N)
Total	2.0**	(1.1)	(359)	4.1	(1.5)	(461)
By university prestige						
First	2.1**	(1.2)	(140)	4.3	(1.6)	(167)
Second	2.1**	(1.2)	(127)	4.2	(1.5)	(156)
Third	1.8**	(1.0)	(92)	3.8	(1.3)	(138)
By occupation						
Teaching at higher education level	2.1**	(1.0)	(28)	3.3	(1.5)	(18)
Teaching at other education level	1.9**	(1.0)	(141)	2.9	(1.3)	(56)
Nursing/pharmacy	2.6**	(1.3)	(39)	4.3	(1.3)	(7)
Other white-collar	2.2**	(1.1)	(106)	4.3	(1.4)	(366)
Secretarial	1.6	(1.0)	(41)	—	—	—
Sales/service	2.3	(2.3)	(4)	3.8	(1.7)	(14)

[a]Respondents were asked to estimate the proportion of women among all those who were performing the job similar to their own in their workplace.

[b]Respondents were asked how many levels they thought they could be promoted from their initial position in the workplace (the number of levels including the initial position).

*$p < .05$, **$p < .01$ in one-tailed t-test for gender differences in means.

than among their third-ranked university counterparts (again controlling for occupational category). Whether this anticipated promotional opportunity is pure subjective perception or a realistic assessment of their career potential in the first job, men from highly prestigious institutions certainly anticipate greater career opportunities than those from less prestigious ones at the beginning of their careers. Yet women from similarly elite institutions do not foresee any greater career prospects than other women.

The gender disparity in the category of "other white-collar occupations" is especially important. Men who entered these occupations clearly perceive greater career potential than those who entered the teaching profession. But for women, other white-collar occupations did not entail any greater promotional opportunities than teaching occupations. This demonstrates that women's jobs in the category of "other white-collar occupations" are fundamentally different from men's. Starting earnings illustrate this as well. Among full-time employees, women overall earn 82 percent of what men earn. But the gender gap is *greatest* among those engaged in other white-collar occupations, where women earn only 76 percent of men's starting salaries. This suggests that women face greater obstacles in these occupations.

Important in the organizational structure of South Korean companies is that one's initial job assignment determines one's long-term career prospects (as in Japan). When women are channeled into different jobs than men, it means that they are assigned different job ranks, base wages, and promotional opportunities. Hence, even if women and men appear to be assigned to different job tasks because of differences in their major fields or other experiences, these differences in initial job tasks become amplified over time and lead to divergence in earnings. Monthly earnings in South Korea include various allowances in addition to the base wage, and these allowances are attached to each job assignment. Initial job assignment is therefore critical for earnings as well as for promotional opportunities (Bai and Cho 1996; Jeong 1994).

The average monthly earnings of women and men who were working at the time of the survey demonstrate how economic rewards by gender had diverged during the first 10 years or so of people's careers. The gender gap in current earnings for full-time employees (72 percent) was greater than the gap in starting earnings (82 percent). This gender gap existed within each university prestige ranking and for each occupational category. According to multivariate analyses (appendix table 8.2), women's earnings in education-related jobs were significantly lower than in other white-collar jobs, illustrating the lower rate of earnings increase with seniority in teaching jobs.[14] A key difference between women's and men's earnings lies in the effect of university prestige, controlling for other occupational characteristics. Neither university prestige nor a graduate degree has any significant effect on women's earnings. This highlights the fact that women's human capital is not a key factor determining their economic rewards (just as it does not determine the female composition rate of their job or their promotional opportunities either). In sharp contrast, men who graduated from top-ranked or second-ranked universities earn significantly more than men from third-ranked universities. (The earnings difference between top-ranked and second-ranked university men is also significant.) This finding supports the common assumption in the South Korean labor market that university prestige is a crucial determinant of career opportunities and economic rewards for men.

In sum, the characteristics of the jobs held by university graduates show the high degree of gender segregation in the South Korean labor market. Women and men are channeled not only into different occupations but also into different career paths, even when they are in supposedly similar occupations. Beyond these pronounced gender differences, we find relatively little difference in women's job characteristics either by university prestige or by the type of occupation. Women's jobs are essentially similar to each other in terms of female composition and intrinsic career potential. Occupational outcomes are simply quite homogeneous across female university graduates. In particular, women's attendance at elite institutions does not lead them into more desirable work settings or generate earnings advantages over time, whereas it does lead to their continuous employment and long-term career commitment.

On the other hand, men's elite university attendance produces substantial benefits both in terms of promotional potential and economic rewards over their early life course. This highlights the gender-segregated nature of the South Korean labor market and the fact that men and women are not treated in the same way, even when women attend the most elite institutions in the country.

WOMEN'S EDUCATION AND MARRIAGE OUTCOMES

Although university-educated women's outcomes in the labor market do not vary much by university prestige, their socioeconomic benefits from marriage do. *All* female university graduates in the sample had married men who were also four-year university graduates, and 43 percent of husbands had a graduate degree as well. Considering the overall sex ratio of two to one in this cohort of four-year university graduates, the fact that all of these women's husbands were also university graduates may not be so surprising. But closer examination of the data reveals that women's university prestige rankings are closely associated with their husbands'. Women in each prestige ranking are likely to be married to men who came from universities of the same prestige ranking, resulting in a pattern of educational homogamy with respect to university prestige. A little over half of all female university graduates in the survey have such homogamous marriages.[15] This pattern of educational homogamy is the most common for women from top-ranked universities (63 percent) and is less so for women from second-ranked (43 percent) and third-ranked universities (45 percent).

This educational homogamy may result from universities functioning as "marriage markets" where young people can meet a potential partner who comes from a university of the same prestige ranking. This marriage market function appears to be particularly important in South Korea, since most secondary schools are single-sex and hence provide relatively few opportunities for dating. Dating opportunities at university are not confined to coed institutions, since friends at university tend to play an active matchmaking role at the inter-university level by arranging many social gatherings for the purpose of dating (the equivalent of the American "blind date"). These gatherings have become an important part of university culture in South Korea. They are usually arranged by friends who attend different universities. These personal ties at the inter-university level are prevalent in South Korea partly because of the concentration of universities in big cities, especially in the Seoul area. The hierarchical prestige structure among universities tends to segregate the formation of personal ties and friends' gatherings according to prestige. About one-third of women in the survey met their husbands at their university or through university friends. These women were more likely to marry men who came from universities of the same prestige ranking, compared to women who met their husbands through other channels.

Another one-third of women met their husbands through other channels such as family members.[16] Even among these women, the largest proportion of women in each prestige ranking consists of those whose marriages are homogamous in terms of university prestige. For women from second- and third-ranked universities, their chances of marrying a man from a top-ranked university are higher if they are from a high social background (e.g., their father is in a professional or administrative occupation). However, even among women from similarly privileged social backgrounds, top-ranked university women have a significantly greater chance (69 percent) of marrying a man from a top-ranked university than women from second-ranked (37 percent) or third-ranked (30 percent) universities. This suggests that a homogamous pattern of marriage by university prestige comes from men's and women's strong preference to marry someone who shares a similar educational background—not just in terms of the level of educational attainment but also in terms of the prestige ranking of the university attended. In other words, strong status consciousness based on university prestige seems to influence the choice of a marriage partner. In fact, when someone tries to play a matchmaking role for young people with university education, he/she first asks which university they attended in order to see whether they will be a good match.

This tendency for status matching in marriage based on university prestige also implies that the traditional conception that women's overeducation is a disadvantage for their marriage prospects—because men expect their wives to have lower status than their own—no longer holds in South Korean society. Education is increasingly viewed by men (and their parents) as a valuable quality in a wife, not necessarily because of its economic benefits (labor market rewards to her education) but because of its symbolic and cultural importance for women's roles as mother and wife (Kim 1997). In a competitive society like South Korea where educational attainment is so heavily emphasized for children from a young age on, a woman's education is regarded as representing her "social and biological competence for motherhood" (Kim 1993: 195).

That marriage patterns among South Korean university graduates tend to be based on status matching of educational background is also evident from the proportions of husbands with graduate degrees. The likelihood of a husband having a graduate degree varies more according to the *woman's* than the man's university prestige; over half of the husbands married to top-ranked university women have a graduate degree (whether the husband is from a top-ranked or third-ranked university), compared to only about one-fifth of the husbands married to third-ranked university women.[17] This suggests that when a woman from an elite university marries a man from a less

TABLE 8.5

Husband's Occupation and Current Income
by Women's University Prestige

Husband's occupation	WOMEN'S UNIVERSITY PRESTIGE			
	First	Second	Third	Total
A. Husband's occupation (%)				
High-prestige prof./adm.[a]	47.3	31.3	28.7	36.6
Other white-collar	42.7	50.8	53.0	48.4
Sales/service	10.0	18.0	18.3	15.0
Total	100.0	100.0	100.0	100.0
(N)	150	128	115	393
B. Husband's current income (thousand in Korean won)				
Mean	1,862.2	1,803.6	1,659.7	1,769.6
(SD)	(814.9)	(844.5)	(697.3)	(793.7)

[a]High-prestige professional/administrative occupations include doctor, lawyer, engineer, professor, business owner with over 10 employees, mid- to high-level business executive, and high-level government official.

prestigious university, this husband's relatively lower educational status is usually supplemented by an advanced degree in order to better match the wife's elite educational status.

Table 8.5 shows that women from high-prestige universities are also more likely to be paired with men in high-prestige professional/administrative occupations and men with higher earnings. (The *t*-tests indicate that the difference in husbands' earnings between top- and third-ranked university women is statistically significant, while the difference between second- and third-ranked university women is not.) Considering that our survey data included female university graduates in their mid-30s whose husbands were still in a relatively early career stage, the differences in husbands' earnings are likely to widen further over time. Moreover, professional occupations such as doctor, lawyer, and high-level government official—to which a large number of husbands of top-ranked university women belong—signify high social status as well as high income in South Korean society. Thus, both the economic and social status gains from marriage are substantially greater for top-ranked university women than for others.

In short, even though women who attended the most prestigious universities do not derive greater benefits from their human capital in the labor market—especially in terms of earnings—their elite university education appears to confer a credential that is valuable in the marriage market. By marrying men from highly prestigious universities who tend to garner high earnings and to be in high-status occupations, these elite women derive greater socioeconomic benefits from marriage than women who attended less prestigious universities. In terms of overall socioeconomic gains, women's attendance at elite universities is a valuable investment—because of its effect on whom they marry.

CONCLUSION

Dramatic increases in university attendance among South Korean women in the past two decades raise the question of how university education contributes to women's socioeconomic outcomes in the labor market and the marriage market. In view of the relatively low rate of postmarital labor force participation among university-educated women, many people in South Korea assume that women seek university education primarily to marry a man of high socioeconomic potential rather than to pursue a career. But this chapter has shown that female university graduates in South Korea are not homogeneous with respect to their propensity for labor force participation and career commitment. Women's employment patterns can be largely divided into two types: one in which women pursue a lifelong career (and are continuously employed), and another in which women work for the period before marriage. Importantly, these patterns are associated both with women's educational background and with the nature of sex discrimination in the labor market.

Women from the most prestigious universities are more likely to participate in the labor force after marriage and are also more likely to be employed continuously over the early life course. This suggests a strong career commitment among elite women that is associated with their human capital, given that the prestige ranking of South Korean universities closely reflects individuals' academic ability and general human capital. At the same time, women in traditional female occupations are more likely to be working long-term than women in other professional and clerical occupations. This difference stems from the fact that most white-collar occupations do not provide equal opportunities to women and men; women tend to be segregated into less desirable jobs with little career potential, which in turn undermines their incentives for long-term employment.

Despite differences in women's career patterns according to university prestige, the characteristics of jobs and the socioeconomic rewards for female university graduates are surprisingly homogeneous and are strikingly different from those of their male counterparts. *Women's attendance at elite universities does not appear to produce any advantages in the labor market* in terms of the gendered nature of the job, the long-term promotional potential, or earnings. In great contrast, men's elite university attendance generates substantial economic benefits, consistent with prevailing beliefs in South Korean society. The white-collar professional jobs that are highly sought after by male university graduates provide greater long-term career opportunities and economic rewards than other occupations such as teaching. For women, these occupations do not involve the same kinds of career prospects. This strongly supports the view that female university graduates face different opportunities and treatment in the South Korean labor market than their male counterparts. *It is striking that women's elite university background does not mitigate the degree of sex discrimination or offer any economic benefit in this gender-segregated labor market.*

South Korean women's university prestige does produce socioeconomic outcomes *via marriage.* Women who attended highly prestigious universities are likely to marry men from similarly prestigious ones. This leads to higher socioeconomic benefits for them because of husbands' occupations and income. It remains ironic that despite their greater career commitment, women from prestigious universities in South Korea have an economic edge over women from less prestigious universities not because of the type of work they do but because of whom they marry.

APPENDIX TABLE 8.1

Discrete-Time Logit Model for Women's Leaving the Labor Force

	Model 1		Model 2	
Constant	−3.499***	(.230)	−3.436***	(.230)
University prestige				
First	−.361**	(.181)	−.291*	(.183)
Second	−.144	(.177)	−.128	(.178)
Third	—		—	
Graduate education				
Received a degree before work	—		−.465***	(.257)
Attended graduate school while working	—		−.121	(.379)
Occupational category				
Education-related	−.828***	(.183)	−.793***	(.183)
Pharmacy/nursing	−.659***	(.275)	−.687***	(.275)
Secretarial	.746***	(.198)	.701***	(.199)
Other white-collar	—		—	
Full-time vs. part-time job	−.839***	(.175)	−.800***	(.177)
Number of previous jobs held	.122**	(.072)	.119*	(.072)
Duration at work	−.010***	(.003)	−.011***	(.002)
Marital status				
Single to married	2.744***	(.280)	2.745***	(.281)
Married	.162	(.239)	.202	(.240)
Husband's social status	.313*	(.202)	.317*	(.204)
Presence of Children				
From pregnancy to childbirth	.848***	(.250)	.839***	(.250)
Any child under age 6	−.063	(.294)	−.053	(.294)
Any child over age 6	−.590***	(.236)	−.560***	(.237)
No child	—		—	
Maximum likelihood	2212.59		2208.78	
n with event	228		228	
Total N	25,542		25,542	

$* p < .10, ** p < .05, *** p < .01$ for one-tailed significance tests. Standard errors are in parentheses.

231

Regression Model for Job Characteristics

	FEMALE COMPOSITION RATE (EMPLOYEES ONLY)		EXPECTED PROMOTION (EMPLOYEES ONLY)		CURRENT EARNINGS (EMPLOYEES ONLY)	
	Women	Men	Women	Men	Women	Men
Constant	44.274**	20.409**	1.240**	1.963**	3.447**	4.276**
	(5.378)	(5.357)	(.206)	(.321)	(.246)	(.172)
University prestige						
First	−.228	−.438	.197	.421**	−.072	.150**
	(4.285)	(1.993)	(.150)	(.160)	(.095)	(.032)
Second	1.510	1.054	.182	.317*	−.090	.099**
	(4.199)	(1.986)	(.147)	(.160)	(.097)	(.032)
Third	—	—	—	—	—	—
Graduate degree	1.208	−7.300**	.186	−.291	−.022	.009
	(5.025)	(2.524)	(.176)	(.205)	(.085)	(.036)
Occupational category						
Education-related	—	—	—	—	—	—
Nursing/pharmacy	11.915**	5.191	.488**	1.052*	.025	—[a]
	(5.766)	(6.724)	(.204)	(.541)	(.158)	
Other white-collar	−5.285	−7.266**	.203	.882**	.313**	.161**
	(3.947)	(2.496)	(.159)	(.203)	(.084)	(.042)
Secretarial	−2.185	−3.808	−.275	.511	.098	.159*
(sales for men)	(5.380)	(4.133)	(.189)	(.333)	(.146)	(.082)
Organizational size	.106	−.258	.089**	.212**	.006	.005
(logged)	(1.016)	(.646)	(.036)	(.052)	(.024)	(.011)
Female incumbency rate			.002	−.010**	.001	−.002**
			(.002)	(.004)	(.001)	(.001)
Years of working					.333**	.139*
(logged)					(.090)	(.059)
Full-time work					.356**	.197*
					(.088)	(.090)
Marital status (single)					−.101	−.028
					(.096)	(.059)
Adjusted R^2	2.7	4.7	8.4	17.9	24.6	14.1
N	359	461	359	461	178	435

*$p < .05$, **$p < .01$ for one-tailed significance tests. Standard errors are in parentheses.

[a]Pharmacy is included in other white-collar occupations (there were no males in nursing jobs).

CHAPTER NINE

Taking Informality into Account

Women's Work in the Formal and Informal Sectors in Taiwan

Wei-hsin Yu

Women in the informal sector constitute a significant proportion of the labor force in many countries, including East Asian societies (Castells and Portes 1989; De Soto 1989; Portes 1994). Although definitions of the informal sector vary, it is common to consider it as composed of nonwage earners as opposed to wage and salaried workers in the formal sector (e.g., Beneria and Roldan 1987; Castells and Portes 1989; Choi 1994; De Sato 1990; Hill 1983). Unlike in Western industrial countries where a large proportion of female workers are wage or salaried employees, wage employment does not tell as much of the story for the female labor force in East Asia. For example, over 90 percent of the female labor force in the United States worked as wage earners in 1995, but in Japan, South Korea, and Taiwan that figure is only about 70 percent (Choi 1994; Yu 1999b). Not only is the proportion of female workers in the informal sector in East Asia relatively high, but women are overrepresented (relative to men) in nonwage employment in Japan and South Korea (e.g., Brinton 1989; Choi 1994; Hill 1983). These facts make it important to analyze informal sector employment in order to understand women's working lives in East Asia.

Despite the increasing attention paid to the informal sector, previous studies have tended to focus on the existence of the informal economy rather than the influence of informal work on individual workers (e.g., Castells and Portes 1989; Portes 1994; Portes and Sassen-Koob 1987). In the absence of adequate research on informal sector workers—namely, nonemployees—it is unclear what it means for women to participate in the labor force in this sector. Are women generally better or worse off in formal employment (i.e., wage or salaried workers), where jobs have fixed time schedules, specific job content, and regular pay? While some researchers argue that getting away from regular paid employment offers women increased flexibility and autonomy at work (Carr 1996; Jurik 1998), others see the use of self-employed female homeworkers as exploitation of women's labor (e.g., Beneria and Roldan 1987; Boris 1994). It is difficult to explain women's concentration in the informal sector and to assess the implications of this for gender inequality in society unless we figure out ways to empirically address this debate.

Just as it is ambiguous whether informal employment signifies opportunities or exploitation to women, the images of women in the informal sector are inconsistent across various studies. The conventional understanding characterizes workers in the informal sector as refugees from poverty who provide a reserve army that depresses the wages of the working class (see Portes 1994 for a review). However, there is evidence that the informal sector phenomenon has persisted in both developing and advanced countries and that not all informal sector workers are poor and therefore eager to enter the formal sector (Castells and Portes 1989; Choi 1994; Jurik 1998; Portes and Benton 1984; Portes and Sassen-Koob 1987; Steinmetz and Wright 1989).

So while a large proportion of women in East Asia have the experience of informal employment, the existing literature is not consistent enough for us to draw conclusions about the meaning of such experience for women in these societies. This chapter provides comparisons between female workers in the formal and informal sectors in Taiwan. By doing so, it contributes to an understanding of the female labor force in that society as well as to the general debate on the impact of informal employment on women. I compare women's individual qualifications as well as earnings, one of the major outcomes of work. The comparisons of worker qualifications across sectors provide a more complete picture of women in the informal sector. The comparisons of earnings indicate workers' well-being in these two sectors, although I certainly do not claim that earnings are a complete representation of women's work experience. Rather, the analyses here answer whether women's concentration in the informal sector increases or decreases their financial well-being. This has implications for the broader consideration of gender inequality in Taiwan.

PERSPECTIVES ON WOMEN, WORK, AND THE INFORMAL SECTOR

There are two main approaches regarding the determinants of women's earnings. On the one hand, human capital theorists provide a gender-neutral explanation of the earnings gap between men and women. A more structural approach, on the other hand, attributes women's lower earnings to gender-specific constraints. According to the former perspective, education, length of work experience, and on-the-job training make up one's human capital and contribute to one's earnings (Becker 1975, 1985; Polachek 1979, 1981). In contrast, many sociologists argue that earnings inequality cannot be interpreted by individual choices alone (e.g., England et al. 1988). For example, occupational sex segregation, as a structural outcome, explains a large proportion of the male-female wage gap (e.g., Goldin 1990; Hartmann 1976; Milkman 1987). This focuses attention on women's assignment to low-skill, dead-end, low-paying occupations through the process of occupational sex stereotyping.

Human capital theorists imply that the importance of human capital is constant across all employment sectors—wage and nonwage—of the economy. This is plausible if human capital is indeed made up of skills that enhance productivity. In contrast, the credentialist position would argue that human capital has only limited influence on earnings or occupational status attainment in unregulated and less institutionalized economic settings compared to large bureaucratic settings (Collins 1979; Faia 1981; Winkler 1987). Rather, "social capital" (Coleman 1988; Granovetter 1985), a concept introduced by sociologists to identify the role of social relations in economic activities, may be more important than human capital for small-business owners or self-employed people, since they may need more "trust" and tighter social networks to run their own businesses.

Like the human capital argument, a theory of sex segregation based on employers' sex stereotypes is an explanation that also largely ignores the informal sector. If women receive relatively low wages because employers assign them to certain occupations based on gender stereotyping, would self-employed women in the informal sector be better off because they are not so affected by employers' preferences? And if this is the case, would working in the informal sector be a way for women to shatter the effects of occupational sex segregation?

Dual-economy theorists clearly see women's work in the informal economy in a different way. They distinguish between "core" and "periphery" economies (also defined as "monopoly" and "competitive" sectors by some scholars) that have different patterns of employee recruitment and advancement, returns to human capital, and job stability. Rosenfeld (1983) shows that men and women have different opportunities to move out of the competitive sector and attain better career trajectories. The informal sector is included as a part of the periphery or competitive labor market in the dual-economy model. According to the theory, workers in the periphery have less job stability and lower incomes than those in the core sector. But by assuming that there are two labor markets corresponding to the core and the periphery sectors, the dual-economy perspective largely ignores variation *within* each sector (Althauser and Kalleberg 1981; Hodson and Kaufman 1982; Wallace and Kalleberg 1981). This may be empirically problematic.

Consistent with the dual-economy approach, previous studies of the informal sector have generally assumed it to be a transitory feature of Third World economies. Informal sector workers are characterized as refugees from poverty and are portrayed as a reserve army that suppresses the wages of the working class. But recent studies show that the informal sector is not limited to Third World settings (Castells and Portes 1989; Portes and Sassen-Koob 1987). And even though workers in the informal sector experience less state protection (in terms of minimum wage regulations, welfare benefits tied to employment, limitations on maximum working hours, etc.), have less stable levels of income, and work in a sector with higher rates of organizational mortality (business failure), to describe them as a homogeneously low-paid and low-skilled reserve army for the formal sector is to oversimplify matters (e.g., Choi 1994; Portes 1994.)

Because many previous studies on women's work either ignore women in the informal sector or provide a contradictory picture of them, we do not have a clear understanding of the implications of women's concentration in this sector for their well-being. This chapter asks two principal questions for the case of Taiwan: (1) Are there differences in female workers' qualifications in the formal and informal sectors? and (2) are there differences in the financial returns from jobs in the two sectors?

I compare working women's human capital (educational levels, work experience, and on-the-job tenure) between sectors in Taiwan in order to explore the adequacy of characterizing informal sector workers as possessing inferior human capital and being excluded from the formal sector. As for worker *outcomes*, I conduct analyses that aim to answer the following questions: Are education and on-the-job training equally relevant for informal sector workers? Are the determinants of women's earnings the same in both sectors? Because women in the informal sector are relatively immune from employers' tastes for discrimination (Goldin 1990), do they face fewer structural constraints on career achievement and therefore receive greater earnings than their formal sector counterparts?

BACKGROUND AND MACROLEVEL TRENDS

This section introduces the macrolevel trends in Taiwanese women's participation in the labor force, especially in the informal sector, over the last several decades. Aggregate data in government reports are the major source for the discussion here.

Women and Work in Taiwan

Female labor force participation by age in Taiwan has had a general U-shaped pattern across the last 40 years (figure 9.1). Industrialization in the postwar era led to a decline in the number of agricultural jobs for women in the beginning, and an increase in female employment in nonagricultural sectors later on. Before the mid-1960s, most women who reported themselves as working were in the agricultural sector (i.e., agriculture, forestry, hunting, and fishery), but current female labor force participation is concentrated mainly in nonprimary industries. Not only have female workers shifted from agricultural to nonagricultural jobs, but the proportion of married women in the labor force as well as in white-collar occupations has increased over time (see Brinton, Lee, and Parish, Chapter 2 this volume).

The employment status of women workers has also changed over time as a result of industrialization (figure 9.2). The proportion of unpaid family workers dropped rapidly as industrialization drastically shrank the relative size of the agricultural sector, while the numbers of self-employed workers declined only slowly. As would be expected, the number of paid female employees increased significantly after the 1970s.

This dynamic may lead some to argue that the informal sector, roughly measured by the proportion of nonwage employment in the labor force, will diminish as the economy grows. But a closer look reveals that for the last de-

Figure 9.1.   Female Labor Force Participation in Taiwan, 1951–1995

SOURCE: Directorate-General of Budget, Accounting, and Statistics, Executive Yuan, ROC, *Yearbook of Manpower Survey Statistics, Taiwan Area, Republic of China*, various years.

NOTE: FLFP = female labor force participation.

cade the proportion of female employers, self-employed workers, and family enterprise workers has dropped only slightly in Taiwan despite continuing economic development. The decline in the number of unpaid family workers and the rise of paid employees in the 1970s instead reflected the historical change in economic structure from agriculture to industry.[1]

The small amount of change in the size of the informal sector after the 1980s makes it unwarranted to conclude, at least for female workers, that

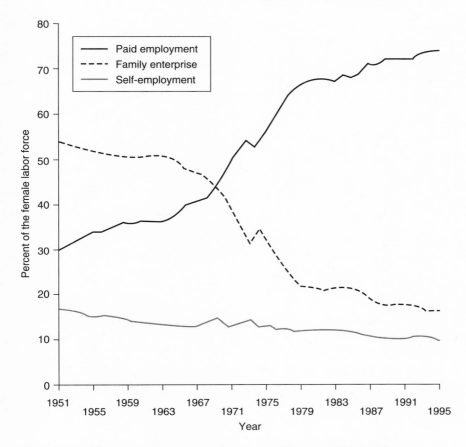

Figure 9.2.   Changes in Employment Structure in Taiwan, 1951–1995

SOURCE: Directorate-General of Budget, Accounting, and Statistics, Executive Yuan, ROC, *Yearbook of Manpower Survey Statistics, Taiwan Area, Republic of China*, various years.

this sector is transitional and destined to disappear as Taiwan becomes highly industrialized. Despite the rapid increase in salaried employment in the early stage of industrialization, a significant proportion of women remain in the informal sector in Japan and South Korea as well (Choi 1994; Yu 1999b). Experiences in none of these East Asian societies support the argument that the informal economy is no more than a transitional stage in the process of industrialization.

TABLE 9.1
Distribution of Employment Status in Selected Countries

	Self-employment	Family enterprise employment	Paid employment
United States	8.4	0.1	91.5
Western countries			
Canada	9.7	0.5	89.8
Germany	9.3	1.3	89.4
France	11.7	(not reported)	88.3
United Kingdom	12.7	0.6	86.7
Sweden	10.7	0.5	88.8
Taiwan	**22.1**	**8.4**	**69.5**
East Asian societies			
Japan	12.1	6.4	81.5
South Korea	27.9	9.5	62.5
Hong Kong	10.1	0.8	89.1
Singapore	10.6	1.2	87.9

SOURCES: Directorate-General of Budget, Accounting, and Statistics, Executive Yuan, ROC, *Yearbook of Manpower Survey Statistics, Taiwan Area, Republic of China*, 1995; International Labour Organisation, *Yearbook of Labor Statistics*, 1996; Statistics Bureau, Japan, *Statistics of Japan*, 1997.

NOTES: All figures are in percentages. Figures do not include workers whose status was not classifiable. Some rows do not add up to 100.0 because of rounding errors. Figures of the United States, France, and Hong Kong are for 1994, and figures of United Kingdom and Canada are for 1993, while the rest are for 1995.

The Informal Sector in Taiwan

The size of the informal sector in Taiwan is large compared to many other societies (table 9.1). Wage or salaried employment constituted only 70 percent of the labor force in 1995, far smaller than in Western industrial countries. I consider the following three groups of workers as informal sector workers: (1) self-employed workers with zero or fewer than five employees, (2) family enterprise workers, and (3) home-based pieceworkers. Workers in these categories are likely to work in environments where job content, job tenure, and earnings are all uncertain. Moreover, these workers are less likely to be protected by existing regulations. The time and place of work for these categories of workers are also relatively flexible, and the characteristics of these types of employment status allow workers to be involved in informal arrangements of production. For example, home-based pieceworkers and self-employed workers are often included in informal, seasonal subcontracting work, and family enterprise workers are likely to have irregular working hours that depend on the weekly or daily demands of work.

I exclude from the informal employment definition those self-employed workers who hire more than five employees. Given the low average size of Taiwanese businesses, the working environments of firms that are this size are relatively stable and their production arrangements are relatively visible to state authorities.[2] In contrast, self-employed workers who operate larger establishments are more likely to be subject to tax law and other regulations.

Taiwan's unique industrial structure to some extent explains the large number of individuals working in the informal sector. The specific organizational structure that is argued to be a result of the role the state played in the early stage of development contributes to the sector's relatively large size (Hamilton and Biggart 1988; Noble 1998). Taiwan's recent economic growth was accomplished through labor-intensive industries and production activities distributed across an unusually large number of small firms throughout the island (Deyo 1989; Galenson 1979). According to Brinton, Lee, and Parish (Chapter 2 this volume), in 1990 only 8 percent of Taiwan's employees worked in companies with over 500 employees, and only 24 percent worked in firms with more than 100 employees. By contrast, in South Korea, one of Taiwan's rapidly developing East Asian counterparts, 35 percent of all employees worked in firms of over 300 people.

Furthermore, because the Taiwanese economy consists mainly of labor-intensive industries, little technology and capital are required for a person to become self-employed. Given their small size, most firms lack the ability to recruit many full-time employees, who request long-term benefits and stable wages. Heavy reliance on an extensive subcontracting system allows firms to respond to macroeconomic changes efficiently and rapidly, but also creates a large number of temporary or home-based pieceworkers, most of whom are female (Shieh 1989). Contract workers, short-term or part-time workers, and home-based pieceworkers constitute a sizable proportion of the informal labor force. Even though some of these workers are regulated by law and pay taxes, most of them work "underground." Thus the size of the informal sector in Taiwan as shown in table 9.1 may actually be greatly underestimated. Statistics measuring the female labor force are even more problematic because most home-based pieceworkers and short-term workers identify themselves as "housewives," a group that believes and is believed to be "not working" even though it is involved in economic activities.[3]

Unpaid or irregularly paid family enterprise workers, another predominantly female group, also contribute to the size of the informal sector in Taiwan (Cheng and Hsiung 1994; also Lu, Chapter 10 this volume). Most Taiwanese firms are family based (Hamilton and Biggart 1988), and many small to medium-sized firms are composed of extended family members and one or two additional nonfamily employees. Because of the low profit and high risk associated with the small enterprise scale, most small family enterprises employ wives of self-employed husbands as unpaid labor because they provide flexible labor at no cost (again see chapter by Lu). Even those family firm-based workers who are paid are likely to have wages below the average market price. It is also common for family enterprise workers to be paid irregularly, particularly in times of economic fluctuation (Ka 1993; Li and Ka 1994).

COMPARISONS BETWEEN SECTORS: WORKER QUALIFICATIONS

Researchers who employ a dual-economy approach characterize the informal sector as having low entry barriers in terms of skills and capital and containing a homogeneous group of poor and less-educated workers. But does such a description fit women in the informal sector in East Asia?

Very few women in Japan, South Korea, or Taiwan start their first job in the informal sector (Choi 1994; Yu 1999b). Nonetheless, nearly 50 percent of married women in Taiwan who are currently working and over 60 percent of their South Korean counterparts, according to Chapter 2, are in the informal sector (see table 2.1). The overall proportion of women in self-employment and family enterprise employment is much smaller in Japan than in Taiwan or South Korea, but Japanese women display the same tendency to move out of regular, full-time wage employment as they age (Yu 1999b). In short, many women working in the informal sector in East Asia have previously held former sector jobs. A dualist approach would not predict the formal and informal sectors to share workers. So the assumption that the formal and informal sectors absorb workers with different qualifications may not be valid for women in East Asia.

I defined above the informal labor force in Taiwan as consisting of self-employed workers with zero or fewer than five employees, family enterprise workers, and part-time, temporary, or home-based pieceworkers. Within the formal sector, I categorize paid employees into government employees and private enterprise employees because the recruitment methods and employment patterns of these two are quite different. All government employees in Taiwan are recruited through national examinations (*gaopukao*),[4] which to a great extent eliminates discrimination against women at the time of recruitment. "Permanent employment" is assumed once one enters civil service;[5] furthermore, most public employees are assured a pension and medical insurance, benefits that cannot be taken for granted in private enterprises. Although there are a few areas of public employment that are traditionally segregated by sex, wages in the government sector are to a large extent based on seniority. Because the government employment system in Taiwan has been designed this way, female public employees are likely to be less affected by gender discrimination in the workplace than their private enterprise counterparts and they generally receive higher income as well. Thus I consider private enterprise and public employees separately even though they are both in the formal sector.

Statistics in the remainder of the chapter are from the Taiwan Women and Family Survey (ROC 1989). I include only women in urban areas.[6] I exclude members of the agricultural population (those whose current job is classified as being in agriculture) because self-employment in the agricultural sector generally has different work conditions than urban self-employment. Further, I include only those women who have been married at least once because their career expectations and work patterns are likely to differ from those of never-married women.[7]

Human Capital of Female Workers across Sectors

Table 9.2 describes worker characteristics (age, human capital, and family background) in the formal and informal sectors, with each sector divided into several groups. To compare human capital, I show by type of employment the means for years of education, total work experience and tenure of the current job, and proportion of women who left the labor force immediately after the time of their first marriage. This last figure reflects employment interruption by marriage, and therefore possible human capital depreciation (Polachek 1979, 1981). I define women whose employment was

TABLE 9.2

Characteristics of Urban Married Women in the Formal and Informal Sectors,
Classified by Employment Status

| | | FORMAL SECTOR | | INFORMAL SECTOR | | |
	No job	Government employees	Private enterprise workers	Self-employed workers	Family enterprise workers	Home-based pieceworkers/ temporary workers
Age	41.0	39.7	38.0	41.4	38.0	39.2
Hours of work	N.A.	45.1	49.0	61.0	61.2	46.7
Human capital						
Education (in years)	7.8	12.3	8.8	7.5	8.2	6.7
Work experience (in years)	7.4	17.7	13.5	18.6	18.1	14.4
Tenure of current job (in years)	N.A.	13.9	6.2	10.3	10.7	5.6
Out of labor force after marriage						
Yes	75.2	9.1	18.6	12.4	8.5	17.8
No	24.8	90.9	81.4	87.6	91.5	82.2
Family background						
Father's employment status[a]						
Employee	34.7	53.9	38.5	31.6	22.6	30.7
Nonemployee	56.6	43.6	57.9	61.2	73.8	65.1
Other	8.8	2.5	3.6	7.2	3.5	4.3
Husband's employment status						
Employee	59.5	83.7	71.9	47.1	9.0	68.1
Nonemployee	30.0	8.7	17.0	42.0	89.4	19.0
Unemployed	7.6	4.1	4.1	4.7	1.0	5.5
Widowed/divorced	2.9	3.6	7.0	6.2	0.5	7.4
N	817	197	442	193	199	163
Percentage of the sample	40.6	9.8	22.0	9.6	9.9	8.1

SOURCE: Taiwan Women and Family Survey, 1989.

NOTES: The employment statuses shown here are based on the current job or the last major job the respondent held in 1988. Values other than averages are percentages; "N.A." signifies "not applicable."

[a]The statuses listed here reflect the father's major job across his life span. "Other" signifies respondents who answered "don't know" or "unemployed."

interrupted by marriage as those who were absent from the labor force the year they got married and remained out of work for at least 24 months.

Looking first at the column for nonemployed women, we can discern a correlation between marriage and employment interruption. A large proportion (75 percent) of those who did not hold a job had withdrawn from the labor force at the time of marriage. The average years of work experience for this group were much lower than for all others. In other words, most women who left the labor force upon marriage spent a relatively short time in the workplace and had a less continuous employment pattern than the rest of the sample. In contrast, women who did not quit right after marrying were likely to remain working for quite a long time.

In addition to the mean values of education, work experience, and on-the-job tenure in table 9.2, I compare human capital among female workers by age cohort to control for age differences between employment groups (figure 9.3). The first chart in the figure shows that with the exception of public employees, a group selected through national examinations, educational differences between workers in the formal and informal sectors are not as great as some studies of the informal sector suggest. Even though on average formal employees in private enterprises have slightly more education than informal sector workers, they have less than one year more than the average self-employed or family enterprise worker.

Moreover, women in the informal sector, specifically self-employed and family enterprise workers, are likely to have much more work experience and on-the-job tenure than formal employees in private enterprises (figure 9.3). The fact that fewer workers in the informal sector quit upon marriage suggests that informal sector workers have a more continuous employment pattern than formal employees in private firms. A continuous employment pattern generally represents greater human capital accumulation and, as Rosenfeld (1978) shows, contributes to higher occupational achievement. The relatively long on-the-job tenure of self-employed and family enterprise workers also implies that job security for certain types of employment in the informal sector may be comparable to formal sector employment in private enterprises.

While the difference in human capital between formal and informal sector workers is not as great as one may imagine, there certainly are differences among workers in education, work experience, and on-the-job tenure *within* the informal sector. Temporary, part-time, and home-based pieceworkers

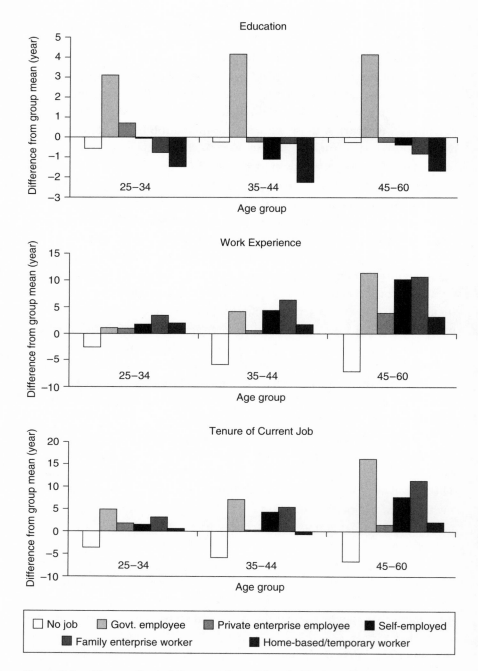

Figure 9.3. Human Capital Composition of Female Workers, by Age and Type of Employment

SOURCE: Taiwan Women and Family Survey, 1989.

NOTES: Each bar indicates the difference between the mean of the employment status group and the mean of the age group. Employment status is recorded based on the primary job the respondents held in 1988.

generally match the conventional expectation of low education and work experience. Even so, this group of workers does not necessarily have less work experience than formal sector employees in private firms. These figures also show differences within the formal sector: government employees have far more education, work experience, and job tenure than private enterprise employees. This is true for all age groups.

These human capital comparisons lead to two conclusions. First, using education and work experience (both over the life span and in on-the-job work experience) as proxies for human capital, we can clearly see considerable variation across job types within the informal sector. While temporary and home-based pieceworkers to some extent match the conventional descriptions of informal sector workers—that is, they are poorly educated and work less continuously and for fewer years of their life—the other two groups of women in the informal sector by no means represent the most disadvantaged in terms of education. Further, the relatively large amount of work experience these two groups possess indicates quite continuous employment patterns over the life span. This is consistent with the argument that informal employment is *not* an outlet for homogeneously poor and unskilled workers.

Second, after excluding full-time government employees who work in environments with greater potential for upward mobility, descriptive statistics do not support the argument that formal sector employees as a whole have more human capital than informal sector workers. Although they have slightly less education, family enterprise workers and the self-employed actually have more work experience on average than paid employees in private enterprises.

Beyond Human Capital: Other Worker Qualifications

Discussions of the informal sector do not consider the possibility that specific qualifications are required for working there. However, lacking institutional arrangements that match individuals with jobs, informal employment relies more on personal relations and social networks than formal employment (Granovetter 1985). If social networks are necessary for entering self-employment, it oversimplifies matters to argue that entry barriers are lower for entering the informal than the formal sector and that the informal labor force possesses fewer skills.

I use qualitative data to illustrate this particular type of qualification (network ties) for informal sector workers. I conducted personal interviews in Taipei in 1994 with women in the informal sector in order to investigate whether women's participation there results from inferior qualifications, a lack of opportunities for formal employment, or necessary compromises between work and family. Respondents were located through snowball sampling. My conversations with these women reveal that in order to enter certain types of informal employment and be productive, one needs social networks that enhance information flows. As a result, it is arguable that some informal sector women are more qualified as workers than women in the formal sector.

Within the informal sector, self-employed women in particular rely on social networks to initiate their work. According to my interviews, women who became self-employed usually knew people in the same business who could provide them with important information and the proper connections. Some of them had enough connections to acquire patrons before they switched from formal to informal sector employment. The three examples below represent the general conditions in which women become employers or self-employed. In the first example, a middle-aged woman describes how she started a videotape rental store with help from a friend who had been in the same business for a long time:

> At that time, my husband worked for his family business and his brother controlled the money. We only got an allowance. So I wanted to work to save some money of our own. I did not know anything about the videotape rental business then. But one of our friends had been in the business for a long time. He told me it was a good business with good profits. At the beginning, he helped me with everything. He told me where to get videotapes, which ones to buy, and many other details about running a videotape store. I picked it up after a while.

Talking about her experience managing the store, she briefly describes how social relations affect her business:

> Other owners of videotape rental stores seem to know each other well. Sometimes they will get together to decide on something about the business. I don't know many of them. They won't invite me to their meetings because I am a woman and they look down on me. Sometimes when there is some trouble in my business I am less able to handle it since I am not in the group of other owners. It is hard for me to compete when I don't know their decisions. Fortunately, the friend who helped me at the beginning gives me some information

from time to time. Besides, if you know the salesmen well [who sell videotapes to individual rental stores], they will tell you some news they have heard, too.

A hairdresser who worked as an employee in a beauty salon for nearly 30 years explains how her self-employment resulted from contacts with her old customers. Her already-established social network reduced the risks of self-employment and encouraged her to launch her own business:

> When I retired from the hair salon, a lot of my old clients asked me to keep working. We had known each other for so long. I felt it wasn't right to let them down. So I put two chairs at home and started my work here. Now I have some new clients, but a lot of them are my old clients, too. They all introduced each other to me. I have known some of them for 10 or 20 years. Now we are really good friends. Some of my customers spend hours traveling to come here to have a hair perm. I have a record for each customer. Sometimes I will contact them to see how they are doing, or remind them it's time to perm their hair again, and so on.

Another example of starting a business is from a woman in her early 30s who owns a home-based interior design firm and has a few employees. She talked about the use of social networks when she described the first time she left the formal sector to initiate a business with three other employees in the same former company:

> We four decided to leave the company partly because we didn't like the policies. We were all managers in the old company. To start, we hired one bookkeeper in addition to us four. We had the salesperson from the former company on our team, and our former design manager was on the team. We got a lot of cases through the manager's personal networks (*ren mai*). He was really good at managing social relations. We were quite busy from the very start.

As revealed in table 9.2, a large proportion of self-employed women have fathers or husbands who are not paid employees. Even though not all self-employed women acquire social connections through family members, being from families with members who are nonemployees helps to provide some social networks in the informal sector. Social connections are also critical for family enterprise workers, since by definition they obtain their work through relatives. Thus it is not surprising that a large number of female workers in this group too have fathers who are not paid employees (table 9.2). The proportion of husbands who are nonemployees is also extremely high (89 percent). In the case of family enterprise workers, social ties bring more obligations than advantages. These workers contribute their labor in exchange for hardly any pay. But the relationship between social ties and family enterprise employment nevertheless indicates that insufficient qualifications are not necessarily the reason why women in family enterprises are where they are.

To sum up, it is inaccurate to claim that informal sector female workers in Taiwan are a group of unskilled individuals eager to enter the formal sector. On the contrary, their levels of human capital are often comparable to workers in the formal sector and they may also have other qualifications. The examples from personal interviews show that social networks play a key role in women becoming self-employed.

EARNINGS OF FEMALE WORKERS ACROSS SECTORS

Does the informal sector then provide a reasonable set of alternatives for women or, conversely, does it increase the exploitation of women's labor? To shed light on this, it is necessary to look at the relative economic well-being of women in the informal versus the formal sector.

Although I showed above that informal sector workers do not necessarily possess less human capital, it is not clear whether it is as useful to them as it would be in the formal sector. If, as neoclassical economists argue, human capital is a stock of skills one invests in through formal education and work experience, we should find equal returns (payment) regardless of sectoral constraints. But if human capital contributes little to productivity but is instead used mainly by employers to justify hiring and promotion decisions, we should find lower or zero returns to human capital in the informal sector, where women's work and earnings are not affected by employer decisions.

Dual-economy theory, in contrast, simply assumes inferior income for informal sector workers. But it overlooks the fact that because of gender discrimination in the workplace, women in the formal sector may not obtain good, promising jobs that guarantee high pay and upward mobility. Thus dual-economy theory oversimplifies matters in assuming that formal sector jobs will necessarily provide more earnings than all types of informal sector jobs.

Table 9.3 shows women's earnings across sectors. Because there is great variation in work hours among female workers in different sectors, I mea-

TABLE 9.3

Hourly Earnings of Female Workers in the Formal
and Informal Sectors

	HOURLY EARNINGS (IN NT$)			
	Government employees	Private enterprise employees	Self-employed workers	Home-based pieceworker/ temporary workers
Percentile				
25%	318.2	166.7	153.1	92.7
50%	437.5	214.3	238.1	139.8
75%	568.2	333.3	428.6	196.2
Mean	456.0	311.2	398.9	153.4
Standard deviation	209.8	276.4	594.2	87.0
N	194	415	159	144

SOURCE: Taiwan Women and Family Survey, 1989.

sure earnings by reported hourly income. (I exclude family enterprise workers here because most of them report no income.)

Full-time government employees have the greatest mean earnings and show relatively low variation. Their high average income is not surprising given that they have the greatest years of education and work experience. Moreover, because the wage levels in government service are regulated by government rules based on objective factors such as seniority and education, we would expect variation to be relatively low. In contrast, part-time, home-based pieceworkers appear to match the dual-economy theorists' expectation: they have the lowest income whether measured at the mean or by quartiles.

Table 9.3 also demonstrates an interesting comparison between self-employed workers and private enterprise employees. Self-employed women have a higher average income but also show greater variation than private enterprise employees. The difference in the two means is not significant by t-test ($t = 2.41$). Nevertheless, the quartiles of the hourly earnings of self-employed women and private enterprise employees reveal that although the former who earn *less* than the median are worse off than low-income female employees in private enterprises, those whose income is *above* the median have a higher average hourly income than their private enterprise counterparts.

TABLE 9.4
Hourly Earnings of Female Private Enterprise Employees
and Self-Employed Workers by Occupation

	PRIVATE ENTERPRISE EMPLOYEES			SELF-EMPLOYED WORKERS		
Occupations	*Hourly earnings (in NT$)*	*Number of cases*	*Percentage*	*Hourly earnings (in NT$)*	*Number of cases*	*Percentage*
Upper-level white-collar	740.3	49	11.8	445.2	74	46.5
Lower-level white-collar	328.0	169	40.7	379.6	66	41.5
Blue-collar	190.0	197	47.4	285.3	19	11.9
N		415			159	

SOURCE: Taiwan Women and Family Survey, 1989.

The comparison of earnings between self-employed and private enterprise workers by occupation provides additional insight into the distribution of income across these two groups. In table 9.4, I divide workers into three occupational categories: (1) upper-level white-collar, including professional and managerial positions, (2) lower-level white-collar, such as clerical, sales, and service jobs, and (3) blue-collar occupations. Although private enterprise employees on average have higher income than self-employed women in the high-prestige occupations—professional, administrative, or managerial—only a small proportion of them (12 percent) are able to reach this level. (In fact, a large proportion of women in private enterprises are manual workers.) In contrast, over 80 percent of the self-employed report that they are in white-collar occupations. That is to say, a large proportion of female private enterprise employees are located in lower-level white-collar and blue-collar occupations with lower mean hourly wages than self-employed workers in the same occupations. Thus the comparison by occupation across sectors shows that with the exception of the top tier of workers, self-employment yields *higher* mean hourly wages for female workers.

The earnings differences between sectors could still conceivably be attributed to individual characteristics such as education and work experience rather than to sectoral constraints. In order to examine the extent to which human capital explains women's earnings by employment status, I use regression analysis to construct a model in which the dependent variable is hourly earnings measured as the natural log of gross hourly individual earnings from employment in 1988 (in New Taiwanese dollars, or NT$). *Years of education* is measured by the level of education the respondent completed.[8] *Work experience* is measured by total years spent in the labor force.[9] Because on-the-job training is often emphasized by human capital theory, I also include *number of years on the current job* as a predictor. In addition to these variables, I control for age. I use a quadratic specification for age (age + age^2) because, as economists would argue, a worker's productivity decreases after reaching a certain age. The age effect could also be curvilinear because of age discrimination against older workers. The results are reported as model 1 in table 9.5.

The results in table 9.5 show that model 1 has far more predictive power in the formal sector, which includes both government and private enterprise employees, than in the informal sector (self-employment and temporary or home-based piecework). As human capital theory would predict, both education and on-the-job work experience have positive and significant effects on women's earnings in the formal sector. The total amount of time spent in the labor force does not contribute to one's wages. Further, for private enterprise employees, age shows a convex curvilinear effect on income. That is, women's earnings initially increase with age, but after a certain point age is associated with lower income. The effects of age are not as significant for government employees as for private enterprise employees, perhaps because wage levels in government service in Taiwan are based on length of service within the sector. Therefore, it is understandable to find instead a positive effect of on-the-job tenure on wages in government service jobs.

By contrast, the human capital model does not do a good job of explaining women's earnings in the informal sector. For self-employment, education is the only significant predictor in model 1. Work experience and on-the-job training show no significant effects. I argue that education has a positive effect on self-employed women's earnings here not only because education represents one's skills or capability but also because education to some extent contributes to the kinds of social networks one has. Both of these functions of education influence the types of self-employment to which one can obtain access and how well one manages business as a self-employed

TABLE 9.5

Unstandardized Coefficients from Regression Models Predicting Log Hourly Earnings

	Government employees		Private enterprise workers		Self-employed workers		Home-based pieceworkers/ temporary workers	
	MODEL 1	MODEL 2	MODEL 1	MODEL 2	MODEL 1	MODEL 2	MODEL 1	MODEL 2
Age	.045† (1.67)	.051† (1.97)	.090** (2.88)	.060* (2.19)	.042 (.59)	.047 (.66)	-.040 (-.62)	-.044 (-.71)
Age²	-.001† (-1.70)	-.001* (-2.10)	-.001** (-2.71)	-.001* (-2.16)	.000 (-.57)	-.001 (-.64)	.000 (.35)	.000 (.46)
Work experience	.000† (1.79)	.000† (1.84)	.000 (.83)	.000 (.80)	.000 (.44)	.000 (.36)	.000 (.42)	.000 (.46)
On-the-job tenure	.012* (2.46)	.009* (2.18)	.013** (2.63)	.008† (1.76)	.005 (.56)	.006 (.67)	.029** (3.04)	.028** (2.95)
Education	.088** (10.79)	.057** (5.19)	.084** (11.87)	.030** (3.65)	.082** (4.24)	.076** (3.80)	-.008 (-.49)	-.010 (-.55)

Occupation	(1)	(2)	(3)	(4)	(5)	(6)	(7)	(8)
Professional	—	.432** (3.22)	—	.986** (11.18)	—	.086 (.40)	—	— (no observation)
Clerical	—	.244† (1.95)	—	.399** (5.66)	—	.927 (1.55)	—	.540 (.98)
Sales	—	.569* (1.25)	—	.572** (5.92)	—	.061 (.28)	—	— (no observation)
Service	—	.046 (.32)	—	.013 (.19)	—	-.140 (.65)	—	-.057 (-.48)
Manual	—	—	—	—	—	—	—	—
Constant	3.850** (6.99)	3.883** (2.13)	2.847** (4.56)	3.766** (6.79)	3.976** (2.65)	3.849* (2.51)	5.846** (4.50)	5.974** (4.55)
Adjusted R-squared	.45	.52	.31	.47	.09	.08	.09	.09
N	193	193	413	413	158	158	144	144

NOTE: Figures in parentheses are t statistics.

†$p < .10$, *$p < .05$, **$p < .01$.

worker. Among temporary or home-based workers, only on-the-job work experience has a significant effect on earnings. Since most part-time or home-based piecework is paid by piece rate, the period of time one stays in the current job is related to how efficiently and skillfully one handles the work; therefore, it positively affects hourly earnings. The fact that age has no significant effect on earnings in the informal sector suggests that there may not be a tight relationship between age and productivity. The effect of age in the formal sector, I would argue, may well be a result of employers' *expectations* for a connection between age and productivity.

Because the occupational distribution varies greatly across employment statuses, perhaps this accounts for the earnings differences between self-employment and private enterprise employment. To see whether this is true I control for occupation in model 2 of table 9.5. Dummy variables for four occupational categories are included: professional and managerial jobs, clerical work, sales work, and service work.

The addition of occupation in model 2 helps explain earnings differences in particular for private enterprise employees, but occupation does not have any significant effect on women's earnings in the informal sector. Among private enterprise employees, the effect of education is reduced from 0.84 to 0.30 after occupation is taken into account. Further, the effect of on-the-job tenure becomes less statistically significant. That is to say, for women who are employed in private enterprises, occupation takes away the importance of human capital. Instead, occupation itself determines earnings to a great extent. The magnitude of the occupational effects shows that among private enterprise employees professional women make the highest earnings, sales workers come in second followed by clerical workers, and manual laborers receive the lowest earnings. Similar regression results are found for government employees, but the wage differences between occupations are not as great and as significant as in private enterprises.

From the results of model 1 in table 9.5, I estimate the earnings of a woman with fixed characteristics in both the formal and informal sectors. I use the averages in the sample of working women for this hypothetical woman: she is 39.2 years old, has 14.5 years of work experience in total, 8.9 years of education, and has been on her current job for 8.4 years.

The hourly earnings of this hypothetical woman would be NT$260, NT$252, NT$275, and NT$147 in government service, private enterprise (as a full-time employee), self-employment, or temporary or home-based piecework respectively. (But see the caution in note 10.)[10] The first three types of work therefore show little earnings difference after controlling for age, education, work experience, and on-the-job tenure. This "average" woman in fact earns slightly more in self-employment than in the formal sector. Temporary or home-based pieceworkers, in contrast, receive less than 60 percent of the earnings of women in the other three groups. Working under contractors or for small satellite factories, home-based pieceworkers resemble wage earners in the sense that they do not own the means of production (Shieh 1992b). But unlike wage earners they are not protected by institutional arrangements. Furthermore, almost all home-based pieceworkers are in low-skilled blue-collar occupations. All of these conditions make them the most disadvantaged workers in terms of earnings.

Discussion

Because of the variation in earnings among informal sector workers, this chapter does not support the idea that formal sector employment is definitely economically better than informal sector work for women in Taiwan. One explanation is the dominant organizational structure in Taiwan. Very small firms make up a large proportion of Taiwanese business. Even though informal sector employment in most economies is riskier and less protected by the state, in an environment like Taiwan where formal establishments are small, there is not as much difference in worker outcomes between formal and informal employment. For example, in Taiwan, self-employed women do not have lower average earnings than do formal sector workers in private enterprises, and both groups are likely to receive medical insurance but unlikely to receive pensions from their jobs.[11]

But organizational structure may not be the only explanation. Occupational differences within each sector also explain why formal sector employment does not necessarily lead to financial well-being for Taiwanese women. Model 2 of table 9.5 shows that some occupations bring greater earnings than others in private enterprises. For example, the top white-collar occupations (professional and managerial occupations) have much higher earnings than all other occupations. The comparisons between formal private enterprise employment and self-employment in table 9.4 show that upper-level white-collar jobs in formal sector employment *do* provide greater average earnings than similar occupations for self-employed workers. But more than 80 percent of female full-time employees in private enterprises are in lower-level white-collar or blue-collar occupations. And the average earnings in these occupations are lower than in the same occupations in self-employment.

Further, the number of women who work in large firms indicates the low likelihood for women to obtain "good jobs"—that is, jobs with potential to move up job ladders within a firm. Survey data show that only 4 percent of married women in formal, private employment worked for firms of 100 or more employees and had upper-level white-collar jobs in 1988 (ROC 1989). When we include all white-collar occupations, the figure increases only to 15 percent. The majority of female workers in the formal sector are either in small private firms that cannot afford much pay or in manufacturing factories that make profits out of cheap labor, as labor-intensive methods are the major way of production in Taiwan. In small firms, unsurprisingly, upward mobility is limited given that there are hardly any job ladders. In short, because most female full-time employees in Taiwan's private enterprises hold low-skilled, dead-end jobs, formal employment does not necessarily generate higher earnings than self-employment

Although the dual-economy approach is not supported by the findings, it would be a mistake to conclude that sectoral constraints are unimportant for women's earnings. Women's earnings are determined differently across sectors and employment statuses in Taiwan's economy. The earnings returns to human capital are more consistent and greater in the formal than the informal sector. Such different dynamics in determining earnings demonstrate that education and on-the-job work experience not only represent the skills required for work but also to some extent function as credentials that serve a signaling purpose in the formal sector. The effect of education on earnings drops by more than one-half when occupations are added into the model. Therefore, I argue that education plays a key role in signaling and placing employees into various occupations. While jobs in the informal sector are more likely to be obtained through kinship or personal ties, educational credentials are more important for attaining positions in a bureaucratic environment.

Compared with formal employment in private enterprises, self-employment has an equivalent or slightly more beneficial effect on earnings. Further, within the informal sector, self-employment has an earnings advantage over irregular or home-based piecework. These findings raise yet more questions related to the informal sector. If self-employment seems to be a good choice, relatively speaking, who is qualified to enter this kind of work? Why would those who hold unfavorable jobs in the formal sector not shift to work as self-employed persons? Is this solely a matter of individual volition? Moreover, since human capital is a poor predictor of earnings in the informal sector, what is an alternative explanation for women's earnings there?

In my discussion of entry barriers to the informal versus formal sector, I suggested that social capital is an important asset in the informal economy as well as a critical entry barrier to self-employment. One can argue that the monetary capital one needs in order to acquire the means of production to be self-employed is a major barrier and that lack of funds may keep women who are located in much worse positions in the formal sector from moving to self-employment. The initial capital is definitely a barrier for many women. But given the typically small scale of operation, the costs are quite low for one to become self-employed in Taiwan.[12] Therefore I doubt that it is sufficient to explain the movement or stasis of workers in different employment statuses. I suspect instead that social capital, which can reduce the risks associated with self-employment, may be a major factor for individuals in making the move to the informal sector and a major asset in determining earnings among self-employed workers. The chapter by Lu in this volume provides additional ethnographic data on social capital and tiny family-based firms.

CONCLUSION

This study began as an exploration of the implications of women's participation in the informal sector. But the findings show that the female informal labor force in Taiwan is so heterogeneous that a simple distinction between the formal and informal sectors is not adequate for studying women's participation in the economy. In many countries, including South Korea and Japan, women are overrepresented in the informal sector, a fact that is often used to explain gender inequality (Beneria and Roldan 1987; Choi 1994; Hadjicostandi 1990; Hill 1983; Truelove 1990; Yu 1999b). The presumed connection between women in the informal sector and gender inequality is based on the assumption that informal employment leads to inferior earnings and requires few qualifications. This study, however, reveals that women in the informal sector in Taiwan are *not* homogeneously unskilled, poor, and inferior to formal sector employees in terms of educational level, work experience, and the earnings they obtain from work.

This should make us question whether the attempt to evaluate informal sector work as a whole is reasonable in the first place. The comparisons of individual qualifications and earnings in this study both show that workers within the informal sector are *not* equal. Informal sector jobs certainly share some characteristics such as uncertain work environments, nonstandardized work content, and low job stability, but the differences between informal sector jobs are not minor. Dividing informal sector workers into three categories (self-employed workers, family enterprise workers, and home-based pieceworkers) by employment status, I have shown that self-employed and family enterprise workers possess human capital comparable to formal sector employees in private enterprises, and self-employed women may even have *more* social capital (i.e., social networks that enhance business performance) and receive slightly higher earnings than formal sector employees. In contrast, home-based pieceworkers match the stereotype of informal sector workers in both qualifications and earnings. They tend to have less human capital and make far less money than their counterparts in other types of employment. All these findings lead to the conclusion that distinctions should be made between types of employment rather than between sectors.

In addition to showing the heterogeneity within the informal sector, my research shows that very different dynamics determine women's earnings in the formal and informal sectors. In the beginning of this chapter, I asked whether the concept of human capital is as useful in the informal as in the formal sector and whether the former has fewer structural barriers to upward mobility for women. As the findings show, education, work experience, and on-the-job tenure are hardly good predictors for women's earnings in Taiwan's informal sector. In short, human capital does not contribute much to earnings in an environment where rules for promotions and earnings increases are not standardized. This finding casts doubt on the argument that human capital influences earnings because it enhances productivity—its effect on productivity theoretically should not differ between sectors.

Certain types of informal employment appear to be more advantageous for women's earnings in Taiwan than the most usual type of formal employment, full-time employment in private enterprises. There are two reasons for this. First, Taiwanese women employed in private enterprises have limited access to promising jobs; most are instead in blue-collar occupations. By contrast, self-employed women are likely to be in white-collar occupations despite their slightly lower education. Women employed in upper-level white-collar occupations in private enterprises *do* receive greater earnings than their self-employed counterparts, but few women in the formal sector belong to this group. The particular occupational composition among female employees in private enterprises implies that there are relatively high structural barriers for women in the formal sector. Unlike self-employment, in private enterprises employers' preferences affect married women's chances of obtaining white-collar jobs. A middle-aged woman, based on her own experience, told me that finding a white-collar job in the private sector could be quite a challenge for married women:

> I moved after I got married and then I had to find a new job. I shifted to a factory job [from an accounting job before marriage] because it's easier to find a blue-collar job for married women. Owners of factories don't care whether you are married since the turnover rate among manual workers is high anyway. To find a job like what I had before, as an accountant, is very difficult. Think about this, they all prefer girls who just graduated from school (because they are cheaper). It's unlikely that an employer will hire a married woman to do accounting.

This woman contrasted employers' inability to be choosy in hiring factory workers with their ability to set more criteria for hiring white-collar workers.

The second reason for the relatively high earnings of self-employed women is related to the Taiwan economy's organizational structure. The contrast between self-employment and formal sector employment reveals the disadvantageous side of women's work in the formal sector, in particular in private enterprises. The average size of private enterprises is quite small in Taiwan (Hamilton and Biggart 1988), limiting their capacity to pay high wages. Labor-intensive methods of production also encourage firms to keep their labor costs low (Yu 1999a). As a result, full-time employees in Taiwan, regardless of gender, receive relatively low earnings compared to their counterparts in both Japan and South Korea (Chapters 2 and 3 this volume; Yu 1999b). Upward mobility is likely to be blocked in small firms, particularly given that in Taiwan most are family-owned. Hence, private enterprise employees in Taiwan generally suffer from blocked mobility and limited labor compensation. This particular context creates a disadvantageous side to formal employment and therefore makes self-employment relatively advantageous for women.

This leads to the more general conclusion that the type of industrial organization predominant in a society determines to a great extent the relative economic benefits of working in the informal sector. There are disadvantages to formal employment in Taiwan that make at least one type of informal work (self-employment) more advantageous. However, formal sector employees may enjoy greater earnings than self-employed workers in economies where the average firm size is larger and more regulations are set to protect formal sector workers. For example, Japanese women in the informal sector, regardless of employment status, generally earn less than their counterparts in full-time, formal employment (Yu 1999b). But in South Korea, interestingly, despite a great number of large firms in the economy, informal employment does not mean income loss for women compared to formal employment (Brinton and Choi, forthcoming). A possible explanation is that although the level of married women's representation in white-collar jobs is low in Japan, the proportion of women in white-collar occupations is even lower in South Korea (Chapter 2 this volume; Lee 1997; Ogasawara 1998 and Chapter 6 this volume; Yu 1999b). As shown in this chapter, women's chances of reaching upper-level white-collar positions in the formal sector determine whether formal employment is advantageous for them. It is also worth noting that the history of employment relations and the demand for high-skilled labor in Japan encouraged firms to offer relatively high labor compensation and extensive welfare benefits for employees (Yu 1999b). South Korea and Taiwan have not followed the same path. Therefore, the benefit of being employed in the formal sector is generally less in South Korea and Taiwan.

This final brief comparison of Taiwan to Japan and South Korea suggests the importance of taking into account a society's economic structure when assessing the advantages to women of participating in a certain type of work. Not only do we need to distinguish types of employment within each sector, but we also need to consider the organizational structure of an economy in order to understand the limits on women's work in the formal sector. Given that the implications of women's participation in the informal sector are relative to their well-being as formal sector employees, taking the context into consideration is the only way to come to a proper understanding of women's work in the two sectors.

CHAPTER TEN

The "Boss's Wife" and Taiwanese Small Family Business

Yu-Hsia Lu

Taiwan's export-led economic development involved a labor-intensive economy dominated by small family enterprises. As other chapters of this book have discussed, this generated types of employment opportunities for many urban Taiwanese married women that allowed them to balance work and family responsibilities. Taiwan's pattern of industrialization also brought about a large and heterogeneous informal sector (as shown in Yu, Chapter 9 this volume), in which married women constitute a significant part. Yu's chapter compares married women's positions and earnings across the formal and informal sectors of the economy. The present chapter looks in depth at married women's working lives within a particular part of the informal sector: small family enterprises, where wives contribute their labor as unpaid workers. Specifically, I investigate how families' economic strategies combine with patriarchal ideology to shape the dynamics of gender relations in Taiwanese family enterprises.

Unlike in Japan and South Korea, where family businesses tend to form large conglomerate enterprises, family businesses in Taiwan are usually small and labor-intensive. Since the early 1960s, medium- and small-scale businesses have accounted for over 90 percent of all industrial enterprises in Taiwan.[1] The average firm employs fewer than 10 workers, and nearly 70 percent of the labor force works in establishments with fewer than 30 workers.[2]

The prevalence of small family businesses in Taiwan can be attributed to a number of economic, political, and social factors that have combined in complex ways to impose intrinsic limits on business expansion. Strong export-led economic growth results in a pattern of dispersed industrialization in which labor-intensive small and decentralized producers can respond quickly to fluctuations in the international market. Untrammeled competition among small firms forces them to keep their costs down in order to stay competitive; their profits are usually only enough to sustain themselves and not enough to expand the scale of their business.

Besides these economic conditions, the Nationalist state's historical experience on the Chinese mainland left it with an anti-big business bias that colored its economic policies (Wade 1984), making it difficult for firms to outgrow their small, familistic skin. The state created an environment in which entrepreneurial opportunities were available primarily to small businesses. The prevalence of the small family business can also be attributed to workers' entrepreneurial energies and strategies and to the particular social relations of production that characterize Taiwan's economic organizations (Stites 1982). As mentioned in Yu's chapter, the organization of production involves a subcontracting system that increases production capacity and flexibility at the same time that it generates opportunities for workers to become their own bosses.

Married women are much more likely than married men or unmarried women to work as unpaid family workers in Taiwan's family businesses. The purpose of this chapter is to explore the consequences of women's work in these businesses. Under the prevailing patriarchal system, does women's work in small family businesses bring them opportunities for empowerment, or does it reproduce relations of exploitation? By examining women's work roles in the particular economic and cultural context of Taiwan's family firms, I explore the dynamics of gender relations. I focus on women's economic power and explore wives' power/autonomy in the business family's production—rather than reproduction—system. Economic power is defined as control over key economic resources such as income, property, and the means of production (Blumberg 1984). Many previous studies in Taiwan have argued that women's economic power is a strong predictor of their power in the household, measured in terms of equality in family decision making and the division of household labor (Lee, Yang, and Yi 2000; Lu and Yi 1998; Yi and Tsai 1989).

Married women constitute an important labor resource in the Taiwanese family business. In 1993, unpaid family workers made up 20 percent of the married female labor force compared to less than 4 percent of the male labor force.[3] Government employees make up a much smaller proportion (11 percent) of the married female labor force, and employees in private firms and self-employed workers constitute the rest. Since married women are much more likely than men and unmarried women to work as unpaid family workers, this status constitutes an important way through which they are integrated into the Taiwanese labor force.

The term "family business" refers to those businesses in which majority ownership or control lies within a single family, with proprietorship and management not clearly differentiated. The organization of the family business is rooted in the Chinese family system (Hamilton and Biggart 1988; Hwang 1983). The kinship network is a basic element of Chinese social structure, and kinship ties are an important source of solidarity in economic organization. Given that the family firm is usually organized on the basis of family relations, personal connections are an essential part of managerial strategy (Hwang 1983).

The great majority of small- and medium-sized factories in the manufacturing sector in Taiwan are in subcontracting networks. These networks consist of several layers in the division of labor for production processes. In the top layer are the factories that receive orders directly from buyers or trading companies (if they are export-oriented factories). Instead of completing the entire production process, these factories put out part or most of the work to subcontracting factories or home-based workers; these subcontracting factories may also further contract out part of the work to lower subcontracting factories or home workers. Subcontracting firms are usually small. When demand exceeds the modest capacity of their own operations, they turn to home-based workers—most of whom are married women— to produce the same components on a piece-rate basis. The existence of the subcontracting system is closely related to the outward-looking, export-oriented economy of Taiwan (Shieh 1992a). As mentioned above, the decentralized nature of the system means that it can quickly adjust to changes in the world market.

WOMEN'S WORK AND STATUS

In response to the rapid growth of female labor force participation in Taiwan, an increasing number of empirical studies have focused on issues related to the impact of industrialization on women's roles and status. Most of these studies suggest that although women's labor force participation has rapidly increased, women's economic status relative to men has not changed

significantly. Married women's class status is shaped both by gender relations at work and by the patriarchal order within the family.

Many studies have suggested that during Taiwan's economic development, women workers have continued to attain only secondary status in the
labor market and are more likely to be in the peripheral or informal sector (as
unpaid family workers, self-employed workers, short-term or part-time wage
workers, or piece-rate workers; Chou 1987; Lu 1992). Significant sex segregation exists in the labor market, with women tending to be concentrated in
traditional female jobs with lower status and income (Tsai 1987; Lin 1988).
Studies of women's status in the labor market in Taiwan are consistent with
the findings of marginalization theorists for other developing countries, who
argue that during capitalist economic development women tend to be confined to the home or to be absorbed into inferior jobs in the peripheral sector of the economy (Saffioti 1976; Scott 1986; Humphrey 1987).

Research in Taiwan on the effects of women's employment on their status in the family, however, has not always produced consistent conclusions.
Some studies argue that because of the persistence of patriarchal norms,
women's status within households has not changed significantly in spite of
their involvement in income-generating activities (Gallin 1984; Lu 1983).
These studies suggest that women's subordinate status in the labor market
and the persistence of a patriarchal gender ideology continue to define gender relations; both of these contribute to the perpetuation of women's inferior status in the family. However, other studies, especially those concerning
women in metropolitan areas of Taiwan, find that women's increased employment has led to an increase in their relative resources in the family. They
argue that this growth in resources has in turn improved their status in the
family power structure (Tsui 1987; Yi and Tsai 1989).

A recent study that compared married women's status in the family
across different generations found that the consequences of women's employment may have changed over time along with economic development in
Taiwan. During the early period of economic development, women's employment did not lead to an increase in their status in the family. However,
accompanying the changes in Taiwan's economic development, work patterns
for married women have changed. In spite of women's persistently inferior
position compared to men, the trends in married women's work during this
later period suggest a shift toward more formal and stable employment (Lu
1996). This is likely to improve women's status in the labor market and to

counteract the domination of traditional gender-role attitudes. Hence more women may be experiencing economic empowerment in the home because of their employment outside the family (Lu and Yi 1998).

WOMEN AND FAMILY BUSINESS

Previous studies have focused mainly on the consequences of women's gainful employment and have ignored the consequences of women's informal work, despite the prevalence of women's employment in Taiwanese family businesses. Research on family businesses has focused mainly on the process of mobilization of family labor. Hsia and Cheng's case study (1989) observed the dynamics of kinship relations in a small-scale plastics factory and illustrated how small firms, through the mobilization of family labor, are able to subsist without investing in the costs of labor management. Ka's study of small-scale factories in the garment industry emphasizes the exploitation of family members as a key factor for the survival of the family business. Family members feel obliged to work for their own family business in order to increase the family's welfare. Consequently they usually work harder than workers who are not relatives (Ka 1993: 82).

A study of women's work in family businesses (Lu 1992b) indicates that the decision to participate in a family business is made within the context of familial ideology. This study reveals that although most wives participated in their family business (if there was one), those with higher education or some experience of nonfamilial work were more likely to work *outside* the family enterprise. This is due to the family's concern for efficiency in the household division of labor. Should a wife's job abilities be such that the value of her time spent in market activity is higher than that of her time at family production work, she may spend more time in market activities; some of the work at home may then be left to other family members or to hired workers. (See the chapter in this book by Lee and Hirata; also see Chapter 3 by Yu for a discussion of how a similar family logic may dictate that women in Taiwan with good income-generating potential may be encouraged to work outside the home and leave a substantial portion of the childrearing tasks to their mothers-in-law.)

Among the few studies related to women's roles and status in the industrial entrepreneurial context, earlier research by anthropologists noted the important role played by Chinese familial ideology in promoting the prosperity of family enterprises (Basu 1991; Gates 1987; Niehoff 1987). Family labor is deployed along the lines of gender and age, with senior males making major decisions, junior males performing labor, and females filling in when and where they are needed (Niehoff 1987). An individual's role in the family enterprise is thus in accordance with the family's conception of the traditional division of labor.

Basu's (1991) study of married women in the overseas Chinese family enterprise in Calcutta points to the possibility of women's development of informal power through their involvement in the family business. She shows how married women in a Calcutta tannery community undertook significant business responsibilities. The study describes a gendered division of labor, with the women engaged in tasks enabling them to remain close to the "domestic" sphere and the men involved in relatively public realms of business activity crucial to the family enterprise. Basu argues that in the Calcutta Chinese community, women's power is based on their close bonds with their sons. According to traditional Chinese family relations, the emotional bond with a son is a significant source of a woman's informal power and ensures her own economic well-being. Married women's participation in the work of family firms is in fact one means of cementing bonds with children and using these bonds to motivate sons to work harder for the family. The study further shows that women's roles in family businesses vary with firm size. Women occupy less important roles in family firms or withdraw from business activities altogether when their families operate larger firms. Basu concludes that due to existing gender roles under the patriarchal system, a woman's power and influence in the family do not increase with her participation in the family firm.

Using case studies in a garment industry community, Li and Ka (1994) show that the division of labor in the firm reproduces a new division of labor in the family. Men play the role of head of firm and family, representing the family business to the outside world. Wives are unpaid managers of the firm and family, managing the routine work and finances in the factory. The author indicates that this family ideology, rooted in traditional patriarchal norms, provides the basis for a division of labor in the family business and at the same time reproduces the patriarchal system and gender relations.

Greenhalgh's study (1994) of 25 Taiwanese enterprises, however, gives another explanation for the gendered division of labor and women's status in family firms. Her study also asserts that men's and women's business roles correspond neatly to their roles in the kinship system. While men's work approximates formal employment (full-time, salaried jobs), married women's work is more like an extension of their household and childrearing responsibilities (part-time, uncompensated labor). Women work at jobs that can be combined with or subordinated to their reproductive duties and are offered few means to enhance their professional skills or pursue career development. She argues that gender differentiation in work and the close correspondence between kinship and business positions are the product of power differentials within the family rather than a natural reflection of tradition or an outcome freely chosen by subordinate family members. The division of labor is a construction of the family head based on traditional inequalities fostering the formation of a stratified workforce, where women hold low-level jobs that do not interfere with their reproductive tasks while men work at more high-powered jobs that advance their careers.

The studies described above show that family obligations spur women's involvement in family firms. Researchers emphasize women's lower status in the power structure of the work organization despite their significant contributions. The earlier studies by Niehoff (1987), Harrell (1985), and Gates (1987) focus on the effects of family ideology on the reproduction of the gender hierarchy in family firms. Basu's (1991) study suggests that women's participation in family firms is unrelated to their status, but that such work can indirectly improve their informal power because family work may cement family bonds. Work is, therefore, a resource for women's informal power under the prescribed traditional Chinese culture. Greenhalgh's argument, however, points out the restrictions imposed by social structure and the mentorship of the firm's head. These studies provide different arguments concerning the consequences of women's entrepreneurial work in family firms, but all of them assert that traditional family hierarchies and the cultural expectations of a patriarchal system confine women to marginal status both in the productive and reproductive spheres of the family.

The generalizations drawn from these studies, however, mask differences in gender relations that may arise from the degree of autonomy and economic responsibility that women have in the family business, factors that vary with the nature of the work organization and the macroeconomic setting. This study will consider the work activities and status of small family business owners' wives as consequences of Taiwan's decentralized industrialization pattern. By examining women's actual work responsibilities, I investigate how economic strategy and family ideology combine to influence married women's power. I also look at a number of factors that differ *across* small family firms and may affect wives' power. These include the developmental stage of the firm, the nature of the industry to which the family business belongs, and both the employer's and the wife's job skill or human capital. Gender relations may vary with the developmental stages of the firm. As revealed by previous studies, women's involvement in a family business often changes with transformations in the size of the family business (Basu 1991; Greenhalgh 1994). Further, whether women are empowered may vary with the nature of the industry as well as the firm's status in the subcontracting system. Finally, husbands' and wives' relative job abilities may be important determinants of women's power and autonomy.

METHODOLOGY

As described above, the majority of the Taiwanese workforce is in enterprises with fewer than 30 persons. This study focuses on family businesses of that size, where both husbands and wives are directly involved in the business on either a full- or part-time basis. Family enterprises with more than 30 employees tend to be more organizationally complex and formal and thus are very different from most small family businesses in terms of the social relations within the organization.

The present study is based primarily on qualitative data generated through in-depth interviews of employers and their wives in 50 firms. The cases come from a two-stage sampling design based on the 1991 Taiwan industry census. I first stratified industries into three groups according to their proportion of female employment (see appendix table 10.1). The higher the density of female workers in a specific industry, the larger the fraction of the sample chosen from that industry. The three industry groups are (1) high-density industries, in which female employment accounts for 50 percent or more of the workforce (including the textile, garment, and electronics industries); (2) middle-density industries, in which female employment constitutes 30–49 percent of the workforce (including the manufacture of plastic products, food manufacturing, and retail sales); and (3) low-density industries, in which female employment constitutes less than 30 percent of the workforce (including manufacturing of bamboo products and paper products, printing, machinery and equipment production, and wholesale trade). Six hundred firms were selected, including 300 high-density firms, 200 middle-density firms, and 100 low-density firms. The agricultural sector is excluded because production and social relations in that sector are substantially different from relations in other industries.

The selection of districts was based on degree of geographical concentration of the selected industries. The sampled firms in each selected industry were chosen from the top two counties with the highest density of the particular industry according to the 1991 industry census. This resulted in the concentration of sampled firms in five districts: Taipei city, Taipei county, Taoyuan county, Taichung county, and Changhua county.

Since the fieldwork for this research was undertaken three years after the census year, I had to determine if the sampled firms had changed, expanded, or shut down during this period. To confirm the status of the firms, I conducted a brief telephone interview for the 600 firms. After excluding from the list those that had shut down, moved, or could not be contacted and those that had no family members participating in the business, 64 firms willing to be interviewed were selected, with the criterion that the distribution of firms across industries be roughly proportional to the distribution of female-labor density across industries. In all, interviews were successfully carried out at 50 firms, including 2 wholesale firms, 3 retail stores, 1 food store, 4 export- or import-trading companies, 13 textile factories, 7 garment factories, 2 paper product factories, 1 printing firm, 3 bamboo product factories, 4 plastic product factories, 6 electronics parts factories, 3 nonmetallic mineral products factories, and 1 machinery/equipment factory.

In terms of firm size, 15 of the firms consist of 2 persons (involving only the married couple), 12 firms have 3–5 persons, 13 firms have 6–10 workers, 6 firms have 11–20 workers, and 4 firms have 21–30 workers (see table 10.2). Among the sampled firms, 18 firms do not hire workers. Among the firms that do, 14 employ only relatives, and 18 hire nonrelatives as some or all of their workers (see table 10.3). Among the 35 manufacturing firms in subcontracting networks, 14 are contractors who contracted out all or part of the production work to subcontractors, and 21 are subcontractors who received out-processing work from contractors but did not contract work out. The family structure of owners includes 30 nuclear families and 20 extended families (with more than two couples living together). Among the extended families, 15 had extended kin involved in the family business.

The contents of the in-depth interview included the organization of

TABLE 10.1

Sampled Firms: Distribution by Industry and District ($N = 50$)

		District	N
	COMMERCE		
Wholesale trade	Machinery equipment	Taipei city	1
	Agricultural, husbandry, and fishery products	Taipei county	1
Retail trade	Food products and non-alcoholic beverages	Taipei city	1
	Agricultural, husbandry, and fishery products	Taipei city	1
	Fabrics, clothes, and apparel accessories	Taichung county	1
Foreign trade	Export trade	Taipei city	1
	Import trade	Taipei city	2
	Import/export trade	Taipei city	1
Eating and drinking places	Catering shops	Taipei city	1
Total			10
	MANUFACTURING		
Textile mill products	Knitting mills	Changhua county, Taichung county, Taipei county	10
	Cotton textile mills	Changhua county	3
Wearing apparel and accessories	Outwear apparel	Taipei county	6
	Accessories manufacturing	Taipei county	1
Wood and bamboo products	Bamboo products	Taichung county	1
	Lumbering	Taichung county	1
	Wooden containers	Taichung county	1
Plastic products manufacturing	Plastic housewares	Taichung county, Taipei county	4
Paper products and printing processing	Printing	Taipei city	1
	Paper containers	Taipei county	1
	Other paper products	Taipei county	1
Nonmetallic mineral products	Pottery, china, and earthenware	Taipei county	3
Electrical and electronic machinery	Electrical machinery, apparatus, appliance, and supplies	Taipei county	1
	Electrical parts and components	Taoyuan county	3
	Other electrical and electronic machinery and equipment	Taipei county, Taoyuan county	2
Machinery and equipment	Special production machinery	Taoyuan county	1
Total			40

TABLE 10.2
Sampled Firms: Distribution by Size

Size (no. of workers)	No. of firms
2	15
3–5	12
6–10	13
11–20	6
21–30	4
Total	50

TABLE 10.3
Status of Workers in Firm

Worker status	No. of firms
Hired labor (relatives only)	14
Hired labor (relatives or nonrelatives)	18
No hired labor	18
Total	50

work, women's work activities and responsibilities, and women's work history. Both employers and their wives were interviewed. Usually the bosses were interviewed about the labor process, business networks, the division of labor, and the history of the development of the family business. The bosses' wives were interviewed about their work both in the household and in the business at different stages in the development of the business, their decision-making roles in both the business and the family, their socialization, and their work history. With detailed questions in hand concerning these topics, the interview was conducted in a conversational style, with the interviewer directing the respondent to the relevant topics. Since each respondent provided a full account of their business situation and their work experience, at least three interviews were carried out in most households. First, the husband was interviewed for general information about the business's status and development. Later, the wife and the husband were interviewed separately and asked different questions depending on who was the best informant for the study.

In the following sections, I first examine the roles of bosses' wives in family businesses in terms of their responsibility and autonomy at work. Then I analyze the factors that account for variations in women's work roles. The latter includes an examination of women's changing roles and status with the development of the business as well as the family life cycle. The processes of how women negotiate and construct their relative position in family businesses are explored under different contexts, including the nature of industries, the stage of business development, and women's relative human capital, all of which may crucially influence their position.

THE ROLE OF BOSSES' WIVES IN FAMILY BUSINESSES

Family businesses are the meeting place of two major social systems, family and work. The interdependence of business organization and family thereby shapes the division of labor and the resources of the business. The labor division between the couple in the family business seems to reproduce the gendered division of labor in the family. In general, a boss's work is based on establishing and expanding market relations, and he may spend considerable time taking orders and negotiating with buyers, customers, or producers. Wives' roles in family management, negotiation, and coordination tend to extend to their business roles. Their familial roles in managing household work usually lead to their responsibility for the routine work inside the factories (or stores), including the supervision of hired workers. However, in many cases, they are also involved in processing tasks.

The in-depth interviews in the 50 family businesses indicate that wives' roles may include business management, financial management, supervision and training of hired workers, processing tasks, and delivery and collection of out-process work. For an employer in a small business, his wife is his most reliable companion and helper. As a textile-factory boss stated: "The thing we [textile-factory bosses] fear the most is a wife's strike. That means you cannot go out, otherwise no one answers the phone, no one checks on the quality of the cloth when it comes out, no one receives the raw goods or semifinished products when they arrive, and no one helps with the packing and shipping to meet the deadline. A wife at home—she can do everything" (Shen42h).[4]

In most family businesses, wives' most important duty is that of financial management. Among the 16 family businesses with a specialized division of labor for financial management, 14 of the wives are themselves accountants or treasurers (table 10.4). Whether wives take the position of

TABLE 10.4
Content of Wives' Work in Family Businesses

Tasks	No. of Firms	Firm ID
Accounting	14	Pan04, Wang17, Lai20, Yeh21, Chiang24, Gu25, Fu27, Lai29, Wu35, Gu37, Chuang43, Liu44, Wang46, Lai48
Processing	31	Pan04, Li05, Chan09, Fu10, Yang11, Gu12, Lu13, Li14, Chen15, Wu16, Wu19, Yeh21, Li22, Gu25, Fu27, Pan28, Lai29, Shen30, Pan32, Shen33, Lo34, Chang36, Shen38, Teng40, Chiu41, Shen42, Chuang43, Lai45, Teng49, Li51, Li53
Supervising	13	Chang02, Pan04, Li05, Chan09, Wang17, Lai20, Sun23, Chiang24, Chen26, Lai29, Chuang43, Liu44, Teng49
Sale	7	Chang01, Chang02, Hau03, Gu07, Shen08, Lai29, Chen52
Taking new orders	3	Chen26, Lai29, Teng49
Taking routine orders	10	Chan09, Wang17, Lai20, Sun23, Chiang24, Gu25, Chen26, Lai29, Liu44, Teng49
Repair or maintenance	4	Chan09, Wu16, Lai29, Chuang43
Contacts with out-workers	3	Wu16, Lai29, Pan32
Business contacts with subcontracting factories	8	Pan04, Sun23, Chiang24, Gu25, Chen26, Lai29, Wu35, Chuang43

NOTE: The number of firms exceeds 50 because many wives carry out multiple tasks.

accountant or not, most of them take responsibility for the financial management of assets and liabilities.

Also among the wives' most important responsibilities are training and supervising workers. Table 10.4 shows that among the family businesses with hired workers, 13 wives were involved in training and supervising. In the case of garment factories, wives are the masters who train workers in processing tasks according to the design required by the contractors for whom the factory work is being done. As a boss's wife in a garment factory with ten in-house female workers said: "I train the in-house workers and my husband trains the home-based workers. We teach them the most efficient way of doing tasks and make sure they have done them correctly" (Chuang43w, age 39). In negotiating and coordinating roles in the family business organization, wives play an important role in consolidating workers' loyalty toward the family business. Working on the shop floor by either supervising workers or working side by side with them, the boss's wife is more likely to deal with the problems workers face on a daily basis. A boss of a sock-knitting factory (Wang17, 20 in-house workers) said that his wife used to deal with virtually all the problems on the shop floor; the problem would come to him only if his wife were unable to handle it.

Among the wives in the 40 manufacturing factories in the sample, 31 were directly involved in processing work (table 10.4), with some of them performing specific processing tasks. In many cases, especially in industries that rely particularly on female labor, wives themselves are skilled workers who are familiar with every kind of processing job on the shop floor. While hired workers do specific processing tasks, wives themselves may do any task to make up for a shortage of labor when it occurs. As a garment-factory boss said: "We have a division of labor, with some doing the task of *ping-che* [sewing] and some doing *kauke* [sealing], but my wife can do everything, usually taking on the job no one else is doing" (Chuang43h).

In manufacturing firms, wives' work varies with the position of the family business in the subcontracting network system. Among the firms in subcontracting networks, 14 are upper-layer factories and 20 are lower-layer factories. Most upper-layer factories contract out all of their production-processing work. Such is the case, for example, with the sock-knitting factory mentioned above. The boss gets orders, negotiates with customers, and sets up the subcontracting networks. All the in-house work, including quality inspection and packing, belongs principally to the wife. Lower-layer subcontracting factories (*dai-gung-chang*) show a less clearly gendered division of labor. To minimize costs, they rely heavily on family labor and usually the couple themselves are the only labor involved in the processing work. The division of labor has to be as flexible as possible due to the shortage of labor in such firms.

At the lower-layer knitting factories (Wu16, Shen38), the employer couples are the only labor in the workshop. The husbands do the skilled work such as setting up the machinery and repairing it, while the wives are in charge of operating the knitting machines and performing the tasks of sewing and tightening. Some wives are also involved to a limited extent in so-called men's tasks, such as shifting the design disk on the machines or doing easy repairs.

Most lower-layer textile factories keep their machines running continuously, and employer couples work day and night in order to meet their deadlines and maximize profits. Usually the couple takes turns. According to the boss of a textile-factory with two hired workers: "My wife works from 10 in the morning until 11 P.M. or midnight, and then my turn is midnight through 4 A.M. Then I take a nap until 10 A.M." (Lu13h, age 51).

The boss of a couple-only textile workshop in a mid-Taiwan township described the division of labor as follows:

> I come here [it is about a five-minute walk from his residence to the workshop] at about 6 A.M. to turn on the machines while my wife prepares breakfast and does the laundry. She comes to work at about nine o'clock so that I am able to get back for breakfast and send out the orders or meet customers [or owners of subcontract-factories with whom they collaborate]. I get back to the factory at about noon to take on my wife's work while she goes home for lunch. Then she comes back after lunch while I go home for a nap. I come back to work at about 4 P.M. in order to let my wife prepare supper, and she comes back at about 6 P.M. to give me a chance to have supper. I come back for the night shift from 8 P.M. to 10 P.M. (Li14h, age 37)

Another couple-only textile factory has no fixed schedule: "My wife and I take turns operating the machines. There is no fixed schedule. When one of us is tired, the other one takes his/her turn. The important thing is that the machines are kept running" (Yang11h, age 45). Generally, the more skilled tasks or technical machine tasks are the husband's job. Wives are also much less likely to be involved in repairs or maintenance of the machinery. Only 4 of the 40 wives in the sampled manufacturing factories do repair jobs (table 10.4).

Because Taiwan family culture generally requires that jobs in the public domain belong to men, wives are less likely to be involved in work pertaining to market relations, with the exception of the routine work of carrying out orders. Ten of the wives interviewed mentioned that they set up contracts with old customers; only three among them had initiated new contracts or had taken orders that did not follow old contracts (table 10.4). In three of these cases, the women had equal or higher job ability than their husbands and are entrepreneurs themselves in the sense that they are full business companions to their husband in the family business.

Women's segregation from market relations stems not only from familial culture but from the prevailing business culture that reproduces patriarchal norms. According to Taiwanese business culture, business talk is a man's job. As Mrs. Chuang, a garment factory boss's wife described: "They won't talk about business with women" (Chuang43w). A printing factory wife, Mrs. Chiang said that she declined to step into business negotiations: "My husband does it. I have no idea about the situation between my husband and them and if what I said is different from what my husband said, it would be hard to handle" (Chiang24w, age 45, college graduated).

Nevertheless, in those family businesses that perform subcontracting work, wives play an important role in consolidating the relationships in the subcontracting network. Among the 35 factories involved in subcontracting networks, eight wives mentioned that they were responsible for the business connections with subcontracting factories (table 10.4). In the production network, the subcontractors (including home-based workers) are independent production units, and there is no formal employment relationship between the contractors and their subcontractors. Managing and maintaining stable and reliable relations with other units in the subcontracting network can be crucial to the survival of a family business. Employers in sock-knitting factories (Wang17, Gu12) portray subcontracting as "putting machines outside." They do not own any production workshops, but rather they "disperse the production units out." The production process in sock-knitting factories involves the purchase of raw materials (e.g., thread) according to the sample; the processing of the main part of the sock either in-house or through contracting the work out; sending work to subcontracting factories or home-based workers; further processing work, such as sewing, tightening, pressing and shaping; and, finally, returning the finished products to the contractors for quality inspection, packing, and shipping.

The level of effort required to maintain network relations is inverse to the substitutability of the subcontracted units. If the subcontracted unit is difficult to replace—that is, if the contractors are highly dependent on the subcontractors—then the contractors must put more effort into maintaining the relationship. If, on the other hand, the subcontracting unit is easily replaced or its replacement will not affect the normal production process, then contractors may put less effort into maintaining the existing relationship.

My observations indicate that the substitutability of subcontracting units is correlated with job skill and with the deployment of machinery in the production process. Mr. Gu, a sock-knitting factory employer, said that the kind of sport socks he produces require particular techniques and machinery. Therefore, he puts out work to subcontracting workshops whose heads are his former colleagues in a big sock-knitting factory that had shut down before they established their own workshops. He has six subcontracting workshops that also work for other contractors. He was worried that if those workshops shut down it would be a heavy blow to his business. The way he maintained the subcontracting network relationships was to cultivate friendships and to invite subcontractors to festival celebrations: "We get along like friends, celebrating *wei-ya* [a custom whereby the employer gives a feast to workers at a festival near the end of the year]. . . . Once in a while, we go on a picnic or go sightseeing together" (Gu12h, age 37, high school graduated). His wife also emphasized that "cultivating friendships with subcontractors' families is important: I chat with the wives of subcontractors when I meet with them. . . . I often give them a ride to the food market so that they can do their shopping" (Gu12w).

Among the 22 factories that have out-workers, three bosses' wives mentioned distributing the out-processed pieces to subcontracting home workers and collecting the pieces when they had finished (table 10.4; Wu16, Lai29, Pan32). Home-based workers are usually married women, and bosses' wives often chat with them during these occasions, so that their friendships are consolidated from daily contact.

Mrs. Chiang, the wife of the boss at a printing factory mentioned her relationships with subcontracting workshops:

> "We often lunch together. . . . We meet every weekend. It is convenient for us, because after being busy working the whole week we need to take a break, sometimes we take it at my residence or sometimes here [the firm's office]. I usually cook, and their kids are also invited. . . . Sometimes the hired workers we are acquainted with come along because we belong to the same business body. . . ." (Chiang24w, age 45, college graduated)

Bosses' wives in the subcontracting network families not only share their leisure hours but also exchange information regarding their work. As the printing-factory wife continued: "Sometimes the wives [of subcontracting workshop heads] come to ask me about the way we do our accounting [she is an experienced accountant]. I point out general things to them—it would not be polite if I were to ask them the details of their accounting" (Chiang24w).

In sum, women tend to be involved in those activities that can be carried out in greater proximity to the domestic sphere; those activities that draw one into the public sphere of bargaining and business relations are mostly men's jobs. Wives' roles are in management, personnel, and money coordination, while husbands are the family head and the firm head. Because the political roles belong to men, wives are less involved in the work of market relations such as negotiation. Most wives are involved in "inside" functions such as finance and production-processing work. Under some circumstances, wives may take the job of distributing unfinished pieces and collecting the finished work from the home workers. Wives also often need to collect money from customers. Therefore, wives' jobs are not *always* confined to the territory of firms. But they are seldom active in the public sphere in terms of regularly negotiating with customers or dealing with the subcontracting or coordinating firms in the network. These are seen as political roles and are designated as the husbands' jobs. While women engage in tasks that enable them to remain close to the "domestic" sphere, this contrasts with the women in Basu's case study of the overseas Chinese tanners (Basu 1991); most Taiwanese bosses' wives engage in tasks inside the firm but not *confined* within the firm. The wives of firm bosses have by far the most responsible positions compared to anyone besides the boss, and they tend to function especially as financial managers and work coordinators.

WIVES' ROLES IN DECISION MAKING

While most wives in Taiwan's family businesses have important responsibilities in running the business, they do not identify themselves subjectively as the decision makers. In most cases the husbands/bosses are the chief decision makers and although wives may be consulted, they seldom have the final say.

Table 10.5 shows that wives have low involvement in decision making, and if they do make decisions, they are more likely to be involved in decisions regarding the tasks they are responsible for. Among the 50 wives, 9 are involved in making decisions about financing, 6 are involved in recruitment decisions, and 7 are involved in decisions about hired workers' pay. Those wives who are involved in decisions about taking new orders, the specifics and design of products, or the partition of production tasks and business contacts to subcontracting factories all have strong job skills and play crucial roles in the production process. The three wives involved in decisions related

TABLE 10.5
Wives' Involvement in Decision Making

Tasks	No. of firms	Firm ID
Taking new orders	3	Chen26, Lai29, Teng49
Financing	9	Chang02, Pan04, Yeh21, Chiang24, Gu25, Lai29, Gu37, Chuang43, Liu44
Hiring	6	Chan09, Wang17, Chen26, Lai29, Liu44, Teng49
Hired worker's payment	7	Chan09, Wang17, Chen26, Lai29, Chuang43, Liu44, Teng49
Species and design of products	4	Chang02, Pan04, Lai29, Teng49
Partition of production tasks	4	Chiang24, Lai29, Chuang43, Teng49
Business contacts with subcontracting factories	2	Lai29, Teng49

to taking new orders are actually involved in the businesses' market relations, which is very unusual. Those three women are themselves entrepreneurs in running the business.

Most wives abstain from decision making under the ideology of patriarchal norms. Mrs. Li talked about her involvement in the process of decision making in the following way: "My husband and I talk to each other about new customers, and we ask around. If a person has been running his business well, the customer he recommends may also be trustworthy. I let my husband make the final decision; I would agree with anything my husband decides to do" (Li05w, age 35, primary school graduated, sock-knitting factory). In other cases, wives may work under their husband and say nothing during the decision making. Mrs. Lu put it this way: "My husband makes every decision; I just follow whatever he has decided" (Lu13w, age 43, junior high graduated, thread-producing factory). Mrs. Yeh runs a textile factory with her husband, and attributes her noninvolvement in decision making to her husband being better equipped in business management: "I care only about changing threads and connecting thread [operating machines]. All the rest is my husband's job, such as purchasing threads. . . . He knows better than I do!" (Yeh21w, age 35, junior high graduated). Likewise, Mrs. Chau, in a trading company, says, "My husband knows better than me, thus he makes the decision. I just help answer phone calls while I take care of the children" (Chau06w, age 31, college graduated).

In many cases the pattern of decision making reproduces marital power in the family. As a food-store owner's wife says: "We discuss our business but he always makes the decision. He tends to be the big man in our family, and my job is to take care of the children, do household chores, and not to care too much" (Fu10w, age 40, junior high graduated).

However, a wife may affect her husband's decision making even on large issues when she carries out vital responsibilities in the family business or is well-equipped to run the business. Mrs. Chang, a boss's wife in a fashion factory, was involved in nearly the entire process of production. She mentioned the experience of objecting to her husband's investment plan: "I quarreled with him when he wanted to make a risky investment, and my mother-in-law also joined with me in order to dissuade him. He ended up agreeing with us" (Chang02w, age 33, primary school graduated).

In sum, in most cases a wife's status is subordinated to her husband's either because of traditional gender relations in the family or because of the way her participation in the family business is structured (to be discussed below). Because wives are more likely to make decisions about the work for which they have direct responsibility, does such responsibility increase their bargaining power? In other words, if wives' empowerment is possible through their role in the family business, what are the mechanisms? To what extent does women's economic responsibility influence the relative power of the sexes in spite of the dominant patriarchal hierarchy? The next section explores more deeply the nature of Taiwanese family business organization and the meaning it gives to wives' work roles.

THE WIFE AS AN "INSIDE PERSON"

The organization of family businesses in Taiwan is based on family ties or simulated family ties (Hwang 1987; Chen 1994) and exemplifies what has been described as the "nesting box" system of Chinese management (Hwang 1983; Redding 1990). A typical family business with hired workers consists of different groups organized according to their connection with the owner. In the small innermost box are those core family members who own the business; in the next box are more distant relatives and workers or staff members who are trusted by the owners and are in a position to influence and be influenced by the owners. In the next outer boxes are unrelated hired workers. Loyalty among unrelated employees is often low, which makes personalistic connections closer to the center an essential part of management strategy (Hamilton and Biggart 1988; Hwang 1983). The members of the inner circle (the innermost box and the next inner box) are called *ze-ji-ren*, or "inside persons," and are viewed as loyal and capable of carrying out the employers' will and orders. They are fully trusted and relied upon by the employers (Chen 1994; Hwang 1987). The *ze-ji-ren* are usually but not always family members or relatives. Most essential is that a "we-consciousness" is shared among the inside persons, against whom the employer contrasts members beyond this circle (Chen 1994).

The employers need *ze-ji-ren* to share the responsibility of running a family business. They need them to take on those jobs crucial to the firms' survival such as supervising the production process, checking the quality of the product, and most importantly, managing finances. Most small family businesses hire only production labor, and in this case the most significant *ze-ji-ren* is the boss's wife. A wife's moral involvement is based on familial obligation and a tacit understanding between the couple that allows her to assume the role of *ze-ji-ren*. This is a primary reason why the wife is always a key person in the family business even if the business grows. In what follows, I explore the wives' role as *ze-ji-ren* and the possibility of wives developing bargaining power from it.

Most family businesses need *ze-ji-ren* to stay within the firm to supervise workers while the employer is busy working outside with customers or with business contacts. As in the case of an electronic-wire factory run by joint-family ownership (Wu35), with five family members and seven hired non-relative workers, the daughter-in-law of the employer, as one of the accountants in the family business, was asked to remain in the business when she proposed quitting her job in the family firm in order to take care of her two small children. According to the daughter-in-law, "We have a hired accountant and an administrative staff (but no clear division of work) and they can handle almost everything. I hoped to stay at home for a while because my two-year-old needs my care, but my parents-in-law (the employer couple) asked me to stay because they need a *ze-ji-ren* here (within the firm office)." She explained that her parents-in-law have another business investment, and her husband is involved in the public realm of family business in marketing and managing subcontracting units. He has to spend most of his time outside the firm while her brother-in-law takes care of processing work at the shop-floor level. Consequently, she has to stay in the office, managing financial affairs, overseeing the workers, paying workers, and doing routine paperwork. She states, "My parents-in-law hope a *ze-ji-ren* can stay here [in the firm's office] to handle things if there is any problem"(Wu35w, age 28, vocational high school graduated).

Another important job in family businesses is checking on quality and measuring the product. This usually is the *ze-ji-ren*'s job, since poor quality is detrimental for the firm and a mistake in measuring the finished product can result in over- or underpayment. In the case of textile factories, most wives take charge of measuring cloth on the measuring machine and mark those pieces of cloth that are flawed. In other factories, such as electronic machinery, sock knitting, and plastic manufacturing, the bosses' wives and immediate family members (if they work in the family business) check the quality, count the product, and pack the finished product.

Wives' position as *ze-ji-ren* results directly from the features of the family firm that stem from its embeddedness in the culture of Chinese familism: an informal organizational structure and the survival mentality of the family economy. Informal organizational structure derives directly from the overlapping of the family and the firm as organizations. Typically, the organization of small family businesses places no boundaries between the work system and the family system, or between production and reproduction. Both the dwelling unit and the business unit are located in the same place. This eases the combination of wives' productive and reproductive roles and also makes wives indispensable for carrying out responsibilities at the intersection of family and firm.

The most significant overlapping responsibility is financing. In most small family businesses, business financing is combined with home financing, and thus the responsibility belongs to those who take charge of the home financing—usually bosses' wives. Many wives report that the family living expenses are mixed with the costs of running the business—"all come from the same drawer," as they said. Mr. Chuang, a boss of a garment factory, reports "the profit earned from business has to pay for the house mortgage, utility, food . . . what is left is our earnings" (Chuang43h).

Many wives who take charge of financial management initially set up the accounting system and establish the informal rules of business administration. When the bosses' wives have some professional training, they prefer there to be clear boundaries between finances for the family and the business. Mrs. Gu, the wife of a machinery factory boss, recalled that before she married into this family, the business and the family had mixed accounts and any family member could withdraw money from the public account. Thus no one had a clear picture of the business's financial status. But because she was an experienced accountant herself, she was able to set up rules separating the business accounts and the family accounts: family expenses belong to the family account, business expenses to the business account. This way she has a clearer picture of the real financial status of the family business (Gu37, age 26, vocational high school graduated).

Adequate financing is obviously critical to both family and business. Mrs. Chiang, the wife of a printing firm boss, puts it this way: "I do my best to separate the household accounts and the firm's accounts, at least in the bookkeeping. For example, I include our salary in the business cost . . . so that I can get a crude estimate of the profit. . . . I think this is important because you should stabilize the family's financial position first. The firm is going up and down, and you shouldn't let the firm pull down the family!" (Chiang24w).

Even when a family business employs professional accountants, those employees usually cannot substitute for a wife's financial work because that work is supposed to be done by a trustworthy insider. As is the case in a box factory (Liu44), with 5 family members and 15 hired workers, the business organization consists of four departments: production, design, accounting, and marketing. The job of the hired accountants is to keep track of the daily expenses and the income accounts without dealing with assets and liabilities, which are the wife's responsibility. Thus in most cases only the wife has information on the real financial state of the business.

Besides wives' crucial responsibility for finances, deriving from the overlap between the family and the firm, wives are indispensable because of the nature of informal business organization itself. Most Taiwanese small family businesses are not governed by formal institutional rules that specify the division of labor, define employment relations, and guide the work activities. Rather, the coordination and control of work activities rely on interpersonal, informal processes. Day-to-day activities proceed by informal rules designed by the persons who actually carry out the roles of management and supervision. The boss's wife, who carries out multiple roles in the family business including managing, coordinating, financing, and supervising, may be the only person who can keep track of every detail. Therefore, a wife's work is not replaceable. Mrs. Chiang, with four hired workers in their printing factory, said, "No one can replace me. The hired workers may help by following my instructions for a few days, but not longer. I honestly think I cannot leave my work for more than three days" (Chiang24w).

The informal rules that wives, as managers and supervisors, design in order to guide the day-to-day work activities are crucial to the survival of family businesses. In an electronics factory run by an extended family (Pan32), with 9 family members and 15 hired workers, one of the daughters-in-law in charge of managing the orders also sets up a detailed procedure and schedule of the processing work for each order, including each step of the production process—from receiving the orders to packing and shipping. According to her mother-in-law, who also works in the family business, "It would be hectic all the time without the arrangements she makes"(Pan32w). In improving the efficiency of running the business, the young boss's wife's contribution markedly increases the survival capabilities of the firm.

The importance of wives' role as *ze-ji-ren* also stems from the economic strategy of the family business. Family firms in Taiwan are more likely to pursue survival strategies than strategies of mobility. And the former is more apt to provide a context in which wives gain economic power through their work involvement. As suggested by previous studies, the poorer the family, the more critical the role played by women (Stoler 1977; Tinker 1994). Following this line of argument, women's role as *ze-ji-ren* in Taiwanese family businesses epitomizes their "strategic indispensability" (Blumberg 1984; Young 1993) to the family firm within a survival economy. Women gain economic power not through the mere generation of income but through their control of productive activities and their responsibility in allocating surplus. Within a Taiwanese family business, wives often control resources because of the prevalent business strategy of relying on *ze-ji-ren*. Thus, a woman's critical role as inside person can become an important source of economic power. As Tinker (1990) noted in her study of street food vendors, personal relationships can be negotiated to produce change even under the prevailing system of patriarchy, particularly in a time of economic crisis. Wives' critical role as inside persons means that bosses *need* their wives' involvement in decision making, especially in regard to financial affairs. Because it is only wives who have complete information on the firm's financial status and on cost calculations, they can play the role of a "car brake," preventing their husbands from over-investment or over-expansion. As is the case in the electric-wire factory run by joint-family ownership (Wu35), the boss's wife manages financing and is responsible for resource allocation, the distribution of earnings, and the purchase of housing or equipment.

As wives' economic power comes directly from their work involvement and to a large extent depends on their own job skill and the nature of the industry, it is important to focus on these features in order to understand variations in women's economic power. In addition, as discussed above, the importance of wives' role as inside person may derive from the organizational structure and economic strategy of the family business. These organizational features may vary with the developmental stage of the family business. The following sections go into these variations.

WIVES' STATUS AND THE DEVELOPMENT OF THE FAMILY BUSINESS

Greenhalgh argues in her comparative study of six developing countries that women's informal employment does not improve their status in the labor market because as family businesses develop, wives' labor becomes unnecessary and this leads to a return to the family roles dictated by the traditional gender ideology dominant in these societies (1991). However, the tendency of Taiwanese family firms to persist as small businesses leads to most wives staying on in the family business. The findings of my study suggest that women may *change* their work patterns during the development of the family business, but they generally do not *leave* the business. In some cases, when family businesses get upgraded, wives are less involved in the labor process but become more involved in the work of management or financing. Such is the case in a paper container factory that started in 1972 and has 20 employees (Liu44); in a top-level lamp-manufacturing factory established in 1983 (Li05); and in a garment factory, established in 1989 (Teng49). In other cases, continuing diversification leads to specialization on both the shop floor and in the administration; here, bosses' wives may have no fixed position but are still needed to "check head and tail." This is the case for a sock-knitting factory (established in 1975) that is at the top level of the subcontracting system (Wang17), and an electric-wire factory (Wu35) with 12 employees and established in 1974.

No matter what stage the family business has reached, when asked about the role of the boss's wife, family business members agree that the boss's wife is very important as a source of inside support. Mrs. Liu, the boss's wife in a box-making factory with 20 workers, recalled her work history throughout the development of the business:

> We started the workshop in 1970, and both my husband and myself were involved in the processing work with two or three home workers (mostly neighborhood housewives). We worked around the clock. When more orders came in and we hired more laborers, I took charge of the accounting and my husband was responsible for the business contacts, but both of us still had to be involved in the shop floor operations until we moved here, expanded the factory, and formally set up four divisions: production, design, finance, and business management. I still take charge of the finance department, but we have hired accountants [actually she supervises them], and I seldom get involved in the shop-floor tasks now since we have a shop-floor head to supervise them. (Liu44w, age 43, vocational high school graduated)

In some cases when the family business has become more developed, the boss's wife has grown experienced enough to share greater responsibility in decision making, especially when the boss needs to put more effort into expanding market relations or setting up subcontracting networks. Mrs. Wang, a boss's wife in a sock-knitting firm with more than 20 workers, used to take charge of in-house work, but she also sometimes took orders on her own when the boss was absent from the factory: "Decisions about business contacts are my husband's . . . when my husband is on a business trip, I make decisions on the parts in which I am capable" (Wang17w).

Mrs. Li, the boss's wife in a lamp factory, recalled how her role has changed from an earlier stage: "At the beginning, we produced a kind of study lamp and sold one hundred of them every day. We worked the whole day in the mill. Now we have hired workers in the mill and I only need to take care of the business management and answer phone calls" (Li05w, age 35, primary school graduated).

In many cases, wives paved the road for the establishment of the family business. They took charge at the beginning stage while their husbands took the family business as a side job while continuing to work in their original careers. Usually, husbands did not quit their original jobs until the family business had become stable. A knitting-sweater factory boss, Mr. Yang set up his own workshop in 1974 while moonlighting at another textile factory. His wife took charge of the workshop at the early stages. He recalled: "My wife operated machines. These were old-fashioned machines. Usually one person can take care of three at most, and she cared for all three. The process of thread knitting was contracted out. When I got home from work, I helped set up the machinery according to the sample designs requested by the customers" (Yang11h, age 48).

Mrs. Gu, the wife of the owner of an export trade company, remembers: "We started up our business in 1989. I was pregnant then and my husband asked me quit my job, and we rented an office near our residence. I went there whenever there was work to do. There was not much business coming in then, and my husband still worked at —X trading company" (Gu25w, age 30, college graduated).

According to Mrs. Chen, who owned an import-export trade company with her husband and had 10 staff members and a subordinate manufacturing factory, "I used to work at a trading company. . . . I left and started up our own business in 1977. My husband still worked for a Japanese trading company and he hoped to learn more in that trade, so he asked me to quit my job first. About two years later, our business generated enough income to support us and he quit his job and we embarked on importing more professional electronic parts" (Chen26w, age 43, college graduated).

INDUSTRY CHARACTERISTICS, HUMAN CAPITAL, AND THE WIFE'S ROLE

Wives' responsibilities and bargaining power may also vary with the industry of the family business and women's own qualifications. My findings show that women's involvement in some productive activities can increase their autonomy, thereby rearranging relations in the patriarchal family. Women in family businesses are usually involved in the less skilled jobs. However, when a woman instead of her husband possesses the job skill that is crucial to the family business, the division of labor between the couple is quite different. Wives are more likely to assume significant responsibility in those industries that utilize female skills, such as the garment industry.

Observations in many subcontracting garment factories reveal that wives play crucial roles because of their job skills. One of the important features of the subcontracting factories system is the partitioning of the production-processing work. The production process is broken down into piecework:

some is done in-house and some is contracted out, but the partition should be made to enhance efficiency (to maximize profits and to meet deadlines). Usually partitioning is the boss's job, since the boss rather than his wife possesses the necessary job skills. This is typically the case in textiles, electronics, machinery, plastics production, box making, and printing factories. In garment factories, however, wives may have better job skills than their husbands. Thus in many cases wives, alone or in collaboration with their husbands, figure out the most efficient way of partitioning the processing work. They break down the work into cutting, sewing, pasting on of designed decorations, buttonhole making, and pressing, so that each task may be done sequentially. Usually the less complicated work or the work compatible with home workers' equipment is out-sourced to home-based workers.

Since wives in garment factories take the responsibility of designing as well as supervising the processing work on the shop floor, they are more involved in business decision making than other wives. A fashion-factory boss noted: "We consult each other in running the business. . . . My wife is very experienced in making decisions, such as cloth purchasing and designing" (Chang02h). Whether the business features female skills or not, a wife's own job skills also influence her role in the family business. In many cases, a wife's work experience before entering the family business provides her with the necessary skills for running a business. Mrs. Chang (Chang02, fashion factory) was the most competent hired worker in her husband's father's fashion factory before she married his son. Mrs. Pan (Pan04, plastic-products factory), Mrs. Li (Li22w, plastic-products factory), Mrs. Wu (Wu35, electric-wire factory), Mrs. Lai (Lai20, lumber factory), and Mrs. Chiang (Chiang24, printing factory) were already experienced accountants before marriage. All of these wives contribute significantly to the family business.

In most garment factories, husbands and wives have comparable job skills, so they collaborate on the processing work. A special case of a wife alone possessing the necessary job skills is that of a bridal-dress firm (Teng49). Unlike other garment factories, this factory takes orders directly from buyers and thus is at the same time a trading company. The wife is an excellent dress designer with fine skills in producing bridal dresses; the husband gained experience working in a trading company. In setting up the business, the wife took charge of designing and monitoring the processing work. Her work includes partitioning the processing work and setting up schedules, determining the piecework rate, supervising and training workers, selecting home-based workers, delivering out-processing work, and inspecting the quality of the product. Her husband took charge of financing, managing, and marketing. According to the wife, "I need not care about financing, my husband takes care of it. The production processes keep me busy around the clock" (Teng49w, age 34, college graduated). In this case, the wife alone has the requisite job skills, so she has full control over the production process from design to quality checking. Meanwhile, for business contacts and financing she relies fully on her husband. Thus, for the survival of this family business, the division of labor and the shared decision-making power were determined by each person's capabilities.

In the family businesses that are largely based on "female-typical" skills, women are more likely to gain some autonomy in the production process because they have more opportunity to accumulate the needed job skills. In some cases, the skill of the boss's wife is the foundation on which the family business is based; in other cases the wives learned skills after the family business started and have since had the opportunity to further develop their skills.

Female control can be seen not only in those industries requiring what are traditionally women's skills, but also in gender-neutral industries. Such is the case in a ceramic business that produces ceramic arts pieces (Lai29). In their mid-30s, both Mr. and Mrs. Lai are professional ceramic artists. In 1991, after about six years of assisting her husband's business, Mrs. Lai started to take full responsibility for running the factory while her husband was absent trying to find new market opportunities in mainland China. She continued to play crucial roles in both production and marketing even after her husband came back to their business.

In contrast, in industries based on what are considered to be male skills, women are not encouraged to take on managerial responsibilities. For example, in the textile industry, because fabric designing is related to manipulating machinery, it is considered a man's job. Women are involved less in designing, and thus they are less likely to take on full responsibility for the production process. It is possible that when a woman possesses the necessary skills, she rather than her husband could head the processing department. But it is not likely that a woman would take the lead in marketing. Even in the clothing industry where women have vital production skills, this rarely occurs. It may be that in Taiwan's business culture, people cannot accept women as negotiators even when the commodity is a product of women's work.

Among the businesses I studied, the importance of professional ability was more salient for women whose families run foreign-trade companies. All of the wives in foreign-trade companies I interviewed are college graduates who had some related work experience before entering the business. As a result, their professional ability has affected the development of the family business. As Mrs. Sun, the boss's wife in an export-trade company said: "I need to learn more (besides import- and export-trade stuff), because finance and accounting are important too. I need to handle the financing of the company. . . . When recruiting new staff, I used to screen those applicants before the interview, although it is my husband who makes the final decision" (Sun23w, age 32, college educated).

Mrs. Chen, however, is not only a boss's wife in their foreign-trade company; she runs her own part of the business independently in addition to supporting her husband's portion: "My husband takes care of the domestic business (inside the country), especially things related to technology. I take care of the business related to foreign countries, but I still need to help him handle factory things, such as building up the institution of administration, the personnel, the labor division in the factory, and dealing with personal relations among the staff. Beside this, I work as a general agent for a big corporation in Europe. . . . I do it on my own; this part is 'my business' " (Chen26w, age 43, college educated). This case suggests that the boss's wife has broken through the stereotypes of traditional roles and become an independent actor alongside the boss.

In short, in the survival economy of the family business, women tend to get more bargaining power when they control the key resources surrounding business survival. Women's job skills, as human capital, give them bargaining power to achieve some autonomy. Through her human capital, the boss's wife is able to negotiate the patriarchal system and construct her own position to some extent.

CONCLUSION

This chapter has explored the status of bosses' wives in Taiwan's small family businesses as well as the possibilities for power and autonomy stemming from their work involvement. Families who own and run businesses are at the same time organizations of commodity production. The family businesses in Taiwan that survive do so through their skillful use of strategies to increase labor productivity and minimize production costs. Family members whose labor is absorbed by the business are inseparable elements in an organic unit. The findings of this study of 50 small family businesses across different industries suggest that the gendered division of labor under patriarchal norms does prevail; men take charge of market relations and outside business contacts, and women take charge of business management within the firm. In most cases, women are subordinated to men in decision making. However, bosses' wives are often in an indispensable position in the family business, which increases their bargaining power.

A whole chain of consequences can emerge from changes in the microlevel gender balance of economic power between males and females (Blumberg 1988). In my study the most important source of women's bargaining power comes from their "strategic indispensability" in production and management. Wives' key position in the family business and the empowerment that comes with that role may be attributed to the particular features of Taiwan's family firms, embedded in Chinese familism: informal organizational structure and the family survival economy. The coordination and control of work activities in the Taiwanese small business rest on interpersonal relations rather than on institutionalized structures. Instead of control by formal procedures, the rules associated with the processes of production, management, and administration are mostly informal and are set by the head of the family business or the persons he trusts. Enterprises are structured around family ties or simulated family ties, and most family business owners trust only their core family members, the insiders. Bosses need the insiders to support them in managing and supervising their factories or stores. The inside person is especially important in matters of finance. Observing wives' roles in family businesses shows that except for the small proportion of family businesses that are run by brothers of joint families, the wife is the most likely individual to be the indispensable "inside person" who takes charge of finance, supervision, and quality inspection. For this reason, most wives remain in important positions even as the family business grows and develops. As indispensable inside persons, wives may assist their employer husbands in establishing the family business and in the early stages of its development. But this study suggests that the roles held by wives of bosses also evolve across different stages of development of the business and that even as their roles change, wives remain indispensable "inside persons."

The survival economy of Taiwanese small businesses actually provides a context in which wives are able to negotiate the patriarchal system and reconstruct their position relative to men, especially when they control key elements of the business. The findings of this study also indicate that women's empowerment through their strategic roles may vary with the nature of industry and with women's personal abilities. In industries using female-typical skills, such as the garment industry, wives' involvement in both the division of labor and in decision making is significantly greater than in other industries. Under these circumstances, wives' job skills are crucial to the survival of the family business. Thus their responsibilities tend to be accompanied by greater autonomy in decision making than is true for women in other industries. Bosses' wives in industries featuring traditionally male skills—such as lumber and machinery—may still have the responsibility of managing finances and checking quality. But these women are less likely to attain the autonomy gained by bosses' wives in businesses that rely on female skills. The study also suggests that wives with professional education and work experience before marriage are more likely to work as female entrepreneurs and to share power and responsibility equally with their husbands.

Given that Taiwan shares Confucian-based cultural values with other East Asian societies, especially Japan and South Korea, comparing women in family businesses across these societies should be illuminating. As Brinton discusses in Chapter 1 of this volume and (with Lee and Parish) in Chapter 2, Taiwan and South Korea not only have similar cultural values, but the labor supply conditions and industrial distributions of the two economies are also very similar. Japan can be included in this statement as well. Given this, how does the status of Japanese and South Korean married women in family businesses compare to Taiwan? Is there an argument to be made that women in these countries as well are empowered by their indispensability in family firms?

A major theme of this volume is the impact on married women of the different types of economic organizations and institutions that Japan, South Korea, and Taiwan have developed. Export-led growth in Taiwan and South Korea has had very different organizational consequences. Taiwan's labor-intensive, dispersed industrialization involved a myriad of small enterprises scattered throughout the island, whereas the South Korean government has promoted large, capital-intensive enterprises by privileging them with foreign loans (Chapter 2 this volume). Family enterprises can more easily get bank loans to expand their scale in South Korea and grow out of their familistic skin, compared to Taiwan. Women who are unpaid workers in family enterprises as part of their family obligation are likely to leave when enterprises expand, since cultural, ideological, and economic forces tend to deter women from contributing to large family enterprises and instead encourage them to contribute to smaller ones (Basu 1991; Greenhalgh 1994). In contrast to Taiwanese women's empowerment from the informal arrangements of small business organizations, South Korean women's participation in family firms tends to be a temporary arrangement at the early stage before an enterprise expands and becomes institutionalized. Therefore, it may be less likely that South Korean women assume vital responsibility, acquire entrepreneurial resources (skills and capital), and thereby become empowered from their involvement. In contrast, the majority of Taiwanese family firms are not likely to evolve to a higher level of formal rules and institutionalized organization.

Research on the Japanese firm has focused much more heavily on large enterprises rather than on the smaller firms that employ the majority of workers. Like women in Taiwan, Japanese women married to self-employed men tend to work in the family firm as part of their familial obligation. The proportion of the Japanese female labor force working in family enterprises is only slightly lower than in Taiwan: 12.5 percent in 1995 compared to 16.1 percent in Taiwan in the same year.[5] However, Japanese women's work status in the family business may be different from Taiwan due to the different family economic context and the different market situation faced by companies. Japanese subcontracting networks tend to be more stable than similar networks in the United States and Western Europe (Arrighi, Ikeda, and Irwan 1991). Instead of competing against one another, large and small Japanese firms cooperate through a division of labor where firms specialize in certain production techniques or processes. The pervasive subcontracting network reproduces itself over time (Eccleston 1989; Whittaker 1997). As a result, it can be argued that Japanese small businesses may be less likely to experience the degree of untrammeled competition facing Taiwanese small family businesses and forcing them to keep their costs down to stay competitive. If this is true, it is possible that Japanese women who work in their family's firm may be less strategically indispensable than women in Taiwanese family businesses. What is more, many studies cite the Japanese cultural emphasis on mothers' focusing on the family and being dedicated to the care and education of children (Kato 1989; Kumagai 1986; White 1987b; Yu and Hirao, Chapters 3 and 7 this volume). As a result, Japanese business families may be less likely to encourage mothers' work commitment or central responsibility in the business compared to Taiwan.

Cyclical economic circumstances in Japan such as the deep recession of the late 1990s and early twenty-first century may bring small family businesses in Japan closer to the survival mode of Taiwanese tiny businesses. How these economic pressures intersect or conflict with the strong Japanese emphasis placed on the mother as an indispensable caretaker is a compelling question for research.

APPENDIX TABLE 10.1

Proportion of Female Workforce in Various Industries, Taiwan

Industry	Ratio	Industry	Ratio	Industry	Ratio
Agri. animal husbandry & hunting	0.25	Chemical products	0.33	Painting, coating, mounting, matting	0.05
		Petroleum, coal prod.	0.13	Other construction	0.12
Forestry, logging	0.15	Rubber products	0.43	Wholesale trade	0.29
Fishing	0.14	Plastic products	0.34	Retail trade	0.37
Coal mining	0.10	Nonmetallic mineral prod.	0.33	Foreign trade	0.45
Crude petroleum, natural gas, & geothermal energy mining	0.12	Basic metal industries	0.12	Restaurants, hotels	0.44
				Transportation	0.15
Metal ore mining	0.20	Fabricated metal prod.	0.17	Storage, warehousing	0.18
Salt mining	0.28	Repair of machinery, equipment	0.16	Communications	0.27
Clay, stone mining	0.13	Manufacture & repair of electrical, electronic machinery & equip.	0.50	Finance	0.50
Chem., fertil. mineral mining	0.13			Insurance	0.63
Other mining	0.15			Brokerage	0.36
Quarrying	0.09	Repair of transport equipment	0.20	Legal, business services	0.44
Food manufacturing	0.32	Precision instruments	0.43	Machinery, equip. rental & leasing	0.22
Beverage, tobacco	0.27	Miscellaneous industrial prod.	0.43	Public admin. & national defense	0.32
Textile industries	0.50	Electric light, power supply	0.11	Sanitary & environmental services	0.27
Wearing apparel, accessories	0.71	Gas supply	0.16	Social and community-related services	0.55
Leather, fur, & their products	0.50	Steam & hot water supply	0.21	Cultural, recreational services	0.42
Wood products, bamboo products, & nonmetallic furniture	0.21	Water supply	0.21	Personal services	0.42
		Construction of infrastructure	0.12	International & other extra-territorial bodies	0.45
Manufacture of paper, paper prod., printing, & publishing	0.28	Construction of electricity, water, gas, & other pipe lines	0.06		
Chemical materials	0.21				

SOURCE: Directorate-General of Budget, Accounting, and Statistics, Executive Yuan, ROC (Republic of China), *General Report on the 1990 Census of Population and Housing,* 1991b.

297

CHAPTER ELEVEN

Daughters, Parents, and Globalization

The Case of Taiwan

Nidhi Mehrotra and William L. Parish

Accepted wisdom suggests that as developing societies become involved in the global economy, the fate of women depends greatly on the patriarchal value system in these societies. At similar levels of economic development and with similar levels of world market involvement, economic opportunities for women vary significantly depending on the degree of patriarchal culture (Mason 1996). Contrasting patterns in Southeast Asia (such as in Indonesia, Malaysia, Thailand) and East Asia (such as Taiwan and South Korea) provide such an example. Southeast Asian societies have typically placed less emphasis than East Asian societies on patrilineal descent and patriarchal authority. As these societies entered the global economy, daughters purportedly reaped significant benefits from their premarital work—getting more discretionary income, accumulating savings for their weddings, and reporting a sense of improved status (e.g., Ong 1991; Wolf 1990, 1992). Ong and Wolf note that this contrasts sharply with what the scholarly literature portrays for the more patriarchal systems of Taiwan and South Korea, where daughters are typically described as getting few positive returns for their work. In these more patriarchal systems, it is argued, parents exploit daughters economically for the sake of their sons. Dependent on sons for support in old age and embedded in a value system that values continuity in the male line, East Asian parents tend to favor sons over daughters in education, work, and subsequent parental investments (e.g., Berheide and Chow 1994; Brinton 1993; Schultz 1993).

For many authors, Taiwan family practices exemplify the East Asian patriarchal pattern. As in Hong Kong, many daughters have traditionally quit school early in order to go to work in "dead-end" jobs. Daughters' income

is purportedly retained not by the daughter but by her parents and her brothers; the latter reap benefits by getting more education and by experimenting
with jobs that provide them a basis for increasing their income over the life
cycle (e.g., Thornton and Lin 1994). In the extreme versions of these pessimistic accounts, daughters are prepared mainly for the job of childrearing
or, by the 1980s, for postmarital work in jobs with distinctly lower pay than
men's (e.g., Bell 1994; Diamond 1979; Gallin 1984a, 1984b; Greenhalgh
1985; Hsiung 1996; Kung 1983; Salaff 1981; Tang 1981).[1]

Even the pessimistic accounts in the literature, however, note some
changes that began to shift more power into single women's hands over time.
Greenhalgh stated that by the 1970s in Taiwan, "parents were willing to increase their investments in their daughters' education . . ." since post-primary
education was "increasingly necessary to obtain a factory, and even more,
an office job" (1985: 276). Even if the primary purpose of daughters' work
was the short-term revenue they could provide to their families, daughters
could conceivably use their increased education to their own advantage once
they married. Moreover, with rapid export-led growth, Berheide and Chow
note, the increased demand for women's work began to give women "resources with which to resist subordination within their families" (Berheide
and Chow 1994: 268).

Taiwan's labor-intensive growth pattern began to produce labor shortages in the 1980s, drawing or keeping married women in the labor force in
a wide variety of jobs (Thornton and Lin 1994; Chapters 1, 2, and 3 this volume). No longer was women's work concentrated among the never-married,
and, in contrast to South Korea and Japan, women's education and other
skills could be used to garner better jobs and income (Chapter 2 this volume).
Moreover, as incomes increased, fewer parents had to make the difficult
choice of sacrificing their daughter's for their son's education (Parish and
Willis 1993; Thornton and Lin 1994). These trends suggest that patriarchal values, while very important, do not irretrievably lock a society into a
certain pattern of gender inequality. The consequences of patriarchal values
can soften in societies that enter the global market with labor-intensive patterns that create a demand for married women's labor (Chapters 1 and 3 this
volume).

The task of this chapter is to explore for Taiwan the argument that the
dynamics of the patriarchal family continue to translate into a situation where
single women's families reap much greater benefits from their work than

women themselves do. Specifically, we examine whether most of the gains from women's premarital work were indeed captured by the patriarchal family through the late 1980s. If so, then several consequences should have followed: Having more younger brothers should have forced single women into the labor force and deprived them of control over their earnings. In turn, a daughter's premarital work should have had little relation to her subsequent marriage dowry, the "quality" of her husband, or her postmarital work and income. Parents would have withheld most of the additional income that might have gone into the daughter's dowry. And, in the extreme version of the patriarchy argument, since premarital work was in dead-end jobs and was mainly for the purpose of generating short-term income to be given to brothers and parents, premarital work should not have led women into better jobs after marriage. This final implication is particularly important given the focus of this book on married women's employment.

We open this chapter, then, with the extreme version of the patriarchal control argument. But we note at the outset that some recent research suggests the more modest hypothesis that both sons and daughters benefit in some ways from parental investment and women's premarital work. For example, in her account of women in home-based factories, Hsiung cites research on the garment industry showing that husbands often start making garments because their wives have the necessary skills and contacts *based on their work prior to marriage* (1996). This implies that women's premarital work even in less-than-ideal conditions can provide skills that are used in later life, although this may be in a small family-run business where the husband is the boss (see also Chapter 10 this volume).

EXPLORING THE TAIWAN SETTING

By the beginning of the last decade of the twentieth century, Taiwan was completing a three-decade-long period of rapid export-led growth. Growth in gross national product per capita in that period had averaged around 9 percent per annum. At the end of the 1980s, export earnings stood at 60 percent of gross national product and made Taiwan one of the most trade-dependent countries in the world (Ranis 1992). Moreover, trade dependence involved a myriad of small firms, often based on family ownership (see Lu, Chapter 10 this volume). At first blush Taiwan may have seemed to exhibit many of the features purported to be negative consequences of globalization. Union power, job security, and fringe benefits were rare, and job turnover and business bankruptcy rates were high (Deyo 1989; Hsiung 1996). At the same time, because of the labor-intensive pattern of growth, urban unemployment remained extremely low, and by the 1980s labor shortages were so severe that more and more married women began to be drawn into the labor force along with illegal migrant workers from abroad (Chang 1987; Galenson 1979, 1992; Speare, Liu, and Tsay 1988; Chapters 1, 2, and 3 this volume). Real incomes continued to grow for both male and female workers. This pattern of *increasing* labor demand accompanied by rising wages in Taiwan set the stage for parental decisions about investment in sons and daughters, and also set the stage for what the long-term consequences of women's early work experience would be.

Our data are from a 1989 society-wide survey of women 25–59 years of age, including 3648 married women. We are particularly interested in the consequences of siblings and work prior to marriage on women's subsequent life chances. We statistically control for several background conditions that would be expected to shape outcomes for women. We use a standard labor supply model, including years of education (which should prepare women for more lucrative jobs); urbanity (which should presumably inhibit work because of longer journeys to work and less flexible work arrangements in cities than in towns and villages; see Chapter 2 in this volume on these factors in South Korea); age (because older women were young at a time prior to Taiwan's full involvement in the global economy, they had fewer work opportunities); and other income sources for the family (including higher-income parents or husbands, meaning that a single woman would not be under great pressure to work because of household economic necessity).

In addition, we pay attention to the distinction between women of "mainland" and "local" origin. The 12 percent of women in our sample who are mainlanders are those who themselves (or more likely, those whose parents) came from the mainland of China around 1949 when the Nationalist Government fled to Taiwan. We do not know exactly how they differ in work experience and in other ways. They tend to have fewer kin and hence may have weaker personal networks available when they search for a job (see Chapter 9 for a discussion of women's use of social capital and personal networks in Taiwan in becoming established in jobs). They are likely to have thought of themselves as higher in status in earlier years and hence they may be less likely to take just "any" job. For these myriad reasons, we include mainlander status as a control variable in the analyses.

FINDINGS

We have data both on patterns of women's work before marriage and the consequences of their work in subsequent years. Since our objective is to explore the various consequences of women's premarital labor force participation, we begin by examining how women's work before marriage has changed over time in Taiwan.

Work before Marriage

Women's likelihood of working before marriage increased rapidly over the last four decades (figure 11.1A). Including unpaid work on the family farm and in small family businesses, most women in the early 1950s were engaged in some kind of work before marriage.[2] Though the total of all kinds of work combined increased in the subsequent four decades, the sharpest increase was in work as paid employees, mostly in the private sector but also in government and public enterprises (see also Chapters 1 and 9). The result of this sharp increase in paid labor was that unmarried daughters increasingly had a pay package of their own.

Many studies in Taiwan have noted that working daughters heretofore turned most of their pay over to their parents. This provides the basis for generalizations that little has changed over time in daughter-parent relations and that daughters' labor is being used for the benefit of others in the family. Our data show that in the early 1950s, nearly half of the women reported that they had no control over the use of their salary and only about one-fourth said that they had complete control (figure 11.1B).

But while it is important to point out how little control unmarried women had over their earnings in the 1950s, it is equally important to note the rapid change in recent decades. By the late 1980s, a little over half of working women reported complete control over how they used their own income, and the percent reporting at least partial control had risen to 85 percent. So while the continuing degree of parental control over daughters' incomes may seem remarkable to Western observers, the situation has in fact been far from static. Increasingly, daughters have gained control over how

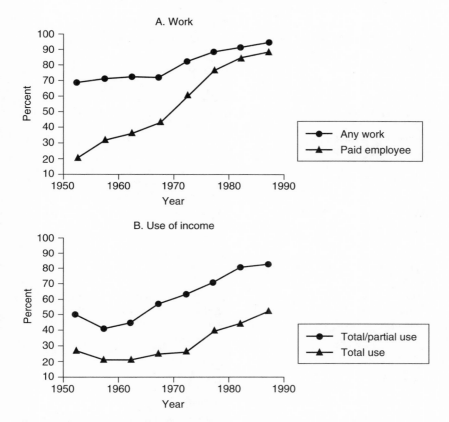

Figure 11.1.   Premarital Work by Year of Marriage

SOURCE: Taiwan Women and Family Survey, 1989.

NOTE: Year of first marriage by five-year age groups, centered on the middle year.

their income is used rather than having it go directly into parents' hands, presumably partly for use in helping sons get started in their careers. This suggests that as Taiwan's global market involvement deepened, patriarchal norms weakened. In short, working daughters in Taiwan began to have greater autonomy, becoming more similar to their counterparts in several Southeast Asian societies.

Another way to test the hypothesis that much of single women's pay in Taiwan is used by parents to help get sons set up in their adult life is to see whether women with many brothers, especially younger brothers, are more likely to enter the labor force while they are single. We analyze the factors

TABLE 11.1
Premarital Work, Control over Earnings, and Presence of Siblings

| Variable description | PREMARITAL WORK | CONTROL OVER PAY (PRIOR TO MARRIAGE) | |
	Work vs. no work	Full vs. no control	Partial vs. no control
Years of education		0.31***	0.14***
Urban background (1 = grew up in city; 0 = did not)	−0.03	−0.06	0.06
Age	−0.03***	0.0002	−0.03**
Mainlander (1 = mainland Chinese origin; 0 = otherwise)	−0.38***	0.11	0.02
Father's economic status (1 = poor; 2 = so-so; 3 = rich)	−0.09*	−0.09	−0.18
Number of:			
older brothers	−0.03	−0.10	−0.04
older sisters	0.01	−0.01	0.01
younger brothers	−0.02	−0.01	0.01
younger sisters	0.01	−0.18***	−0.05
Constant	2.58	−1.86***	0.42
N	3287	1204	
Pseudo R^2	.05	.08	

NOTES: The first column of coefficients has been obtained from a probit model, where 1 = worked before marriage and 0 = did not work. Coefficients reported in the second and third columns come from a multinomial logit model. Unless stated otherwise, all variables refer to the respondent. All statistical analyses refer to women married after 1949.

*$p < .10$, **$p < .05$, ***$p < .01$

that affect unmarried women's labor force participation as well as the factors that affect how much control women exercise over their own earnings. The results show the overwhelming influence of two variables: the woman's age and whether or not her parents came from the mainland (table 11.1, column 1). To some extent, parental affluence appears to keep daughters out of the labor market. Most of the other possible background features are not related in any of the expected directions. This is particularly striking for number of siblings. The number of older brothers, older sisters, younger brothers, and younger sisters a woman has are all unrelated to whether she worked before marriage.[3] This finding is consistent with several things. First, it is consistent with the idea that single women have been increasingly drawn into the labor force because of "pull" (labor demand) factors such as rising wages. If daughters have simply been driven into the work force because of family poverty, then the presence of younger brothers and sisters should have contributed to the probability of labor force participation because of the economic needs of the household. One "push" factor from the family, parental economic status, does seem to affect the probability of daughters' premarital labor force participation, but only modestly so. Second, as argued by Parish and Willis, one of the most common ways in which daughters helped families strapped for cash because of poverty and too many children was not by going to work early, but instead by leaving the family permanently via marriage (1993). The results here are consistent with the interpretation that older daughters help poor parents and siblings not so much by going to work at an early age but rather by marrying at a young age.

Control over earnings is an additional indicator of whether parents use the earnings of daughters to help sons. If younger brothers soak up the earnings of older sisters, then unmarried women with many younger brothers should have less control over the use of their earnings. In the survey, women reported whether they had full, partial, or no control over the use of their premarital earnings. To isolate the impact of younger brothers on an unmarried woman's control over her earnings, we controlled for family background and personal characteristics. In particular, we controlled for women's age, education, rural/urban background, mainland origin, and fathers' socioeconomic status. We expected to find that women who had grown up in cities, had higher educational attainment, and were younger would be less "traditional" and would have greater control over their earnings. We also expected that women from high socioeconomic backgrounds would have greater control because their parents would have less need to rely on them financially.

In the analysis where both full and partial control over premarital earnings are each compared to the situation of no control, fewer of these background conditions are important than we expected (table 11.1, final columns). As we anticipated, education provides a woman with greater control over her earnings. Also, younger women are somewhat more likely to have partial control. But little else is related. Most importantly, number of younger brothers has no effect on the control a woman has over her earnings.

Does something statistically hide the impact of younger brothers? Perhaps education does; it could be that daughters receive less education if their parents are eager to push them into the labor force and appropriate their earnings to finance the education of younger sons. However, leaving education out of the analysis (as in column 1 of table 11.1) does little to change the results of the earnings-control analysis. This suggests that there may be other mechanisms at work that have hitherto been overlooked in the literature on women, economic development, and patriarchal norms.

It may be that there is some effect from the total number of siblings that is obscured by our detailed separation into younger/older, brother/sister categories. Redoing the analysis including simply the number of siblings does indeed show a significant sibling effect. Daughters with many siblings are less likely to have full control over the use of their income (details not shown). However, what remains striking about the sibling figures in table 11.1 is that contrary to expectation, *it is not younger brothers but younger sisters who are the greatest threat to a daughter's full control over the use of her earnings.*[4] It may be that the family's important need for resources stems not so much from the necessity for younger brothers to pursue more education and job training but for younger sisters to accumulate a dowry so that they can find a suitable spouse.

The argument that a daughter's earnings are used to advance the career of younger brothers can be further questioned by the finding that father's socioeconomic status has little impact on a woman's control over her pay. If indeed daughters' earnings were being spent on sons' education, that should happen most often among financially strapped parents. But this is not borne out in our findings; parental socioeconomic status is unrelated to a woman's control over her pay.

In sum, from our analysis it is not clear that single women's earnings in Taiwan have greatly benefited their siblings. It is clear, however, that the women in our sample did work many years before marriage (six on average) and that many of them had less than full control over the use of their earnings. Our findings suggest that some of these earnings were redistributed to other family members, both male and female. The central issue, then, is what proportion of single women's income was utilized by parents and siblings and whether premarital work eventually helped or hurt women's long-term life chances. We will focus on four aspects of life chances: amount of dowry, "quality" of husband, postmarital labor force participation, and current earnings (similarly, see Lee, Chapter 8 this volume, which focuses specifically on the role of higher education for women's work and marriage in South Korea).

Marriage Finance

If parents use up most of what their daughters earn, then little remains for later gifts to daughters. One occasion on which parents can potentially give sizable gifts to daughters is at the time of marriage. In Taiwan, as in other Chinese populations, marriage finance involves an indirect dowry system. The groom's family pays a bride price which is typically used by the bride's family to provide a dowry of furniture, bedding, clothing, and other goods of roughly equal value (e.g., Johnson, Parish, and Lin 1987). Thus, bride price and dowry typically coexist. This is illustrated in our sample of marriages: over 80 percent of women who provided a dowry also received a bride price. Bride price and dowry arrangements are usually negotiated by parents and/or a third party mediator. Given the rapid rise in the number of free choice marriages, in which individuals choose their own mate (as opposed to entering into an arranged marriage), it is reasonable to expect that dowry and bride price arrangements declined rapidly by the 1990s (on free choice trends, see Freedman, Chang, and Sun 1982; Gallin 1984b; Thornton, Chang, and Sun 1984). Things were not quite that simple, however.

Our data show that things changed considerably over time, with the prevalence of dowry rising from about two-fifths to over half of all marriages and bride price falling from two-thirds to about two-fifths of all marriages (figure 11.2A). These changes are consistent with four changes in marriage finance that occurred due to a transformation in the marriage market in Taiwan. First, the loss of the Chinese mainland to Communist rule in 1949 caused a large contingent of young males in the defeated Nationalist army and in other forms of public service to retreat to Taiwan. This produced a highly imbalanced marriage market in the 1950s, with many migrant males "bidding" for a small pool of available females. In this context, it is not surprising that it was much more likely for a husband to give a bride price while the girl's family gave little or no dowry. In the 1960s, as the sex ratio of young people of marriageable age began to equalize, the gap between those giving

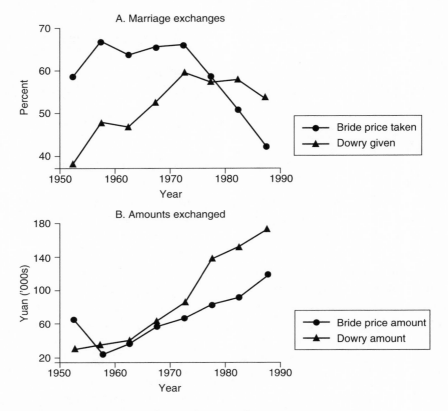

Figure 11.2.   Marriage Exchanges by Year of Marriage

SOURCE: Taiwan Women and Family Survey, 1989.

NOTE: Amounts in constant 1988 NT$, calculated only for those who gave or received some amount.

bride price and receiving dowry also began to narrow. Second, this narrowing tendency was accelerated by the rapid shift of young, unmarried women into the paid labor force. In popular understandings of the time, this new source of income for young unmarried women allowed them (or, more frequently, their families) to bid up the frequency and size of dowry payments (William Parish, personal communication). This was the second source of change.

The third source of change was that with increasing free choice in marriage, financial exchanges at marriage, typically negotiated by elders in the family, began to decline. This decline was more rapid for bride price than for dowry. We suspect that this was because the unmarried women who worked had the means to offer a dowry. The fourth change was the rising prosperity of brides, grooms, and their families. This increasing prosperity translated into higher values in marriage exchanges (even after adjusting for inflation; figure 11.2B). The increase was more rapid for dowry than for bride price, which is consistent with the argument that part of daughters' new earnings was being used to finance their dowries.

The combination of the second and fourth changes outlined above meant that the value of dowries rose more rapidly than the value of bride price. In our sample, among people who had married at different times over the last several decades, there were four possible outcomes:

1. A bride's parents could keep most of the bride price payments from the groom's parents and presumably use the funds for the parents' own needs or for the needs of children other than the daughter. In fact, only 15 percent of brides' parents followed this pattern.

2. Both the bride's and the groom's parents could eschew interparental financial exchanges, instead letting the new couple fund most household start-up expenses on their own. About 30 percent of parents followed this pattern. We would expect this to occur most often among more urbanized and higher-status parents, whose children have better jobs and higher incomes.

3. The bride's parents could simply pass on all monetary gifts from the groom's family, returning the gifts to the young couple as the daughter's dowry of bedding, furniture, clothing, and other household goods. This is the traditional "indirect dowry" system, which remained common through the late 1980s (45 percent of cases).

4. A small minority of brides' parents paid all or most of the expenses for their daughters' dowry (9 percent).

If seen as a bargaining game between the bride's parents and their daughter, the greatest gains to the parent (and the daughter's siblings) is in situation one. The greatest gains to the daughter are in situation four. Situation three might also provide some gain to the daughter, particularly when her parents negotiate a "good deal" with the groom's parents. However, her gains are more the result of her parents' negotiating skills and resources than of their direct financial contributions.

In our analysis, we want to know whether parents cluster more toward solution one (parents win) or toward solution four (daughter wins). In particular, we want to know whether the shift among solutions is influenced by a woman's work before marriage, with solution four serving as a kind of re-

TABLE 11.2
Marriage Finance and Daughter's Premarital Work

	MARRIAGE FINANCE FLOWS		
	None	*Indirect dowry*	*Bride's parents pay*
Year of marriage	.00	.01	.04***
Urban background (1 = grew up in city, 0 = did not)	.05	−.13	−.13
Father's economic status	.07	−.10*	.09
Years of education	.11***	.09***	.23***
Age at marriage	.10***	.02	.10***
Years worked before marriage (logged)	−.16**	.24***	.08
Number of (logged):			
older brothers	−.36***	.02	−.27*
older sisters	−.13	−.05	−.18
younger brothers	−.21*	.07	.07
younger sisters	−.32***	−.05	−.33**
Percentage of all responses	31%	45%	9%

NOTES: Multinomial logit coefficients from a single equation that uses the financial flow from a groom's parents to the bride's parents as the comparison. The coefficients show how likely it is that one of the other three flows will emerge rather than the comparison. $N = 3424$. Pseudo $R^2 = .06$.

$*p < .10$, $**p < .05$, $***p < .01$

payment for her previous economic contributions to the family. We also want to know whether competition from brothers moves the daughter more toward the first "parents win" option.

We note at the outset that few daughters "won" significant financial exchanges at marriage. Only 9 percent (table 11.2, column 3) received significant financial contributions from their own parents. When they did "win" in this manner, they got back on average about 10 months of an average female worker's salary. Women who worked before marriage typically worked a total of five to six years. Increasingly, that work was away from home, and if we take into account the costs incurred for room and board, 10 months of salary represents a significant amount of savings. Even so, to the extent that only a small minority of women reaped any net dowry contributions from their parents, dowry was only a minor way for working daughters to recoup the income contributions they had made to the family.

We investigate these patterns in greater detail with a multivariate analysis that includes the range of conditions that shape marital finance. Our primary interest is in whether premarital work leads to exchanges that favor daughters more and whether competition from brothers leads to exchanges in the other direction. But a number of other conditions will also shape marital finance. These include the following. Year of marriage should be important because of the changing sex ratios and other influences in the larger society. (These influences were suggested in the over-time patterns we discussed.) Urban background should also be important, as urban families are more likely to shift away from traditional patterns of exchange toward a pattern of letting the new couple manage their own start-up expenses. This should occur not only because of changing values but also because urban couples are more likely to have ample incomes for their initial household expenses. Father's economic status should help determine whether a daughter's parents need to keep the groom's payments to themselves or pass them on to the new couple.

In addition, women's educational attainment should have several consequences for marital finance. Educated women are more likely to defy traditional norms of marriage finance. Nevertheless, high educational attainment can be associated with a bigger dowry due to the positive association between women's education and parental wealth and due also to the fact that well-educated women have a weaker bargaining position in the marriage market because social norms generally dictate that women should "marry up" in the status hierarchy. Finally, higher age at marriage increases a woman's autonomy relative to her parents, making it more likely that parents will either be totally uninvolved in marriage exchanges or that they will give into demands for more assistance from their daughters.[5]

In our multivariate analysis, all of these background conditions have an influence (table 11.2). In recent years more daughters have gotten a net contribution from their parents (see column 3). In cities, more parents eschew overt financial exchanges and choose instead to let the young couple fund their own household set-up expenses (although this effect is not statistically significant; column 1). Higher-status parents are more likely to be non-involved in marriage finances or to contribute to their daughter's dowry, rather than to garner some of their daughter's earnings or to simply pass on as indirect dowry the groom's contribution.[6] Undoubtedly for a variety of reasons, the income of educated daughters tends not to be used by their parents, and in some cases these daughters actually receive additional resources from parents. As expected, daughters who marry at an older age either circumvent parental finance entirely or gain additional resources from their parents. Thus, both age and education substantially improve a daughter's economic bargaining position relative to her parents.

Marital finance is also shaped by a daughter's premarital work. The longer a woman works before marriage, the less likely it is that parents are completely uninvolved in marital financing. However, parents are less likely to garner resources from their daughter than to pass on all of the groom's parents' payments to the new couple. This pattern fits our earlier conclusion that daughters have few direct opportunities to recoup their work contributions through marriage finance. Though they gain greater control over contributions from the groom's parents, they fail to gain major new dowry resources from their own parents. In other words, *single women's work provides few immediate monetary benefits to them at the time of marriage.*

Finally, single women's economic rewards and losses are shaped by competition from siblings. Older sisters have little effect on a woman's marital finance. As suggested by Parish and Willis, the major way older sisters help is by early exit from the family via marriage (1993). In contrast, other siblings appear to lead parents to be involved in marital finance, often to the daughter's financial loss. Contrary to the accounts that emphasize how daughters' economic well-being is sacrificed for younger sons, the greatest threat to a daughter's economic rewards comes from both her older brothers and her younger sisters. Both sets of siblings keep daughters from receiving dowry contributions from their parents.

These analyses show that competition from siblings forces daughters to sacrifice more, but often in patterns that are more complex than in the usual patriarchy explanation. When a woman marries, younger sisters compete for family resources just as much as older brothers. In sum, financial exchanges at the time of marriage provide daughters with few chances to recoup their premarital work contributions to the family.

Do daughters receive any additional contributions from parents *after* marriage? Historically in Taiwan, a daughter could expect only modest postmarital contributions from parents. In our sample, years worked before marriage failed to improve a woman's chances of getting either land or buildings at the time of family property partition.[7] Daughters' early work was also unrelated to in-kind assistance from parents to daughters. For example, parents' assistance (in contrast to her husband's parents' assistance; see Chapter 3 this volume) with childcare remained minimal even when the daughter had worked for many years before marriage.

In short, over the past three decades, if parents' repayment for a daughter's work and financial contributions to the family before marriage took place at all, it was restricted to dowry payments at the time of marriage. In this way family behavior remained very much in a traditional, patrilineal mold, with financial ties to daughters tapering off rapidly after marriage.

"Quality of Spouse"

Women's work before marriage can have multiple consequences for their long-term economic security. Even if in the short run, parents and siblings reap many of the rewards from single women's work, it may be that the long-term benefits to women are nevertheless substantial. Several factors could help a woman find a more educated husband, including she herself having more education, her parents having more income, her marrying in a more recent year when education was more common for everyone, her growing up in a city as opposed to a village, and her being a member of the urbanized, politically dominant mainlander minority that arrived after World War II. Our results for marriages over the last four decades suggest that all these factors were important (table 11.3, column 1). Most significantly for the themes of this volume, the longer a woman worked before marriage, the more educated was the man she married.

This effect of work before marriage may be two-pronged. First, work before marriage can enhance a woman's chances of finding a more educated husband by enabling her to meet such men at her place of work. Second, parents who accumulate earnings from a daughter's work may be able to engage in more successful negotiation with the parents of more educated sons. Any assessment of this second "ability to pay" effect is necessarily imprecise because of the feedback effect between quality of prospective mate and the size of dowry. That is, size of dowry could be both a cause and a consequence of better quality husbands. It is a consequence when a woman's parents discover after the match has been initiated that a high status groom's parents expect far more in dowry than they had planned to give. Conversely, know-

TABLE 11.3
Husband's Years of Schooling by
Women's Premarital Work and Dowry

Variable description	Short model	Long model
Years of education	0.68***	0.66***
Urban background (1 = grew up in city; 0 = did not)	0.24**	0.24**
Year of marriage	−0.014*	−0.02**
Mainlander (1 = mainland Chinese origin; 0 = otherwise)	1.50***	1.53***
Father's economic status (1 = poor; 2 = so-so; 3 = rich)	0.42***	0.41***
Amount of bride price in real Taiwan $, logged		−0.05***
Amount of dowry in real Taiwan $, logged		0.05***
Years worked before marriage	0.05***	0.05***
Constant	29.64**	33.76**
N	3101	3101
Adjusted R^2	.509	.513

$*p < .10, **p < .05, ***p < .01$

ing that their son is desired by many prospective brides, the parents of more-educated grooms will be disinclined to give large bride prices. Thus, it is difficult to sort out the precise direction of causation among bride price, dowry, and quality of husband. Nevertheless, we can get some assessment of causal effects when background conditions are included in the equation at the same time (table 11.3, column 2).

The results are consistent not only with explanations that emphasize marriage finance being a consequence of husband's quality (better-quality husbands provide less bride price and demand more dowry) but also with explanations that emphasize how women who have worked and acquired more resources can pay the dowries that allow them to marry more desirable husbands. The quantitative results imply that part of the influence of the respondent's own education, father's socioeconomic status, and work before marriage comes through the intermediate influence of how generous a dowry she can provide. Her education and years of work should increase her accumulated earnings, and her father's status should increase the amount her parents can contribute to her dowry. Each of these background influences on ability to pay declines in influence once amount of dowry is included in the analysis (compare columns 1 and 2, table 11.3). This suggests that part of the influence of these conditions is indeed being mediated through amount of dowry.

Work before marriage, then, appears to have both a direct effect (the opportunity to meet a more educated husband) and an indirect effect (the ability to pay expected dowry) on the quality of husband a woman marries. Some of the benefits of work before marriage thereby pass to the daughter through her increased ability to marry a husband who can provide greater financial security in the years to come.

Postmarital Labor Force Participation

According to the extreme version of patriarchy explanations, daughters are educated only to the point where they can successfully enter the nonagricultural labor market in dead-end, lackluster jobs with flat earnings profiles. If indeed women were being forced to take up undesirable jobs by their parents, one would expect them to give up these jobs once they got married. However, in our sample almost three-fourths of the women who worked before marriage continued to do so after marriage.

This continued work after marriage was part of a rising trend in married women's labor force participation that followed the inception of export-led growth in the mid-1960s (figure 11.3A; see also Chapters 1 and 2 this volume). Because Taiwan women tended to have their first child immediately after marriage, the period just after marriage was a time when the demands of tending to a young child kept many women at home. Those women who did return to work after moving to their husband's home often took jobs in self-employment, out-work for larger enterprises, and unpaid family employment (helping in their husband's business rather than in their own parents' business). Fewer women returned to work as full-time paid employees (compare the total and paid employee lines in figures 11.1A and 11.3A). These

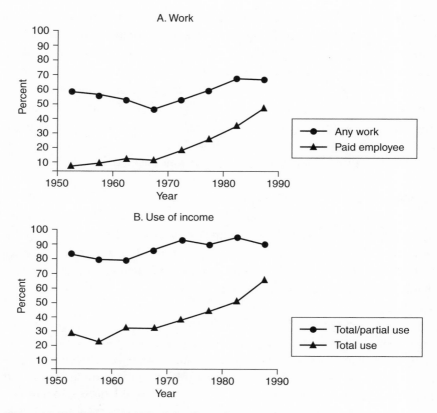

Figure 11.3.   Postmarital Work by Year of Marriage

SOURCE: Taiwan Women and Family Survey, 1989.

NOTE: Working three years after year of marriage.

are traditional trends, very much in keeping with what one expects in a society with strong patriarchal norms that require women to move between
households at the time of marriage and to invest much in their children for
the sake of family continuity.

Nevertheless, despite these strong patriarchal forces, married women's
work began to increase rapidly after the start of export-led growth in the
middle 1960s. The increase was particularly dramatic for work as paid employees, which more than quadrupled in two decades (figure 11.3A). This
growth in paid employment also had consequences for women's use of their

own income. In contrast to unmarried women, who often had little control over the use of their earnings in the initial decades, virtually all married women always had at least partial control over their earnings (figure 11.3B). Even in a family business, they were frequently the ones who staffed the cash register and kept the books (see Chapter 10 this volume). In addition to this partial control, in the last two decades they increasingly gained total control over the use of their earnings (bottom line of figure 11.3B). Thus, though the tenacity of tradition is in some ways surprising, what is equally surprising is how fast some things have changed for married women.

The question with which we began was whether women's work before marriage redounded only to the benefit of a woman's parents and siblings or also to the woman herself. We can continue that inquiry by asking whether women who worked before marriage were more likely to continue work immediately after marriage. Whether a woman works or not at any point in time is likely to be shaped primarily by individual labor supply factors including education, age, husband's income, and husband's education (see early part of Chapter 1, on women's work during late industrialization). These are included in our next analysis along with year of marriage and urban origin.

We examine whether these types of factors influenced a woman's work three years after marriage, by which time any temporary disturbances of work caused by migration to the husband's place of residence would have passed (table 11.4). Except for the nonsignificant consequences of year of marriage and of having a child, all the other standard background conditions influence postmarital work in the predicted direction. Married women are more likely to work if they are more educated, younger, non-mainlander, and in rural areas. They are also more likely to work when their husbands are poorer and more educated. These are quite predictable findings. More importantly for our purposes, women are also more likely to work after marriage if they had worked before marriage. In the context of standard labor supply theories, this could again be seen as a predictable finding—accumulated prior experience makes women more valuable to potential employers. Where the finding is more exceptional is in the context of the pessimistic theories arguing that young women's work before marriage was only in dead-end jobs where all the rewards were reaped by parents. In this context, it is surprising that premarital work continued to increase women's chances for work after marriage.[8] (Also see the comparative chapters in this volume for

TABLE 11.4
Work after Marriage

Variable description	Probit coefficient
Years of education	0.08***
Urban background (1 = grew up in city; 0 = did not)	−0.13***
Year of marriage	−0.004
Mainlander (1 = mainland Chinese origin; 0 = otherwise)	−0.22***
Age 3 years after marriage	−0.06***
Child within 3 years of marriage (1 = had a child; 0 = did not)	−0.02
Husband's socioeconomic status	−0.57***
Husband's education level	0.03***
Years worked before marriage	0.12***
Constant	13.06**

NOTES: The coefficients have been obained from a probit model, where 1 = working three years after marriage and 0 = not working. $N = 3452$. Pseudo $R^2 = .07$.

$^*p < .10, ^{**}p < .05, ^{***}p < .01$

the stronger effect of women's premarital work on work after marriage in Taiwan than in Japan and South Korea.)

Current Earnings

How are married women's earnings affected by their premarital work experience? If women worked mainly in dead-end jobs with flat earnings profiles, work experience would not have a positive impact on their later wages. However, if premarital work experience did have a positive impact on women's current wages, it would demonstrate that they reaped long-term benefits from that experience.

Assessing current wages requires controls for standard human capital variables, including years of education and experience (as proxied by age and age-squared). We also control for husband's earnings and employment status to net out the effect these variables can have on a woman's current earnings.[9] One would expect a priori that improvements in husband's economic status would reduce a woman's need for supplementing household income with her own earnings. This expectation is confirmed by the negative

TABLE 11.5
Premarital Work and
Women's Current Earnings

Variable description	Regression coefficient
Years of education	0.15***
Rural residence (1 = city; 2 = town; 3 = village)	−0.16**
Mainlander (1 = mainland Chinese origin; 0 = otherwise)	0.24
Age	0.19***
Age^2	−0.002***
Husband employed (1 = employed; 0 = unemployed)	−2.11***
Husband's income, logged	−0.29***
Years worked before marriage	0.06**
Lambda	−1.71**
Constant	−1.64

NOTE: N = 1734. Adjusted R^2 = .106. The analysis controls for self-selection by including Heckman's lambda. Dependent variable is current hourly wages (logged) in Taiwan dollars.

*$p < .10$, **$p < .05$, ***$p < .01$

coefficients associated with these variables (table 11.5). Our results are also consistent with those predicted by human capital models. Current wages rise significantly with increases in women's level of education. Also, they rise with age (a proxy for experience), with the rate of increase declining with age (captured by the negative coefficient of age-squared). Background influences—city, town, or village residence and whether or not the women is a mainlander—are also discounted for reasons described earlier. Even with these controls, we find the relationship between years worked before marriage and real wages later in life to be positive and statistically significant (table 11.5). Thus, work before marriage has continuing benefits for women after they marry.[10]

DISCUSSION

When a considerable literature on women, export-led economic development, and patriarchy has been so negative, how can the findings in this chapter be so positive about the consequences of women's work before marriage?

Have we overlooked something very obvious? We were concerned about this issue, for we did not expect quite the results that we obtained. To that end, we delve into some of our more nagging concerns below.

Parental Self-Interest

We want to emphasize that we are by no means arguing that a woman's pre-marital labor force participation is not linked to parental self-interest. What we are arguing instead is that even in a patriarchal society such as Taiwan, globalization may advantage women in ways that are often overlooked in the research literature. This implies neither that daughters are able to retain all the benefits from their work nor that parents do not discriminate between sons and daughters. Given the paucity of public old-age support in Taiwan and the continuing dependence of parents on sons in old age (see also Chapter 3 by Yu), it is to be expected that parents of modest means will focus their attention on sons who will support the parents in old age. That tendency is likely to moderate somewhat with growing prosperity and a low birth rate, both of which allow parents to accumulate more savings before retirement. But as late as the 1990s, all of daughters' earnings were not being returned to them through dowry or in any other form.

Nevertheless, women in Taiwan have been better off as a consequence of getting more education and working before marriage. Even when parents, brothers, and (importantly) sisters were the major early beneficiaries of a woman's education and work, she still acquired human capital that, when combined with a high-demand labor market, could serve her well in later life.

Comparing Men

We have examined in this chapter the bold hypothesis that global involvement in a patriarchal society worsens women's situation. The proponents of this hypothesis might well complain that what they had in mind was a much more modest hypothesis: Although women may make absolute gains in income and autonomy when compared to their mothers, they still fail to keep up with their brothers and other males in the same generation. Patriarchal discrimination in the family is an important source of women's lagging gains.

This is not an easy hypothesis to test. Many things other than parental decisions shape a woman's adult life chances, including discrimination by adult men (such as employers) outside a woman's own family. Nevertheless, there are several statistics that give one pause. One is that with globalization and the movement of women outside the home to work, women are increasingly receiving their own income. Increasingly, few women work as unpaid family laborers, and more women state that they have significant control over the use of their income (figures 11.1 and 11.3). This suggests that women have made major gains on this dimension. Though far short of an egalitarian ideal, women are closer to men in terms of control over their income than when Taiwan's global market involvement began.

Also important is the ratio of women's to men's incomes. Working as paid employees, women in Taiwan in 1996 made 64 percent as much as men.[11] Again, while short of full egalitarian ideals, this figure is about the same as in the United States until recently. And it is higher than in much of Southeast Asia, where patriarchal norms are weaker. Thus, 30 years of global market involvement in a society with strong patriarchal values seems to have produced results that are not inferior to societies with weaker patriarchal values. Patriarchal values, while important, are to some extent malleable and can soften over time.

CONCLUSION

Once the long-term as well as the short-term outcomes for women are considered together, the strong argument that patriarchal exploitation characterizes women's premarital labor force behavior in Taiwan is seriously undermined. We definitely find evidence of continuity in patriarchal values. However, the story is one of persistence combined with significant changes. On the one hand, daughters do not generally maintain total control over their own income, they do not recoup all their earnings in dowry, financial relations between parents and daughters largely cease at marriage, and daughters tend to move away at marriage. However, there are many areas of dramatic change. Compared to two decades ago, young unmarried women are now much more likely to work as paid employees and to have greater say over how their incomes are used. Even in the case when much of their earnings goes to parents and siblings, daughters reap many long-term advantages. They get slightly better dowry financing, better-quality husbands, and are more likely to work after marriage. Finally, premarital work experience helps raise their earnings later in life.

As other chapters in this volume have argued, a plethora of small firms that are labor- rather than capital-intensive meant that rapid export-led growth in Taiwan raised labor demand significantly. This generated more choices for women over the kinds of jobs they would take and the terms and conditions of those jobs. Real earnings have increased significantly for women in Taiwan, and women have acquired increasingly greater control over how these earnings will be spent. We suggest that the very pessimistic conclusions for Taiwan drawn by much of the literature on export-led growth may stem from a focus on the early stages of economic growth or on portions of the female population who lack the education, skills, and locational advantages to help them participate in new forms of employment. In our view, this scenario is increasingly inaccurate for Taiwan.

Chapter One

I wish to thank Matthew Di Carlo, Zun Tang, and other participants in the Comparative Societal Analysis workshop at Cornell University for their insightful suggestions on an earlier draft of this chapter. I am also grateful to Yutaka Horiba of Tulane University for his comments.

1. There is also a strong tradition of research on the lives of factory women in other parts of Asia such as Indonesia; see Wolf 1992.

2. This literature built on Ester Boserup's classic work outlining the negative consequences of development for the valuation of women's productive activities (1970), and is in stark contrast to the rosy predictions of the earlier prevalent modernization theory in sociology. The integration thesis in modernization theory posited that the growth of individualism and modern norms stressing achievement rather than ascription, coupled with the expansion of education and the increasing utility of educational credentials in the labor market, would lead to greater equality between men and women (Goode 1970; Moore 1963). In this optimistic scenario, women enter wage employment in increasing numbers with industrialization, and patriarchy is gradually replaced by egalitarian sex roles (Davis 1984; Inkeles and Smith 1974).

3. In organizing the volume to be highly oriented toward urban women, it is important to acknowledge the importance of earlier studies, particularly by anthropologists, of rural women's work lives in East Asia (Bernstein 1983; Gallin 1984a; Smith 1982; Tamanoi 1998; Wolf 1972; also see Gills 1999 for a recent study of rural women's work in South Korea).

4. I use the terms service sector and tertiary sector interchangeably, as with manufacturing sector and secondary sector, and agricultural and primary sector.

5. These latter countries are particularly egalitarian either in their legal commitment to gender equality in the labor market (the United States and Canada) or in the state support they offer to working parents (Northern European countries). This is discussed more fully in Chang (2000).

6. Among non-Asian OECD countries, only in Ireland, Italy, Mexico, Portu-

gal, and Spain does the proportion of the labor force in wage or salaried employ-ment fall below 85 percent (OECD 2000b).

7. The decline with age in economic participation by women in Taiwan (fig-ure 1.3) seems to be due principally to a cohort rather than an age effect. That is, women's labor force participation rates historically went up so rapidly in Taiwan that the rate for women in their 20s is much higher than the rate for older middle-aged women. Even so, the pattern of dropping out of the labor force with marriage and child rearing was much less common even for older women in Taiwan than in the other two East Asian countries (Yu 1999b).

8. While the Japanese colonial government set up a formal school system in each country, it limited Koreans to primary education (Lett 1998; Mason et al. 1980). In Taiwan, some middle schools were mainly for Taiwanese (Tsurumi 1977). Educational attainment increased very rapidly in both South Korea and Taiwan once colonial rule ended.

9. Reports in the Japanese media and in scholarly articles in the 1990s repeat-edly emphasized women's increasing postponement of marriage and the possibility that the rates of permanent singlehood were rising in that country. A recent com-parative survey reported that only about half of Japanese women expect to be hap-pier if they marry than if they remain single, whereas 70 percent of South Korean women expect happiness with marriage (American women's expectations fall squarely between these two; Inoue 1998).

10. See Buchmann and Charles for a comparison of women's labor force par-ticipation in six European countries, based on the hours of childcare facilities, stores, and other institutions affecting married women's everyday lives (1995).

11. Tadashi Hanami, Research Director General at the Japan Institute of La-bor, states baldly, "the EEOL was born as an ugly duckling and has never meta-morphosed into a swan" (Hanami 2000). The law, which went into effect in 1986, was not so much the result of forces within Japan but rather pressure from the in-ternational community on Japan to conform to the U.N. Declaration on the Elimi-nation of All Forms of Discrimination against Women (Brinton 1993; Lam 1992). In the consultations leading up to the formulation of the law's provisions, labor and women's groups were pitted against Japan's powerful federation of employers, Nikkeiren. The latter largely triumphed, succeeding in the promulgation of a law that "encouraged" employers to refrain from discrimination on the basis of sex and that made female employees' recourse to the courts nearly impossible (given the provisions regulating how employer-employee conflicts were to be mediated; see below and Upham 1987). The number of changes in employment-related law in the past few years in Japan has been significant. These present a complicated mosaic that, in tandem with strong gender norms, create cross-cutting pressures on mar-ried women (especially mothers) in the labor force (see the discussions by Boling 2000, and Shire and Imai 2000).

12. This being said, tax law provides greater incentives for Japanese married women to work part-time than full-time; this is not the case in Taiwan (Yu 1999b).

Still, this does not explain the M-shaped curve of female labor force participation itself in Japan, as this curve counts part-time as well as full-time employment.

13. Greater bureaucratization and formalization of personnel practices has been shown to have a positive effect on the proportion of female managers in the United States, particularly in large firms (Reskin and McBrier 2000).

14. I could not locate similar research comparing women's earnings in the private sector and in government jobs in South Korea.

Chapter Two

This is a slightly revised version of our earlier paper published as "Married Women's Employment in Rapidly Industrializing Societies: Examples from East Asia," *American Journal of Sociology* 100: 1099–1130. Research support from the Spencer Foundation, the National Institutes of Child Health and Human Development (grant R01 HD23322), and the Chiang Ching Kuo Foundation is gratefully acknowledged. We also thank the Korean Women's Development Institute for allowing us to use the Korean data. Charles Chi-hsiang Chang provided research assistance for the paper. We received helpful comments from participants in the Labor Workshop and the Demography Workshop at the University of Chicago and from several anonymous readers.

1. For examples of the earlier literature on the patterns in each society, see Chang 1982; Chiang and Ku 1985; Cho and Koo 1983; Directorate-General of Budget, Accounting, and Statistics, *Social Indicators* 1991; Galenson 1992; Kang 1993; Kim 1990; KWDI 1986; and Liu 1984.

2. To correct for a slight underrepresentation of large cities, the Taiwan data were weighted to accurately reflect the distribution of the urban population across different city sizes.

3. To the extent that either society had direct foreign investment, some scholars conclude that the employment effects were either neutral or positive (Koo 1985; Ranis and Chi 1985; Tu 1990).

4. As Amsden (1989) notes, the pattern of high returns to education in the midst of high unemployment among the educated is very curious, and is difficult to explain.

5. In order to eliminate differences between the two countries' occupational distributions that might be produced by educational differences in the samples of women, we standardized South Korea's educational distribution against Taiwan's for the purpose of this table.

6. While it would be desirable to retain junior college and university as distinct categories, the number of women with university education is too low to permit this.

7. We do this for two reasons: (1) Classifying self-employed or family enterprise workers by occupation is probably not conceptually meaningful; and (2) our interest in the occupational distribution lies in the prediction of a flow of married

women out of white-collar occupations. This is predicated on the idea of a marriage bar resulting from the actions of employers, who are only relevant in cases where women are employees.

8. For various reasons, married women aged 25–29 are underrepresented in the Taiwan sample. But because these are the women most likely to be in paid employment (table 2.1), age biases in the sample serve not to overstate but to understate the differences we ascribe to Taiwan and South Korea. Moreover, aggregate statistics from government labor force surveys parallel the patterns we report here.

9. In models combining all three types of employment (not shown here), education has little effect on women's overall employment in Taiwan because of its offsetting effects on different types of employment. Only college education has a significant positive relationship with women's employment. In South Korea, on the other hand, education has consistently negative effects on all three types of employment and thus shows a very strong negative relationship with aggregate employment. For both countries, the effect of the husband being an employer or a self-employed worker is also strongly related in a positive direction to the wife working. This is because the positive effect on the wife's probability of being a family enterprise worker (as well as self-employed in the case of Taiwan) overrides the negative effect on her probability of being an employee. These patterns hold in both the short and long models.

10. Although not shown here, the relationship between wife's education and husband's logged income, controlling for wife's age, is positive and strong in both countries. But the regression coefficient for wife's education is larger in South Korea than in Taiwan. The relationship between husband's and wife's education is also stronger in South Korea, all of which fits the social science literature describing how educated Korean women divert their energies from the labor market to the marriage market (e.g., Kim 1990; Park 1991).

11. The intersociety differences in the effects of work experience and youngest child's age are substantial but not statistically significant.

12. The percentage differences in this comparison are muted because the comparison includes unmarried as well as married women and because it includes women of all ages.

Chapter Three

Support from the National University of Singapore (Academic Research Fund, RP #112-000-007-107/11), Hosei University, and the Chiang Ching Kuo Foundation is gratefully acknowledged. I would also like to thank Professor Mary Brinton and the Social Stratification and Social Mobility (SSM) Survey Committee for permission to use a portion of the 1995 SSM data for my doctoral dissertation research. An earlier draft of this research was presented at the Annual Meetings of the Association for Asian Studies in San Diego, March 2000, where I received valuable comments.

1. I use data from Questionnaire A of the survey.

2. While the cross-sectional data seem to imply that Taiwanese women retire from the labor force quite early, the gap in the labor force participation rate for older women between Japan and Taiwan actually results from cohort differences. Due to rapid social change, younger cohorts in Taiwan are far more active in the labor force than older cohorts were during their young ages. These cohort differences lead to a decline in labor force participation across successively older age groups. In fact, for every cohort the labor force participation rate has increased as the cohort moved out of the early stage of childrearing (see Yu 1999b for more details).

3. I further examined the association between cohort and women's gender-role attitudes as well as employment status and gender-role attitudes. However I categorized the samples, Taiwanese women tend to agree more with traditional gender roles than their Japanese counterparts.

4. The demand for caring for aged or ill household members can also keep a wife out of the labor force, but the demand for childcare is relevant to a larger number of households.

5. But just as there are times when working in a small firm benefits women, there are also times when the employer's needs come first. For example, a Taiwanese woman with whom I spoke gave the following story in explaining why she preferred to work in a large rather than a small firm: "At the time I got married, I was entitled to have a marital leave, you know, for our honeymoon. But in a small firm, you can't just take a leave when you want to. My boss didn't let me because it was quite busy at that time. He asked me to get back to work right after the wedding and have my honeymoon trip when the company was less busy. It is sometimes really annoying to work for a small firm."

6. The same can generally be said when we compare the sizes of other major cities in the two countries.

7. While the charge at public daycare centers depends on household income, it is by no means low for most households. It is often said that if a household has two or more children in daycare centers, a working mother will have little left from her salary after paying the daycare expenses. Private daycare centers are usually too expensive for mothers to feel that their stay in the labor force is worthwhile.

8. Although I call it a type of household division of labor, in some cases the three generations do not live under one roof. Grandparents may live close to the nuclear family composed of the two succeeding generations. Even though the three generations do not live under the same roof, the way in which they share household responsibilities and family income makes them functionally close to one household.

9. The office atmosphere for Taiwanese women in white-collar jobs is quite different from that of their counterparts in Japan, but it would still be a mistake to assume that male managers in Taiwan do not have any preference between single and married women. A woman with whom I spoke said that a male manager explicitly asked her during her job interview not to become pregnant in the near future. (At the time she had just gotten married.) Another woman who worked in a

bank told me that she heard a male manager speak in public about his intention to avoid recruiting women who had recently married, because "they will get pregnant soon and ask for maternity leave." It is also common for employers to reduce, or withdraw completely, a woman's year-end bonus when she has taken maternity leave during the year. Cohort differences also exist. Older women whom I spoke to are more likely to report that they had encountered or heard about difficulties in taking maternity leave, while this is rarely the case for women in their 30s. As stated above, labor demand conditions in Taiwan have forced management to compromise gradually and to accept more young mothers who continue to work.

Chapter Four

1. As the labor economics and sociology literatures document, it is often hard to distinguish empirically between voluntary and involuntary job separations. For instance, so-called voluntary job separation is often in fact driven by circumstances related to the labor market.

2. This does not mean that there is no competition based on achievement or that there are no differences in promotion among workers who have the same length of tenure. There is indeed variation in salaries and also competition for promotion within internal labor markets (Ariga, Ōkusa, and Brunello 1997; Imada and Hirata 1995; Ishida, Spilerman, and Su 1997).

3. The Equal Employment Opportunity Law was revised and its regulations became stricter in 1999.

4. Exceptions to this are young women from rural areas who migrated massively during the 1960s and 1970s to work in urban factories, but these women's dormitories or other independent living situations were arranged because of severe economic pressure on their families for them to work.

5. This would be the case apart from the confounding effect of how the timing of marriage is related to women's strategic choices.

6. Women who leave their jobs at marriage may reenter the labor market later in their life course. In the Japanese data set, "job separators" also include a minority of women (less than 10 percent) who change their jobs but move immediately to a different job. In the Taiwan and South Korea data, job separators include only women who have a time interval between their pre- and postmarital jobs. These slight differences in the coding schemes are because of differences in the survey data structure for the three countries. For further details, readers should refer to the methods section in this chapter.

7. With small rural populations and with occupation before marriage (including agriculture) controlled in the multivariate analysis, the effects of other independent variables would not be affected to any significant degree by excluding rural residents from the sample.

8. We note that for women not currently married, first husband's information is missing.

9. In Taiwan, the survey asked directly whether women quit their jobs because of marriage. In the Japanese data, women's occupational history is recorded by the beginning and ending years of employment at every firm where the woman worked. If the year of ending the latest employment before marriage is the same as the age at marriage or earlier, job separation is coded as 1. Among the women who left their jobs, a small minority immediately started another job, often as unpaid family workers. In this case job separation is coded as 0. In the South Korean data, work and marital history were recorded by age regardless of employers or jobs; so we construct the variable of job separation based on yearly records. If previously working women are not working at the time of marriage or in the next year after marriage, then job separation is coded as 1. If previously working women are still working at the next age after marriage, job separation is coded as 0.

10. In preliminary analyses we also examined other interaction models, including interactions between education and work duration, between occupation and age at marriage, and between education and age at marriage. These interaction effects were minimal.

11. In a comparative study of Japan and South Korea, Liao (1998) finds that extended family living significantly increases working wives' role strain in South Korea, but not in Japan. He argues that this is because gender roles are more egalitarian in Japan than in South Korea, and that there exists stronger normative resistance on the part of husbands and in-laws to married women's work outside the home in South Korea.

12. The South Korean finding is probably due to sample selectivity. Among women who work in agriculture, rural residents (who are highly likely to continue working after marriage) are not in the sample.

13. Across occupations where gender barriers are relatively weak, the magnitudes of the negative coefficients appear to be smaller, although most differences are not statistically significant. In Japan, professional workers show the smallest duration effect (not statistically significant). In South Korea, sales and service and manufacturing workers show somewhat smaller duration effects than those in other occupations.

Chapter Five

Early versions of this chapter were presented at the Social Science History Association meetings, Minneapolis, October 1990, and the International Institute of Sociology 30th World Congress, Kobe, Japan, August 1991. We are grateful to the Spencer Foundation for funding this research. John Craig, Moonkyung Choi, Gay-Young Cho, Amy Lee-Boonstra, and Pamela Barnhouse Walters provided helpful input on previous drafts.

1. In the United States, for example, women's attendance at two- and four-year colleges doubled between the mid-1960s and the early 1980s. These gains outpaced those of men, and by the mid-1990s a higher proportion of women than men

attended college (Mare 1995). The labor force participation rates of American women also increased dramatically in the past thirty years. Whereas employment previously had been a temporary experience for women before marriage, it has now become a long-term commitment for many (Bianchi 1995; Goldin 1990; McLaughlin et al. 1988; Reskin and Hartmann 1986).

2. Benavot (1989) focused on different schooling levels (primary and secondary education) and examined the relationship between economic growth and educational change for men and women for the period 1960–1985 in a large sample of countries.

3. Men's higher education had already become quite institutionalized by the period Walters considered, and the greater discretionary nature of women's education may have meant that it was more responsive to structural change in the economy.

4. In order to make comparisons across figures, we take the age-eligible population as the denominator in each case. This means that the rates are unaffected by the percentage of people completing the previous level of schooling.

5. This gap shrank after 1992, as employment rates for all young women plummeted with the onset of Japan's worst post–World War II recession.

6. Enrollment measures would also be complicated at the university level in both countries by the fact that some percentage of each high school graduation cohort enters university late, as we discuss shortly. We can adjust for this in the advancement figures, but for enrollment it would be less clear what the age-eligible population would be. Finally, required military service for South Korean men means that many enter university and subsequently leave for a period of one and a half to three years, then return to university again. The measurement of university attendance is simplified in this case by using advancement figures, as nearly all men initially advance to university *before* entering military service.

7. These students are called *rōnin* in Japanese, and *jaesusang* in Korean. The percentage of university entrance cohorts made up of students who graduated from high school in a year other than the current one is now over 40 percent in Japan (Kaneko 1987). It is also quite high in Korea.

8. We follow the formulas used by Kaneko (1987):

Direct entrants to university from high school graduates in year t = (number of high school graduates in year t who advanced to higher education) − (number of junior college entrants in year t)

Late entrants to university from high school graduates in year t = (number of university entrants in year $(t + 1)$) − (direct entrants to university in year $(t + 1)$)

Total university entrants among high school graduates of year t = direct entrants + late entrants

9. We also used the percentage engaged in blue-collar work, but this was, as we would have predicted, unrelated in any of our analyses to changes in higher-education advancement. We therefore omit discussion of it here.

10. In the South Korean case, the denominator is the number of females 15 years old and over, in nonagricultural areas. The numerator is the subset of these females who are in the labor force. This is a slightly different measure than in Japan, where figures are available to calculate the proportion of the female labor force in non-agricultural industries. The difference in the measures does not pose a problem because it is mainly a difference between countries in the level of the rate, and measurement is consistent across years within each country.

11. We ran a model for high school advancement in Japan for the period of most rapid expansion at that educational level, 1955–1975. In this model only the floor effect—the effect of the number of junior high school graduates—was statistically significant. Neither our measures of female labor force participation nor occupational change had any bearing on changes in women's advancement to high school. These results are consistent with the reasoning that if a certain level of education is becoming taken-for-granted in society, changes in the structure of the economy will not produce changes in students' advancement to that educational level (Walters 1984). By contrast, in a model of high school advancement for South Korea over the period 1965–1995, we found significant effects of all variables—the size of the age cohort, the floor effect, the nonagricultural labor force participation rate, and the proportions of the labor force in nonclerical white-collar, clerical, and service sector occupations. These effects are consonant with the very rapid expansion of high school enrollments for young women in South Korea from an initial low level in 1965. (The advancement rate for Japanese women was approximately 65 percent compared to a rate of under 20 percent for women in South Korea in 1965.)

12. The proportion of the Japanese labor force working in professional/technical jobs rose from 8 to 13 percent between 1960 and 1995, whereas the proportion in clerical jobs showed only a slight increase (from 20 to 23 percent) (*Basic Survey on Employment Structure* 1996 [Statistics Bureau, Management and Coordination Agency, Japan]).

13. An example is "marriage bars" that formally or informally prohibit married women from working in many occupations. See Goldin (1990) for discussion of marriage bars in the United States. Cohn (1985) discusses their use in Great Britain in the late nineteenth century, and Pyle discusses their use in Ireland (1990); Upham (1987) and many other sources discuss marriage bars in Japan in the 1960s and 1970s.

14. One could argue that such a preference is irrational if women are cheaper to hire. But on-the-job training practices and strong internal labor market structures in many Japanese and Korean firms make it economically rational for employers to hire men into the starting positions, because men typically do not have the discontinuous employment histories that many women do. This, at least, has been Japanese employers' typical explanation of their preferences (Upham 1987).

Chapter Six

1. On the history of the expansion and feminization of clerical work in Japan, refer to Minako Konno (2000).

2. Mitani (1996) reports only a slight increase in the number of women promoted to *kakarichō*, the lowest rank with any managerial responsibilities, between 1980 and 1994. Women promoted to *kakarichō* were mostly university graduates in their 30s in middle-sized and large companies, while in smaller establishments they tended to be high school graduates in their 40s.

3. See Susan Pharr (1984) for a rare study of Japanese women's rebellion against tea pouring.

4. There are many journalistic books in Japanese on OLs which, in an analogous fashion, emphasize their unconventional values and flamboyant lifestyles. Some of the more well known books include: *All That's OL!*; *Gendai OL Repōto: Shūki de Miru Shigoto, Jōshi, Kekkonkan*; *Imadoki OL Daizukan*; *It's OL Show Time!: Torendi OL no 24 Jikan o Yomu 42 Kō*; *Josei ga Wakaranakunatta Ojisamatachi e*; *Ojisan Kaizō Kōza: OL 500-nin Iinkai*; *Ojisan Kaizō Kōza Part 2: OL 800-nin Iinkai*; *Saigo ni Warau OL wa Dareda?*; and *Tonari no OL Zubari 36 Gyōkai*.

5. "Tōzai" is a pseudonym that means "east and west." The names of men and women working there have also been changed to protect their identity.

6. I worked four days a week from ten in the morning to four in the afternoon for approximately six months, from October 1991 to March 1992.

7. *Sararīman* (literally "salaried man") is an English expression coined in Japan and is usually used to indicate a male white-collar worker. Among the 30 OLs were some women who were no longer actively employed. In line with definitions most commonly used in government statistics and in studies of Japanese employment (e.g., Brinton 1989; Brinton, Ngo, and Shibuya 1991; Cole 1979; Hashimoto and Raisian 1985), firms employing at least 1000 people are considered here and elsewhere in the paper to be large. However, in most cases, the informants that I talked to were members of very large companies, famous worldwide and often employing more than 5000 workers.

8. Of course, factors besides the length of service with the bank also affected how much respect was paid to a person. For example, how well one knew a person was also taken into account: the more intimate one was with a person, the less elaborate the formality.

9. Some firms adopted a more subtle policy of paying first-year university graduates slightly less than third-year junior-college graduates to ease the complaints of the latter, who were more familiar with the work than the more highly educated new employees. However, it was usually the case that their compensations would converge as the years passed.

10. Brinton (1991) reports that more than twice as many Japanese male as female workers experience job rotation in their first job. This is because employers

often restrict job rotation—a particularly important type of training in the Japanese workplace—to employees who can be expected to remain with the firm over a long period of time. In her study of women in the managerial track, Ouchi (1999) found that job rotation was one of the most important factors promoting continued employment.

11. A parallel observation is made by England and Farkas (1986) based on their reformulations of marriage exchange. According to their analysis, youth and associated beauty in women are the currency through which women can "buy" higher-earning men in the marriage market. Furthermore, they argue that it is not rare for divorced women to find themselves disadvantaged in their subsequent marital search, partly because they are older and typically judged to be less attractive.

12. Yamada (1999) coined the term "parasite single" to describe young unmarried men and women who continue to live with and depend on their parents even after graduation.

13. Approximately 15 percent of the women hoped to continue work after marriage and childbirth, while 6 percent replied that they would marry but have no children and remain employed. The remaining 4 percent wished to stay single. The OLs studied were limited to single women between the ages of 20 and 35. We do not know how many OLs failed to answer the questionnaire, which was to be filled out and returned to the insurance company.

14. Because of the absence of young men on the floor, the phenomenon of younger women *chiyahoya sareru* by men in the workplace was not as apparent as described by some informants.

15. See Roberts's (1994) study of a Japanese garment manufacturer, where she reports a similar phenomenon.

16. Hochschild (1989) similarly describes how traditional structures of work are devised for people free of family responsibilities.

Chapter Seven

1. Kindergartens in Japan are run separately from elementary school and cover ages three to five. They are regarded as institutions for precompulsory education. Day nurseries, on the other hand, are daycare institutions for working mothers and those who cannot take care of their children at home for various reasons. Accredited day nurseries are under the auspices of the Ministry of Health and Welfare, with their program content being very similar to that of kindergartens.

2. The second baby boom generation is the cohort born between 1971 and 1974.

Chapter Eight

1. The similar preference for a four-year university education among women and men in South Korea, however, does not mean that the content of their education (e.g., major field of study) has also been similar.

2. For Japan, see Ishida (1993).

3. But see Strober and Chan (1999) for a study of Tokyo University graduates from the class of 1981.

4. The survey was conducted together with Mary C. Brinton and was supported by a grant from the Spencer Foundation.

5. Of the total number of four-year university graduates in 1982, the base graduation year for the sample, slightly over half attended universities in Seoul.

6. In contrast to the admissions process in the United States, students in South Korea apply to a specific department in a specific university.

7. For men, the proportion was greater for third-ranked than second-ranked university graduates. For the total four-year university graduate cohort in South Korea in 1982, only 15 percent of men and 10 percent of women advanced to graduate school. The proportions of men and women with a graduate degree in our sample were quite high compared to this. This is probably because our sample was restricted to universities in the Seoul area, where there is a higher proportion of top-ranked universities than in the national population.

8. Empirical findings in the United States on this argument are mixed at best. Some find that both women and men with interrupted work histories are more likely to be in predominantly female occupations than predominantly male ones (Wolf and Rosenfeld 1978). But others find that women with continuous work histories are no more apt to be in predominantly male occupations than to be in predominantly female ones (Corcoran, Duncan, and Ponza 1984; England 1982).

9. The jobs included in this category were mostly entry-level office workers (about 50 percent), writers/journalists, dieticians, and so on.

10. Female university graduates constituted about 37 percent of the total four-year university graduates in 1990 and about 41 percent in 1996.

11. As Lee and Hirata discuss in Chapter 4 in this volume, the organizational culture of South Korean companies makes it uncomfortable for male employers and colleagues to interact with married women. In addition, many companies view paid maternity leave of married women as generating too heavy a financial burden for the company and hence expect or pressure married women to quit voluntarily (Jang 1990; Jeong 1994). A continuous large supply of male university graduates or high school graduates who could easily fill the positions of female university graduates further makes it possible for companies to continue to discriminate against married women.

12. The units of analysis are labor force spells measured in months, which implies multiple spells for some women. Since some labor force spells consist of more than one job record, specific job characteristics such as occupational category and full-time versus part-time status are included as time-varying variables. Also, to assess the effects of women's varying human capital and family characteristics at each time period, graduate schooling, marital status, and children's ages are included as time-varying variables.

13. Since 60 percent of husbands were concentrated in professional/adminis-

trative occupations, husbands who were in high-prestige professional/administrative occupations were distinguished from others who were in other professional or white-collar occupations. The high-prestige professional/administrative occupations included doctor, lawyer, engineer, professor, business owner with over 10 employees, mid- to high-level business executive, and high-level government official. Overall, about 37 percent of husbands were engaged in these occupations.

14. Starting earnings were lower for other white-collar occupations than for education-related occupations among women, whereas there was no significant difference between these two occupations among men. That was in part because the starting salaries for teaching jobs were relatively high for both women and men. But women's starting earnings in other white-collar occupations were lower not only relative to women's earnings in education-related occupations, but also relative to men's earnings in the same white-collar occupations.

15. Of all homogamous marriages, only 29 percent were marriages between women and men who attended the very same university; the rest were marriages between women and men who attended different universities of the same prestige ranking.

16. This suggests that marriage in South Korean society still remains an important concern for immediate and extended family members, even though the traditional view that marriage should be arranged by parents has given way to a more "modern" view of marriage that is based on love and individual choice (Kong et al. 1992).

17. Women's own graduate school attendance could also have influenced whether their husbands had a graduate degree, for instance, through meeting each other in a graduate school. Among top-ranked university women overall, those who attended graduate school were more likely to be married to men with a graduate degree than those who did not (70 percent vs. 53 percent). But even among top-ranked university women who did not have a graduate degree, similar proportions of their husbands had a graduate degree across prestige rankings of their husbands.

Chapter Nine

1. Of the labor force over age 15, the proportion in agriculture declined from 57 percent in 1951 to 31 percent in 1971.

2. According to the 1991 *Report on Industrial and Commercial Census, Taiwan—Fukien Area*, the average size of establishments, including the self-employed, was only eight employees. In 1991, 74 percent of businesses had fewer than five employees.

3. When in 1994 I interviewed women who were doing piecework at home, some of them denied that they were working (*you gong zuo*). They typically reported being "housewives," and therefore not holding a job or working.

4. The national examinations to recruit employees into government service are normally held once a year. Since they are very competitive, most employees in government service have relatively high levels of education. According to the *Survey*

of Examination and Administration in the Republic of China, Taipei (Zhonghua-minkuo kaoxuan xingzheng gaikuang), published by the Ministry of Examination in 1990, in 1989 the passing rate of the examination for recruiting higher-rank government employees (*gaokao*), in which only people who have more than senior high school education can participate, was 17.6 percent. The rate was 13.4 percent for the lower-rank recruitment examination (*pukao*), which is open to those who have beyond eight years of education. In 1989, according to the same source, about 1222 females and 1603 males passed the *gaokao*. Among those who passed the *pukao* in the same year there were 1605 females and 654 males.

5. Jobs in the government sector are often called "iron bowl [*tie fan wang*] jobs," meaning that they provide unbreakable financial support.

6. I define an area as urban if the percentage of agricultural and mining workers is equal to or less than 25 percent of the labor force and service industry workers account for more than 40 percent of all workers.

7. For convenience, I will use the term "married women" to refer to both currently and formerly married women. According to the *Report on Fertility and Employment of Married Women, Taiwan Area, Republic of China*, 1990 (Directorate-General of Budget, Accounting, and Statistics), among married women between ages 15 and 64 in Taiwan, 22 percent have been out of the labor force because of getting married and 10 percent have left the labor force to give birth. Marriage thus serves as an important life-course event in women's decisions about work.

8. Since the number of years required to complete certain educational levels in Taiwan is highly standardized and the drop-out rate is quite low, the estimated years of education based on corresponding educational levels should be a reliable measure.

9. If a woman remained in a job for less than one year, I assigned that job 0.5 years of work experience.

10. Unfortunately, since human capital variables do not explain much of the variance in women's earnings in the informal sector (model 1, table 9.5), we should be cautious about drawing strong conclusions from these figures on predicted earnings.

11. According to my interview data, most self-employed women can purchase medical insurance (*raobao*) from the government, although they have to bear a higher percentage of the premium than regular employees.

12. In my interviews with self-employed women, the range of start-up capital was generally between U.S.$4,000 and $40,000. Most of the women with whom I spoke obtained their capital from their own savings from former jobs.

Chapter Ten

1. Source: *Report on Industrial and Commercial Census, Taiwan-Fukien Area, the Republic of China* 1962–1992 (Directorate-General of Budget, Accounting, and Statistics).

2. *Yearbook of Manpower Statistics, Taiwan Area, Republic of China* 1994 (Directorate-General of Budget, Accounting, and Statistics).

3. Statistics on men and women's work status are from the 1994 *Yearbook of Manpower Statistics, Taiwan Area, Republic of China* (Directorate-General of Budget, Accounting, and Statistics). Statistics on married women's work status in particular are from the 1994 *Report on Fertility and Employment of Married Women in Taiwan Area, Republic of China* (Directorate-General of Budget, Accounting, and Statistics).

4. A firm's ID is a pseudo surname followed by a sequence number, and a respondent's ID is his (her) firm's ID followed by "h" or "w" to denote husband or wife, respectively.

5. Source: *Labor Statistics 1997* (Statistics Bureau, Management and Coordination Agency, Japan), and 1995 *Yearbook of Manpower Survey Statistics, Taiwan Area, Republic of China* (Directorate-General of Budget, Accounting, and Statistics).

Chapter Eleven

1. For reviews of the large literature on the dubious consequences of globalization for women workers around the globe, see Beneria and Feldman 1992; Nash and Fernández-Kelly 1983; Ong 1991; Pyle 1990; Sassen 1988; Tinker 1990; Wolf 1990.

2. In comparison to official statistics from earlier years, these data produce unusually high figures for women at work. Two reasons are likely. First, in these data it is a woman who is reporting on her work rather than, as in government surveys, the usual male household head. Second, as the economy has become more marketized and a price put on labor that heretofore was exchanged among family and kin without any direct compensation, women have begun to redefine activities done for the family and kin as work (Rita Gallin, personal communication). In Marxist parlance, the commodification of work has affected how women define their activities.

3. Other formulations of sibling relationships produced similar negative conclusions. Number of brothers, number of sisters, total siblings, and birth order were all unrelated to work before marriage.

4. A reanalysis with logged number of siblings to avoid potential problems with outliers (e.g., a single person with 10 younger sisters) produces similar results.

5. Of course, "marriage age" has both collinearity and endogeneity issues. It is collinear with years worked before marriage ($r = .40$) and, much like marital exchanges, it is potentially influenced by competition for family resources from siblings. Older daughters with many siblings, particularly younger sisters, are forced to marry earlier (see Parish and Willis 1993). Nevertheless, redoing the analysis with marriage age excluded produces similar patterns of results.

6. For both "urban background" and "father's economic status" in table 11.2, the negative and positive coefficients are statistically different from one another at $p < .05$.

7. When compared to women who had not worked before marriage, daughters with premarital work experience got 30 percent more cash when the family

property was divided. However, given the close relationship between receiving cash, work, and other family characteristics, this tendency soon disappeared in a more refined analysis (details not shown). This analysis controlled for age, urban residence, level of education, father's socioeconomic status, and dowry (net of bride price).

8. A more detailed analysis reveals that the impact of premarital work on labor force participation after marriage was positive across all sectors—work as a paid employee, self-employee, and unpaid family work. In short, married women were not consigned to the informal sector.

9. Since women who continue to work after marriage may be self-selected, we also control for Heckman's lambda to ensure that the results are not driven by self-selection.

10. The result holds even when unpaid family workers are excluded from the sample—that is, it is not being driven by the dichotomy between paid and unpaid workers.

11. From the 1996 Social Change Survey, an island-wide survey run by Academia Sinica, Taipei. For debates over whether the wage gap between women and men is narrowing, see Greenhalgh (1985) for negative arguments and Kao, Polachek, and Wunnava (1994) for positive arguments.

REFERENCES

Akachi, Mayuko. 1998. "Kikon josei no chī tassei katei ni okeru sedaiteki henka" (Intergenerational change in the process of married women's status attainment). In *1995 SSM chōsa shirīzu: Josei no kyaria kōzō to sono henka* (1995 SSM survey series: Changing career structures of women), edited by Kazuo Seiyama and Sachiko Imada. Tokyo: SSM Chōsa Kenkyūkai.

Akaoka, Isao. 1996. "Ereganto na rōmukanri o motomete" ("Elegant" personnel management). *Soshiki Kagaku* 29: 4–14.

Allison, Anne. 1994. *Nightwork: Sexuality, Pleasure, and Corporate Masculinity in a Tokyo Hostess Club.* Chicago: University of Chicago Press.

———. 1996. *Permitted and Prohibited Desires: Mothers, Comics, and Censorship in Japan.* Boulder, Colo.: Westview Press.

Althauser, Robert, and Arne Kalleberg. 1981. "Firms, Occupations and the Structure of Labor Markets: A Conceptual Analysis." In *Sociological Perspectives on Labor Markets*, edited by Ivar Berg, 119–149. New York: Academic Press.

Amsden, Alice H. 1989. *Asia's Next Giant: South Korea and Late Industrialization.* New York: Oxford University Press.

———. 1991. "Big Business and Urban Congestion in Taiwan: The Origins of Small Enterprise and Regionally Decentralized Industry (Respectively)." *World Development* 19: 1121–1135.

Aries, Philippe. 1962. *Centuries of Childhood: Social History of Family Life.* New York: Knopf.

Ariga, Kenn, Yasushi Ōkusa, and Giorgio Brunello. 1997. "Fast Track: Is It in the Genes? The Promotion Policy of a Large Japanese Firm." Kyoto Institute of Economic Research Discussion Paper Series, no. 452. Kyoto: Kyoto University.

Arnold, Fred, and Eddie C. Y. Kuo. 1984. "The Value of Daughters and Sons: A Comparative Study of the Gender Preferences of Parents." *Journal of Comparative Family Studies* 15: 299–318.

Arrighi, Giovanni, Satoshi Ikeda, and Alex Irwan. 1991. "The Rise of East Asia: One Miracle or Many?" Working Paper, Fernand Braudel Center for the Study of Economies, Historical Systems, and Civilizations, State University of New York at Binghamton.

Asahi Shimbun. 1997. "Shō ichi ni nen ha nen 70 jikan gen" (70 hours cut from lower grade school curriculum). 6 September.

———. 1998. "Gakushū naiyō o san wari sakugen" (Thirty percent cut in school curriculum content). 23 June.

Badinter, Elizabeth. 1981. *The Myth of Motherhood: An Historical View of the Maternal Instinct.* London: Souvenir Press.

Bai, Moo Ki, and Woo Hyun Cho. 1996. "Women's Employment Structure and Male-Female Wage Differentials in South Korea." In *Women and Industrialization in Asia,* edited by Susan Horton, 165–206. London: Routledge.

Basu, Ellen Oxfeld. 1991. "The Sexual Division of Labor and the Organization of Family and Firm in an Overseas Chinese Community." *American Ethnologist* 18: 700–718.

Baxter, Janeen, and Emily W. Kane. 1995. "Dependence and Independence: A Cross-National Analysis of Gender Inequality and Gender Attitudes." *Gender and Society* 9: 193–215.

Becker, Gary S. 1957. *The Economics of Discrimination.* Chicago: University of Chicago Press.

———. 1965. "A Theory of the Allocation of Time." *Economic Journal* 75: 493–517.

———. 1975. *Human Capital.* New York: National Bureau of Economic Research, Columbia University Press.

———. 1981. *A Treatise on the Family.* Cambridge: Harvard University Press.

———. 1985. "Human Capital, Effort, and the Sexual Division of Labor." *Journal of Labor Economics* 3 (suppl.): s33–s58.

Beggs, John J. 1995. "The Institutional Environment: Implications for Race and Gender Inequality in the U.S. Labor Market." *American Sociological Review* 60: 612–633.

Bell, Lynda S. 1994. "For Better, For Worse: Women and the World Market in Rural China." *Modern China* 20: 180–210.

Benavot, Aaron. 1989. "Education, Gender, and Economic Development: A Cross-National Study." *Sociology of Education* 62: 14–32.

Beneria, Lourdes, and Gita Sen. 1981. "Accumulation, Reproduction, and Women's Role in Development: Boserup Revisited." *Signs* 7: 279–298.

Beneria, Lourdes, and Martha Roldan. 1987. *The Crossroads of Class and Gender: Industrial Housework, Subcontracting, and Household Dynamics in Mexico City.* Chicago: University of Chicago Press.

Beneria, Lourdes, and Shelley Feldman, eds. 1992. *Unequal Burden: Economic Crises, Persistent Poverty, and Women's Work.* Boulder, Colo.: Westview Press.

Berheide, Catherine White, and Esther Ngan-ling Chow. 1994. "Perpetuating Gender Inequality: The Role of Families, Economies, and States." In *Women, the Family, and Policy: A Global Perspective,* edited by Ester Ngan-ling Chow and Catherine White Berheide, 257–275. Albany: State University of New York Press.

Berk, Richard A., and Sarah Fenstermaker Berk. 1983. "Supply-Side Sociology of the Family: The Challenge of the New Home Economics." *Annual Review of Sociology* 9: 375–395.

Berk, Sarah Fenstermaker. 1985. *The Gender Factory: The Apportionment of Work in American Households.* New York: Plenum Press.

Bernstein, Gail Lee. 1983. *Haruko's World: A Japanese Farm Woman and Her Community.* Stanford, Calif.: Stanford University Press.

Bianchi, Suzanne M. 1995. "Changing Economic Roles of Women and Men." In *State of the Union: America in the 1990s*, edited by Reynolds Farley. Vol. 1, *Economic Trends*, 107–154. New York: Russell Sage Foundation.

Bianchi, Suzanne M., and Daphne Spain. 1986. *American Women in Transition.* New York: Russell Sage Foundation.

Bielby, Denise D. 1992. "Commitment to Work and Family." *Annual Review of Sociology* 18: 281–302.

Bielby, William T., and Denise D. Bielby. 1992. "I Will Follow Him: Family Ties, Gender-Role Beliefs, and Reluctance to Relocate for a Better Job." *American Journal of Sociology* 97: 1241–1267.

Biggart, Nicole Woolsey. 1990. "Institutionalized Patrimonialism in Korean Business." *Comparative Social Research* 12: 113–133.

Blank, Grant, and William Parish. 1990. "Rural Industry and Non-Farm Employment." In *Chinese Urban Reform*, edited by Reginald Kwok, William L. Parish, and Anthony Yeh. Armonk, N.Y.: M. E. Sharpe.

Blau, Francine. 1993. "Gender and Economic Outcomes: The Role of Wage Structure." *Labour* 7: 73–92.

Blumberg, Rae Lesser. 1984. "A General Theory of Gender Stratification." In *Sociological Theory*, edited by Randall Collins, 23–101. San Francisco: Jossey-Bass.

———. 1988. "Income Under Female Versus Male Control." *Journal of Family Issues* 9: 51–84.

———. 1991. *Gender, Family, and Economy: The Triple Overlap.* Newbury Park, Calif.: Sage.

Boling, Patricia. 2000. "Contradictions Abound: Japan's Family Support Policies." Paper presented at the Annual Meetings of the Association for Asian Studies, San Diego.

Boocock, Sarane Spence. 1991. "The Japanese Preschool System." In *Windows on Japanese Education*, edited by Edward R. Beauchamp, 97–126. New York: Greenwood Press.

Boris, Eileen. 1994. *Home to Work: Motherhood and the Politics of Industrial Homework in the United States.* Cambridge: Cambridge University Press.

Bornstein, Marc H. 1989. "Cross-Cultural Developmental Comparison: The Case of Japanese-American Infant and Mother Activities and Interactions. What We Know, What We Need to Know, and Why We Need to Know." *Developmental Review* 9: 171–204.

Boserup, Ester. 1970. *Women's Role in Economic Development*. New York: St. Martin's Press.

Bowlby, John. 1969. *Attachment and Loss*. New York: Basic Books.

Brines, Julie. 1994. "Economic Dependency, Gender, and the Division of Labor at Home." *American Journal of Sociology* 100: 652–688.

Brinton, Mary C. 1988. "The Social-Institutional Bases of Gender Stratification: Japan as an Illustrative Case." *American Journal of Sociology* 94: 300–334.

———. 1989. "Gender Stratification in Contemporary Urban Japan." *American Sociological Review* 54: 549–564.

———. 1990. "Intrafamilial Markets for Education: An Empirical Example." In *Social Institutions: Their Emergence, Maintenance, and Effects*, edited by Michael Hechter, Karl-Dieter Opp, and Reinhard Wippler, 307–330. New York: Aldine.

———. 1991. "Sex Differences in On-The-Job Training and Job Rotation in Japanese Firms." *Research in Social Stratification and Mobility* 10: 3–25.

———. 1992. "Christmas Cakes and Wedding Cakes: The Social Organization of Japanese Women's Life Course." In *Japanese Social Organization*, edited by Takie Sugiyama Lebra. Honolulu: University of Hawaii Press.

———. 1993. *Women and the Economic Miracle: Gender and Work in Postwar Japan*. Berkeley: University of California Press.

———. 1998a. "The Evolution of the Clerical Sector: A Comparative-Historical Study of the United States and Japan" (in Japanese). In *A Comparative Study of Women's Careers and Life Course*. Research Report no. 112, pp. 95–115. Tokyo: Japan Institute of Labor.

———. 1998b. "From High School to Work in Japan: Lessons for the United States?" *Social Service Review*, December, 442–451.

———. 1998c. "Jimushoku no kakudai: Josei no shūgyō patān ni kansuru beikoku to higashiajia no hikaku rekishiteki kenkyū" (The evolution of the clerical sector: A comparative-historical view of women's work patterns in the U.S. and East Asia). *Nihon Rōdō Kenkyū Zasshi* 453: 36–49.

Brinton, Mary C., Hang-Yue Ngo, and Kumiko Shibuya. 1991. "Gendered Mobility Patterns in Industrial Economies: The Case of Japan." *Social Science Quarterly* 72: 807–816.

Brinton, Mary C., and Moonkyung Choi. Forthcoming. "Women's Incorporation into the Urban Economy of South Korea." In *Korea: Toward an Industrial Society*, edited by Yunshik Chang. Seattle: University of Washington Press.

Brown, Charles, and James Medoff. 1989. "The Employer Size-Wage Effect." *Journal of Political Economy* 97: 1027–1059.

Brown, Clair, Yoshifumi Nakata, Michael Reich, and Lloyd Ulman. 1997. *Work and Pay in the United States and Japan*. New York: Oxford University Press.

Buchmann, Marlis, and Maria Charles. 1995. "Organizational and Institutional Factors in the Process of Gender Stratification: Comparing Social Arrangements in Six European Countries." *International Journal of Sociology* 25: 66–95.

Buckley, Sandra. 1993. "Altered States: The Body Politics of 'Being-Women.'" In *Postwar Japan as History*, edited by Andrew Gordon, 347–371. Berkeley: University of California Press.

Carr, Deborah. 1996. "Two Paths to Self-Employment: Women's and Men's Self-Employment in the United States, 1980." *Work and Occupations* 23: 26–53.

Carter, Rose, and Lois Dilatush. 1976. "Office Ladies." In *Women in Changing Japan*, edited by Joyce Lebra, Roy Paulson, and Elizabeth Powers. Boulder, Colo.: Westview Press.

Cassidy, Margaret L., and Bruce O. Warren. 1996. "Family Employment Status and Gender Role Attitudes: A Comparison of Women and Men College Graduates." *Gender and Society* 10: 312–329.

Castells, Manuel, and Alejandro Portes. 1989. "World Underneath: The Origins, Dynamics, and Effects of the Informal Economy." In *The Informal Economy: Studies in Advanced and Less Developed Countries*, edited by Alejandro Portes, Manuel Castells, and Lauren A. Benton, 11–37. Baltimore: Johns Hopkins University Press.

Caudill, William A., and Helen Weinstein. 1969. "Maternal Care and Infant Behavior in Japan and America." *Psychiatry* 32: 12–43.

Cha, Jongchun. 1992. "The Structure and the Process of Social Stratification" (in Korean). In *Inequality and Equity in South Korean Society*, edited by Il-Chung Hwang, 71–140. Seoul: Nanam.

Chang, Ching-hsi. 1982. "The Labor Force Participation of Married Women in Taiwan" (in Chinese). In *The Chinese Economic Association Annual Conference Proceedings*, 97–127. Taipei: Chinese Economic Association.

———. 1987. "Foreign Workers: A Preliminary Economic Analysis" (in Chinese). *The Fiftieth Symposium on Social Sciences*, 198–216. Taipei: Institute of the Three Principles of Peoples, Academia Sinica, 1987.

Chang, Kyung-Sup. 1995. "Gender and Abortive Capitalist Social Transformation: Semi-Proletarianization of South Korean Women." *International Journal of Comparative Sociology* 36: 61–81.

Chang, Mariko Lin. 2000. "The Evolution of Sex Segregation Regimes." *American Journal of Sociology* 105: 1658–1701.

Chant, Sylvia. 1991. *Women and Survival in Mexican Cities*. Manchester: Manchester University Press.

Chen, Jie-Hsuan. 1994. *Cooperation Network and Life Structure*. Taipei: Lian-jing.

Cheng, Lucie, and Ping-Chun Hsiung. 1994. "Women, Exported-Oriented Growth, and the State: The Case of Taiwan." In *The Role of the State in Taiwan's Development*, edited by Joel D. Aberbach, David Dollar, and Kenneth L. Sokoloff, 321–353. Armonk: M. E. Sharpe.

Cheng, Tun-jen. 1993. "Regulating Access to Higher Education in South Korea and Taiwan." In *Social Issues in Korea: Korean and American Perspectives*, edited by Lawrence B. Krause and Fun-koo Park, 219–260. Seoul: Korea Development Institute.

Chiang, Lan-Hung Nora, and Yen-Lin Ku. 1985. *Past and Current Status of Women in Taiwan*. Taipei: Population Studies Center, National Taiwan University.

Cho, Uhn, and Hagen Koo. 1983. "Economic Development and Women's Work in a Newly Industrializing Country: The Case of Korea." *Development and Change* 14: 515–532.

Chodorow, Nancy. 1978. *The Reproduction of Mothering: Psychoanalysis and the Sociology of Gender*. Berkeley: University of California Press.

Choe, Minja Kim. 1998. "Changing Marriage Patterns in South Korea." In *The Changing Family in Comparative Perspective: Asia and the United States*, edited by Karen O. Mason, Noriko O. Tsuya, and Minja K. Choe, 43–62. Honolulu: East-West Center.

Choi, Elizabeth. 1994. "Status of the Family and Motherhood." In *Women of Japan and Korea*, edited by Joyce Gelb and Marian Lief Palley. Philadelphia: Temple University Press.

Choi, Moonkyung. 1994. "Lifetime Occupational Achievement of Female Workers: The Case of the Republic of Korea." Ph.D. diss., University of Chicago, Department of Sociology.

Choi, Sungook, and Sungho Kim. 1995. "Seventy-six Percent of School Children with Experience of *Kwawei*." *Hankook Daily Newspaper*, 25 January.

Choi, Young-Pyo. 1989. *Problems of Higher Education and Policy Directions* (in Korean). Seoul: Korean Educational Development Institute.

Chou, Bih-Er. 1987. "Industrialization and Change in Women's Status: A Re-evaluation of Some Data from Taiwan." In *Taiwan: A Newly Industrialized State*, edited by Hsin-Huang M. Hsiao et al. Taipei: Department of Sociology, National Taiwan University.

Chung, In-Soo, and Yoon, Jin-Ho. 1994. *Levels of Subcontracted Employment and Policy Issues* (in Korean). Seoul: Korea Labor Institute.

Chung, Kae H., Hak Chong Lee, and Akihiro Okumura. 1988. "The Managerial Practices of Korean, American, and Japanese Firms." *Journal of East and West Studies* 17: 45–74.

Cohn, Samuel. 1985. *The Process of Occupational Sex-Typing*. Philadelphia: Temple University Press.

Cole, Robert E. 1971. "The Theory of Institutionalization: Permanent Employment and Tradition in Japan." *Economic Development and Cultural Change* 20: 47–70.

Cole, Robert E. 1979. *Work, Mobility, and Participation: A Comparative Study of American and Japanese Industry*. Berkeley: University of California Press.

Coleman, James. 1988. "Social Capital in the Creation of Human Capital." *American Journal of Sociology* 94 (suppl.): S95–S120.

Collins, Randall. 1979. *The Credential Society: An Historical Sociology of Education and Stratification*. New York: Academic Press.

Collver, Andrew, and Eleanor Langlois. 1962. "The Female Labor Force in Metropolitan Areas: An International Comparison." *Economic Development and Cultural Change* 10: 367–385.

Condon, Jane. 1985. *A Half Step Behind: Japanese Women Today*. Rutland, Vt.: Tuttle.

Corcoran, Mary, Greg J. Duncan, and Michael Ponza. 1984. "Work Experience, Job Segregation, and Wages." In *Sex Segregation in the Workplace*, edited by Barbara Reskin, 171–191. Washington, D.C.: National Academy Press.

Crawcour, Sydney. 1978. "The Japanese Employment System." *Journal of Japanese Studies* 4: 225–245.

Cumings, Bruce. 1984. "The Origins and Development of the Northeast Asian Political Economy: Industrial Sectors, Product Cycles, and Political Consequences." *International Organizations* 38: 1–40.

Davis, Kingsley. 1984. "Wives and Work: The Sex Role Revolution and Its Consequences." *Population and Development Review* 10: 397–417.

Dentsū Ōeru Pawā, ed. 1991. *Saigo ni warau OL wa dareda?* (Who is the last OL to laugh?). Tokyo: Dentsū.

Desai, Sonalde, and Soumya Alva. 1998. "Maternal Education and Child Health: Is There a Strong Causal Relationship?" *Demography* 35: 71–81.

De Soto, Hernando. 1989. *The Other Path: The Invisible Revolution in the Third World*. New York: Harper & Row.

Deyo, Frederic C. 1989. *Beneath the Miracle: Labor Subordination in the New Asian Industrialism*. Berkeley: University of California Press.

Diamond, Norma. 1979. "Women and Industry in Taiwan." *Modern China* 5: 317–340.

Dinnerstein, Dorothy. 1976. *The Mermaid and the Minotaur: Sexual Arrangements and Human Malaise*. New York: Harper & Row.

Directorate-General of Budget, Accounting, and Statistics, Executive Yuan, ROC (Republic of China). 1966. *Statistical Abstract of the Republic of China*. Taipei.

———. 1986. *Statistical Yearbook of the Republic of China: Taiwan Area*. Taipei.

———. 1991a. *Statistical Yearbook of the Republic of China: Taiwan Area*. Taipei.

———. 1991b. *General Report on the 1990 Census of Population and Housing*. Taipei.

———. Various years. *Monthly Bulletin of Manpower Statistics*. Taipei.

———. Various years. *Report on Fertility and Employment of Married Women, Taiwan Area, Republic of China*. Taipei.

———. Various years. *Report on Industrial and Commercial Census, Taiwan— Fukien Area, the Republic of China*. Taipei.

———. Various years. *Report on the Manpower Utilization Survey, Taiwan Area, Republic of China*. Taipei.

———. Various years. *Social Indicators in the Taiwan Area, Republic of China*. Taipei.

————. Various years. *Yearbook of Manpower Survey Statistics, Taiwan Area, Republic of China.* Taipei.

Doeringer, Peter B., and Michael J. Piore. 1971. *Internal Labor Markets and Manpower Analysis.* Lexington, Mass.: Heath.

Doi, Takeo. 1973. *The Anatomy of Dependence.* Translated by John Bester. Tokyo: Kōdansha International.

Doman, Glenn. 1964. *How to Teach Your Baby to Read.* New York: Random House.

————. 1984. *How to Multiply Your Baby's Intelligence.* New York: Doubleday.

Dore, Ronald. 1976. *The Diploma Disease: Education, Qualification, and Development.* Berkeley: University of California Press.

Durand, John. 1975. *The Labor Force in Economic Development: A Comparison of International Census Data, 1946–1966.* Princeton, N.J.: Princeton University Press.

Durbin, Nancy E., and Lori Kent. 1989. "Post-Secondary Education of White Women in 1900." *Sociology of Education* 62: 1–13.

Eccleston, Bernard. 1989. *State and Society in Post-War Japan.* Cambridge, England: Polity Press.

Elkind, David. 1987. *Miseducation: Preschoolers at Risk.* New York: Knopf.

Ellington, Lucien. 1992. *Education in the Japanese Life-Cycle.* Lewiston, N.Y.: E. Mellen Press.

England, Paula. 1982. "The Failure of Human Capital Theory to Explain Occupational Sex Segregation." *Journal of Human Resources* 17: 358–370.

England, Paula, and George Farkas. 1986. *Households, Employment, and Gender: A Social, Economic, and Demographic View.* New York: Aldine.

England, Paula, George Farkas, Barbara Stanek Kilbourne, and Tomas Dou. 1988. "Explaining Occupational Sex Segregation and Wages: Findings from a Model with Fixed Effects." *American Sociological Review* 53: 544–558.

Evans, Peter, and Michael Timberlake. 1980. "Dependence, Inequality, and the Growth of the Tertiary." *American Sociological Review* 45: 531–552.

Faia, Michael A. 1981. "Selecting by Certification: A Neglected Variable in Stratification Research." *American Journal of Sociology* 86: 1093–1111.

Fantasia, Rick. 1988. *Cultures of Solidarity: Consciousness, Action, and Contemporary American Workers.* Berkeley: University of California Press.

Felmlee, Diane H. 1984. "A Dynamic Analysis of Women's Employment Exit." *Demography* 21: 171–183.

Field, Norma. 1995. "The Child as Laborer and Consumer: The Disappearance of Childhood in Contemporary Japan." In *Children and the Politics of Culture,* edited by Sharon Stephens, 51–78. Princeton, N.J.: Princeton University Press.

Fields, Gary S. 1985. "Industrialization and Employment in Hong Kong, Korea, Singapore, and Taiwan." In *Foreign Trade and Investment: Economic Development in the Newly Industrializing Asian Countries,* edited by Walter Galenson. Madison: University of Wisconsin Press.

Firestone, Shulamith. 1970. *The Dialectic of Sex*. New York: Bantam Books.

Folbre, Nancy. 1988. "The Black Four of Hearts: Toward a New Paradigm of Household Economics." In *A Home Divided: Women and Income in the Third World*, edited by Daisy Dwyer and Judith Bruce. Stanford, Calif.: Stanford University Press.

Frank, Robert. 1998. "Winner-Take-All Markets and Wage Discrimination." In *The New Institutionalism in Sociology*, edited by Mary C. Brinton and Victor Nee, 208–223. New York: Russell Sage Foundation.

Freedman, Ronald, Ming-Cheng Chang, and Te-hsiung Sun. 1982. "Household Composition, Extended Kinship, and Reproduction in Taiwan: 1973–1980." *Population Studies* 36: 395–411.

Frobel, Folker, Jurgen Heinrichs, and Otto Kreye. 1980. *The New International Division of Labour: Structural Unemployment in Industrialised Countries and Industrialisation in Developing Countries*. Cambridge: Cambridge University Press.

Fujii, Harue. 1975. *Gendai hahaoya-ron* (Contemporary motherhood). Tokyo: Meiji Tosho Shuppan.

Fujimura-Fanselow, Kumiko. 1985. "Women's Participation in Higher Education in Japan." *Comparative Education Review* 29: 471–489.

———. 1995. "College Women Today: Options and Dilemmas." In *Japanese Women*, edited by Kumiko Fujimura-Fanselow and Atsuko Kameda, 125–154. New York: Feminist Press.

Fukaya, Masashi. 1977. *Ryōsai kenboshugi no kyōiku* (Education and the ideology of good wife, wise mother). Nagoya: Reimei Shobō.

Fukuhara, Fumihiko. 1992. "Hanako san no raifu dezain" (The life design of Hanako san). *LDI Monthly Report* 1: 3–23.

Galenson, Walter. 1979. "The Labor Force, Wages, and Living Standards." In *Economic Growth and Structural Change in Taiwan*, edited by Walter Galenson. Ithaca, N.Y.: Cornell University Press.

———. 1992. *Labor and Economic Growth in Five Asian Countries: South Korea, Malaysia, Taiwan, Thailand and the Philippines*. New York: Praeger.

Gallin, Rita S. 1984a. "The Entry of Chinese Women into the Rural Labor Force: A Case Study from Taiwan." *Signs* 9: 383–398.

———. 1984b. "Women, Family, and the Political Economy of Taiwan." *Journal of Peasant Studies* 12: 76–92.

Gates, Hill. 1987. "Money for the Gods." *Modern China* 13: 259–277.

Gereffi, Gary, and Donald L. Wyman, eds. 1990. *Manufacturing Miracles: Paths of Industrialization in Latin America and East Asia*. Princeton, N.J.: Princeton University Press.

Gerson, Kathleen. 1985. *Hard Choices: How Women Decide about Work, Career, and Motherhood*. Berkeley: University of California Press.

———. 1987. "Emerging Social Divisions Among Women: Implications for Welfare State Politics." *Politics and Society* 15: 235–239.

Gills, Dong-Sook Shin. 1999. *Rural Women and Triple Exploitation in Korean Development*. New York: St. Martin's Press.

Glass, Jennifer. 1992. "Housewives and Employed Wives: Demographic and Attitudinal Change, 1972–1986." *Journal of Marriage and the Family* 54: 559–569.

Goldin, Claudia. 1990. *Understanding the Gender Gap: An Economic History of American Women*. New York: Oxford University Press.

———. 1995. "The U-Shaped Female Labor Force Function in Economic Development and Economic History." In *Investment in Women's Human Capital*, edited by T. Paul Schultz, 61–90. Chicago: University of Chicago Press.

Goode, William. 1970. "Industrialization and Family Change." In *Industrialization and Society*, edited by Bert Hoselitz and Wilbert Moore, 237–259. Mouton: UNESCO.

Granovetter, Mark. 1985. "Economic Action and Social Structure: The Problem of Embeddedness." *American Journal of Sociology* 91: 481–510.

Greenhalgh, Susan. 1985. "Sex Stratification in East Asia: The Other Side of 'Growth with Equity.'" *Population and Development Review* 11: 265–314.

———. 1991. "Women in the Informal Enterprise: Empowerment or Exploitation?" Working Paper no. 33. New York: Population Council.

———. 1994. "De-Orientalizing the Chinese Family Firm." *American Ethnologist* 21: 746–775.

Grubb, W. Norton, and Marvin Lazerson. 1982. "Education and the Labor Market: Recycling the Youth Problem." In *Work, Youth, and Schooling*, edited by Harvey Kantor and David Tyack, 110–141. Stanford, Calif.: Stanford University Press.

Hadjicostandi, Joanna. 1990. "'Facon': Women's Formal and Informal Work in the Garment Industry in Kavala, Greece." In *Women Workers and Global Restructuring*, edited by Kathryn Ward, 64–81. Ithaca, N.Y.: ILR Press, School of Industrial and Labor Relations, Cornell University.

Hakim, Catherine. 1996. *Key Issues in Women's Work: Female Heterogeneity and the Polarisation of Women's Employment*. London: Athlone Press.

Hamilton, Gary, and Nicole Woolsey Biggart. 1988. "Market, Culture, and Authority: A Comparative Analysis of Management and Organization in the Far East." *American Journal of Sociology* 94 (suppl.): s52–s94.

Hanami, Tadashi. 2000. "Equal Employment Revisited." *Japan Labor Bulletin* 39: 5–7.

Harrell, Stevan. 1985. "Why Do the Chinese Work so Hard? Reflections on an Entrepreneurial Ethic." *Modern China* 11: 203–226.

Hartmann, Heidi. 1976. "Capitalism, Patriarchy, and Job Segregation by Sex." In *Women and the Workplace: The Implications of Occupational Segregation*, edited by Martha Blaxall and Barbara Reagan, 137–169. Chicago: University of Chicago Press.

Hashimoto, Masanori, and John Raisian. 1985. "Employment Tenure and Earnings Profiles in Japan and the United States." *American Economic Review* 75: 721–735.

Heckman, James. 1974. "Shadow Prices, Market Wages, and Labor Supply." *Econometrica* 42: 679–694.

Hill, C. Russell, and Frank P. Stafford. 1974. "Allocation of Time to Preschool Children and Educational Opportunity." *Journal of Human Resources* 9: 323–341.

Hill, M. Anne. 1983. "Female Labor Force Participation in Developing and Developed Countries—Consideration of the Informal Sector." *Review of Economics and Statistics* 65: 459–468.

Hirai, Yoshinobu. 1984. *"Kokoronokichi" wa okāsan* (Mothers as the psychological base). Tokyo: Kikakushitsu.

Hirao, Keiko. 1997. "Work Histories and Home Investment of Married Japanese Women." Ph.D. diss., University of Notre Dame, Department of Sociology.

———. 1998. "Saishūshoku no taiming: Kekkon/shussan taishokugo no rōdōshijō saisanyū katei no hazādo bunseki" (Hazard analyses on the timing of re-entry to the labor force). Paper presented at the Annual Meetings of the Japanese Sociological Society, Kwansei Gakuin University, Nishinomiya, Japan.

———. 1999. "Josei no shoki kyaria keiseiki ni okeru rōdōshijō eno teichakusei: Gakureki to kazoku ibento o megutte" (The effect of education on the rate of labor-force exit for married Japanese women). *Nihon Rōdō Kenkyū Zasshi* 41: 29–41.

Hirata, Shūichi. 1995. "Josei no shokugyō keireki" (Women's occupational career). In *Shokugyō to katei seikatsu ni kansuru zenkoku chōsa hōkokusho* (National survey report on occupation and family life), edited by Nihon Rōdō Kenkyū Kikō. Tokyo: Nihon Rōdō Kenkyū Kikō.

———. 1998a. "Introduction" (in Japanese). In *A Comparative Study of Women's Career and Life Course*, Research Report no. 112, 3–18. Tokyo: Japan Institute of Labor.

———. 1998b. "Joseiteki shokugyō to shokugyō keireki" (Female occupations and occupational career). In *1995 SSM chōsa shirīzu: Josei no kyaria kōzō to sono henka* (1995 SSM survey series: Changing career structures of women), edited by Kazuo Seiyama and Sachiko Imada. Tokyo: SSM Chōsa Kenkyūkai.

Hirschman, Albert O. 1970. *Exit, Voice, and Loyalty: Responses to Decline in Firms, Organizations, and States.* Cambridge: Harvard University Press.

Hochschild, Arlie R. 1983. *The Managed Heart: Commercialization of Human Feeling.* Berkeley: University of California Press.

———. 1989. *The Second Shift.* New York: Avon Books.

Hodson, Randy, and Robert L. Kaufman. 1982. "Economic Dualism: A Critical Review." *American Sociological Review* 47: 727–739.

Hong, Doo-Seung, and Hagen Koo. 1993. *Social Stratification and Class Theory* (in Korean). Seoul: Dasan.

Hong, Won-tack. 1979. *Trade, Distortions, and Employment Growth in Korea.* Seoul: Korea Development Institute.

———. 1983. "Export Promotion and Employment Growth in South Korea." In *Trade and Employment in Developing Countries*, edited by Anne O. Krueger. Vol. 1. Chicago: University of Chicago Press.

Horton, Susan. 1996. "Women and Industrialization in Asia: Overview." In *Women and Industrialization in Asia*, edited by Susan Horton, 1–42. London: Routledge.

Hosaka, Nobuto. 1994. *Abunai kumonshiki sōkikyōiku* (Kumon abuse). Tokyo: Tarōjirōsha.

Houseman, Susan, and Machiko Osawa. 1997. "The Growth of Part-Time Employment in Japan." Unpublished paper.

Hsia, Lin-Ching, and Chun-Chi Cheng. 1989. "A Case Study of a Small Subcontracting Factory." *Taiwan: A Radical Quarterly in Social Science* 2: 189–214.

Hsiung, Ping-Chun. 1996. *Living Rooms as Factories: Class, Gender, and the Satellite Factory System in Taiwan.* Philadelphia: Temple University Press.

Humphrey, John. 1987. *Gender and Work in the Third World.* London: Tavistock.

Hwang, Kwang-Kuo. 1983. "Business Organizational Patterns and Employee's Working Morale in Taiwan." *Bulletin of the Institute of Ethnology, Academia Sinica* 56: 85–133.

———. 1987. "Face and Favor: The Chinese Power Game." *American Journal of Sociology* 92: 944–974.

IBRD (International Bank for Reconstruction and Development). 1988. *World Development Report 1988.* Washington, D.C.: Oxford University Press.

Ibuka, Masaru. 1976. *Yōchien dewa ososugiru* (Kindergarten is too late). Tokyo: Goma Shobō.

———. 1991. *Zerosai* (Zero-year-old). Tokyo: Gomashobō.

———. 1992. *Taijikara* (From embryo). Tokyo: Tokumashobō.

Imada, Sachiko. 1996. "Joshi shūgyō to shūgyō keizoku" (Women's employment and employment continuation). *Nihon Rōdō Kenkyū Zasshi* 433: 37–48.

Imada, Sachiko, and Shuichi Hirata. 1995. *Howaito karā no shōshin kozo* (The structure of white collar workers' promotions). Tokyo: Japan Institute of Labor.

Inkeles, Alex, and David Smith. 1974. *Becoming Modern.* Cambridge: Harvard University Press.

Inoue, Shunichi. 1998. "Family Formation in Japan, South Korea, and the United States: An Overview." In *The Changing Family in Comparative Perspective: Asia and the United States*, edited by Karen Oppenheim Mason, Noriko O. Tsuya, and Minja Kim Choe, 19–41. Honolulu: East-West Center.

Inoue, Teruko, and Yumiko Ehara. 1999. *Josei no dētabukku: Sei, karada kara seiji sanka made* (Women's data book: From sex and body to policy participation). 3d ed. Tokyo: Yūhikaku.

International Labour Organisation. 1996. *Yearbook of Labour Statistics.* Geneva: International Labour Organisation.

Ishida, Hiroshi. 1993. *Social Mobility in Contemporary Japan*. Stanford, Calif.: Stanford University Press.

Ishida, Hiroshi, Seymour Spilerman, and Kuo-Hsien Su. 1997. "Educational Credentials and Promotion Chances in Japanese and American Organizations." *American Sociological Review* 62: 866–882.

Ishihara, Kyoko. 1993. "Onna no sentaku: Yōji kyōshitsu" (Women's choice: Extra-preschool institutions). *Asahi Shimbun*, 7 June.

Iwabuchi, Keiko. 1990. *Josei ga wakaranakunatta ojisamatachi e* (For men who could no longer understand women). Tokyo: Dentsū.

Iwao, Sumiko. 1993. *The Japanese Woman: Traditional Image and Changing Reality*. Cambridge: Harvard University Press.

James, Estelle, and Gail Benjamin. 1988. *Public Policy and Private Education in Japan*. New York: St. Martin's Press.

Janelli, Roger L., and Dawnhee Yim. 1993. *Making Capitalism: The Social and Cultural Construction of a South Korean Conglomerate*. Stanford, Calif.: Stanford University Press.

Janelli, Roger L., and Dawnhee Yim Janelli. 1982. *Ancestor Worship and Korean Society*. Stanford, Calif.: Stanford University Press.

Jang, Ji-Yeon. 1990. "Occupational Sex Segregation and Economic Inequality in South Korea" (in Korean). In *Women and Family in South Korean Society*, edited by South Korean Social History Research Associates, 121–185. Seoul: Munhak kwa Jisung Press.

Jeong, Yeon-Ang. 1994. *A Study on Management Practices for Female Workers in South Korean Firms* (in Korean). Seoul: Korea Labor Institute.

Johnson, Marshall, William Parish, and Elizabeth Lin. 1987. "Chinese Women, Rural Society, and External Markets." *Economic Development and Cultural Change* 35 (January): 257–277.

Jones, Gavin W. 1984. "Economic Growth and Changing Female Employment Structures in the Cities of Southeast and East Asia." In *Women in the Industrial Workforce: Southeast and East Asia*, edited by Gavin W. Jones. Canberra: Australian National University.

Joo, Chul An. 2000. "The Entrance Examination System." In *Higher Education in Korea: Tradition and Adaptation*, edited by John C. Weidman and Namgi Park, 89–107. New York: Falmer Press.

Jurik, Nancy C. 1998. "Getting Away and Getting By: The Experiences of Self-Employed Homeworkers." *Work and Occupations* 25: 7–35.

Ka, Chih-Ming. 1993. *Market, Social Networks, and the Production Organization of Small-Scale Industry in Taiwan: The Garment Industries in Wufenpu* (in Chinese). Taipei: Institute of Ethnology, Academia Sinica.

Kalleberg, Arne, and James R. Lincoln. 1988. "The Structure of Earnings Inequality in the United States and Japan." *American Journal of Sociology* 94 (suppl.): S121–S153.

Kaneko, Motohisa. 1987. *Enrollment Expansion in Postwar Japan*. Hiroshima: Research Institute for Higher Education, Hiroshima University.

Kang, Seyoung. 1993. "Differences in the Process of Earnings Determination and Inequality between Women and Men in South Korea." *Korea Journal of Population and Development* 22: 215–238.

Kanter, Rosabeth Moss. 1977. *Men and Women of the Corporation*. New York: Basic Books.

Kao, Charng, Solomon W. Polachek, and Phanindra V. Wunnava. 1994. "Male-Female Wage Differentials in Taiwan: A Human Capital Approach." *Economic Development and Cultural Change* 42: 351–373.

Kato, Ryoko. 1989. "Japanese Women: Subordination or Domination?" *International Journal of Sociology of the Family* 19: 49–57.

Katsuura-Cook, Noriko. 1991. *Nihon no kosodate, Amerika no kosodate* (Child-rearing in Japan and the United States). Tokyo: Saiensu.

Kawai, Hayao, Noboru Kobayashi, and Chie Nakane. 1984. *Oya to ko no kizuna: Gakusaiteki apurōchi* (Parent-child bonding: An interdisciplinary approach). Tokyo: Sōgensha.

Kawai, Hiroshi. 1989. *Ikuji to shigoto no baransushīto* (Balancing work and family). Tokyo: Fureberukan.

KAWF (South Korea Association of Women Friends). 1989. *The Reality of Women Clerical Workers*. Seoul: Seok-Tap.

Kelsky, Karen. 1994. "Postcards from the Edge: The 'Office Ladies' of Tokyo." *U.S.-Japan Women's Journal* 6 (English suppl.): 3–26.

Kentor, Jeffrey. 1981. "Structural Determinants of Peripheral Urbanization: The Effects of International Dependence." *American Sociological Review* 46: 201–211.

KEPB (Korea Economic Planning Board). 1969. *1966 Population and Housing Census Report*. Seoul: Author.

Kim, Changsoo. 1989. "Labor Market Developments of Korea in Macroeconomic Perspectives." KDI Working Paper no. 8909. Seoul: Korea Development Institute.

Kim, Choong Soon. 1992. *The Culture of South Korean Industry: An Ethnography of Poongsan Corporation*. Tucson: University of Arizona Press.

Kim, Eun-Shil. 1993. "The Making of the Modern Female Gender: The Politics of Gender in Reproductive Practices in South Korea." Ph.D. diss., University of California, San Francisco.

Kim, Kyung-Keun. 1990. "Schooling and Married Women's Work in a Developing Country: The Case of the Republic of South Korea." Ph.D. diss., University of Chicago.

Kim, Seung-Kyung. 1997. *Class Struggle or Family Struggle?* New York: Cambridge University Press.

Kim, Sun-Uk. 1995. "Measures of Personnel Administration for the Equal Employment of Women Civil Servants" (in Korean). *Women's Studies* 13: 5–37.

Kim, Tae-Hong. 1995. "Female Clerical Workers' Position in the Labor Market and Its Prospects" (in Korean). *Women's Studies* 13: 43–69 (Korean Women's Development Institute).

———. 1996. "The Current State of Women's Lifetime Labor Force Participation" (in Korean). *Women's Studies* 14: 103–120 (Korean Women's Development Institute).

Klaus, Marshall H., and John H. Kennell. 1976. *Maternal-Infant Bonding: The Impact of Early Separation or Loss on Family Development*. St. Louis: Mosby.

Klaus, Marshall H., Treville Leger, and Mary Anne Trause, eds. 1975. *Maternal Attachment and Mothering Disorders: A Round Table*. Sausalito, Calif.: Johnson & Johnson Baby Products.

KMA (South Korea Managers' Association). 1992. *Personnel Management in Competitive Era* (in Korean). Seoul: KMA.

———. 1995. *Management of Female Employees* (in Korean). Seoul: KMA.

Koike, Kazuo. 1983. "Internal Labor Markets: Workers in Large Firms." In *Contemporary Industrial Relations in Japan*, edited by Taishiro Shirai, 29–61. Madison: Wisconsin University Press.

———. 1987. "Human Resource Development and Labor-Management Relations." *The Political Economy of Japan*, edited by Kozo Yamamura and Yasukichi Yasuba. Vol. 1, 289–330. Stanford, Calif.: Stanford University Press.

Kondo, Dorinne K. 1990. *Crafting Selves: Power, Gender, and Discourses of Identity in a Japanese Workplace*. Chicago: University of Chicago Press.

Kong, Sae Kwon, and Minja Kim Choe. 1989. "Labor Force Participation of Married Women in Contemporary Korea." *Journal of Population and Health Studies* 9: 116–136.

Kong, Sae Kwon, Ejo Cho, Seongkwon Kim, and Sunghee Sohn. 1992. *The Family Formation and Fertility Behavior in the Republic of Korea*. Seoul: Korea Institute for Health and Social Affairs.

Konno, Minako. 2000. *OL no sōzō: Imisekai toshite no jendā* (Creation of OLs: Gender as meaning world). Tokyo: Keisō Shobō.

Koo, Bohn Young. 1985. "The Role of Direct Foreign Investment in Korea's Recent Economic Growth." In *Foreign Trade and Investment: Economic Development in the Newly Industrializing Asian Countries*, edited by Walter Galenson, 176–216. Madison: University of Wisconsin Press.

Koo, Hagen. 1990. "From Farm to Factory: Proletarianization in Korea." *American Sociological Review* 55: 669–681.

Koo, Hagen, and Doo-Seung Hong. 1990. "Class and Income Inequality in South Korea." *American Sociological Review* 45: 610–626.

Korean Educational Development Institute. 1986. *Educational Indicators in Korea*. Seoul: Korean Educational Development Institute.

Korean Women's Development Institute. 1986. *Socioeconomic Indicators of Women's Position*. Seoul: Author.

————. 1999. *Statistical Yearbook on Women*. Seoul: Author.

Korea Survey (Gallup) Polls Limited. 1987. "Life Style and Value System of Housewives in Korea." Seoul: Korea Survey.

Koyama, Shizuko. 1991. *Ryōsai kenbo to iu kihan* (Norms of good wife, wise mother). Tokyo: Keisōshobō.

KPHI (Korea Population and Health Institute). 1987. *Report of 1985 Fertility and Family Health Survey*. Seoul: KPHI.

Krueger, Anne O. 1983. *Trade and Employment in Developing Countries: Synthesis and Conclusions*. Vol. 3. Chicago: University of Chicago Press.

Kumagai, Fumie. 1986. "Modernization and the Family in Japan." *Journal of Family History* 11: 371–382.

Kumon Kyōiku Kenkyūkai. 1998. *Company Profiles*. Tokyo: Kumon Kyōiku Kenkyūkai.

Kung, Lydia. 1983. *Factory Women in Taiwan*. Ann Arbor: UMI Research Press.

Kyodo Advertising Planning Dept. LIPS, ed. 1989. *It's OL Show Time!: Torendī OL no 24 jikan o yomu 42 kō* (It's OL show time: 42 lessons on fashionable OLs' 24 hours). Tokyo: PHP Kenkyūjo.

————, ed. 1991. *All That's OL!* Tokyo: PHP Kenkyūjo.

Kyūtoku, Shigemori. 1979. *Bogenbyō* (Mother-caused diseases). Tokyo: Sanmāku.

L. MIT, ed. 1991. *Imadoki OL daizukan* (The encyclopedia of contemporary OLs). Tokyo: Nihon Keizai Shinbunsha.

Lam, Alice. 1992. *Women and Japanese Management: Discrimination and Reform*. London: Routledge.

Lantican, Clarita P., Christina H. Gladwin, and James L. Seale, Jr. 1996. "Income and Gender Inequalities in Asia: Testing Alternative Theories of Development." *Economic Development and Cultural Change* 44: 235–263.

Lebra, Takie Sugiyama. 1981. "Japanese Women in Male Dominant Careers: Cultural Barriers and Accommodations for Sex-Role Transcendence." *Ethnology* 20: 291–306.

Lee, Changwon. 1994. "Social Capital, Social Closure, and Human Capital Development: The Case of Managerial Workers in South Korean Chaebol." Ph.D. diss., University of Chicago.

Lee, Hyo-Soo. 1984. *The Theory of the Labor Market Structure in South Korea* (in Korean). Seoul: Bupmunsa.

Lee, Kwang-kyu. 1985. "Development of the Korean Kinship System with Special Reference to Influence from China." *Bulletin of the Institute of Ethnology, Academia Sinica* 59: 163–189.

Lee, Mee-Sook. 1994. "Differences in Parental Role Behaviors and the Quality of Parent-Child Relationship in the Context of College Entrance Exam: The Korean Case." Paper presented at the Annual Meetings of the American Sociological Association, Los Angeles, August.

Lee, Mei-Lin, Ya-Jie Yang, and Chin-Chun Yi. 2000. "Division of Family Labor:

Employment Determination or Gender Equality?" Paper presented at the Annual Meetings of the Taiwan Sociological Association, Taipei, January.

Lee, Sunhwa. 1997. *Elite Education for Career or Marriage: The Case of Female University Graduates in South Korea.* Ph.D. diss., Department of Sociology, University of Chicago.

Lee, Sunhwa, and Mary C. Brinton. 1996. "Elite Education and Social Capital: The Case of South Korea." *Sociology of Education* 69: 177–192.

Lee, Yean-Ju, and Seehwa Cho. 1999. "Gender Differences in Children's Schooling during Industrialization: South Korea from 1965 to 1994." *Society and Development* 28: 285–312.

Lee, Yean-Ju, William L. Parish, and Robert J. Willis. 1994. "Sons, Daughters, and Intergenerational Support in Taiwan." *American Journal of Sociology* 99: 1010–1041.

Leibowitz, Arleen. 1975. "Education and the Allocation of Women's Time." In *Education, Income, and Human Behavior*, edited by F. Thomas Juster, 171–197. New York: McGraw-Hill.

Lett, Denise Potrzeba. 1998. *In Pursuit of Status: The Making of South Korea's "New" Urban Middle Class.* Cambridge: Harvard University Press (Harvard University Asia Center).

Li, Yueh-Tuan, and Chih-Ming Ka. 1994. "Sexual Division of Labor and Production Organization in Wufenpu's Small-Scale Industries." *Taiwan: A Radical Quarterly in Social Science* 17: 41–81.

Liao, Tim F. 1998. "Dealing with a Double Day: Role Strain among Married Working Women in Japan and South Korea." In *The Changing Family in Comparative Perspective: Asia and the United States*, edited by Karen O. Mason, Noriko O. Tsuya, and Minja K. Choe, 137–154. Honolulu: East-West Center.

Lim, Linda Y. C. 1990. "Women's Work in Export Factories: The Politics of a Cause." In *Women Workers and Global Restructuring*, edited by Kathryn Ward. Ithaca, N.Y.: ILR Press, School of Industrial and Labor Relations, Cornell University.

Lin, Chung-Zeng. 1988. "Gender Wage Differential among First-Entry Workers." *Economic Essay* 16: 305–322.

Lincoln, James R., and Kerry McBride. 1987. "Japanese Industrial Organization in Comparative Perspective." *Annual Review of Sociology* 13: 289–312.

Liu, Paul K. C. 1984. "Trends in Female Labor Force Participation in Taiwan." In *Women in the Industrial Workforce: Southeast and East Asia*, edited by Gavin W. Jones. Canberra: Australian National University.

Lo, Jeannie. 1990. *Office Ladies, Factory Women: Life and Work at a Japanese Company.* New York: M. E. Sharpe.

London, Bruce. 1987. "Structural Determinants of Third World Urban Change." *American Sociological Review* 52: 28–43.

Lu, Yu-Hsia. 1983. "Women's Labor-Force Participation and Family Power Structure in Taiwan." *Bulletin of the Institute of Ethnology Academia Sinica*, no. 56: 111–143.

———. 1991. Family Organization and Married Women's Work Experience in a Developing Society: Taiwan. Ph.D. diss., University of Michigan.

———. 1992a. "Married Women's Informal Employment in Taiwan." Proceedings of the National Science Council, part C. *Humanities and Social Science* 2: 202–217.

———. 1992b. "Family Business and Married Women's Work Pattern in Taiwan." Paper presented at the Conference on Small Business in Taiwan, Academia Sinica, Taipei, May.

———. 1996. "Changes in Women's Work Patterns during Taiwan's Economic Development: 1980–1988." In *Family, Human Resources, and Social Development*, edited by Hsiao-Hung Chen, Yia-Ling Liu, and Mei-O Hsieh, 159–194. Taipei: National Chengchi University.

Lu, Yu-Hsia, and Chin-Chun Yi. 1998. "Married Women's Employment and Family Status under Taiwan's Social Change." Paper presented at the Conference on the Chinese Family and Its Ethics, Center for Chinese Studies, Taipei, April.

Lundberg, Erik. 1979. "Fiscal and Monetary Policies." In *Economic Growth and Structural Change in Taiwan*, edited by Walter Galenson. Ithaca, N.Y.: Cornell University Press.

Manabe, Rinko. 1998. "Nijussaidai no shūrō teishi to kekkon shussan" (Women's marriage, childbirth, and job-leaving). In *1995 SSM chōsa shirīzu: Jendā to raifu kōsu* (1995 SSM survey series: Gender and the life course), edited by Hachirō Iwai. Tokyo: SSM Chōsa Kenkyūkai.

Mare, Robert D. 1995. "Changes in Educational Attainment and School Enrollment." In *State of the Union: America in the 1990s*, edited by Reynolds Farley. Vol. 1, 155–214. New York: Russell Sage Foundation.

Mason, Edward S., Mahn Je Kim, Dwight H. Perkins, Kwang Suk Kim, and David C. Cole. 1980. *The Economic and Social Modernization of the Republic of Korea*. Cambridge: Council on East Asian Studies, Harvard University; distributed by Harvard University Press.

Mason, Karen Oppenheim. 1996. *Wives' Economic Decision-Making Power in the Family in Five Asian Countries* (East-West Center Working Papers, Population Series, no. 86, November). Honolulu: East-West Center.

McGinn, Noel F., Donald R. Snodgrass, Yung Bong Kim, Shin-Bok Kim, and Quee-Young Kim. 1980. *Education and Development in Korea*. Cambridge: Council on East Asian Studies, Harvard University; distributed by Harvard University Press.

McLaughlin, Steven, Barbara D. Melber, John O. G. Billy, Denise M. Zimmerle, Linda G. Winges, and Terry R. Johnson. 1988. *The Changing Lives of American Women*. Chapel Hill: University of North Carolina Press.

McLendon, James. 1983. "The Office: Way Station or Blind Alley?" In *Work and*

Lifecourse in Japan, edited by David W. Plath. Albany: State University of New York Press.

Michael, Robert. 1985. "Consequences of the Rise in Female Labor Force Participation Rates: Questions and Probes." *Journal of Labor Economics* 3: S117-S146.

Michell, Tony. 1988. *From a Developing to a Newly Industrialized Country: The Republic of Korea, 1961–82.* Geneva: International Labour Office.

Milkman, Ruth. 1987. *Gender at Work: The Dynamics of Job Segregation by Sex during World War II.* Urbana: University of Illinois Press.

Mincer, Jacob. 1962. "Labor Force Participation of Married Women." In *Aspects of Labor Economics,* edited by H. Gregg Lewis. Princeton, N.J.: Princeton University Press.

———. 1985. "Intercountry Comparisons of Labor Force Trends and of Related Developments: An Overview." *Journal of Labor Economics* 3 (suppl. to no. 1): S1–S32.

Mincer, Jacob, and Solomon W. Polachek. 1974. "Family Investments in Human Capital: Earnings of Women." *Journal of Political Economy* 82 (suppl.): S76–S108.

Ministry of Education, Japan. 1994. *Survey Report on Juku and Other Extra-School Programs.* Tokyo: Author.

———. Various years. *Basic School Statistics.* Tokyo: Author.

Ministry of Education, ROC (Republic of China). 1994. *Statistical Yearbook of Education.* Taipei: Ministry of Education.

Ministry of Education, ROK (Republic of Korea). Various years. *Statistical Yearbook of Education.* Seoul: Author.

Ministry of Examination, ROC (Republic of China). 1990. *Survey of Examination and Administration in the Republic of China: Taipei.* Taipei: Author.

Ministry of Health and Welfare, Japan. 1991. *Survey on Children's Environment.* Tokyo: Government Printing Office.

———. 1996, 1998. *Vital Population Statistics.* Tokyo: Government Printing Office.

Ministry of the Interior, ROC (Republic of China). 1998. *Survey on Women's Living Conditions.* Taipei: Author.

Ministry of Labor, Japan. Various years. *Yearbook of Labor Statistics.* Tokyo: Author.

Ministry of Labor, ROK (Republic of Korea). 1993, 1994. *Establishment-Level Labor Conditions Survey.* Seoul: Author.

———. 1994, 1998. *Wage Structure Survey.* Seoul: Author.

Mitani, Naoki. 1996. "Kintōhō shikōgo no josei koyō" (Women's employment after the enforcement of the Equal Employment Opportunity Law). *Nihon Rōdō Kenkyū Zasshi* 433: 24–36.

Mitsuishi, Yukiko. 1988. *Tensaiji o tsukuru!* (Creating prodigies). Tokyo: Fōyu.

Moore, Wilbert. 1963. "Industrialization and Social Change." In *Industrialization and Society*, edited by Bert Hoselitz and Wilbert Moore, 299–370. Mouton: UNESCO.

Nakano, Yumiko. 1990. "Sansaiji no shikiji nōryoku no hattatsu to sodachi no baransu" (The relationship between degree of literacy and profile of development in three years). *Journal of the Family Education Research Center* 12: 115–128.

———. 1993. "Nyūyōjiki no sōkikyōiku: Sōki no shikiji kyōiku to Kodomo no Hattatsu (The relationship between degree of literacy and profile of development in 3 and 6 years)." *Journal of the Family Education Research Center* 15: 86–98.

Nakata, Yoshifumi, and Carl Mosk. 1987. "The Demand for College Education in Postwar Japan." *Journal of Human Resources* 22: 377–404.

Nash, June, and Maria Patricia Fernández-Kelly, eds. 1983. *Women, Men, and the International Division of Labor*. Albany: State University of New York Press.

National Institute of Employment and Vocational Training, Japan. 1987. Joshi rōdō no shinjidai: Kyacchi appu wo koete (New era of female labor). Tokyo: Tokyo University Press.

National Institute of Population and Social Security Research, Japan. 1997. *Kekkon to shussan ni kansuru zenkoku chōsa* (Attitudes toward marriage and the family among unmarried Japanese youth). Tokyo: National Institute of Population and Social Security Research.

National Statistical Office, ROK (Republic of Korea). 1991a. *Population Projection*. Seoul: Author.

———. 1991b, 1998. *Social Indicators in Korea*. Seoul: Author.

———. 1993. *Life Table*. Seoul: Author.

———. 1995a. *Korean Census*. Seoul: Author.

———. 1995b. *Vital Registration Statistics*. Seoul: Author.

———. Various years. *Annual Report on the Economically Active Population Survey*. Seoul: Author.

———. Various years. *Population and Housing Census Report*. Seoul: Author.

———. Various years. *Report on the Employment Structure Survey*. Seoul: Author.

———. Various years. *Statistical Yearbook of Korea*. Seoul: Author.

NHK (Nihon Hōsō Kyōkai). 1995. *Dētābukku: Kokumin seikatsu jikan* (Databook on national time utilization survey). Tokyo: Nihon Hōsō Shuppan Kyōkai.

Niehoff, Justin D. 1987. "The Villager as Industrialist: Ideologies of Household Manufacturing in Rural Taiwan." *Modern China* 13: 278–309.

Nihon Keizai Shinbun. 1993. "Katsute yūgūsaku, imaya yūdōsaku? Kekkon shussan taishoku iwaikin" (A courteous treatment in the past but now a solicitous device? Marriage and childbirth retirement gifts). 15 December.

Noble, Gregory W. 1998. *Collective Action in East Asia: How Ruling Parties Shape Industrial Policy*. Ithaca, N.Y.: Cornell University Press.

O'Brien, Mary. 1981. *The Politics of Reproduction*. Boston: Routledge & Kegan Paul.

Ochiai, Emiko. 1989. *Kindai kazoku to feminizumu* (Modern families and feminism). Tokyo: Keisōshobō.

OECD. 2000a. *Education at a Glance*. Paris: OECD.

———. 2000b. *Labour Force Statistics: 1978–1998*. Paris: OECD.

Ogasawara, Yuko. 1998. *Office Ladies and Salaried Men: Power, Gender, and Work in Japanese Companies*. Berkeley: University of California Press.

Ōhinata, Masami. 1982. "Hahaoya no shinriteki antei to jūsoku o motomete" (For the mental stability and fulfillment of mothers). In *Ikuji noirōze* (Childrearing depression). Tokyo: Yūhikaku.

Okamoto, Hideo, and Michiko Naoi, eds. 1990. *Josei to shakaikaisō* (Women and social stratification). Tokyo: Tokyo University Press.

Oketani, Sotomi. 1987. *Oketani sotomi no shin bonyū ikuji no hon* (Oketani school of breast feeding). Tokyo: Shufunotomo.

Okuyama, Akira. 1996. "Kintōhō jūnen no genjō to kadai" (Current conditions and remaining problems ten years since the introduction of the Equal Employment Opportunity Law). *Nihon Rōdō Kenkyū Zasshi* 433: 2–13.

Onēsama Company, ed. 1991. *Tonari no OL zubari 36 gyōkai* (OLs next door in 36 industries speak frankly). Tokyo: Futabasha.

Ong, Aihwa. 1991. "The Gender and Labor Politics of Postmodernity." *Annual Review of Anthropology* 20: 279–309.

Ono, Hiroshi. 2000. "An Empirical Look at the Earnings of Japanese Men: The Significance of College Quality, Occupations, and Firm Size." Paper presented at the Annual Meetings of the American Sociological Association, Washington, D.C.

Oppenheimer, Valerie K. 1970. *The Female Labor Force in the United States*. Westport, Conn.: Greenwood. (Reprint of Population Monograph Series, no. 5, University of California, Berkeley, 1970.)

———. 1988. "A Theory of Marriage Timing: Assortative Mating under Varying Degrees of Uncertainty." *American Journal of Sociology* 94: 563–591.

———. 1997. "Men's Career Development and Marriage Timing during a Period of Rising Inequality." *Demography* 34: 311–330.

Orru, Marco, Nicole Woolsey Biggart, and Gary G. Hamilton. 1991. "Organizational Isomorphism in East Asia." In *The New Institutionalism in Organizational Analysis*, edited by Walter W. Powell and Paul J. DiMaggio, 337–360. Chicago: University of Chicago Press.

Osawa, Machiko. 1988. "Changing Role of Education and Women Workers in Japan." *Keio Business Review* 24: 1–15.

———. 1993. *Keizai henka to joshi rōdō: Nichibei no hikaku kenkyū* (Economic change and female labor: A comparative study of Japan and the United States). Tokyo: Nihon Keizai Hyōronsha.

Osawa, Mari. 1993. *Kigyō chūshin shakai o koete: Gendai Nihon o "jendā" de yomu* (Beyond the company-centered society: Reading contemporary Japan by gender). Tokyo: Jiji Tsūshinsha.

Ōshima, Kiyoshi. 1988. *Taikyō* (Prenatal education). Tokyo: Gomashobō.

Osterman, Paul. 1979. "Education and Labor Markets at the Turn of the Century." *Politics and Society* 9: 103–122.

Ōuchi, Akiko. 1999. "Daisotsu josei howaito Karā no kigyōnai kyaria keisei" (Corporate career development of white-collar female university graduates). *Nihon Rōdō Kenkyū Zasshi* 471: 15–28.

Pampel, Fred C., and Kazuko Tanaka. 1986. "Economic Development and Female Labor Force Participation: A Reconsideration." *Social Forces* 64: 599–619.

Panayotova, Evelina, and April Brayfield. 1997. "National Context and Gender Ideology: Attitudes toward Women's Employment in Hungary and the United States." *Gender and Society* 11: 627–655.

Papanek, Hanna. 1990. "To Each Less Than She Needs, From Each More Than She Can Do." In *Persistent Inequalities*, edited by Irene Tinker. New York: Oxford University Press.

Parish, William L., and Robert J. Willis. 1993. "Daughters, Education, and Family Budgets: Taiwan Experiences." *Journal of Human Resources* 28: 863–898.

Park, Fun-Koo, and Se-Il Park. 1984. *Income Structure in South Korea* (in Korean). Seoul: Korea Development Institute.

Park, Mee-Hae. 1991. "Patterns and Trends of Educational Mating in South Korea." *Korea Journal of Population and Development* 20: 1–15.

Park, Se-Il. 1982. "An Analysis of Male-Female Wage Differentials in South Korea" (in Korean). *Korea Development Review* 4: 59–89.

Park, Sook-Ja. 1992. "Structural Aspects of Sex Discrimination in the South Korean Labor Market: Screening Process in Recruitment." *Korean Social Science Journal* 18: 49–72.

Performance Yuki, ed. 1987. *Gendai OL repōto: Shuki de miru shigoto, jōshi, kekkonkan* (Report on OLs today: Their work, bosses, and marriage views disclosed in diaries). Tokyo: Nihon Nōritsu Kyōkai.

Petersen, Trond, and Seymour Spilerman. 1990. "Job Quits from an Internal Labor Market." In *Event History Analysis in Life Course Research*, edited by Karl U. Mayer and Nancy B. Tuma, 69–95. Madison: University of Wisconsin Press.

Pharr, Susan J. 1984. "Status Conflict: The Rebellion of the Tea Pourers." In *Conflict in Japan*, edited by Ellis S. Krauss, Thomas P. Rohlen, and Patricia G. Steinhoff, 214–240. Honolulu: University of Hawaii Press.

Polachek, Solomon W. 1975. "Discontinuous Labor Force Participation and Its Effect on Women's Market Earnings." In *Sex, Discrimination, and the Division of Labor*, edited by Cynthia B. Lloyd, 90–122. New York: Columbia University Press.

———. 1979. "Occupational Segregation among Women: Theory, Evidence, and a Prognosis." In *Women in the Labor Market*, edited by Cynthia Lloyd, 137–157. New York: Columbia University Press.

———. 1981. "Occupational Self-Selection: A Human Capital Approach to Sex

Differences in Occupational Structure." *Review of Economics and Statistics* 68: 60–69.

Portes, Alejandro. 1994. "The Informal Economy and Its Paradoxes." In *The Handbook of Economic Sociology*, edited by Neil J. Smelser and Richard Swedberg, 427–449. Princeton, N.J.: Princeton University Press.

Portes, Alejandro, and Lauren Benton. 1984. "Industrial Development and Labor Absorption: A Reinterpretation." *Populations and Development Review* 10: 589–611.

Portes, Alejandro, and Saskia Sassen-Koob. 1987. "Making It Underground: Comparative Material on the Informal Sector in Western Market Economies." *American Journal of Sociology* 93: 30–61.

Potuchek, Jean L. 1992. "Employed Wives' Orientations to Breadwinning: A Gender Theory Analysis." *Journal of Marriage and the Family* 54: 548–558.

Psacharopoulos, George, and Zafiris Tzannatos. 1989. "Female Labor Force Participation: An International Perspective." *World Bank Research Observer* 4: 187–202.

Pyle, Jean Larson. 1990. *The State and Women in the Economy: Lessons from Sex Discrimination in the Republic of Ireland*. Albany: State University of New York Press.

Ranis, Gustav. 1979. "Industrial Development." In *Economic Growth and Structural Change in Taiwan*, edited by Walter Galenson, 206–262. Ithaca, N.Y.: Cornell University Press.

———, ed. 1992. *Taiwan: From Developing to Mature Economy*. Boulder, Colo.: Westview Press.

Ranis, Gustav, and Chi Schive. 1985. "Direct Foreign Investment in Taiwan's Development." In *Foreign Trade and Investment: Economic Development in the Newly Industrializing Asian Countries*, edited by Walter Galenson. Madison: University of Wisconsin Press.

Rebick, Marcus E. 1993. "The Persistence of Firm-Size Differentials and Labor Market Segmentation in Japan." *Journal of Japanese and International Economies* 7: 132–156.

Redding, S. Gordon. 1990. *The Spirit of Chinese Capitalism*. New York: W. de Gruyter.

Reskin, Barbara F., and Debra Branch McBrier. 2000. "Why Not Ascription? Organizations' Employment of Male and Female Managers." *American Sociological Review* 65: 234–255.

Reskin, Barbara F., and Heidi Hartmann. 1986. *Women's Work, Men's Work: Sex Segregation on the Job*. Washington, D.C.: National Academy Press.

Reskin, Barbara F., and Patricia A. Roos. 1990. *Job Queues, Gender Queues*. Philadelphia: Temple University Press.

Retherford, Robert D., Naohiro Ogawa, and Rikiya Matsukura. 1999. "Late Marriage and Less Marriage in Japan." Honolulu: East-West Center. Mimeo.

Rich, Adrienne C. 1976. *Of Woman Born: Motherhood as Experience and Institution*. New York: Norton.

Roberts, Glenda S. 1994. *Staying on the Line: Blue-Collar Women in Contemporary Japan*. Honolulu: University of Hawaii Press.

Rohlen, Thomas P. 1974. *For Harmony and Strength: Japanese White-Collar Organization in Anthropological Perspective*. Berkeley: University of California Press.

———. 1983. *Japan's High Schools*. Berkeley: University of California Press.

Rosenbaum, James E., and Takehiko Kariya. 1989. "From High School to Work: Market and Institutional Mechanism in Japan." *American Journal of Sociology* 94: 1334–1365.

Rosenfeld, Rachel A. 1978. "Women's Employment Patterns and Occupational Achievements." *Social Science Research* 7: 61–80.

———. 1979. "Women's Occupational Careers." *Sociology of Work and Occupations* 6: 283–311.

———. 1983. "Sex Segregation and Sectors: An Analysis of Gender Differences in Returns from Employer Changes." *American Sociological Review* 48: 637–655.

Rozman, Gilbert. 1991. *The East Asian Region: Confucian Heritage and Its Modern Adaptation*. Princeton, N.J.: Princeton University Press.

Saffioti, Heleieth. 1976. "Relationships of Sex and Social Class in Brazil." In *Sex and Class in Latin America*, edited by June Nash and Helen Icken Safa. York: Praeger.

Sakamoto, Arthur, and Daniel A. Powers. 1995. "Education and the Dual Labor Market for Japanese Men." *American Sociological Review* 60: 222–246.

Salaff, Janet. 1981. *Working Daughters of Hong Kong*. New York: Cambridge.

———. 1994. "Foreword to the Morningside edition." *Factory Women in Taiwan*, by Lydia Kung, xi–xx. New York: Columbia University Press.

Sano, Yoko. 1988. *Kigyō-nai rōdō shijō* (Intra-corporation labor markets). Tokyo: Yūhikaku.

Sasaki, Yuzuru, and Atsushi Ishizuki. 1988. *Hikō ga katarsu oyako kankei* (Juvenile delinquency and parenting style). Tokyo: Iwanami.

Saso, Mary. 1990. *Women in the Japanese Workplace*. London: H. Shipman.

Sassen, Saskia. 1988. *The Mobility of Labor and Capital: A Study in International Investment and Capital Flow*. Cambridge: Cambridge University Press.

Schultz, T. Paul. 1980. "Estimating Labor Supply Functions for Married Women." In *Female Labor Supply: Theory and Estimation*, edited by James P. Smith, 25–89. Princeton, N.J.: Princeton University Press.

———. 1990. "Women's Changing Participation in the Labor Force: A World Perspective." *Economic Development and Cultural Change* 38: 457–488.

———. 1993. "Investments in the Schooling and Health of Women and Men." *Journal of Human Resources* 28: 694–734.

Scott, Alison M. 1986. "Women and Industrialization: The Female Marginalization Thesis." *Journal of Development Studies* 22: 649–680.

Seiyama, Kazuo. 1998. "Trends in Educational Attainment and Labor Force Participation of Japanese Women." In *1995 SSM chōsa shirīzu: Josei no kyaria kōzō to sono henka* (1995 SSM survey series: Changing career structures of women), edited by Kazuo Seiyama and Sachiko Imada. Tokyo: SSM Chōsa Kenkyūkai.

———. 1999. "Josei no kyaria kōzō no tokusei to dōkō" (Characteristics of Japanese women's career structure). *Nihon Rōdō Kenkyū Zasshi* 472: 36–45.

Semyonov, Moshe. 1980. "The Social Context of Women's Labor Force Participation." *American Journal of Sociology* 86: 534–550.

Shichida, Makoto. 1983. *Kiseki ga okiru shichidashiki zerosai kyōiku* (Miraculous education for zero-year-olds). Tokyo: Homeidō.

———. 1985. *Akachan wo kashikoku sodateru himitsu* (Tips on raising an intelligent baby). Tokyo: Nihon Keizai Shimbunsha.

Shieh, Gwo-Shyong. 1989. "Putting-Out System: A Comparative Historical Overview" (in Chinese). *Taiwan: A Radical Quarterly in Social Studies* 2: 29–69.

———. 1992a. *"Boss" Island: The Subcontract in Network and Micro-Entrepreneurship in Taiwan's Development.* New York: Peter Lang.

———. 1992b. "Invisible Factory: Subcontracting Points and Homeworkers in Taiwan" (in Chinese). *Taiwan: A Radical Quarterly in Social Studies* 13: 137–160.

Shimada, Haruo, and Yoshio Higuchi. 1985. "An Analysis of Trends in Female Labor Force Participation in Japan." *Journal of Labor Economics* 3 (suppl. to no. 1): S355–S374.

Shimizu, Chinami, and Yoshi Furuya. 1986. *Ojisan kaizō kōza: OL 500-nin iinkai* (Lessons for transforming men: 500 OLs' committee). Tokyo: Nesko.

———. 1989. *Ojisan kaizō kōza, Part 2: OL 800-nin iinkai* (Lessons for transforming men, part 2: 800 OLs' committee). Tokyo: Nesko.

Shiomi, Toshiyuki. 1993. *Konomama de iinoka chōsōkikyōiku* (Can we accept the present state of accelerated education). Tokyo: Ōtsukishoten.

———. 1996. *Yōji kyōiku sangyō to kosodate* (Education industry and childrearing). Tokyo: Iwanami Shoten.

Shirahase, Sawako, and Hiroshi Ishida. 1994. "Gender Inequality in the Japanese Occupational Structure: A Cross-National Comparison with Great Britain and the United States." *International Journal of Comparative Sociology* 3–4: 188–206.

Shirasa, Izumi. 1990. "Sōki kyōiku ni kansuru kahaoya no taidō" (Attitude of mothers on early education). Master's paper, University of Tokyo.

Shire, Karen A., and Jun Imai. 2000. "Flexible Equality: Men and Women in Employment in Japan." Paper presented at the Annual Meetings of the Association for Asian Studies, San Diego.

Smith, Robert J. 1982. *The Women of Suye Mura.* Chicago: University of Chicago Press.

Smith, James P., and Michael P. Ward. 1985. "Time-Series Growth in the Female Labor Force." *Journal of Labor Economics* 3 (suppl. to no. 1): S59–S90.

Smits, Jeroen, Wout Ultee, and Jan Lammers. 1998. "Educational Homogamy in 65 Countries: An Explanation of Differences in Openness Using Country-Level Explanatory Variables." *American Sociological Review* 63: 264–285.

Smock, Audrey C. 1981. *Women's Education in Developing Countries*. New York: Praeger.

Sohn, Seong Young, and Jung-Ah Cho. 1993. "A Study of College-Educated Women in the Workplace" (in Korean). *Journal of Women's Studies* 10: 183–243.

Sorensen, Annemette. 1995. "Women's Education and the Costs and Benefits of Marriage." In *The New Role of Women: Family Formation in Modern Societies*, edited by Hans-Peter Blossfeld, 229–235. Boulder, Colo.: Westview Press.

Sorensen, Clark. 1994. "Success and Education in South Korea." *Comparative Education Review* 38: 10–35.

Speare, Alden, Paul K. C. Liu, and Ching-Lung Tsay. 1988. *Urbanization and Development*. Boulder, Colo.: Westview Press.

Spilerman, Seymour, and Takeshi Ishida. 1996. "Stratification and Attainment in a Large Japanese Firm." In *Generating Social Stratification*, edited by Alan C. Kerckhoff, 317–342. Boulder, Colo.: Westview Press.

Standing, Guy. 1976. "Education and Female Participation in the Labor Force." *International Labor Review* 114: 281–297.

———. 1981. *Labour Force Participation and Development*. 2d ed. Geneva: International Labour Office.

Statistics Bureau, Management and Coordination Agency, Japan. 1997a. *Labor Statistics*. Tokyo: Author.

———. 1997b. *Statistical Indicators of Social Life*. Tokyo: Author.

———. 1997c. *Statistics of Japan*. Tokyo: Author.

———. Various years. *Basic Survey on Employment Structure*. Tokyo: Author.

———. Various years. *Labor Force Survey*. Tokyo: Author.

———. Various years. *Population Census*. Tokyo: Author.

Steinmetz, George, and Erik Olin Wright. 1989. "The Fall and Rise of the Petty Bourgeoisie: Changing Patterns of Self-Employment in the Postwar United States." *American Journal of Sociology* 94: 973–1018.

Stevenson, Harold W. 1992. "Learning from Asian Schools." *Scientific American* 267 (December): 70–76.

Stevenson, Harold W., and James W. Stigler. 1992. *The Learning Gap: Why Our Schools Are Failing and What We Can Learn from Japanese and Chinese Education*. New York: Summit Books.

Stites, Richard. 1982. "Small-Scale Industry in Yingge, Taiwan." *Modern China* 8: 247–279.

———. 1985. "Industrial Work as an Entrepreneurial Strategy." *Modern China* 11: 227–246.

Stoler, Ann. 1977. "Class Structure and Female Autonomy in Rural Java." *Signs* 3: 74–89.

Strober, Myra H., and Agnes Miling Kaneko Chan. 1999. *The Road Winds Uphill All the Way*. Cambridge: MIT Press.

Sun, Te-Hsiung, Hui-sheng Lin, and Ronald Freedman. 1978. "Trends in Fertility, Family Size Preferences, and Family Planning Practice: Taiwan, 1961–76." *Studies in Family Planning* 9: 54–70.

Tachibanaki, Toshiaki. 1993. "The Employer Size Effect on Wage Differentials in Japan Revived." Kyoto Institute of Economic Research Discussion Paper Series, no. 377. Kyoto: Kyoto University.

Taga, Mikiko. 1991. "OL ryūgaku būmu no hikari to kage" (Hope and despair of the study abroad boom among OLs). *Gekkan Asahi*, October, 130–133.

Taipei Ministry of Education. 1999. *Survey of Primary and Middle School Students' Learning Life in Taiwan*. Taipei: Ministry of Education.

Takahashi, Shigehiro, Takehiro Amino, and Reihō Kashiwame, eds. 1996. *Hairaito kodomo katei hakusho* (White paper on children's households). Tokyo: Kawashima Shoten.

Takahashi, Yukichi. 1997. "The Labor Market and Lifetime Employment in Japan." *Economic and Industrial Democracy* (Tokyo), 18: 55–66.

Takara, Kiyoshi, ed. 1996. *Keikoku! Sokikyōiku ga abunai: Rinshōgenba karano hōkoku* (Dangerous early intervention programs: Report from clinics). Tokyo: Nihonhyōronsha.

Tamanoi, Mariko Asano. 1998. *Under the Shadow of Nationalism: Politics and Poetics of Rural Japanese Women*. Honolulu: University of Hawaii Press.

Tanaka, Kazuko. 1987. "Women, Work, and Family in Japan: A Life Cycle Perspective." Ph.D. diss., University of Iowa.

———. 1995. "Work, Education, and the Family." In *Japanese Women*, edited by Kumiko Fujimura-Fanselow and Atsuko Kameda, 295–308. New York: Feminist Press.

Tanaka, Shigeto. 1996. "Shokugyō kōzō to josei no rōdō shijō teichakusei" (Occupational structure and women's continued participation in the labor market). *Soshioroji* 41: 69–85.

———. 1997. "Kōgakureki to seibetsubungyō" (Higher education and the sexual division of labor). *Japanese Sociological Review* 48: 130–141.

———. 1998. "Kōgakureki to seibetsubungyō" (Higher education and the sexual division of labor). In *1995 SSM chōsa shirizu: Josei no kyaria kōzō to sono henka* (1995 SSM survey series: Changing career structures of women), edited by Kazuo Seiyama and Sachiko Imada, 1–16. Tokyo: SSM Chōsa Kenkyūkai.

———. 1999. "Seibetsubungyō no bunseki: Sono jittai to henyō no jōken" (An analysis of the sexual division of labor: Current realities and prospects for change). Ph.D. diss., Osaka University.

Tang, Stephen Lung Wai. 1981. "The Differential Educational Attainment of Children: An Empirical Study of Hong Kong." Ph.D. diss., University of Chicago.

Taniguchi, Yuji. 1988. *Mama, kamiomutsu wo tsukawanaide!* (Mommy, don't use disposable diapers!). Tokyo: Bunensha.

Thornton, Arland, and Hui-Sheng Lin. 1994. *Social Change and the Family in Taiwan*. Chicago: University of Chicago Press.

Thornton, Arland, Hui-Sheng Lin, Jui-Shan Chang, and Li-Shou Yang. 1994. "Determinants of Historical Changes in Marital Timing." In *Social Change and the Family in Taiwan*, edited by Arland Thornton and Hui-Sheng Lin, 225–244. Chicago: University of Chicago Press.

Thornton, Arland, Ming-cheng Chang, and Te-hsiung Sun. 1984. "Social and Economic Change, Intergenerational Relationships, and Family Formation in Taiwan." *Demography* 21: 475–499.

Thurow, Lester. 1969. *Poverty and Discrimination*. Washington, D.C.: Brookings Institution.

———. 1975. *Generating Inequality*. New York: Basic Books.

Timberlake, Michael, ed. 1985. *Urbanization in the World-Economy*. Orlando: Academic Press.

Tinker, Irene. 1990. "A Context for the Field and for the Book." In *Persistent Inequalities: Women and World Development*, edited by Irene Tinker, 3–13. New York: Oxford University Press.

———. 1994. "The Urban Street Food Trade: Regional Variations of Women's Involvement." In *Women, the Family and Policy: A Global Perspective*, edited by Esther Chow and Catherine Berheide, 163–187. Albany: State University of New York Press.

———, ed. 1990. *Persistent Inequalities: Women and World Development*. New York: Oxford University Press.

Tōkai Ginkō. 1997. *Ankēto chōsa kodomo no kyōikuhi* (Survey on educational expenses). Tokyo: Tōkai Ginkō.

Trow, Martin. 1961. "The Second Transformation of American Secondary Education." *International Journal of Comparative Sociology* 2: 144–165.

Truelove, Cynthia. 1990. "Disguised Industrial Proletarians in Rural Latin America: Women's Informal-Section Factory Work and the Social Production of Coffee Farm Labor in Colombia." In *Women Workers and Global Restructuring*, edited by Kathryn Ward, 48–63. ILR Press, School of Industrial and Labor Relations, Cornell University.

Tsai, Su-Lin. 1987. "Occupational Segregation and Education Attainment: An Analysis of Gender Difference. *Chinese Journal of Sociology* 11: 61–91.

Tsui, Yi-Lan. 1987. "Are Married Daughters 'Spilled Water'?" Monograph no. 4. Taipei: Women's Research Program, Population Studies Center, National Taiwan University.

Tsurumi, E. Patricia. 1977. *Japanese Colonial Education in Taiwan, 1895–1945*. Cambridge: Harvard University Press.

Tu, Jenn-hwa. 1990. *Direct Foreign Investment and Economic Growth: A Case*

Study of Taiwan. Monograph Series, no. 48. Nankang, Taipei: Academia Sinica, Institute of Economics.

United Nations. 1998. *Demographic Yearbook.* New York: United Nations.

Uno, Kathleen S. 1993. "The Death of 'Good Wife, Wise Mother'?" In *Postwar Japan as History,* edited by Andrew Gordon. Berkeley: University of California Press.

Upham, Frank K. 1987. *Law and Social Change in Postwar Japan.* Cambridge: Harvard University Press.

U.S. Bureau of the Census. 1997. *Statistical Abstract of the United States: 1997.* 117th ed. Washington, D.C.: U.S. Government Printing Office.

Vogel, Ezra F. 1963. *Japan's New Middle Class.* Berkeley: University of California Press.

Wade, Robert. 1984. "Deregime Taiwan Style." In *Developmentalist States in East Asia: Capitalist and Socialist,* edited by Robert Wade and Gordon White. *IDS Bulletin* 15: 65–70.

Wallace, Michael, and Arne L. Kalleberg. 1981. "Economic Organization of Firms and Labor Market Consequences: Toward a Specification of Dual Economy Theory." In *Sociological Perspectives on Labor Markets,* edited by Ivar Berg, 77–117. New York: Academic Press.

Walters, Pamela Barnhouse. 1984. "Occupational and Labor Market Effects on Secondary and Postsecondary Educational Expansion in the United States: 1922 to 1979." *American Sociological Review* 49: 659–671.

———. 1986. "Sex and Institutional Differences in Labor Market Effects on the Expansion of Higher Education, 1952 to 1980." *Sociology of Education* 59: 199–211.

Ward, Kathryn B. 1984. *Women in the World System.* New York: Praeger.

———, ed. 1990. *Women Workers and Global Restructuring.* Ithaca, N.Y.: ILR Press, School of Industrial and Labor Relations, Cornell University.

Weekly Economist. 1995. "An Anatomy of New Salarymen" (in Korean). No. 305 (15 September): 70–78.

West, Candace, and Don H. Zimmerman. 1987. "Doing Gender." *Gender and Society* 1: 125–151.

White, Merry. 1987a. *The Japanese Educational Challenge: A Commitment to Children.* New York: Free Press.

———. 1987b. "The Virtue of Japanese Mothers: Cultural Definitions of Women's Lives." *Daedalus* 116: 149–163.

Whittaker, David Hugh. 1997. *Small Firms in the Japanese Economy.* Cambridge: Cambridge University Press.

Wilensky, Harold L. 1968. "Women's Work: Economic Growth, Ideology, and Structure." *Industrial Relations* 7: 235–248.

Winkler, Donald R. 1987. "Screening Models and Education." In *Economics of Education: Research and Studies,* edited by George Psacharopoulos, 287–291. Oxford: Pergamon Press.

Wolf, Diane L. 1990. "Linking Women's Labor with the Global Economy." In *Women Workers and Global Restructuring*, edited by Kathryn Ward. Ithaca, N.Y.: ILR Press, School of Industrial and Labor Relations, Cornell University.

———. 1992. *Factory Daughters: Gender, Household Dynamics, and Rural Industrialization in Java*. Berkeley: University of California Press.

Wolf, Margery. 1972. *Women and the Family in Rural Taiwan*. Stanford, Calif.: Stanford University Press.

Wolf, Wendy C., and Rachel Rosenfeld. 1978. "Sex Structure of Occupations and Job Mobility." *Social Forces* 56: 823–844.

Wood, Adrian. 1994. *North-South Trade, Employment, and Inequality: Changing Fortunes in a Skill-Driven World*. Oxford: Clarendon Press.

Yamada, Makoto. 1989. *Kosodate minna sukina yō ni yarebaī* (Let us choose our parenting style). Tokyo: Tarōjirōsha.

Yamada, Masahiro. 1999. *Parasaito shinguru no jidai* (The age of parasite singles). Tokyo: Chikuma Shobō.

Yamaguchi, Kazuo. 1997a. "Continuing Major Disruption: Determinants of Historical Changes in the Rate of Job Separations due to Marriage or Childbirth/Childcare among Japanese Women" (in Japanese). In *A Comparative Study of Women's Careers and Life Course*, Research Report no. 112, 55–92. Tokyo: Japan Institute of Labor.

———. 1997b. "Continuing Major Interruption: Determinants of Historical Changes in the Rate of Job Separation Due to Marriage or Childbirth/Childcare among Japanese Women." Discussion Paper Series, Population Research Center, University of Chicago.

Yano, Masakazu. 1982. "Joshikyōiku no keizaigaku" (Economics of women's education). In *Kyōiku no keizaigaku* (Economics of the education), edited by Shōgo Ichikawa, Jyōji Kikuchi, and Masakazu Yano. Tokyo: Daiichi Hōki Shuppan.

Yee, Jaeyeol. 1990. "The Formation and Reproduction of Self-Employment in a Developing Economy: Analysis of Job Shift Rates in the South Korean Urban Labor Market." Paper presented at the Annual Meetings of the American Sociological Association. Washington, D.C., August.

Yi, Chin-Chun, and Yuay-Ling Tsai. 1989. "An Analysis of Marital Power in the Taipei Metropolitan Area: An Example of Familial Decision-Making (in Chinese)." In *Social Phenomena in Taiwan: An Analysis*, edited by Chin-Chun Yi and Cathy Chu. Taipei: Sun Yat-Sen Institute, Academia Sinica.

Yi, Eunhee Kim. 1993. "From Gentry to Middle Class." Ph.D. diss., University of Chicago, Department of Anthropology.

Young, Gay. 1993. "Gender Inequality and Industrial Development: The Household Connection." *Journal of Comparative Family Studies* 24: 1–20.

Yu, Wei-hsin. 1998. "Gender, National Markets, and Career Mobility: Comparing Japan and Taiwan." Paper presented at the Annual Meetings of the American Sociological Association, San Francisco, August.

————. 1999a. "Different Labor Markets, Different Choices: Women's Labor Force Participation in Japan and Taiwan." Paper presented at the Annual Meetings of the American Sociological Association, Chicago, August.

————. 1999b. "Unequal Employment, Diverse Career Paths: Gender Stratification in Japan and Taiwan." Ph.D. diss., University of Chicago, Department of Sociology.

INDEX

Administrative/managerial jobs
male/female ratio (1995), 17
women in (1995), 15
work before and after marriage, 54
Age and aging
clerical work opportunities, 152
elderly dependence on young, 90
female labor force participation and,
58–61, 72
low-paying clerical jobs, 175
at marriage, 46, 117, 167
monthly earnings, by gender, 18
wage gap and, 16–18
women's work patterns and, 10–12
work before marriage, 109
youthful attractiveness, 165–66
Agricultural (primary) sector
labor force, 6
women in (1995), 15
work before and after marriage, 54
work before marriage, 111

Benefits
childcare leave, 172
maternity leave, 28, 172
retirement programs, 90
Birth rate, 23, 46
Bosses' wives, in family-owned businesses,
270–89
Bride price, 307–9, 314

Capitalism, gender inequality and, 2
Career tracks, 39–40, 84, 152–53, 206
Careers, motherhood and, 172–73
Chaebol, 33, 48, 52
Childcare, 34
availability of, 87–91

commuting times and, 86–87
father's participation in, 181
gender roles and, 74
hoikuen centers, 87
mother's attitudes toward, 200
women's employment and, 81–85
Childcare leave, 172, 173
Children
childrearing standards, 91–92
daughters and industrial globalization,
299–322
education of, in Japan, 180–203
female labor force participation and,
58–61
mother-child relationship, 193–95
prodigies, obsession with, 184–88
women, characteristics of urban married, 56
China, 13–14
Clerical jobs
employment in middle age, 152
jimushoku track, 84, 152–53
male/female first job characteristics,
222–24
male/female ratio (1995), 17
marriage, job separation at, 99–102,
115
office ladies (OLs), 151–79
women in (1995), 15
work before and after marriage, 54
work before marriage, 111
Colleges and universities. See Universities
Commuting, 34, 52, 85–87
Confucianism, 20–21, 24–25

Daughters and industrial globalization, in
Taiwan, 299–322

371